White Ash

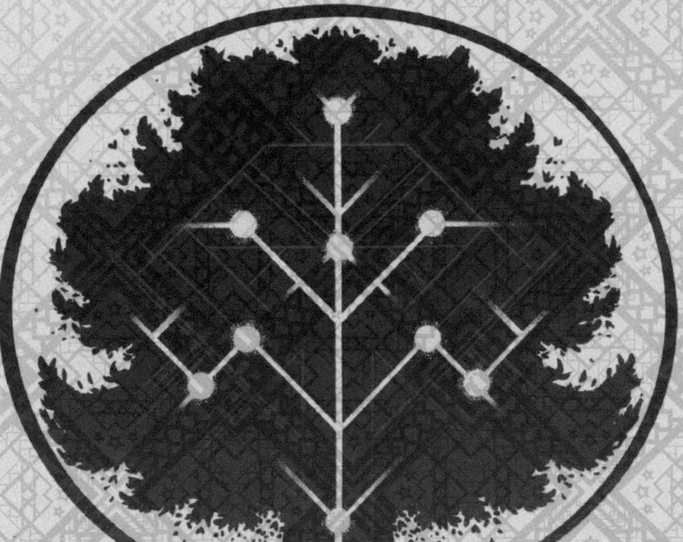

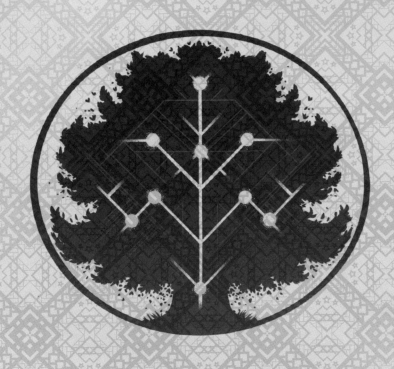

THE
SMALLER
THE
TOWN

THE
BIGGER
THE
ECRET

WRITER:
CHARLIE STICKNEY

ARTIST/LETTERER:
CONOR HUGHES

COLORIST:
FIN CRAMB

Trade Paperback Production by: **Joel Rodriguez**

SCOUT COMICS

Brendan Deneen, *CEO*
James Haick III, *President*
Tennessee Edwards, *CSO*
Don Handfield, *CMO*

James Pruett, *CCO*
David Byrne, *Co-Publisher*
Charlie Stickney, *Co-Publisher*
Joel Rodriguez, *Head of Design*

 FB/TW/IG:
@SCOUTCOMICS

LEARN MORE AT:
WWW.SCOUTCOMICS.COM

CHAPTER ONE

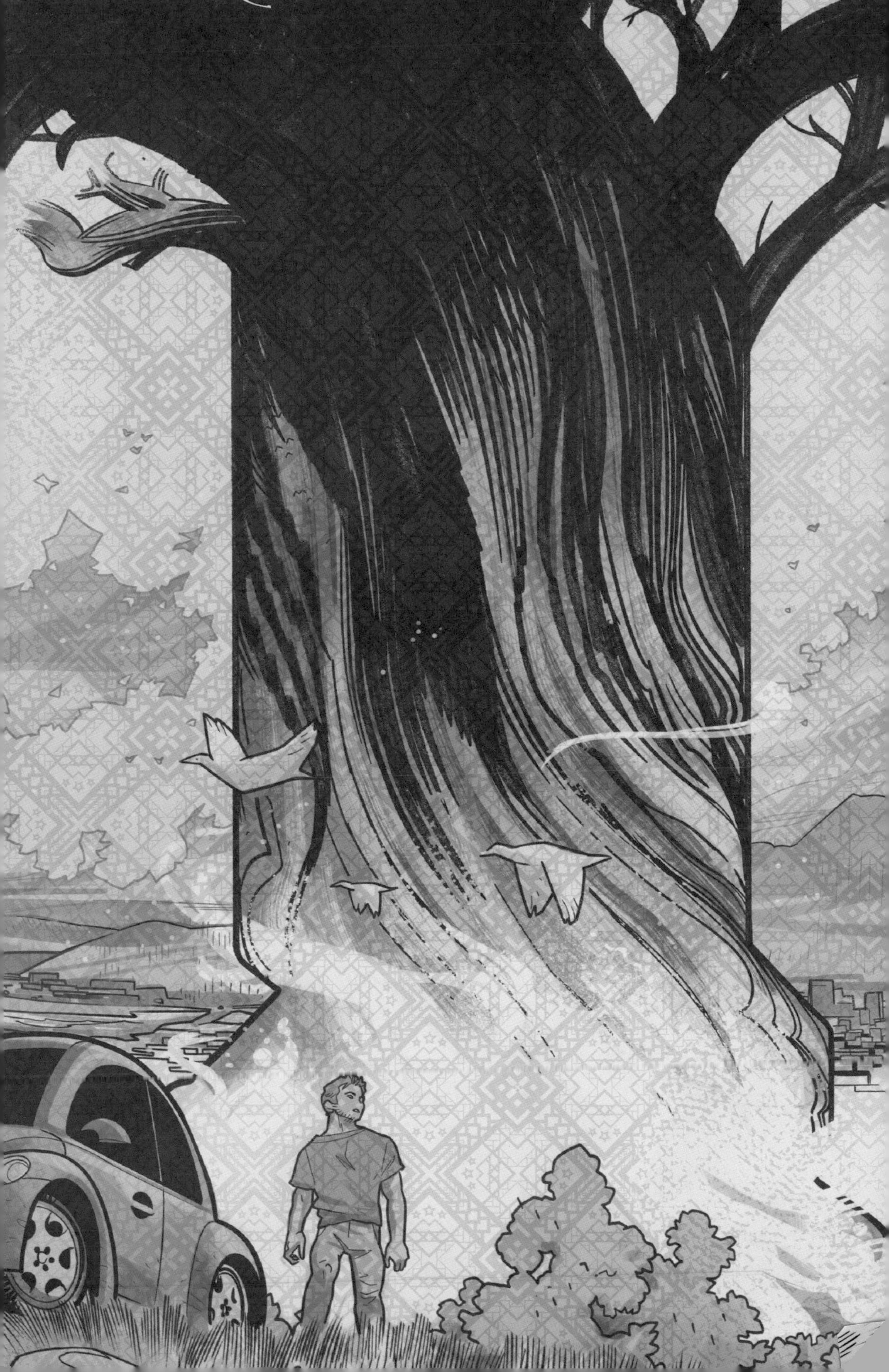

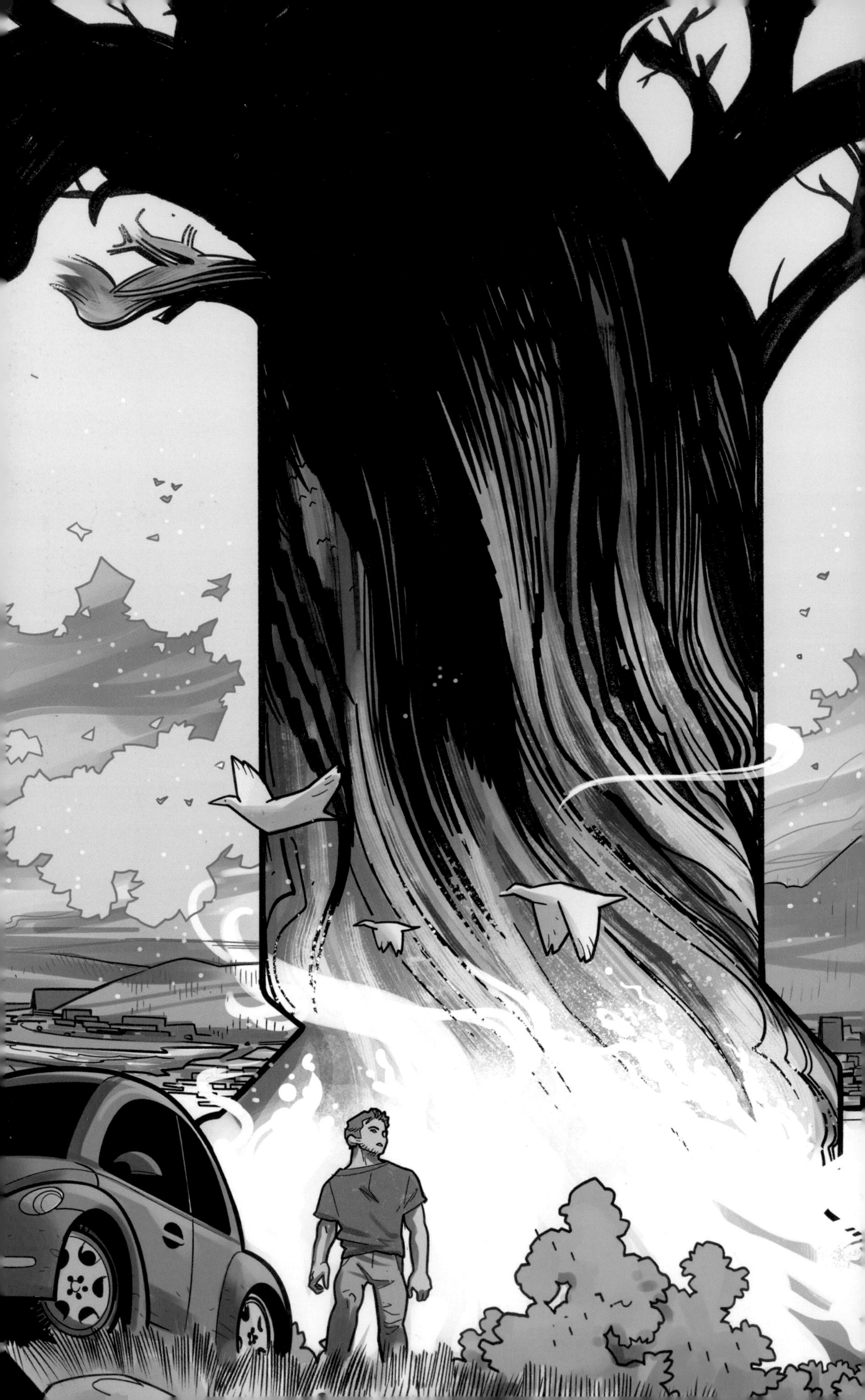

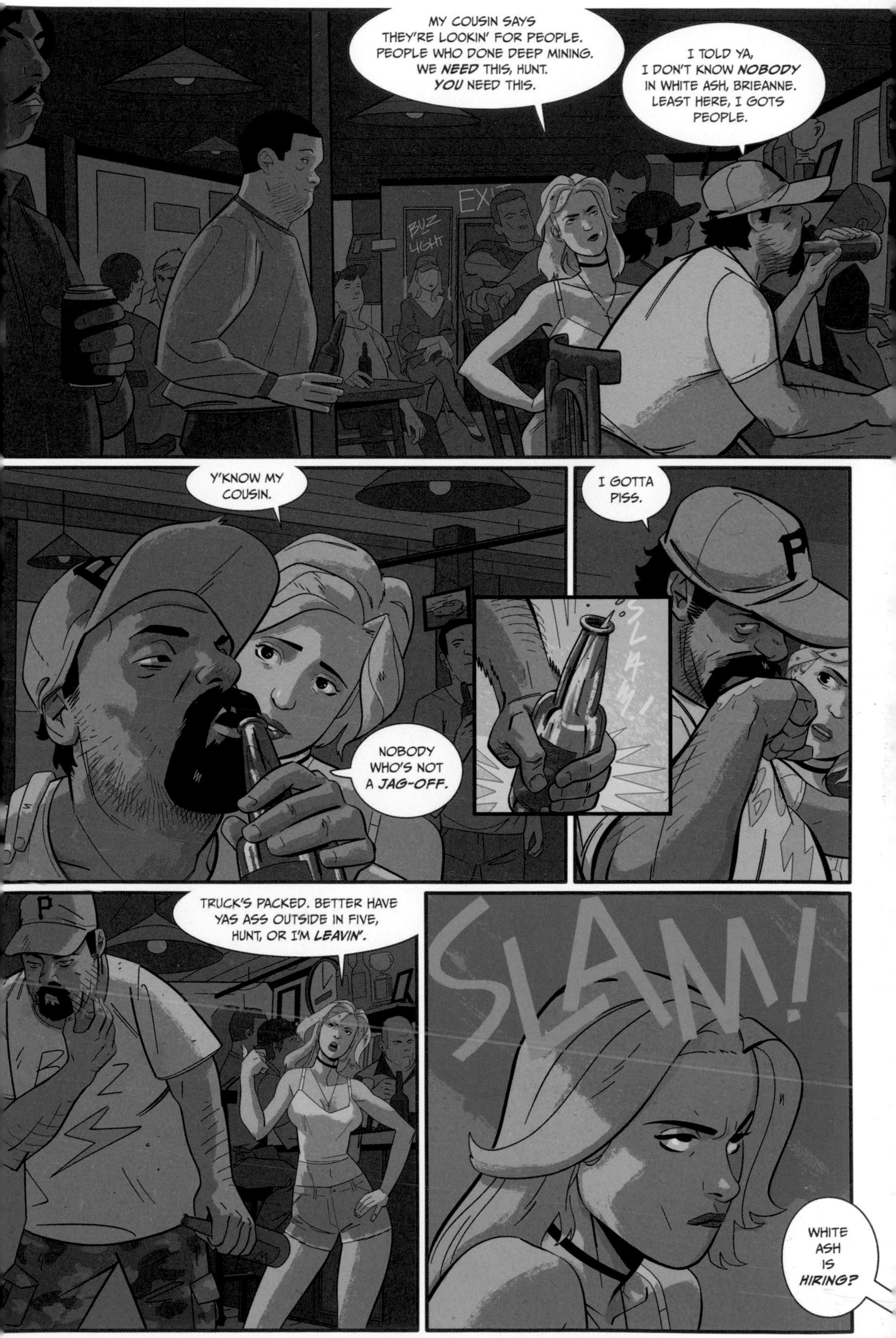
MY COUSIN SAYS THEY'RE LOOKIN' FOR PEOPLE. PEOPLE WHO DONE DEEP MINING. WE NEED THIS, HUNT. YOU NEED THIS.
I TOLD YA, I DON'T KNOW NOBODY IN WHITE ASH, BRIEANNE. LEAST HERE, I GOTS PEOPLE.
EXIT
Y'KNOW MY COUSIN.
NOBODY WHO'S NOT A JAG-OFF.
I GOTTA PISS.
SLAM!
TRUCK'S PACKED. BETTER HAVE YAS ASS OUTSIDE IN FIVE, HUNT, OR I'M LEAVIN'.
SLAM!
WHITE ASH IS HIRING?

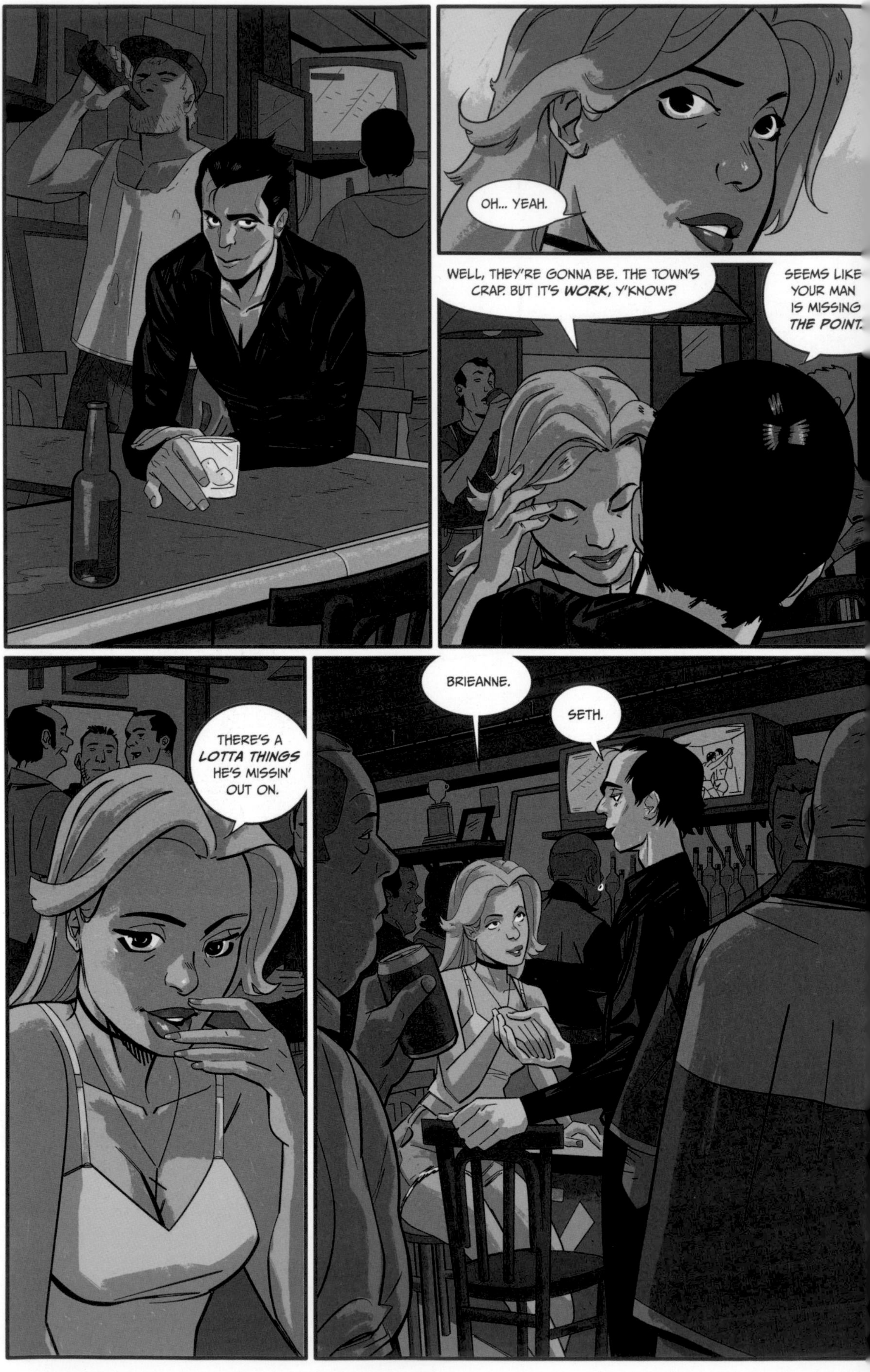
OH... YEAH.
WELL, THEY'RE GONNA BE. THE TOWN'S CRAP. BUT IT'S WORK, Y'KNOW?
SEEMS LIKE YOUR MAN IS MISSING THE POINT.
THERE'S A LOTTA THINGS HE'S MISSIN' OUT ON.
BRIEANNE.
SETH.

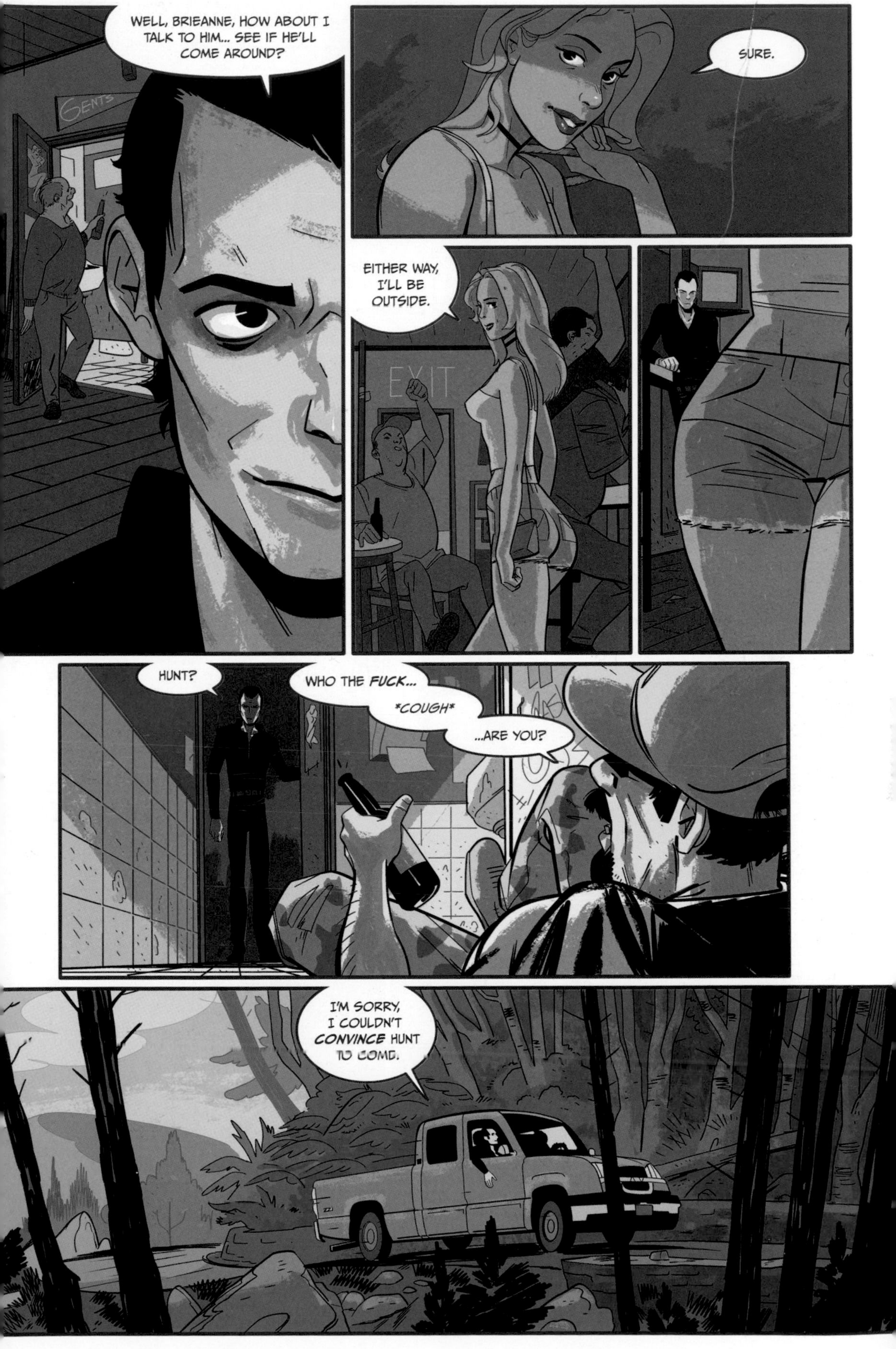
WELL, BRIEANNE, HOW ABOUT I TALK TO HIM... SEE IF HE'LL COME AROUND?
GENTS
SURE.
EITHER WAY, I'LL BE OUTSIDE.
EXIT
HUNT?
WHO THE FUCK...
COUGH
...ARE YOU?
I'M SORRY, I COULDN'T CONVINCE HUNT TO COME.

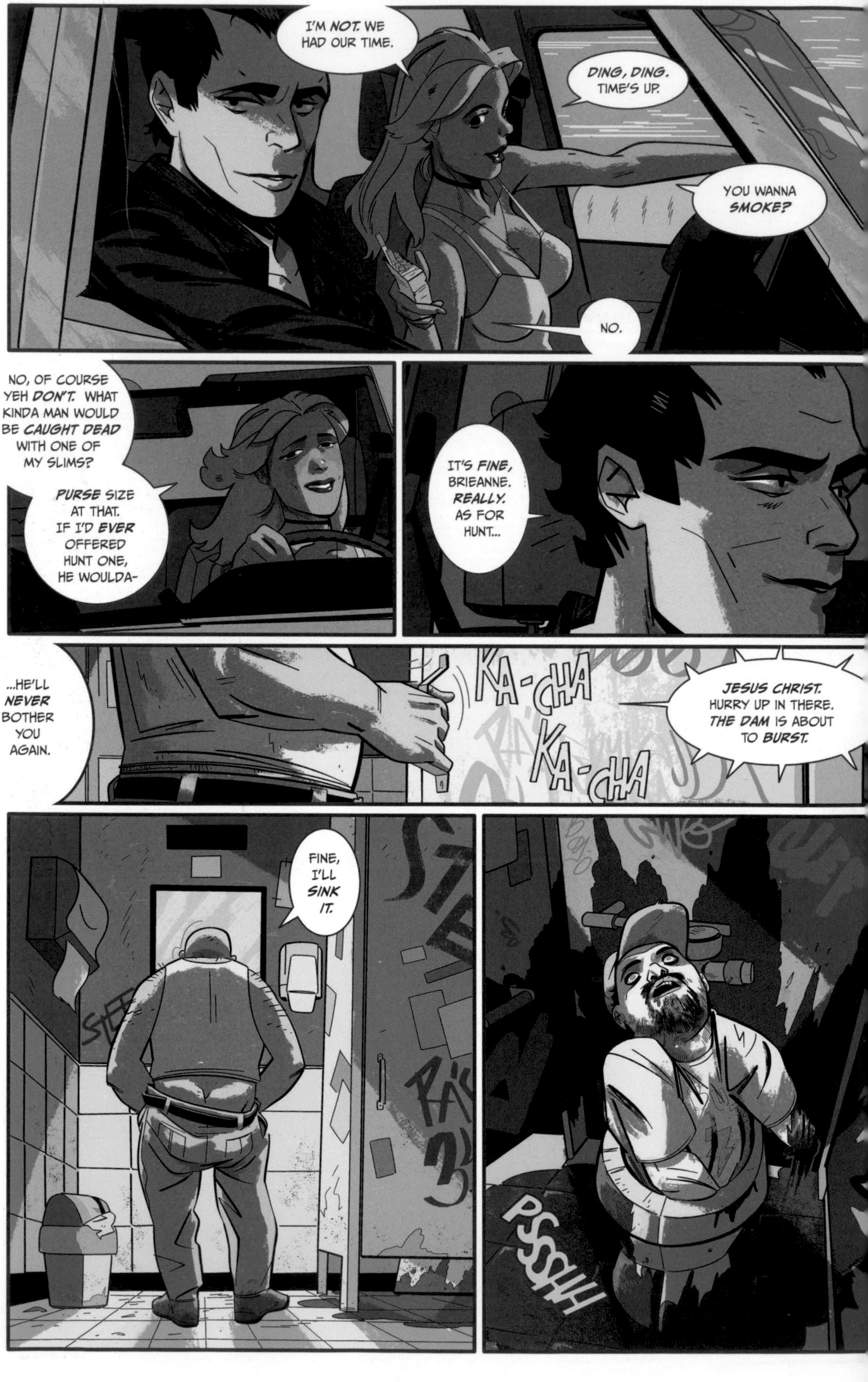
I'M NOT. WE HAD OUR TIME.
DING, DING. TIME'S UP.
YOU WANNA SMOKE?
NO.
NO, OF COURSE YEH DON'T. WHAT KINDA MAN WOULD BE CAUGHT DEAD WITH ONE OF MY SLIMS?
PURSE SIZE AT THAT. IF I'D EVER OFFERED HUNT ONE, HE WOULDA-
IT'S FINE, BRIEANNE. REALLY. AS FOR HUNT...
...HE'LL NEVER BOTHER YOU AGAIN.
KA-CHA
KA-CHA
JESUS CHRIST. HURRY UP IN THERE. THE DAM IS ABOUT TO BURST.
FINE, I'LL SINK IT.
PSSSHH

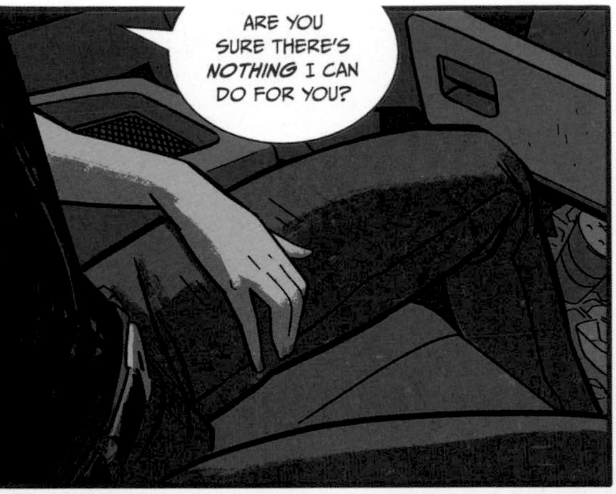
ARE YOU SURE THERE'S *NOTHING* I CAN DO FOR YOU?

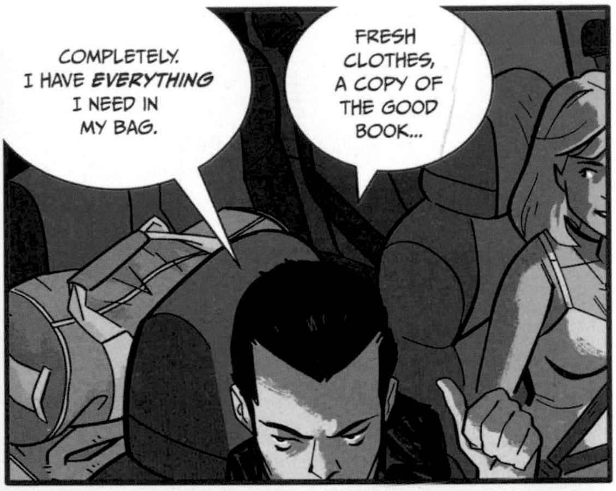
COMPLETELY. I HAVE *EVERYTHING* I NEED IN MY BAG.
FRESH CLOTHES, A COPY OF THE GOOD BOOK...

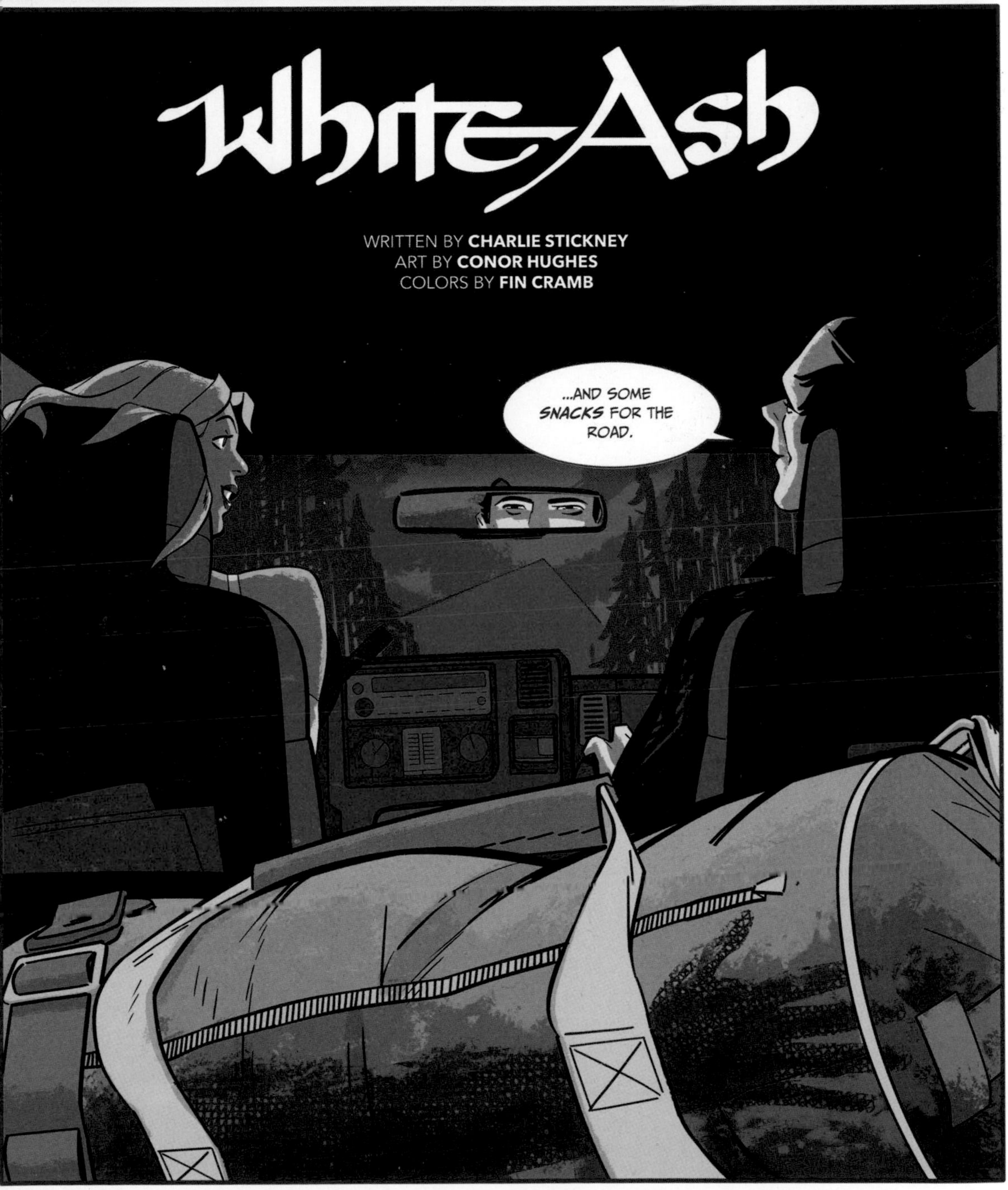
White Ash
WRITTEN BY **CHARLIE STICKNEY**
ART BY **CONOR HUGHES**
COLORS BY **FIN CRAMB**
...AND SOME *SNACKS* FOR THE ROAD.

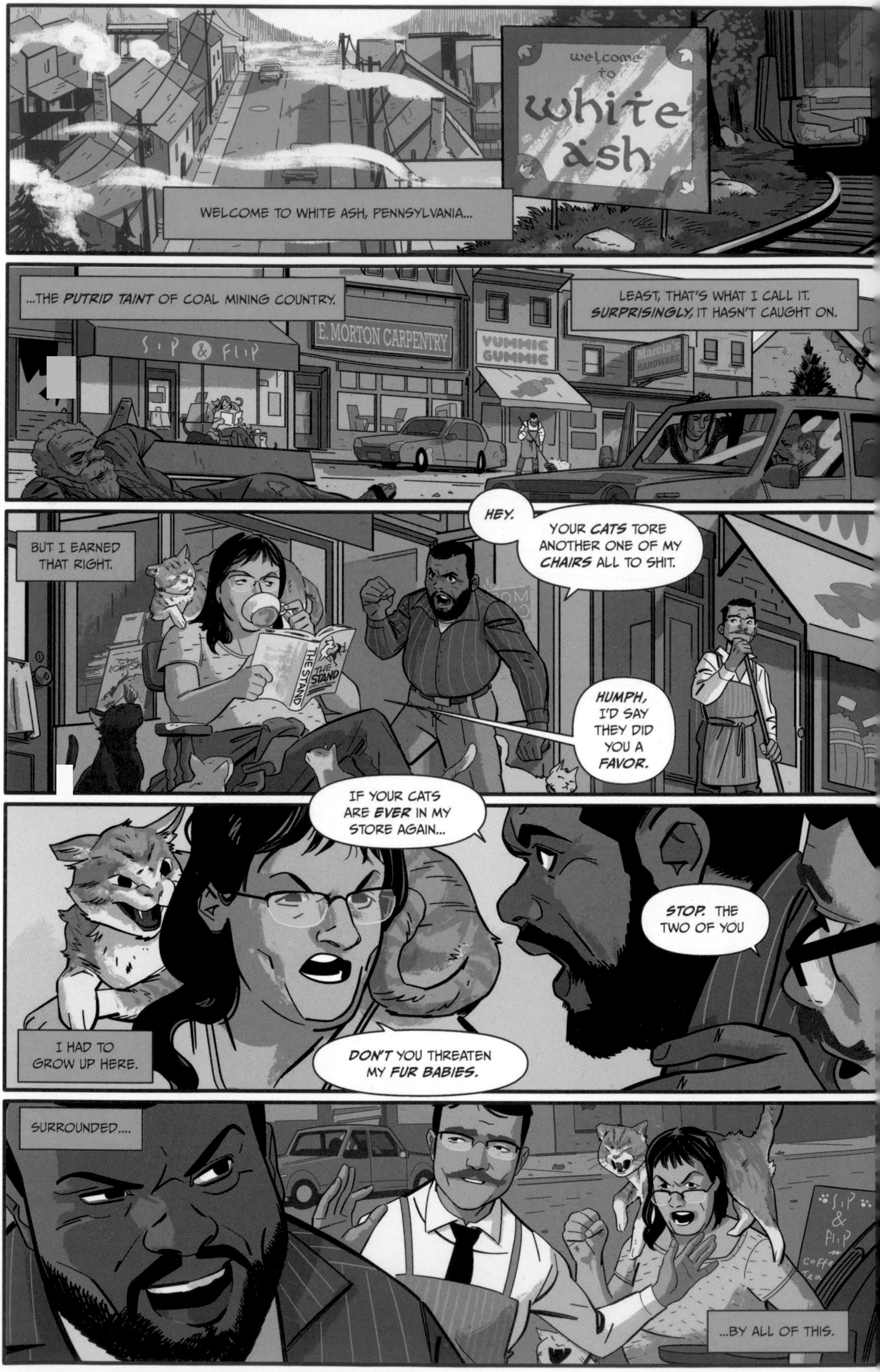
welcome to white ash
WELCOME TO WHITE ASH, PENNSYLVANIA...
...THE PUTRID TAINT OF COAL MINING COUNTRY.
LEAST, THAT'S WHAT I CALL IT. SURPRISINGLY, IT HASN'T CAUGHT ON.
SIP & FLIP
E. MORTON CARPENTRY
YUMMIE GUMMIE
Marcia's HARDWARE
BUT I EARNED THAT RIGHT.
HEY.
YOUR CATS TORE ANOTHER ONE OF MY CHAIRS ALL TO SHIT.
THE STAND
HUMPH, I'D SAY THEY DID YOU A FAVOR.
IF YOUR CATS ARE EVER IN MY STORE AGAIN...
STOP. THE TWO OF YOU
I HAD TO GROW UP HERE.
DON'T YOU THREATEN MY FUR BABIES.
SURROUNDED....
SIP & FLIP
...BY ALL OF THIS.

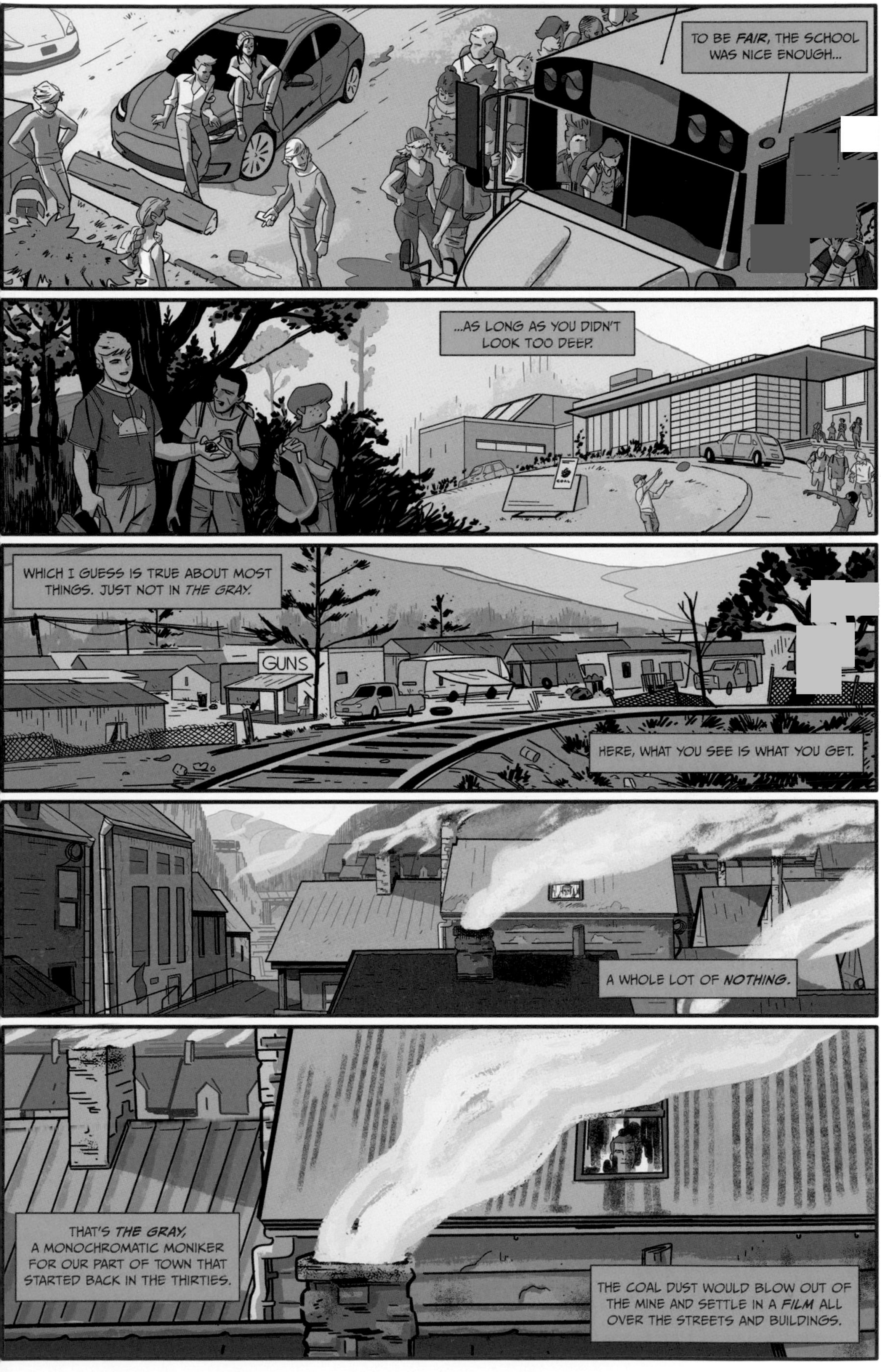
TO BE FAIR, THE SCHOOL WAS NICE ENOUGH...
...AS LONG AS YOU DIDN'T LOOK TOO DEEP.
WHICH I GUESS IS TRUE ABOUT MOST THINGS. JUST NOT IN THE GRAY.
GUNS
HERE, WHAT YOU SEE IS WHAT YOU GET.
A WHOLE LOT OF NOTHING.
THAT'S THE GRAY, A MONOCHROMATIC MONIKER FOR OUR PART OF TOWN THAT STARTED BACK IN THE THIRTIES.
THE COAL DUST WOULD BLOW OUT OF THE MINE AND SETTLE IN A FILM ALL OVER THE STREETS AND BUILDINGS.

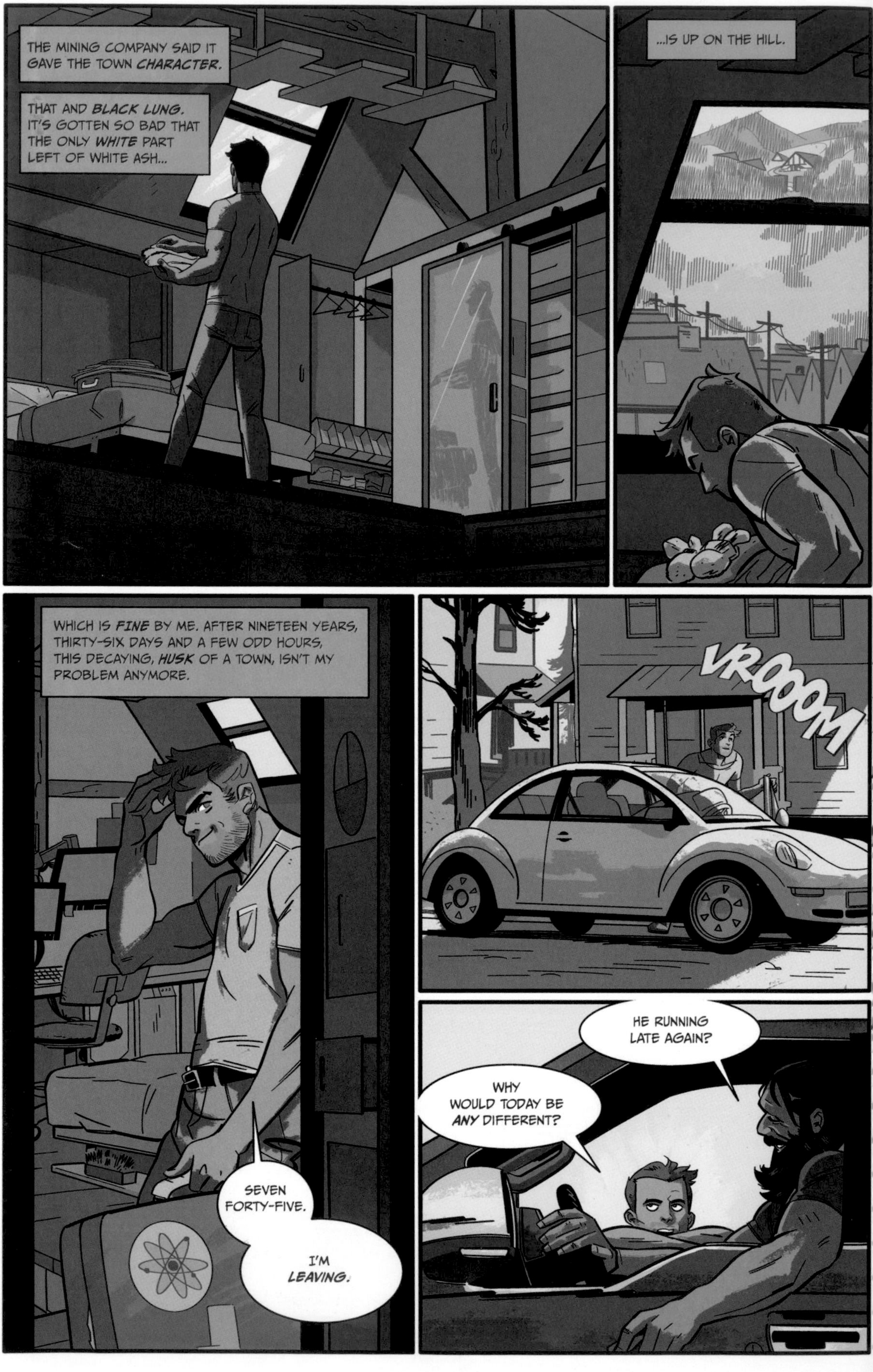
THE MINING COMPANY SAID IT GAVE THE TOWN CHARACTER.
THAT AND BLACK LUNG. IT'S GOTTEN SO BAD THAT THE ONLY WHITE PART LEFT OF WHITE ASH...
...IS UP ON THE HILL.
WHICH IS FINE BY ME. AFTER NINETEEN YEARS, THIRTY-SIX DAYS AND A FEW ODD HOURS, THIS DECAYING, HUSK OF A TOWN, ISN'T MY PROBLEM ANYMORE.
SEVEN FORTY-FIVE.
I'M LEAVING.
VROOOM
HE RUNNING LATE AGAIN?
WHY WOULD TODAY BE ANY DIFFERENT?

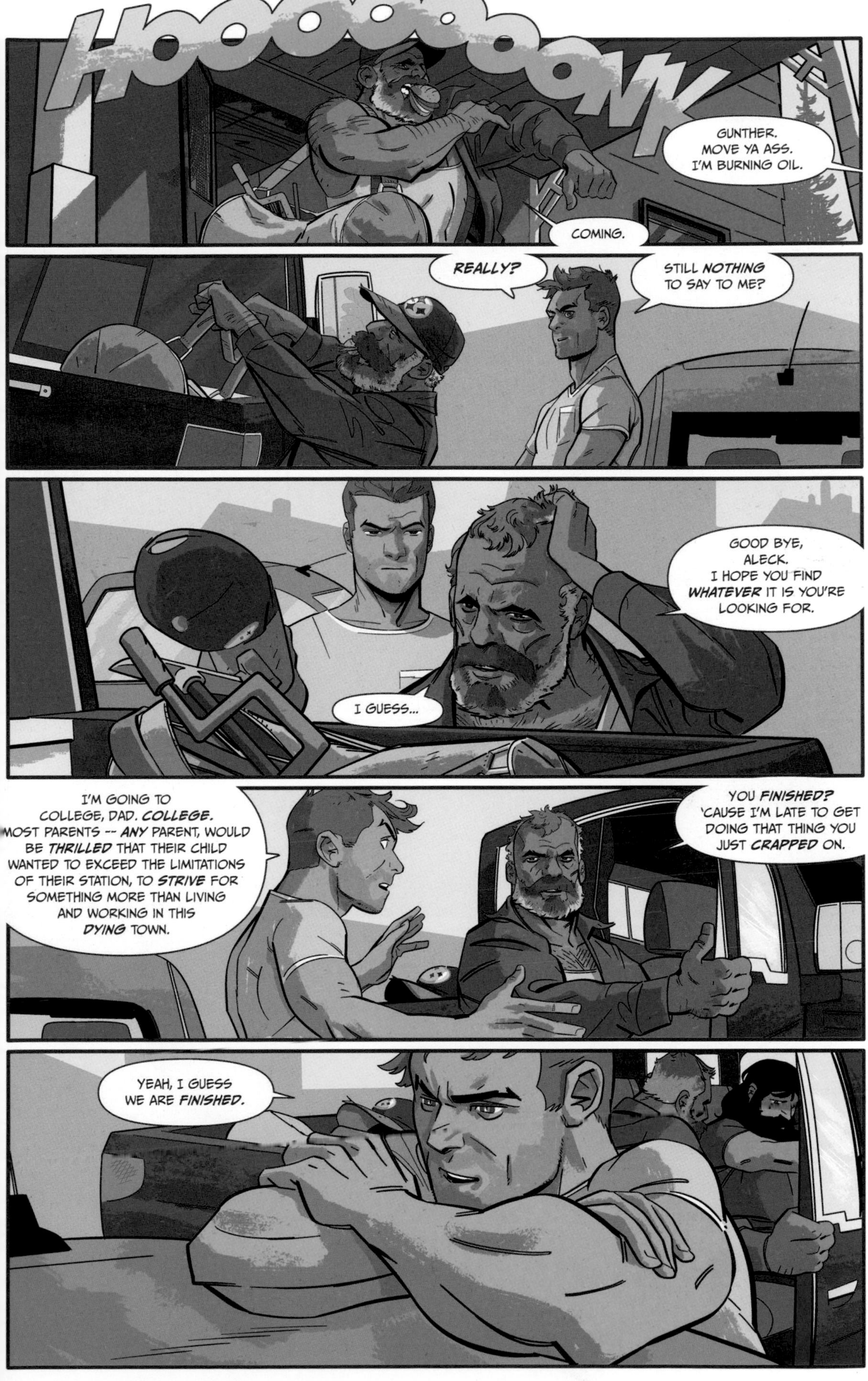
HOOOOOOONK
GUNTHER. MOVE YA ASS. I'M BURNING OIL.
COMING.
STILL NOTHING TO SAY TO ME?
REALLY?
GOOD BYE, ALECK. I HOPE YOU FIND WHATEVER IT IS YOU'RE LOOKING FOR.
I GUESS...
I'M GOING TO COLLEGE, DAD. COLLEGE. MOST PARENTS -- ANY PARENT, WOULD BE THRILLED THAT THEIR CHILD WANTED TO EXCEED THE LIMITATIONS OF THEIR STATION, TO STRIVE FOR SOMETHING MORE THAN LIVING AND WORKING IN THIS DYING TOWN.
YOU FINISHED? 'CAUSE I'M LATE TO GET DOING THAT THING YOU JUST CRAPPED ON.
YEAH, I GUESS WE ARE FINISHED.

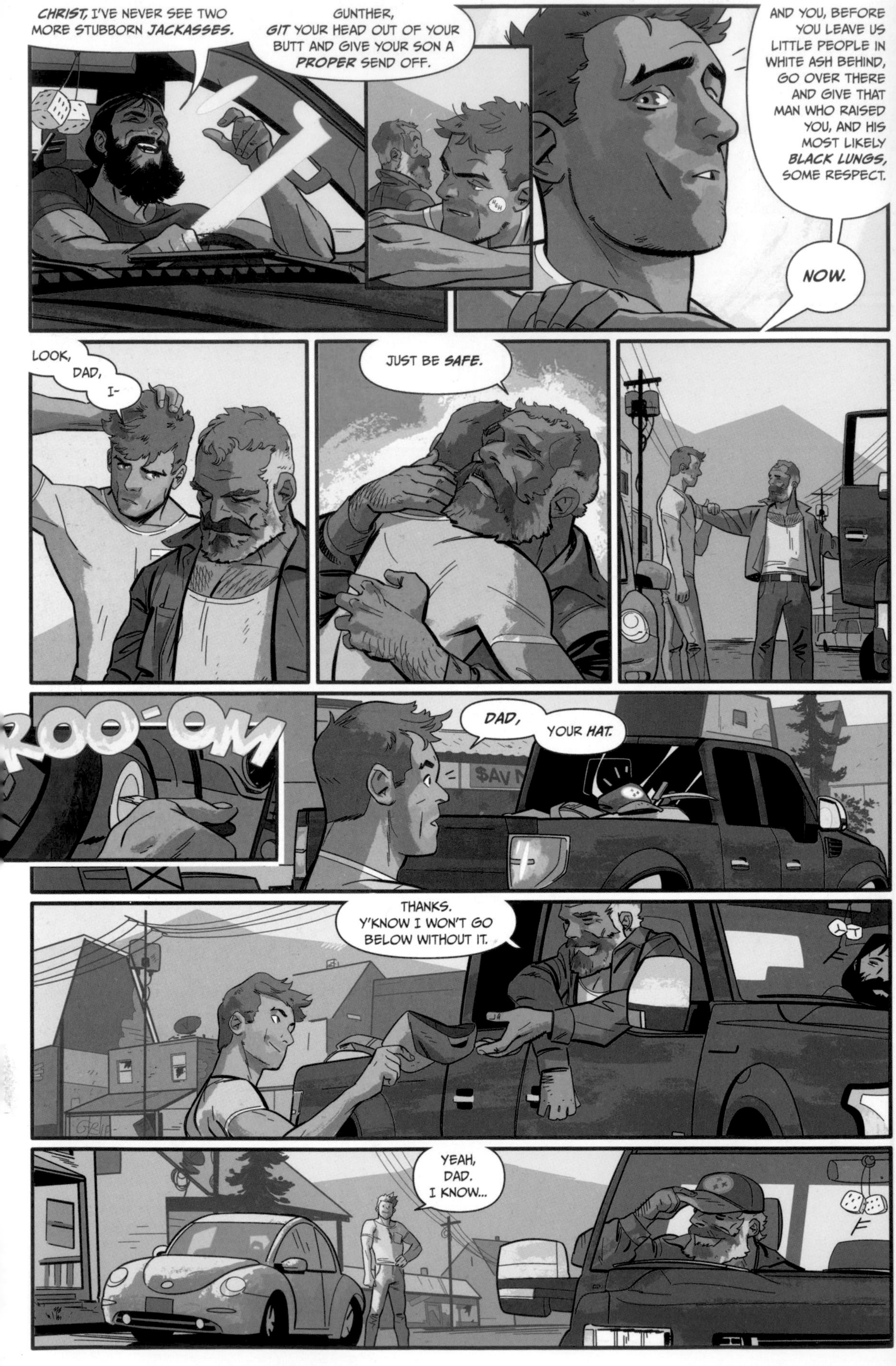
CHRIST, I'VE NEVER SEE TWO MORE STUBBORN JACKASSES.
GUNTHER, GIT YOUR HEAD OUT OF YOUR BUTT AND GIVE YOUR SON A PROPER SEND OFF.
HEH
AND YOU, BEFORE YOU LEAVE US LITTLE PEOPLE IN WHITE ASH BEHIND, GO OVER THERE AND GIVE THAT MAN WHO RAISED YOU, AND HIS MOST LIKELY BLACK LUNGS, SOME RESPECT.
NOW.
LOOK, DAD, I-
JUST BE SAFE.
ROO-OM
DAD, YOUR HAT.
$AV
THANKS. Y'KNOW I WON'T GO BELOW WITHOUT IT.
YEAH, DAD. I KNOW...

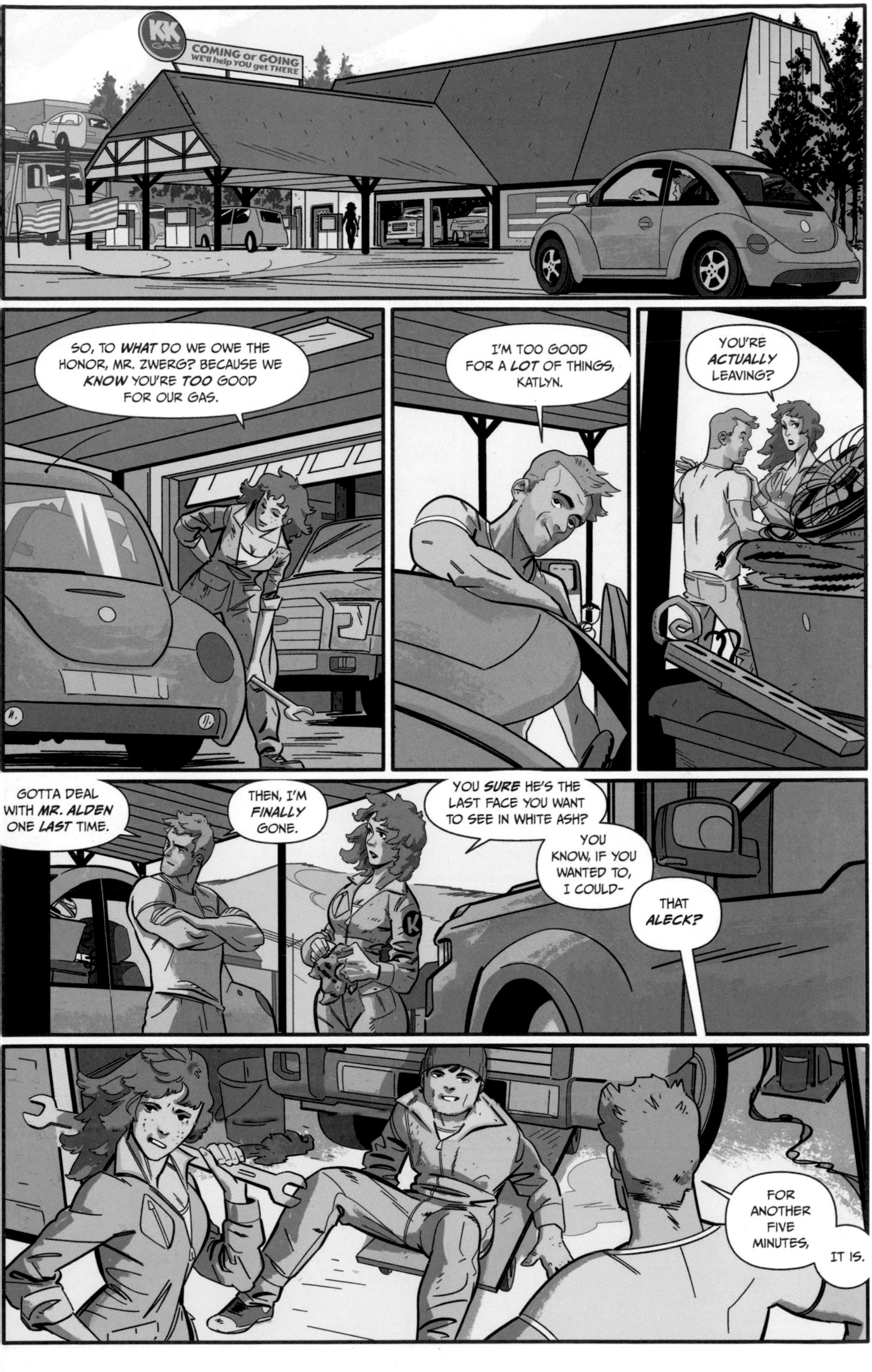
KK GAS
COMING or GOING WE'LL help YOU get THERE
SO, TO WHAT DO WE OWE THE HONOR, MR. ZWERG? BECAUSE WE KNOW YOU'RE TOO GOOD FOR OUR GAS.
I'M TOO GOOD FOR A LOT OF THINGS, KATLYN.
YOU'RE ACTUALLY LEAVING?
GOTTA DEAL WITH MR. ALDEN ONE LAST TIME.
THEN, I'M FINALLY GONE.
YOU SURE HE'S THE LAST FACE YOU WANT TO SEE IN WHITE ASH?
YOU KNOW, IF YOU WANTED TO, I COULD-
THAT ALECK?
FOR ANOTHER FIVE MINUTES,
IT IS.

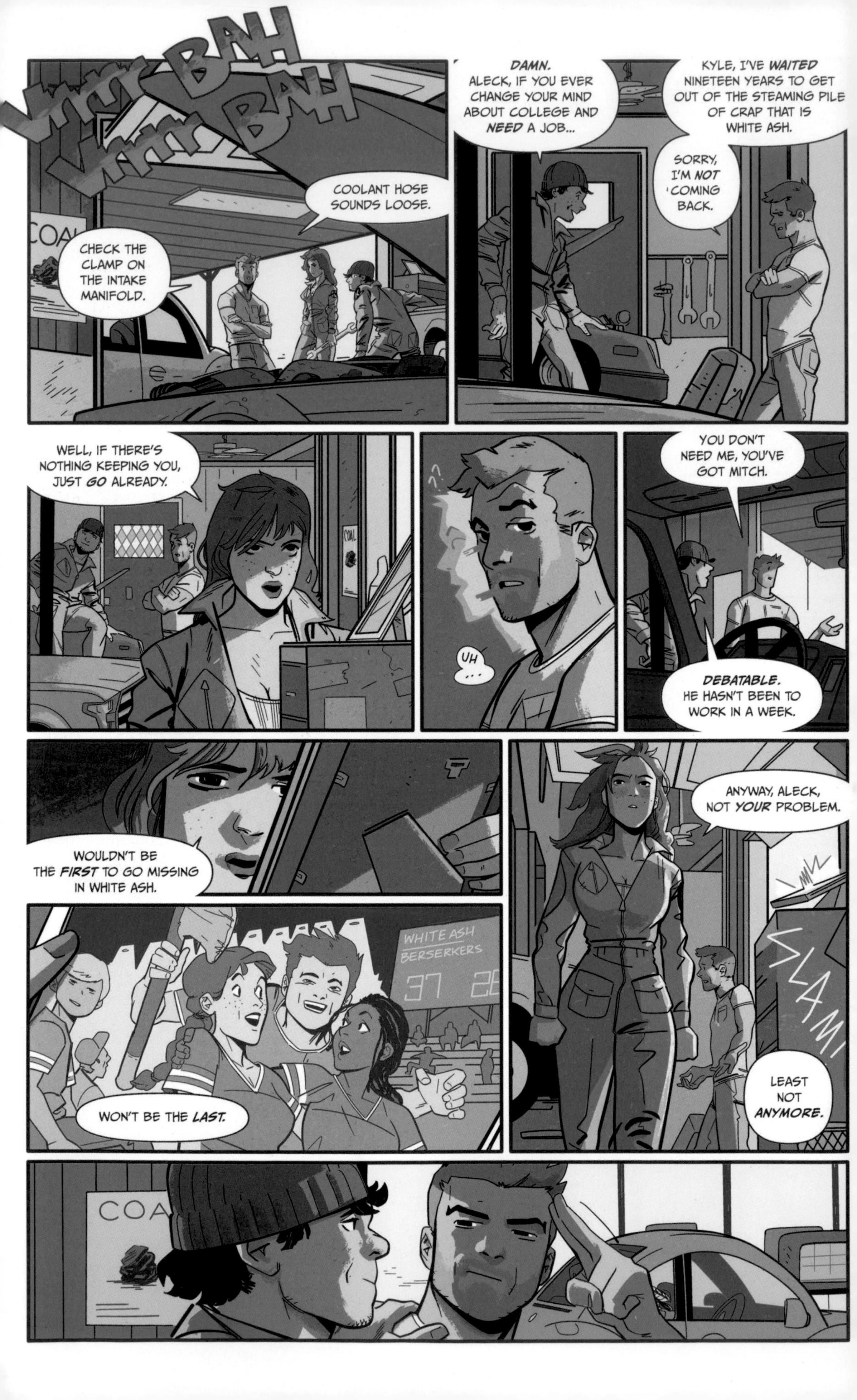
VRRR BAH VRRR BAH
COOLANT HOSE SOUNDS LOOSE.
CHECK THE CLAMP ON THE INTAKE MANIFOLD.
DAMN. ALECK, IF YOU EVER CHANGE YOUR MIND ABOUT COLLEGE AND NEED A JOB...
KYLE, I'VE WAITED NINETEEN YEARS TO GET OUT OF THE STEAMING PILE OF CRAP THAT IS WHITE ASH.
SORRY, I'M NOT COMING BACK.
WELL, IF THERE'S NOTHING KEEPING YOU, JUST GO ALREADY.
??
UH ...
YOU DON'T NEED ME, YOU'VE GOT MITCH.
DEBATABLE. HE HASN'T BEEN TO WORK IN A WEEK.
WOULDN'T BE THE FIRST TO GO MISSING IN WHITE ASH.
WHITE ASH BERSERKERS
37
WON'T BE THE LAST.
ANYWAY, ALECK, NOT YOUR PROBLEM.
SLAM!
LEAST NOT ANYMORE.
COA

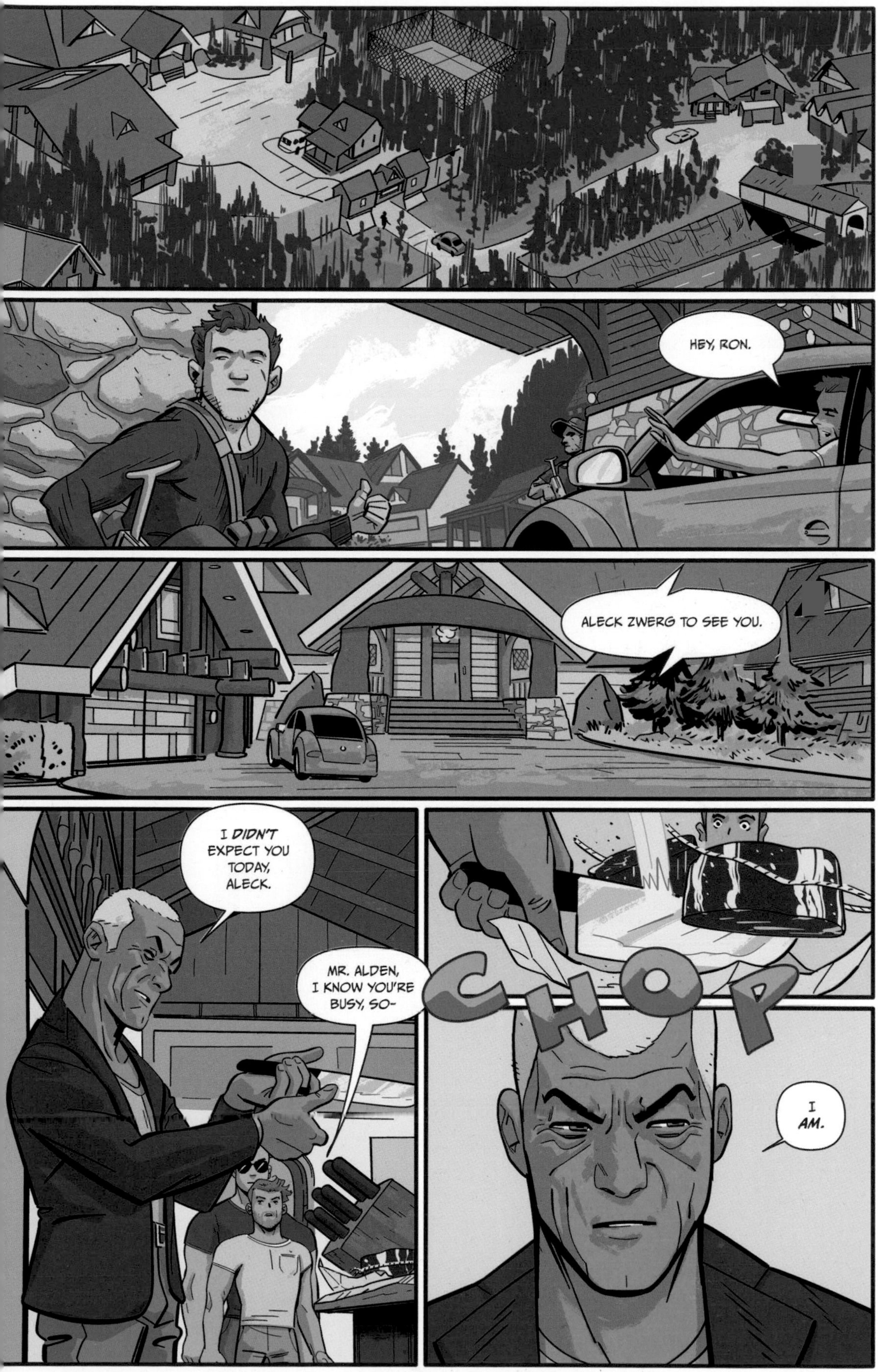
HEY, RON.
ALECK ZWERG TO SEE YOU.
I DIDN'T EXPECT YOU TODAY, ALECK.
MR. ALDEN, I KNOW YOU'RE BUSY, SO-
CHOP
I AM.

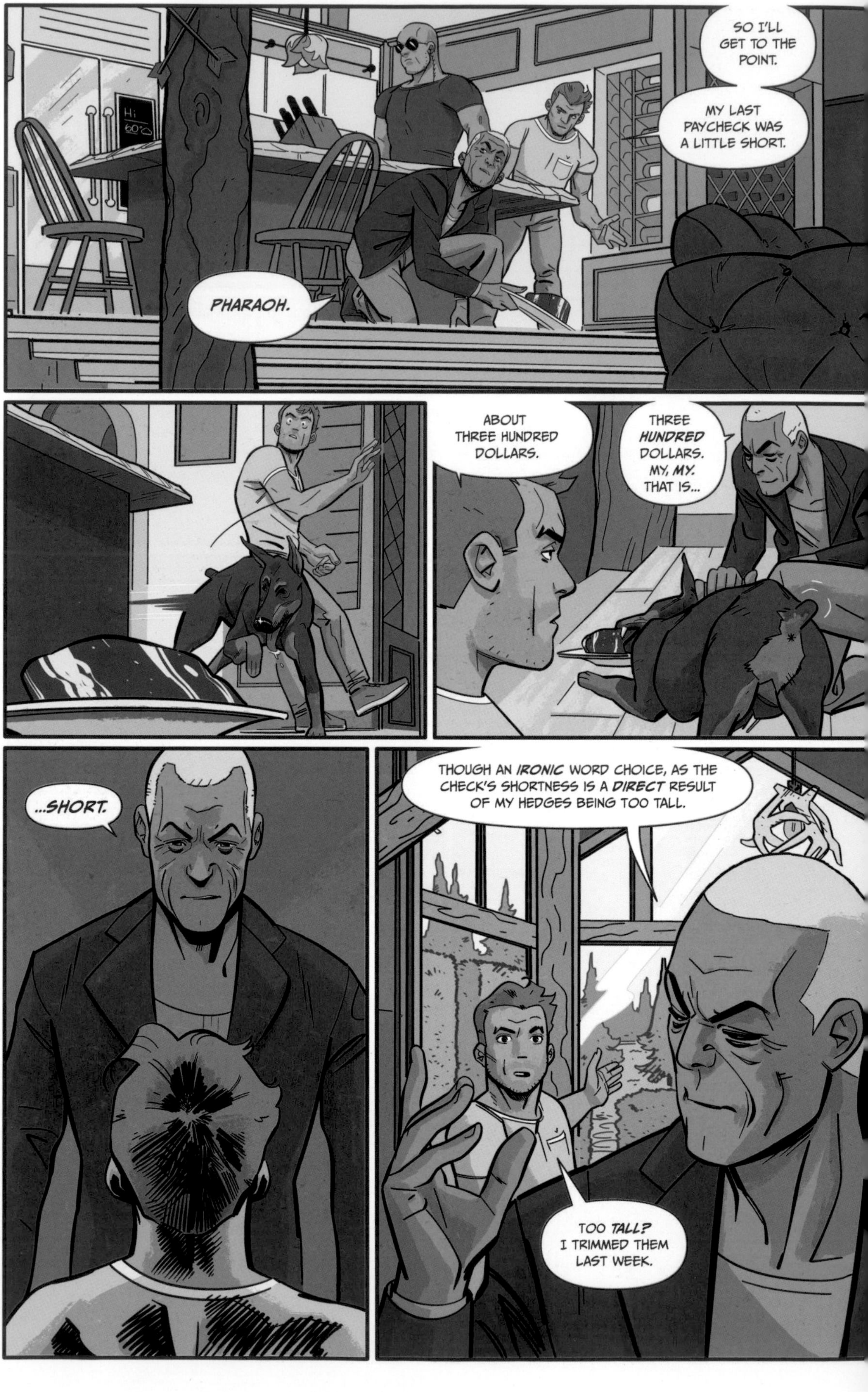
Hi
60°
SO I'LL GET TO THE POINT.
MY LAST PAYCHECK WAS A LITTLE SHORT.
PHARAOH.
ABOUT THREE HUNDRED DOLLARS.
THREE HUNDRED DOLLARS. MY, MY. THAT IS...
...SHORT.
THOUGH AN IRONIC WORD CHOICE, AS THE CHECK'S SHORTNESS IS A DIRECT RESULT OF MY HEDGES BEING TOO TALL.
TOO TALL? I TRIMMED THEM LAST WEEK.

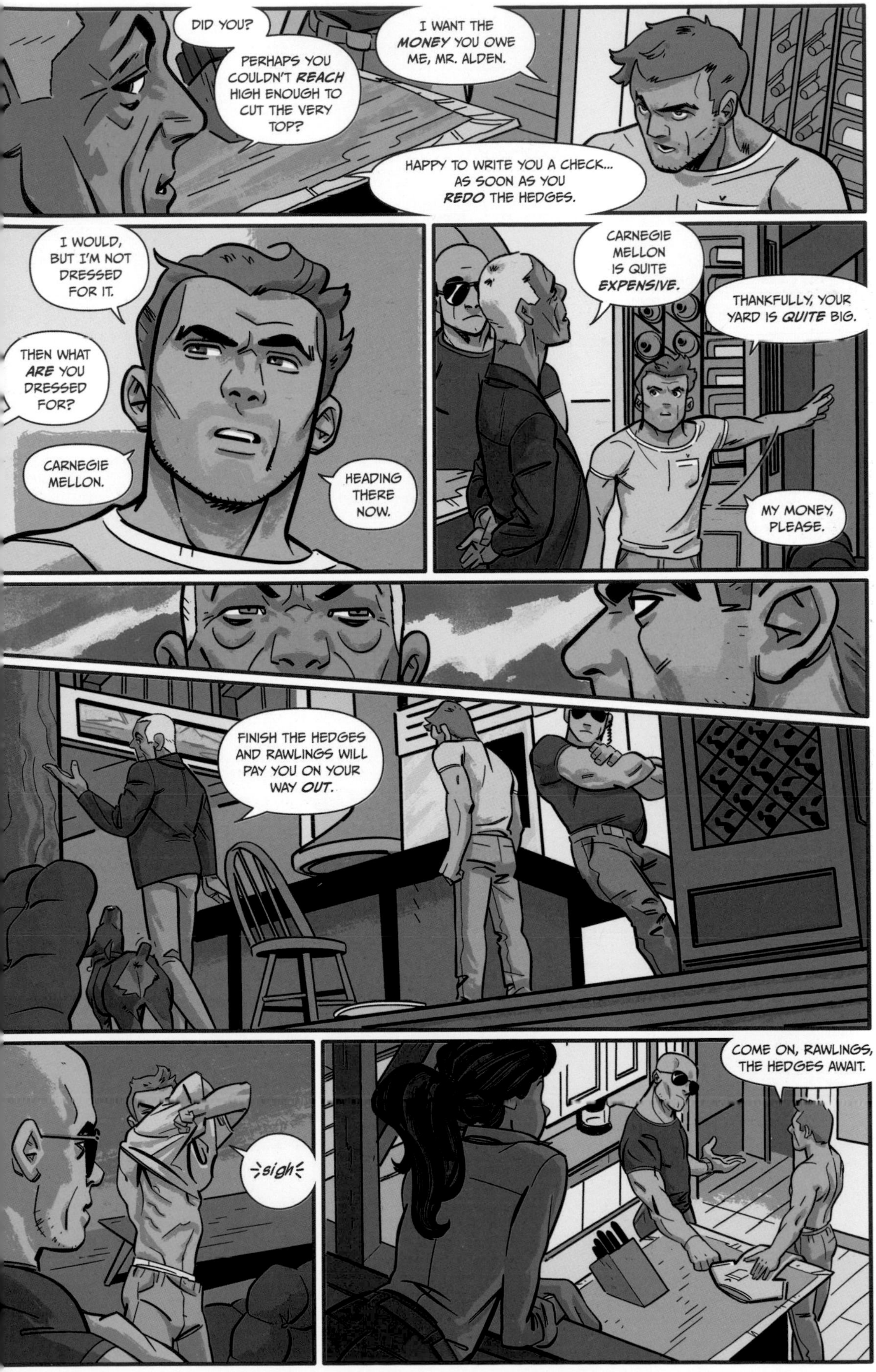
DID YOU?
PERHAPS YOU COULDN'T *REACH* HIGH ENOUGH TO CUT THE VERY TOP?
I WANT THE *MONEY* YOU OWE ME, MR. ALDEN.
HAPPY TO WRITE YOU A CHECK... AS SOON AS YOU *REDO* THE HEDGES.
I WOULD, BUT I'M NOT DRESSED FOR IT.
THEN WHAT *ARE* YOU DRESSED FOR?
CARNEGIE MELLON.
HEADING THERE NOW.
CARNEGIE MELLON IS QUITE *EXPENSIVE.*
THANKFULLY, YOUR YARD IS *QUITE* BIG.
MY MONEY, PLEASE.
FINISH THE HEDGES AND RAWLINGS WILL PAY YOU ON YOUR WAY *OUT*.
sigh
COME ON, RAWLINGS, THE HEDGES AWAIT.

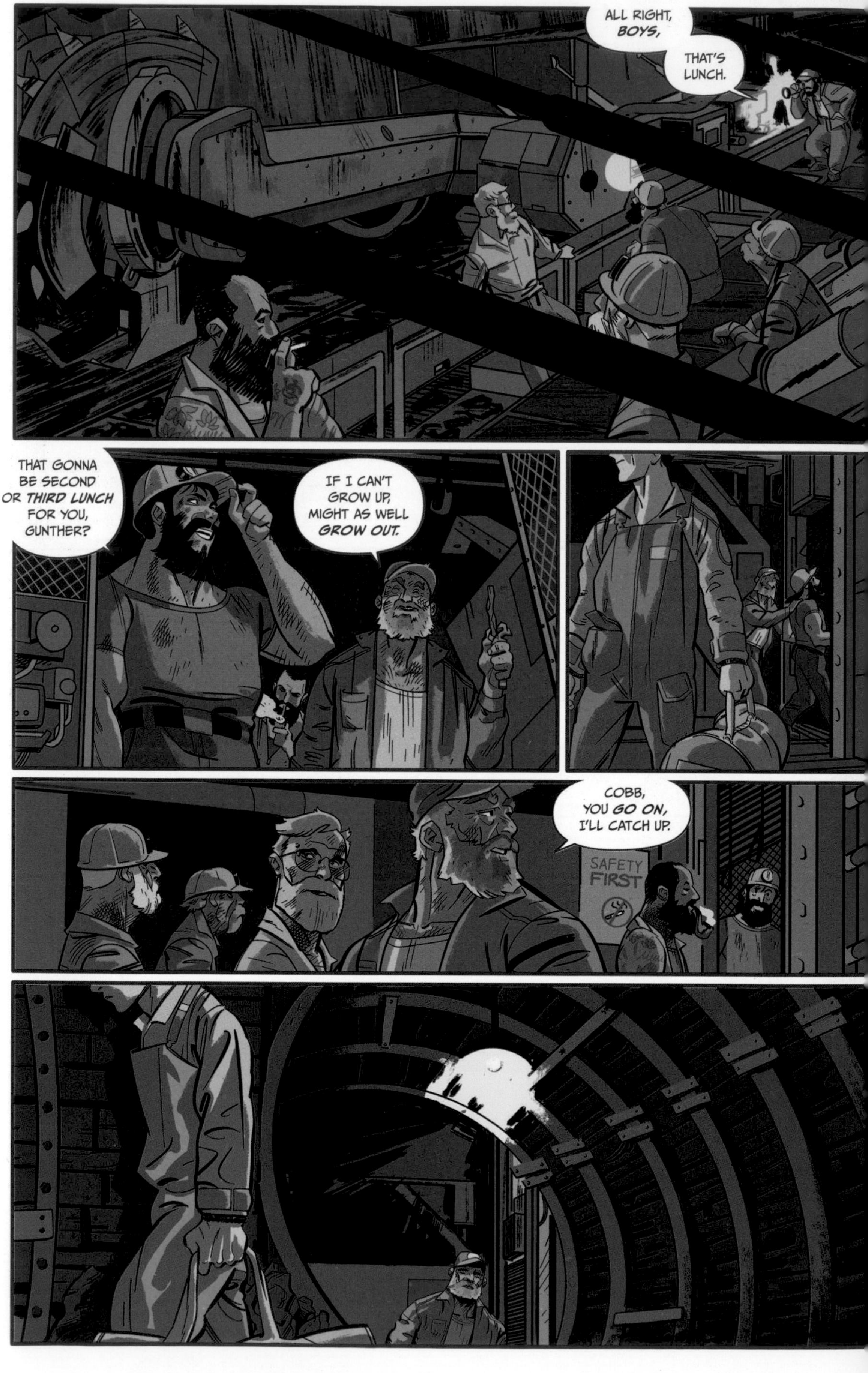
ALL RIGHT, BOYS,
THAT'S LUNCH.
THAT GONNA BE SECOND OR THIRD LUNCH FOR YOU, GUNTHER?
IF I CAN'T GROW UP, MIGHT AS WELL GROW OUT.
COBB, YOU GO ON, I'LL CATCH UP.
SAFETY FIRST

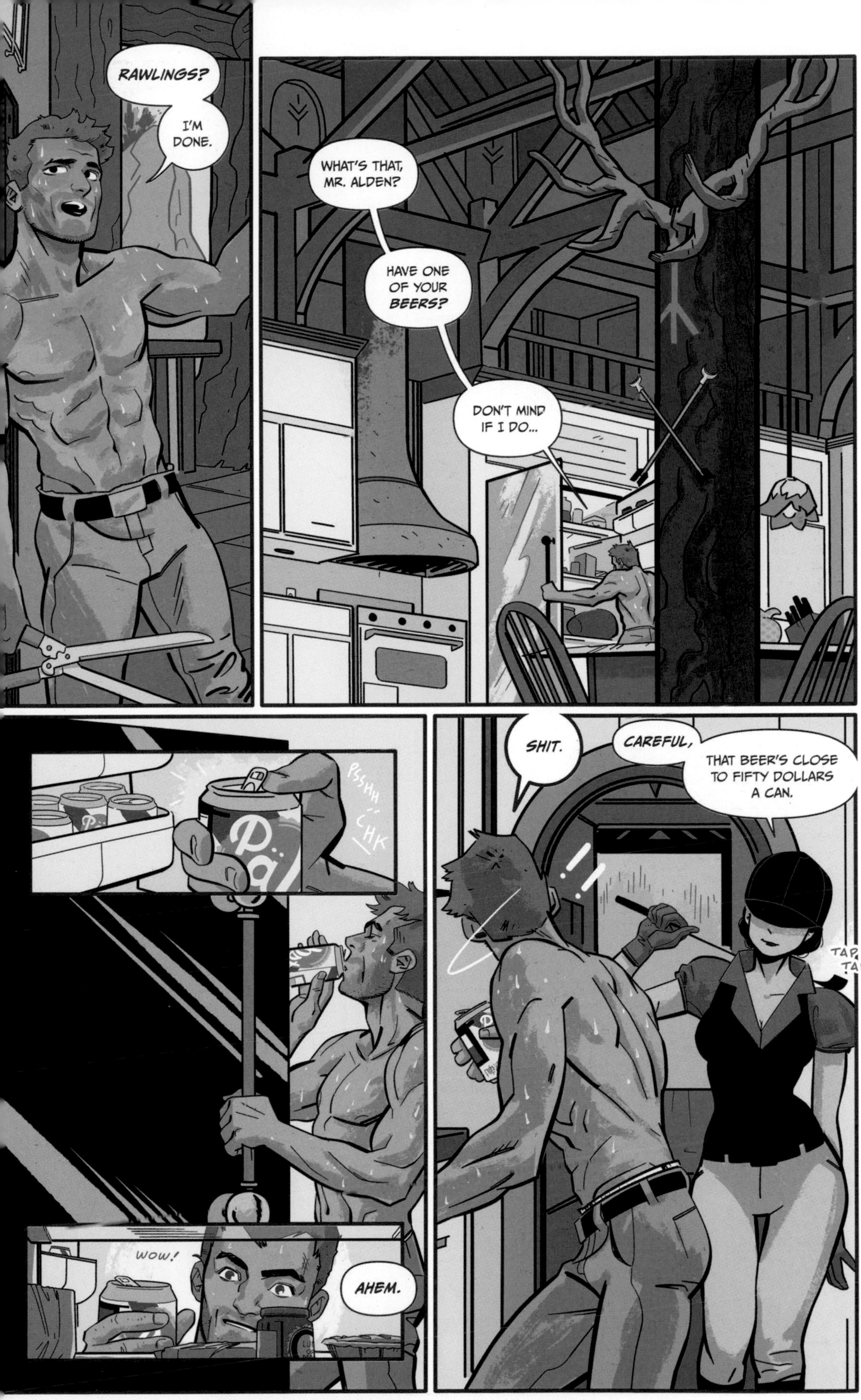
RAWLINGS?
I'M DONE.
WHAT'S THAT, MR. ALDEN?
HAVE ONE OF YOUR BEERS?
DON'T MIND IF I DO...
PSSHH CHK
WOW!
AHEM.
SHIT.
CAREFUL,
THAT BEER'S CLOSE TO FIFTY DOLLARS A CAN.
TAP TAP

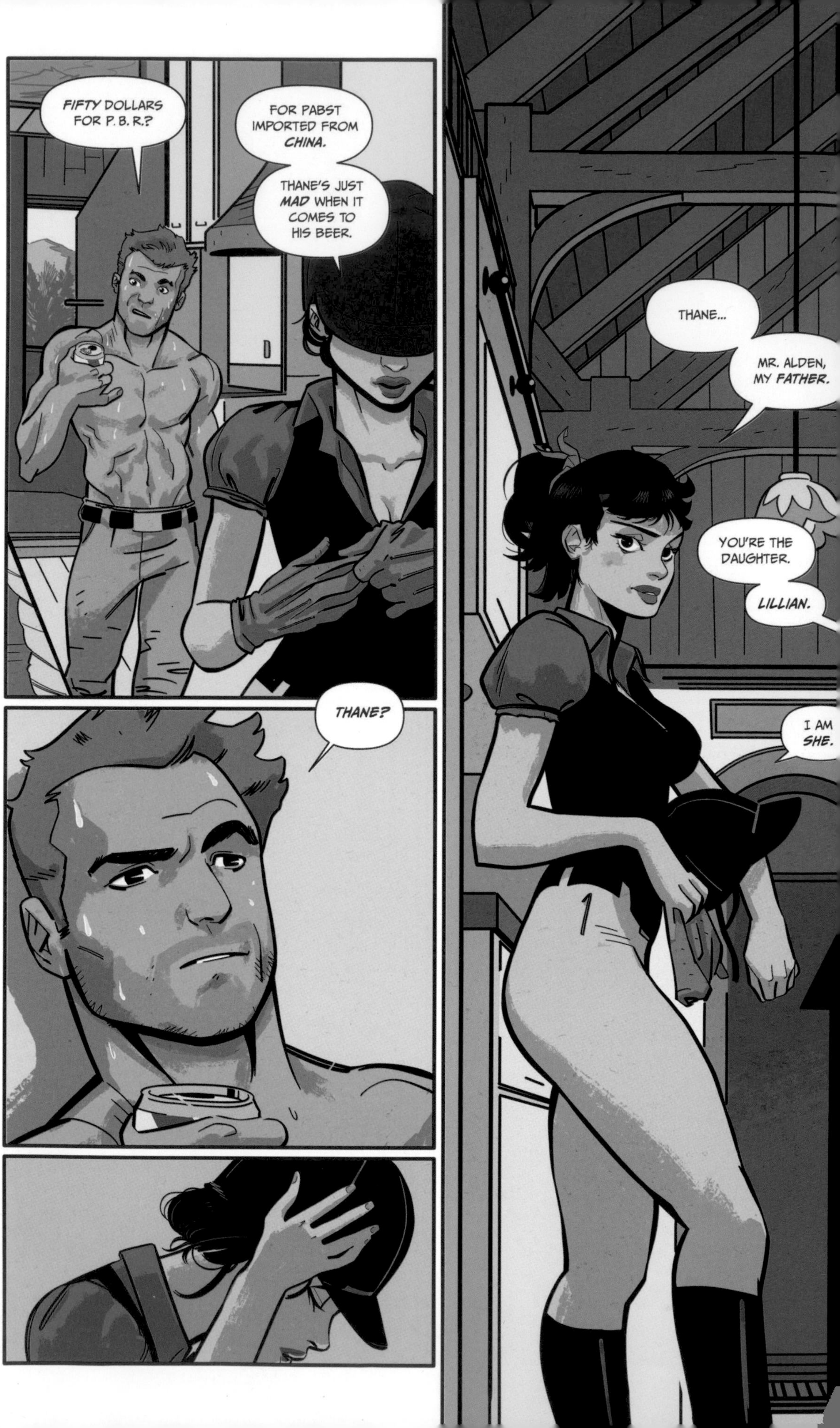
FIFTY DOLLARS FOR P.B.R.?
FOR PABST IMPORTED FROM CHINA.
THANE'S JUST MAD WHEN IT COMES TO HIS BEER.
THANE?
THANE...
MR. ALDEN, MY FATHER.
YOU'RE THE DAUGHTER.
LILLIAN.
I AM SHE.

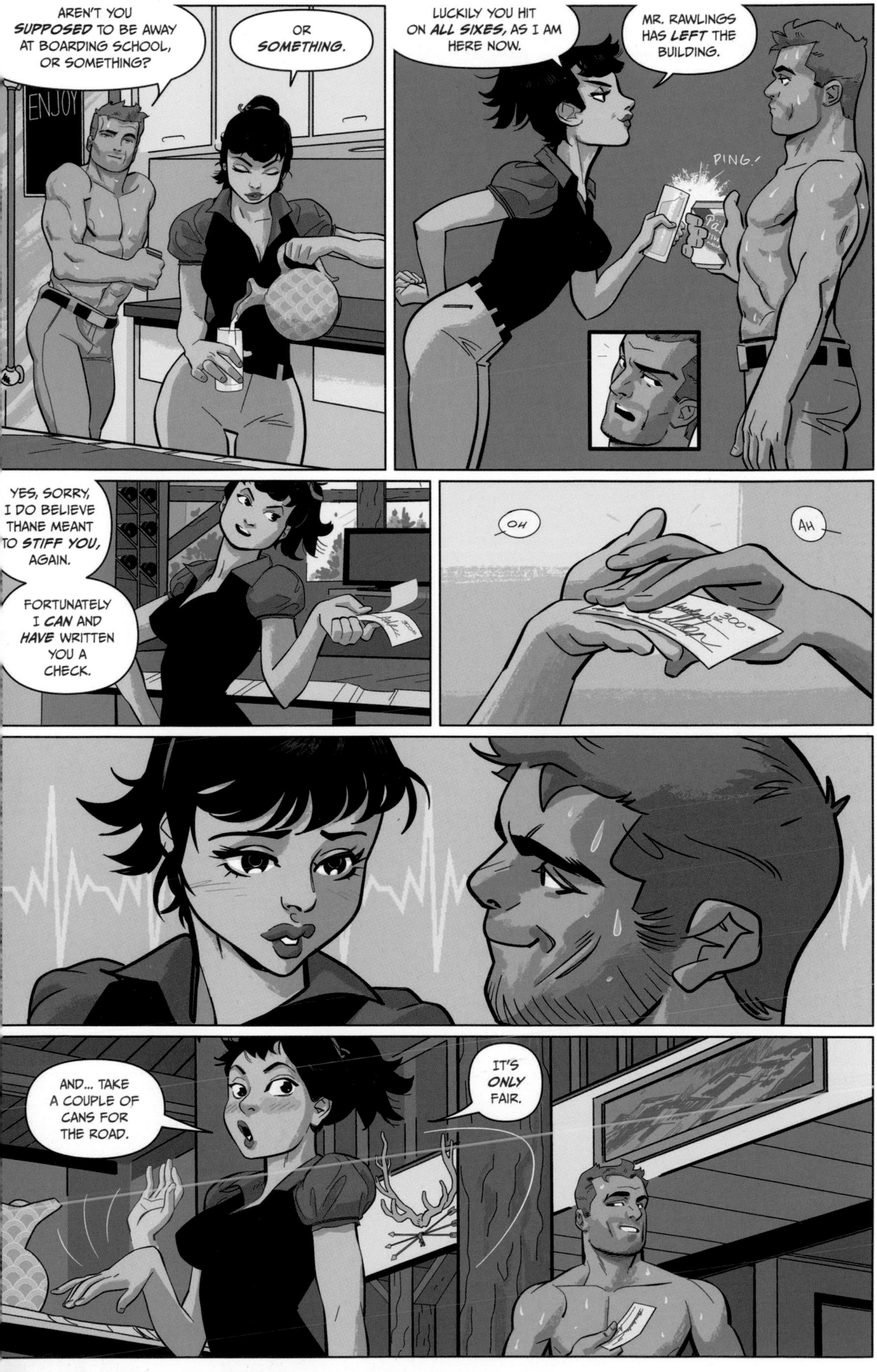
AREN'T YOU SUPPOSED TO BE AWAY AT BOARDING SCHOOL, OR SOMETHING?
OR SOMETHING.
LUCKILY YOU HIT ON ALL SIXES, AS I AM HERE NOW.
MR. RAWLINGS HAS LEFT THE BUILDING.
PING!
YES, SORRY, I DO BELIEVE THANE MEANT TO STIFF YOU, AGAIN.
FORTUNATELY I CAN AND HAVE WRITTEN YOU A CHECK.
OH
AH
AND... TAKE A COUPLE OF CANS FOR THE ROAD.
IT'S ONLY FAIR.

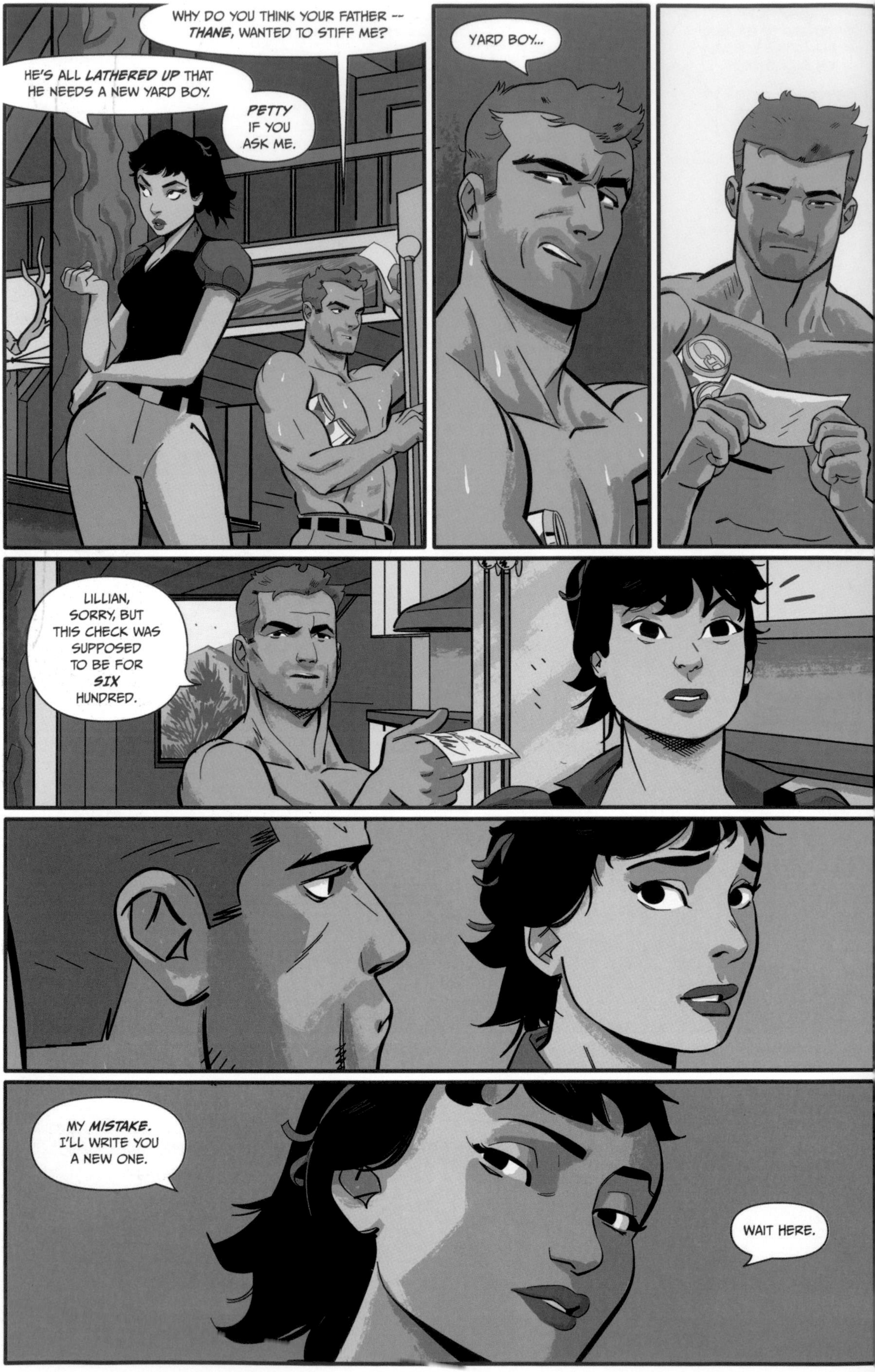

WHY DO YOU THINK YOUR FATHER -- THANE, WANTED TO STIFF ME?
HE'S ALL LATHERED UP THAT HE NEEDS A NEW YARD BOY.
PETTY IF YOU ASK ME.
YARD BOY...
LILLIAN, SORRY, BUT THIS CHECK WAS SUPPOSED TO BE FOR SIX HUNDRED.
MY MISTAKE. I'LL WRITE YOU A NEW ONE.
WAIT HERE.

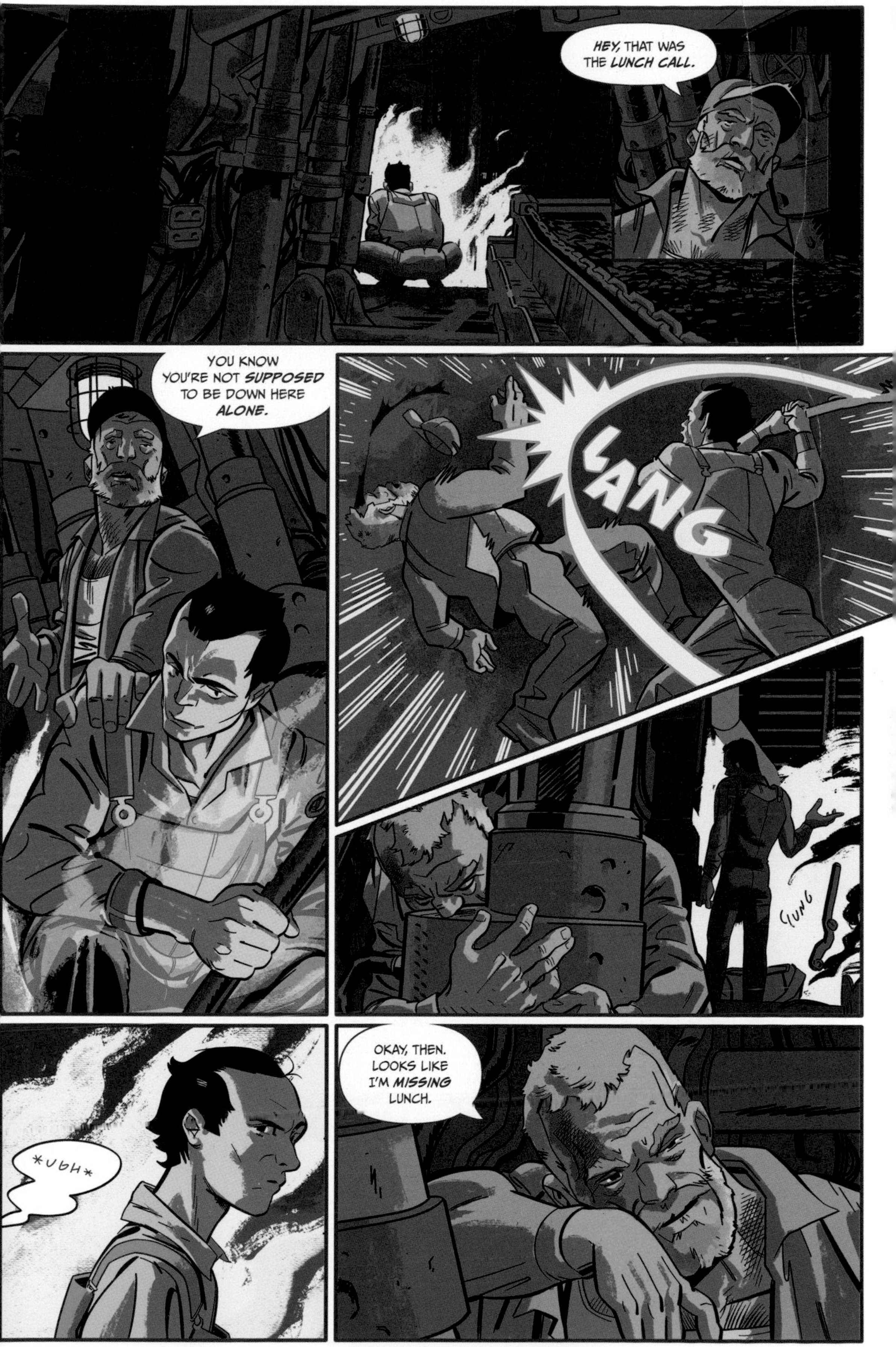
HEY, THAT WAS THE LUNCH CALL.
YOU KNOW YOU'RE NOT SUPPOSED TO BE DOWN HERE ALONE.
LANG
CLUNG
UGH
OKAY, THEN. LOOKS LIKE I'M MISSING LUNCH.

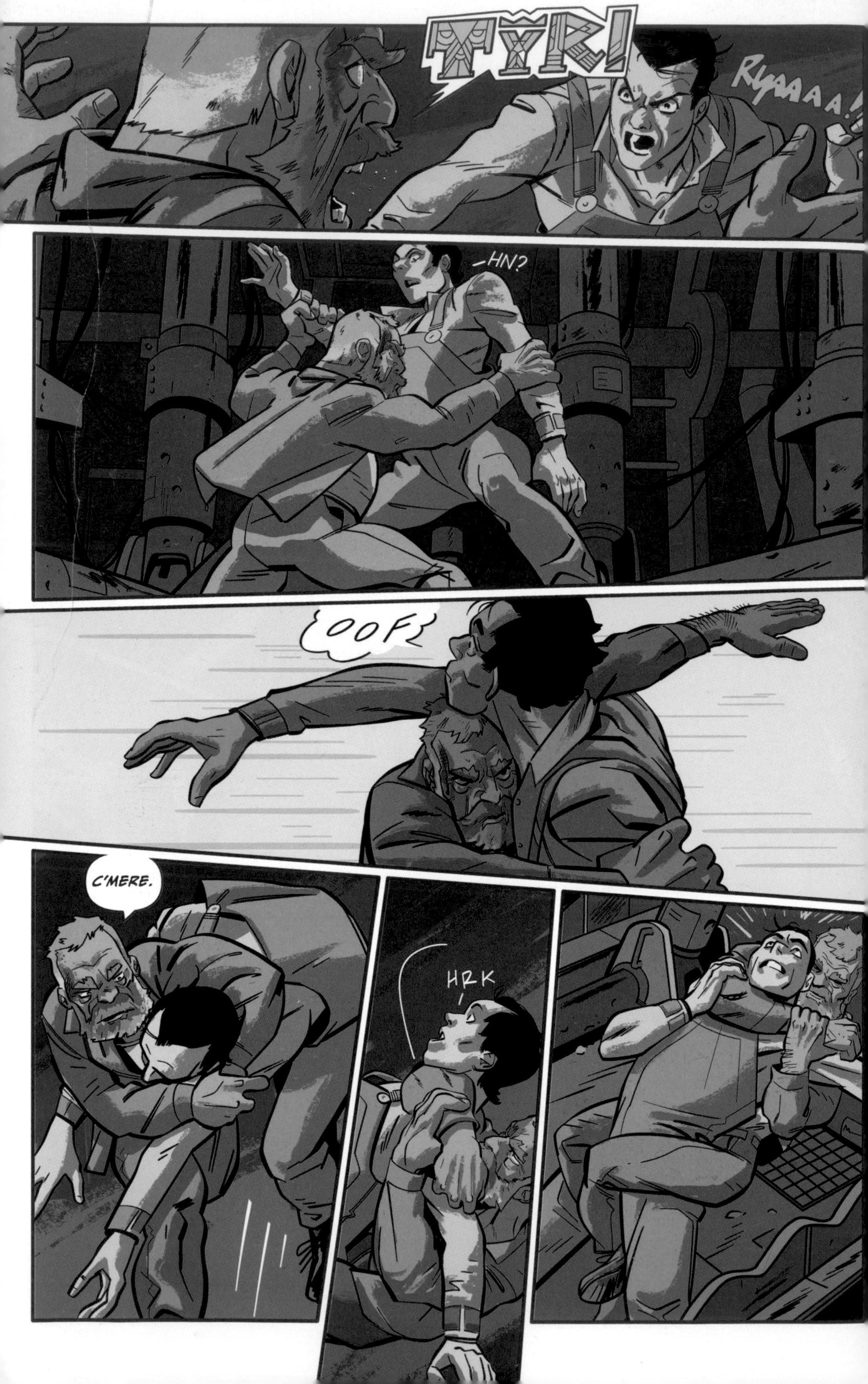
TYR!
Ryaaaa!!
-HN?
OOF
C'MERE.
HRK

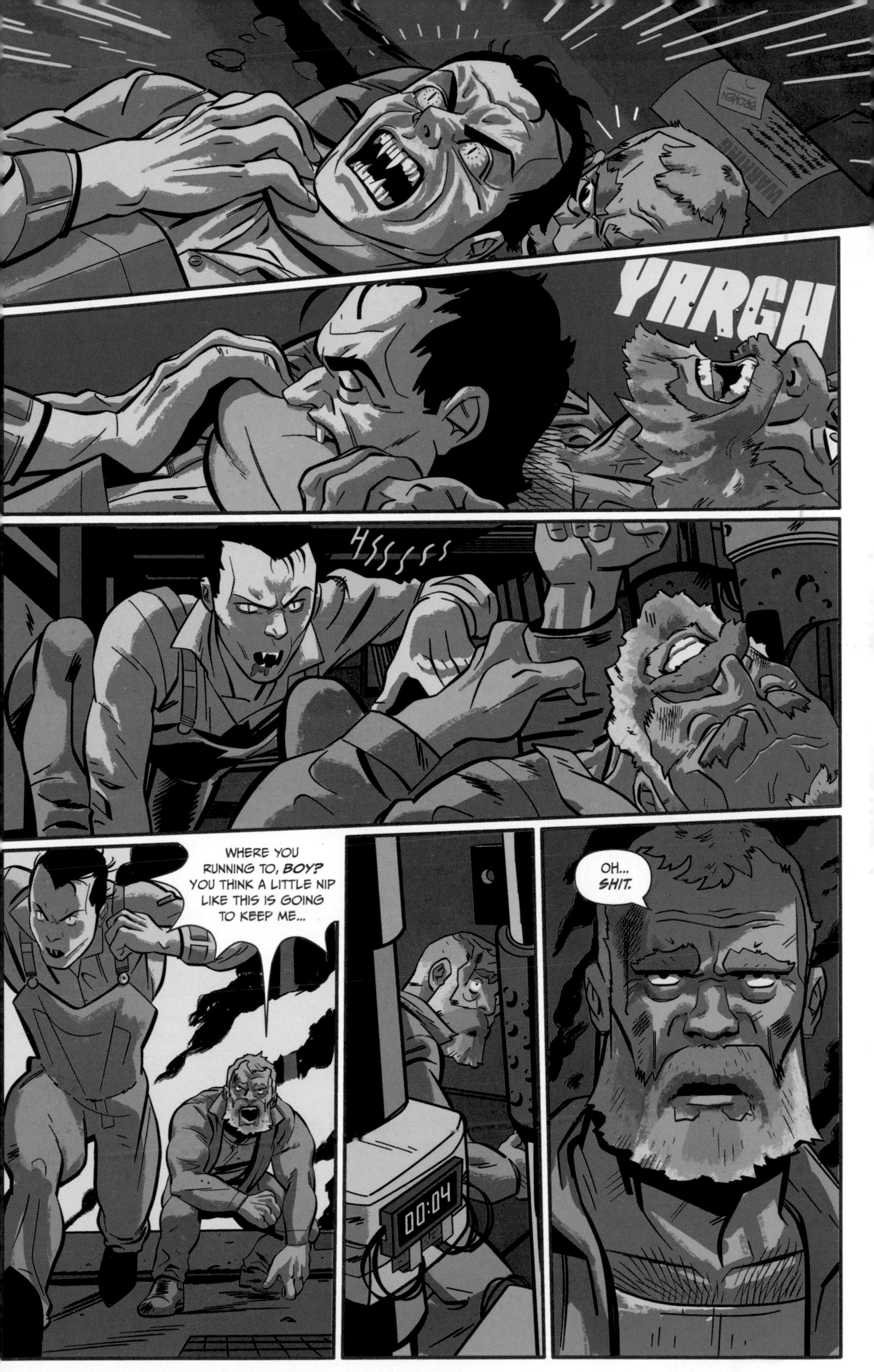
YARGH
HSSSSS
WHERE YOU RUNNING TO, *BOY?* YOU THINK A LITTLE NIP LIKE THIS IS GOING TO KEEP ME...
00:04
OH... *SHIT.*

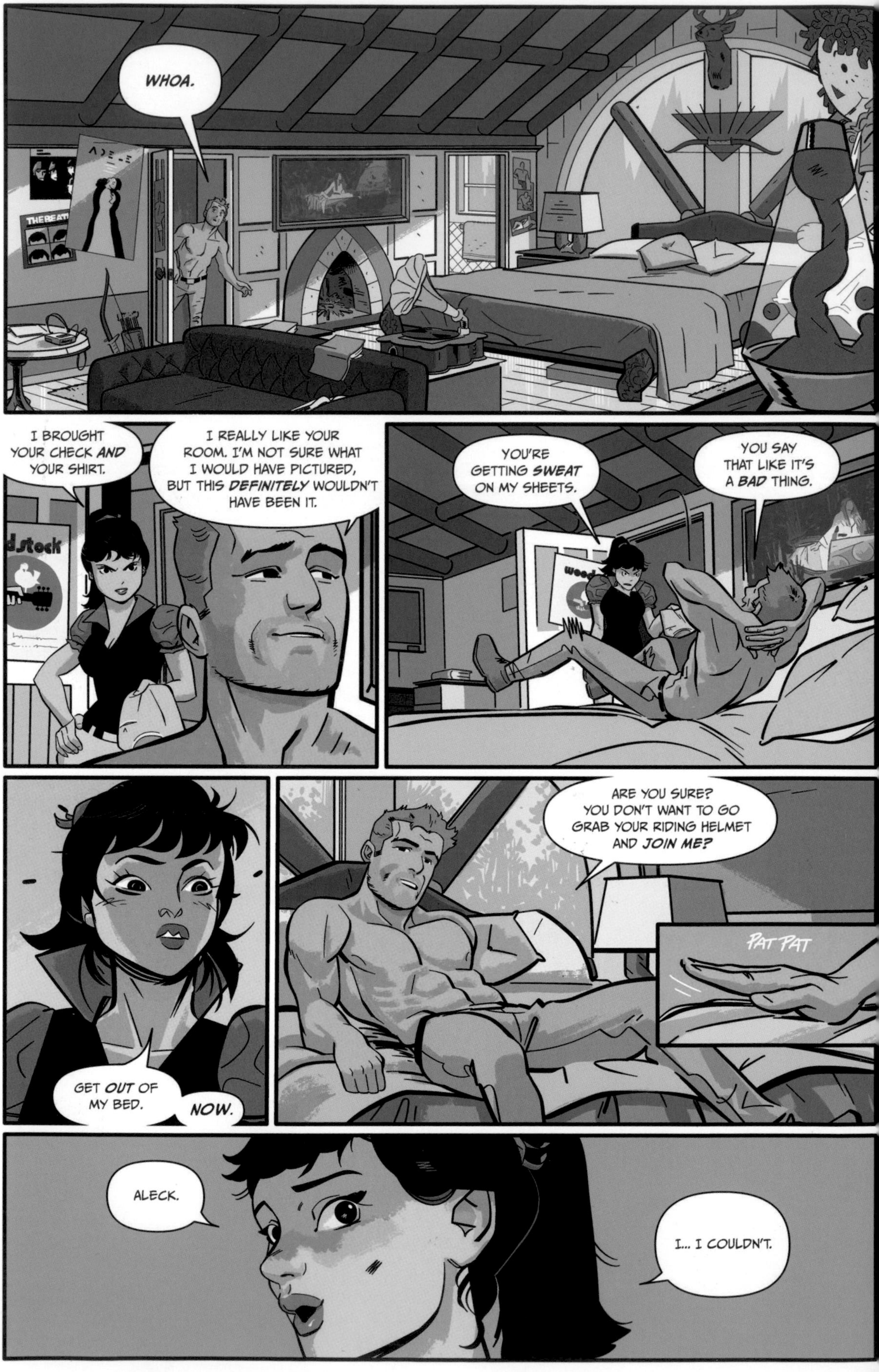
WHOA.
I BROUGHT YOUR CHECK AND YOUR SHIRT.
I REALLY LIKE YOUR ROOM. I'M NOT SURE WHAT I WOULD HAVE PICTURED, BUT THIS DEFINITELY WOULDN'T HAVE BEEN IT.
YOU'RE GETTING SWEAT ON MY SHEETS.
YOU SAY THAT LIKE IT'S A BAD THING.
GET OUT OF MY BED.
NOW.
ARE YOU SURE? YOU DON'T WANT TO GO GRAB YOUR RIDING HELMET AND JOIN ME?
PAT PAT
ALECK.
I... I COULDN'T.

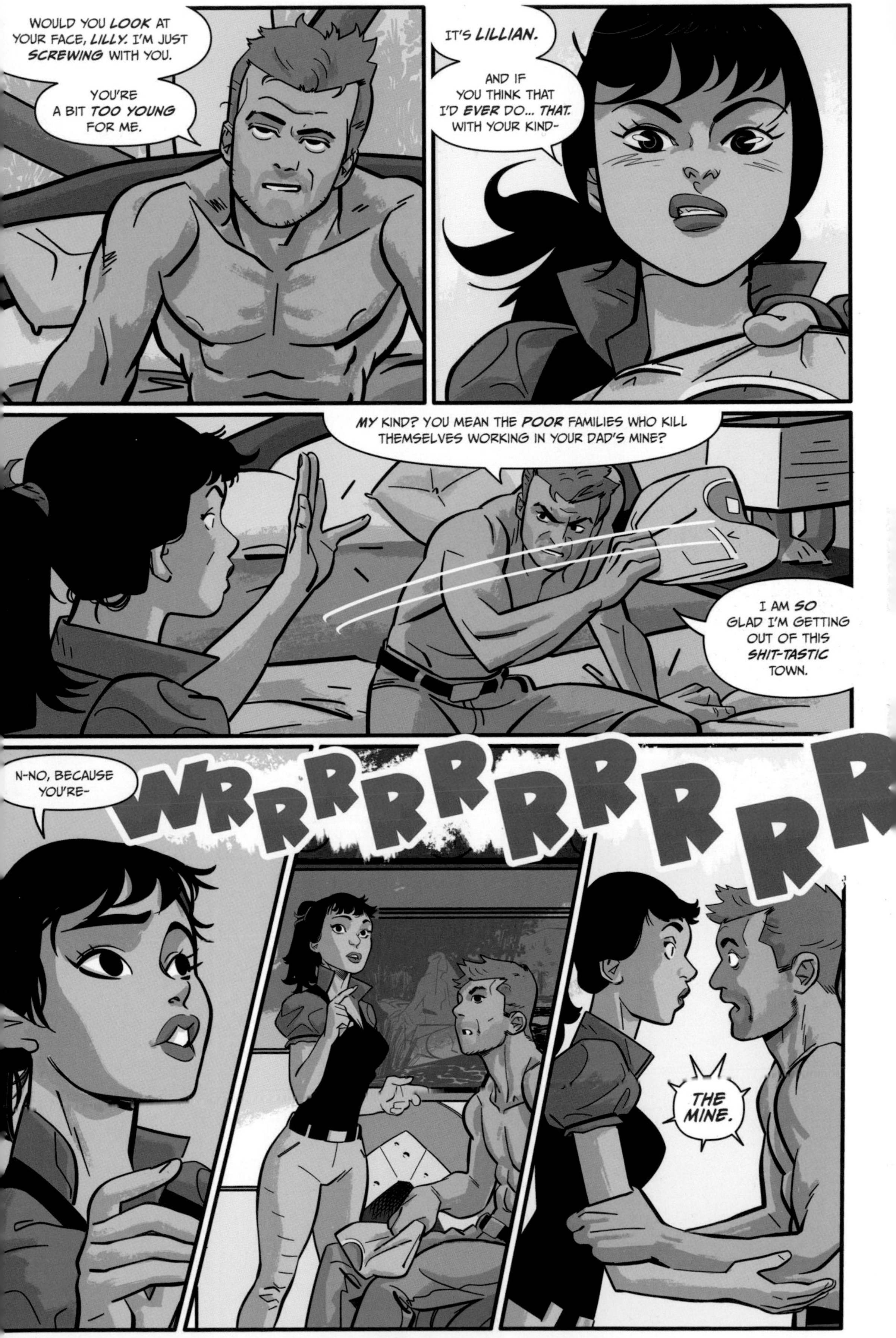
WOULD YOU LOOK AT YOUR FACE, LILLY. I'M JUST SCREWING WITH YOU.
YOU'RE A BIT TOO YOUNG FOR ME.
IT'S LILLIAN.
AND IF YOU THINK THAT I'D EVER DO... THAT. WITH YOUR KIND-
MY KIND? YOU MEAN THE POOR FAMILIES WHO KILL THEMSELVES WORKING IN YOUR DAD'S MINE?
I AM SO GLAD I'M GETTING OUT OF THIS SHIT-TASTIC TOWN.
N-NO, BECAUSE YOU'RE-
WRRRRRRRRRR
THE MINE.

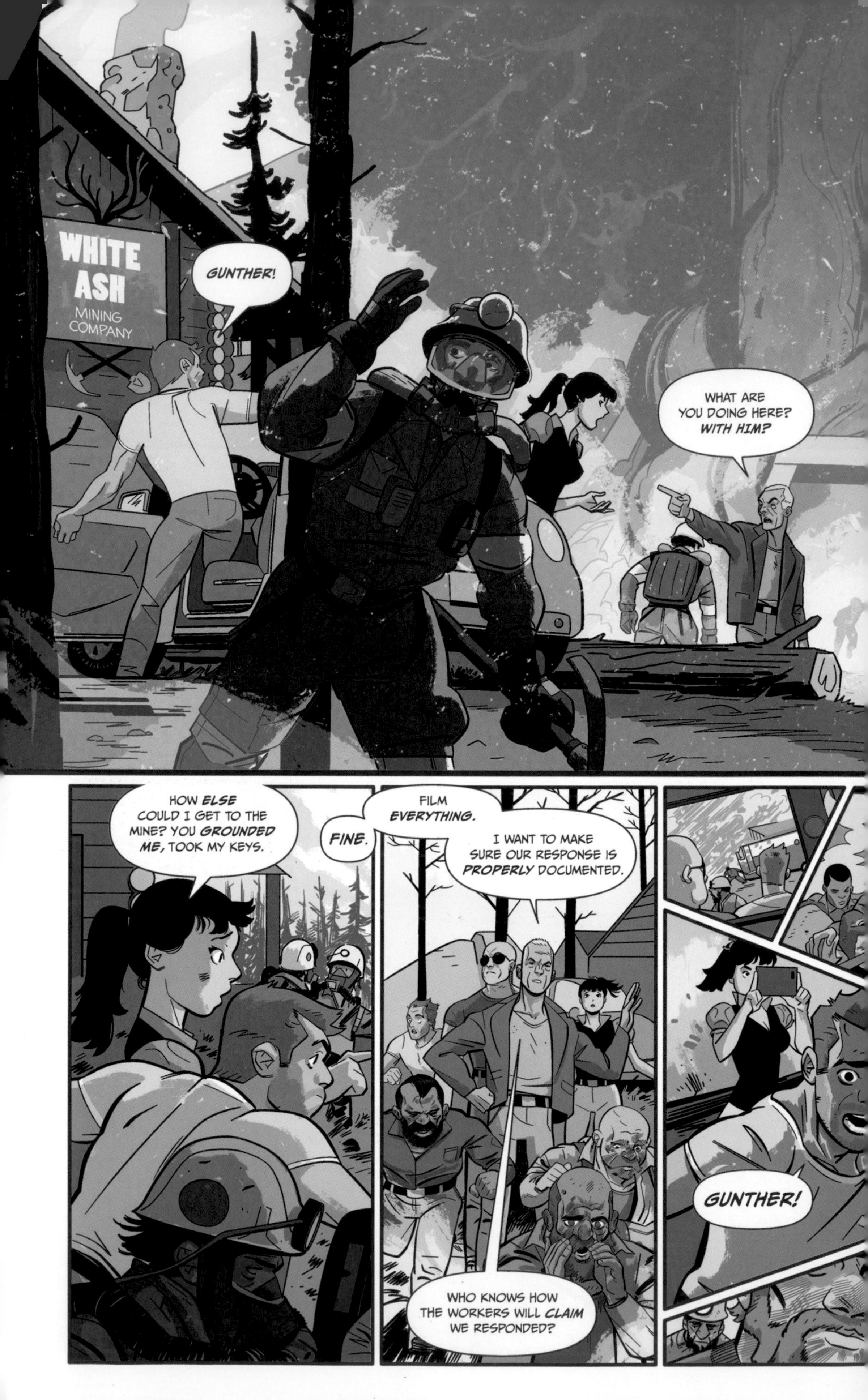
WHITE ASH MINING COMPANY
GUNTHER!
WHAT ARE YOU DOING HERE? WITH HIM?
HOW ELSE COULD I GET TO THE MINE? YOU GROUNDED ME, TOOK MY KEYS.
FINE.
FILM EVERYTHING.
I WANT TO MAKE SURE OUR RESPONSE IS PROPERLY DOCUMENTED.
WHO KNOWS HOW THE WORKERS WILL CLAIM WE RESPONDED?
GUNTHER!

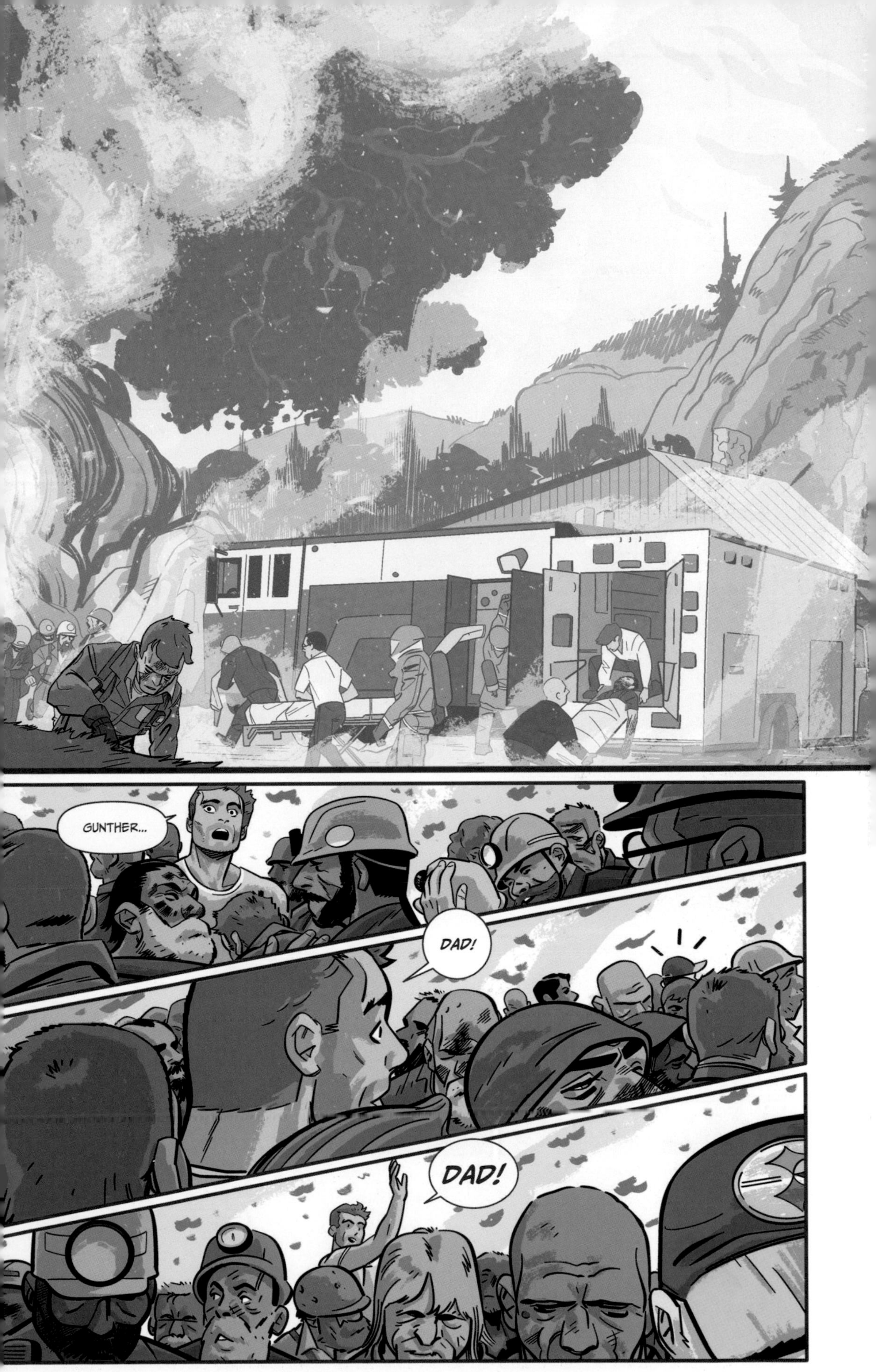
GUNTHER...
DAD!
DAD!

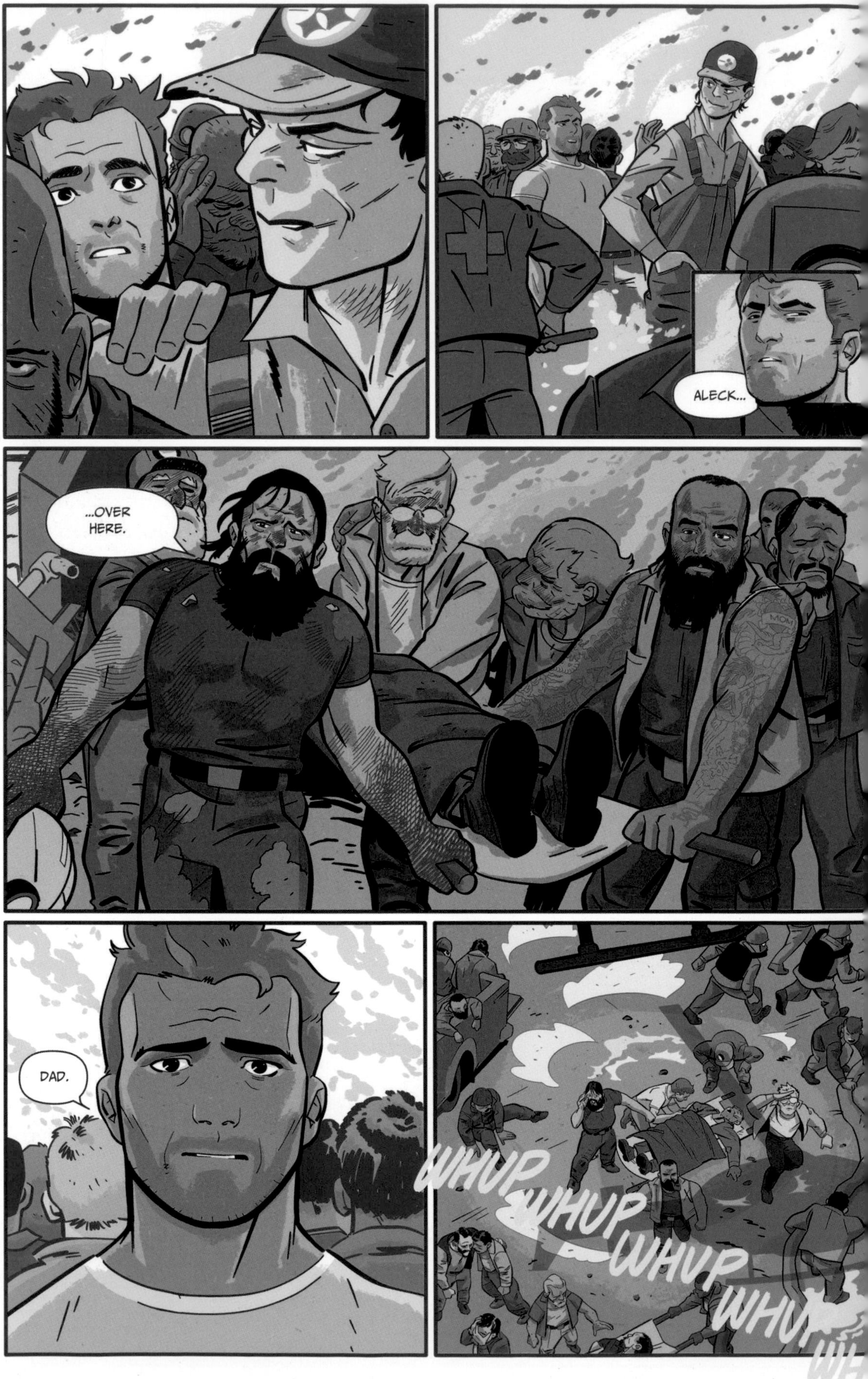
ALECK...
...OVER HERE.
DAD.
WHUP
WHUP
WHUP
WHUP
WH

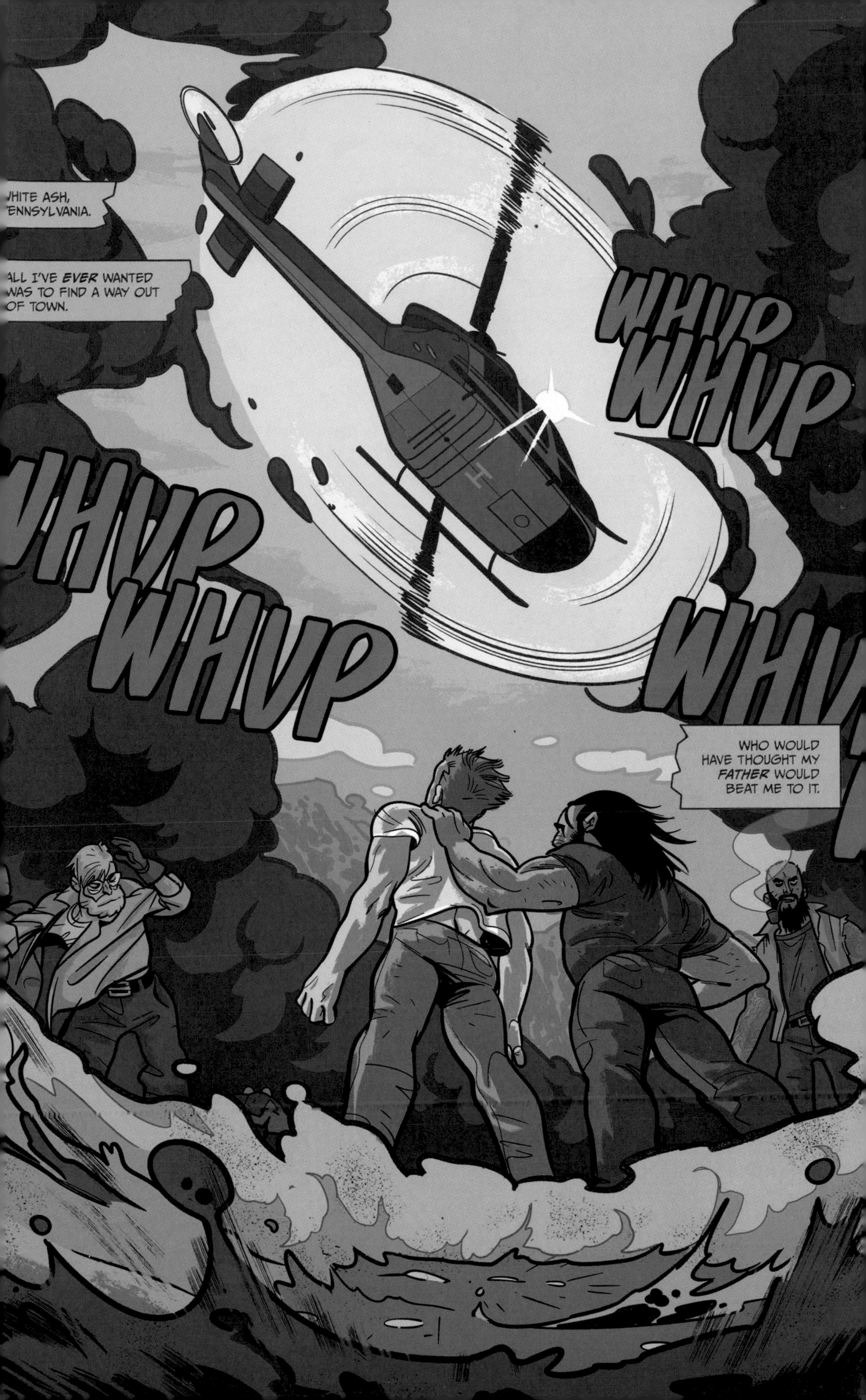
WHITE ASH, PENNSYLVANIA.
ALL I'VE *EVER* WANTED WAS TO FIND A WAY OUT OF TOWN.
WHUP WHUP
WHUP WHUP
WHU
WHO WOULD HAVE THOUGHT MY *FATHER* WOULD BEAT ME TO IT.

CHAPTER TWO

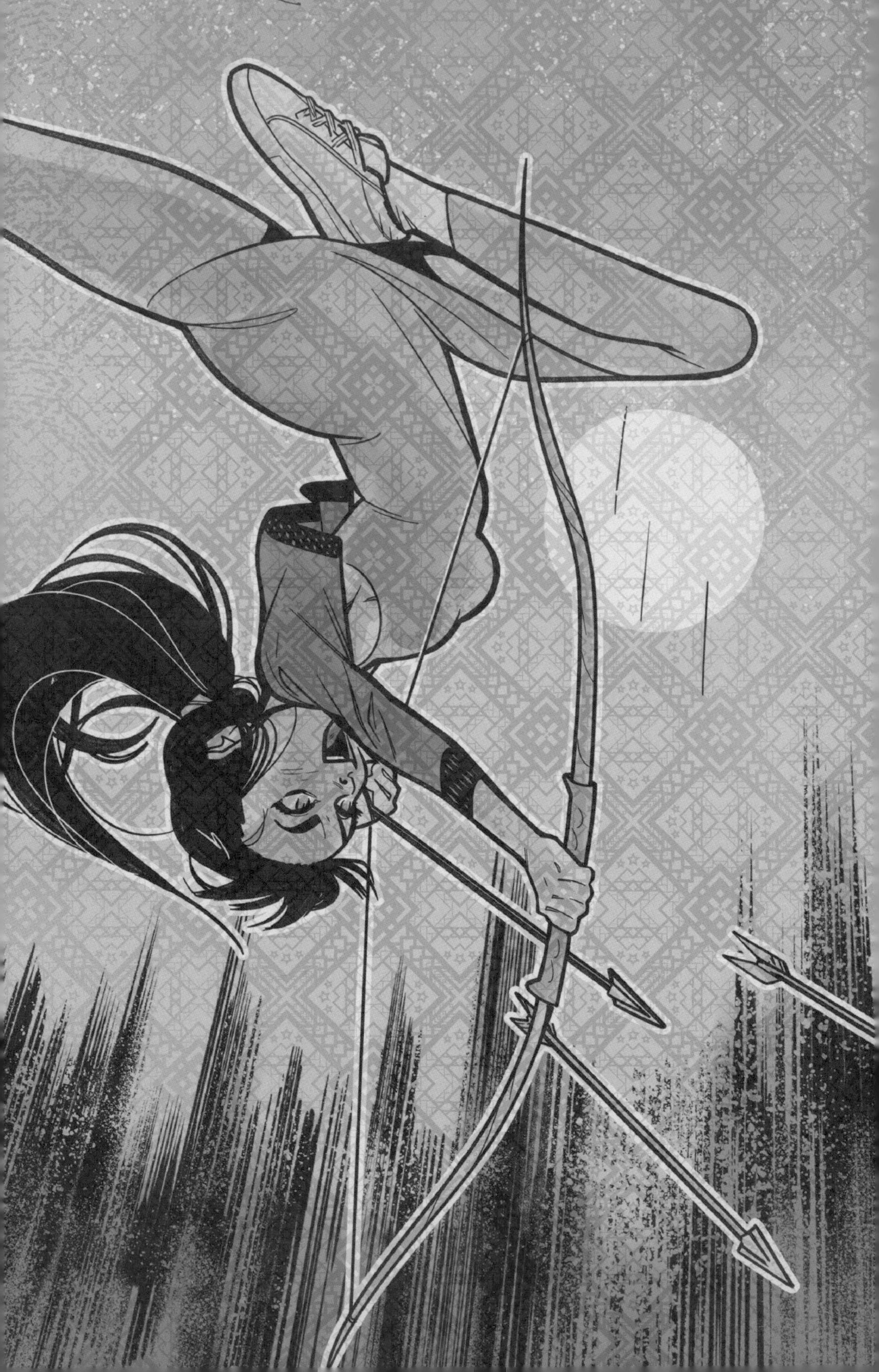

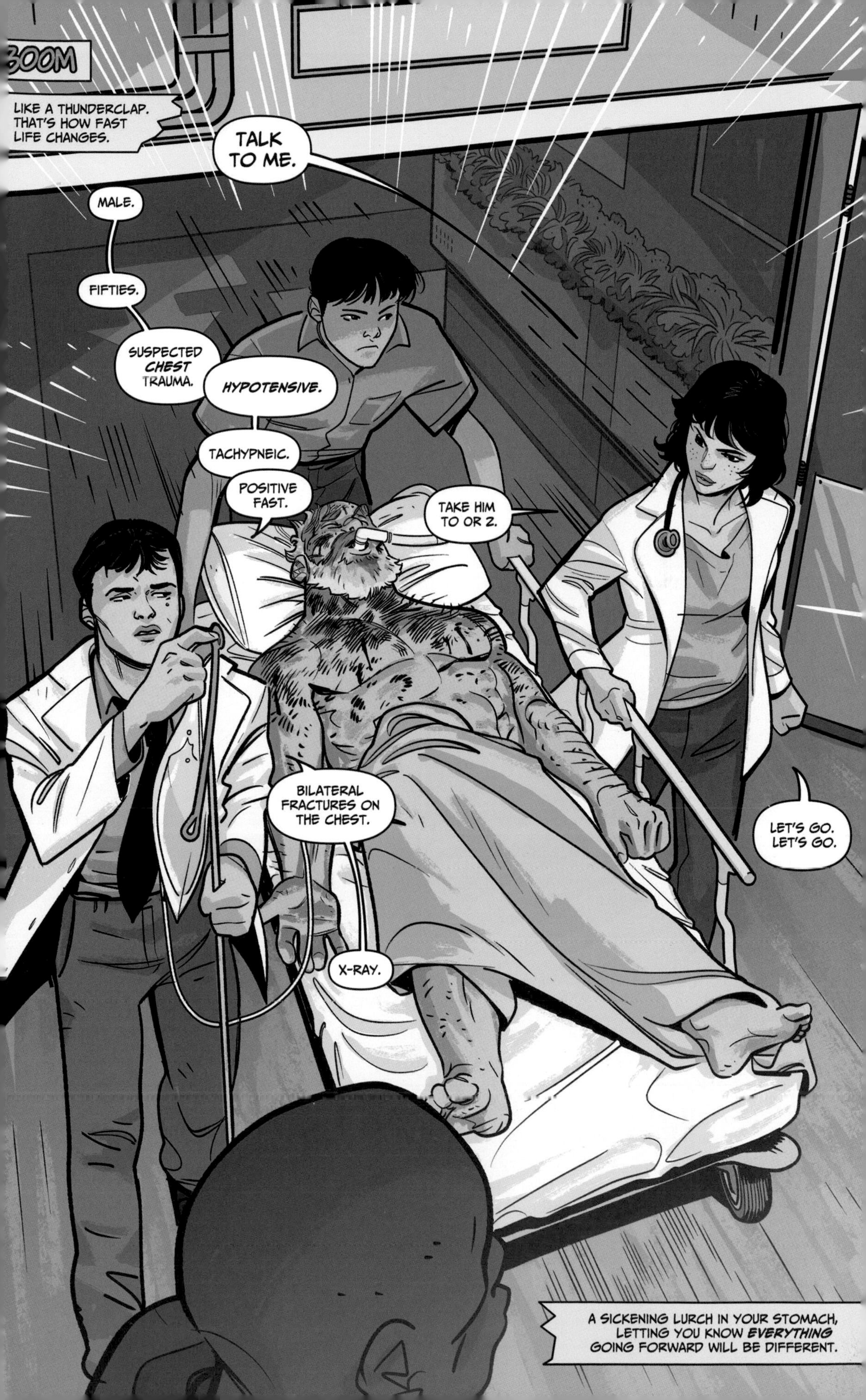
BOOM
LIKE A THUNDERCLAP. THAT'S HOW FAST LIFE CHANGES.
TALK TO ME.
MALE.
FIFTIES.
SUSPECTED *CHEST* TRAUMA.
HYPOTENSIVE.
TACHYPNEIC.
POSITIVE FAST.
TAKE HIM TO OR 2.
BILATERAL FRACTURES ON THE CHEST.
X-RAY.
LET'S GO. LET'S GO.
A SICKENING LURCH IN YOUR STOMACH, LETTING YOU KNOW *EVERYTHING* GOING FORWARD WILL BE DIFFERENT.

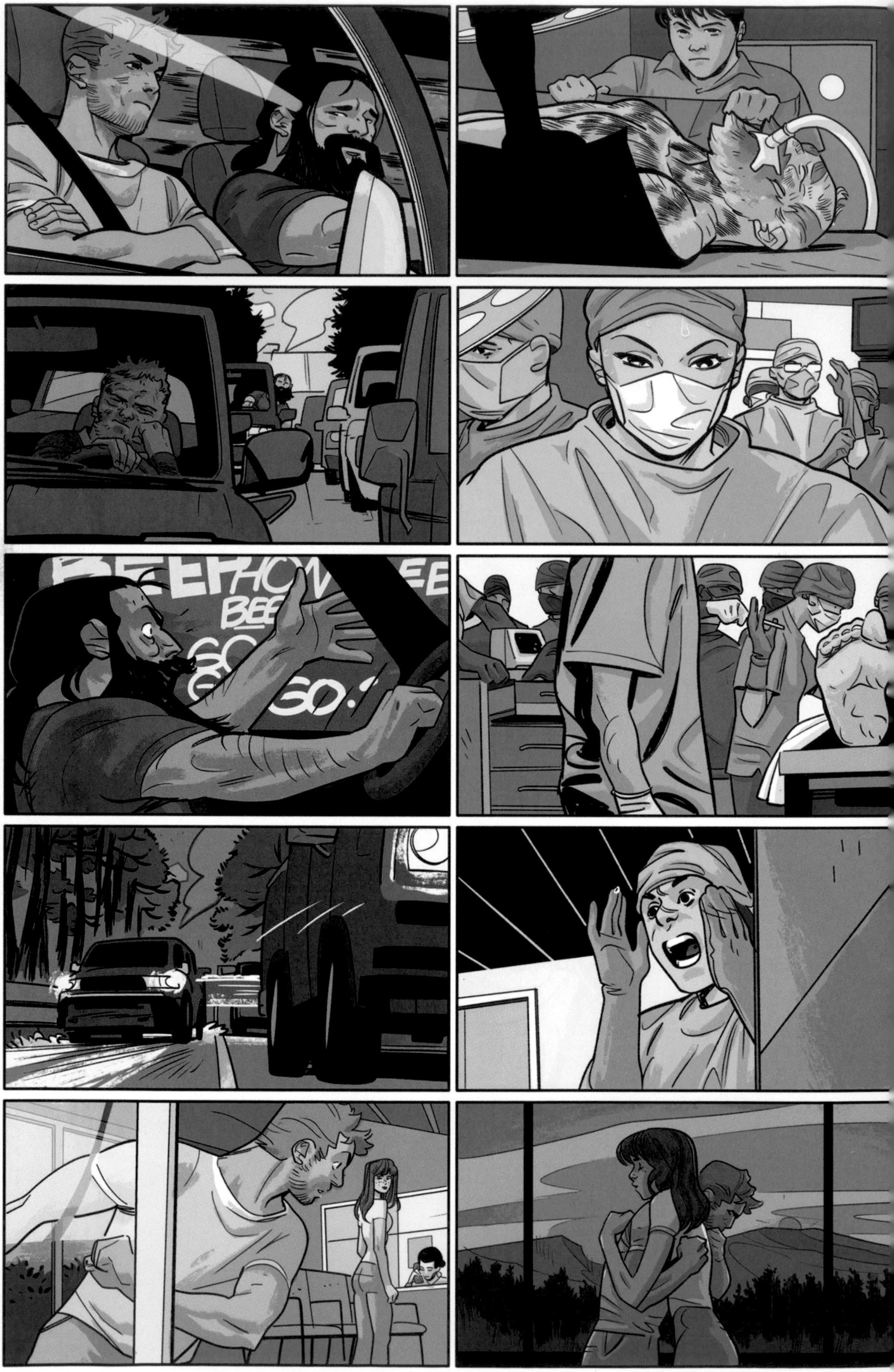

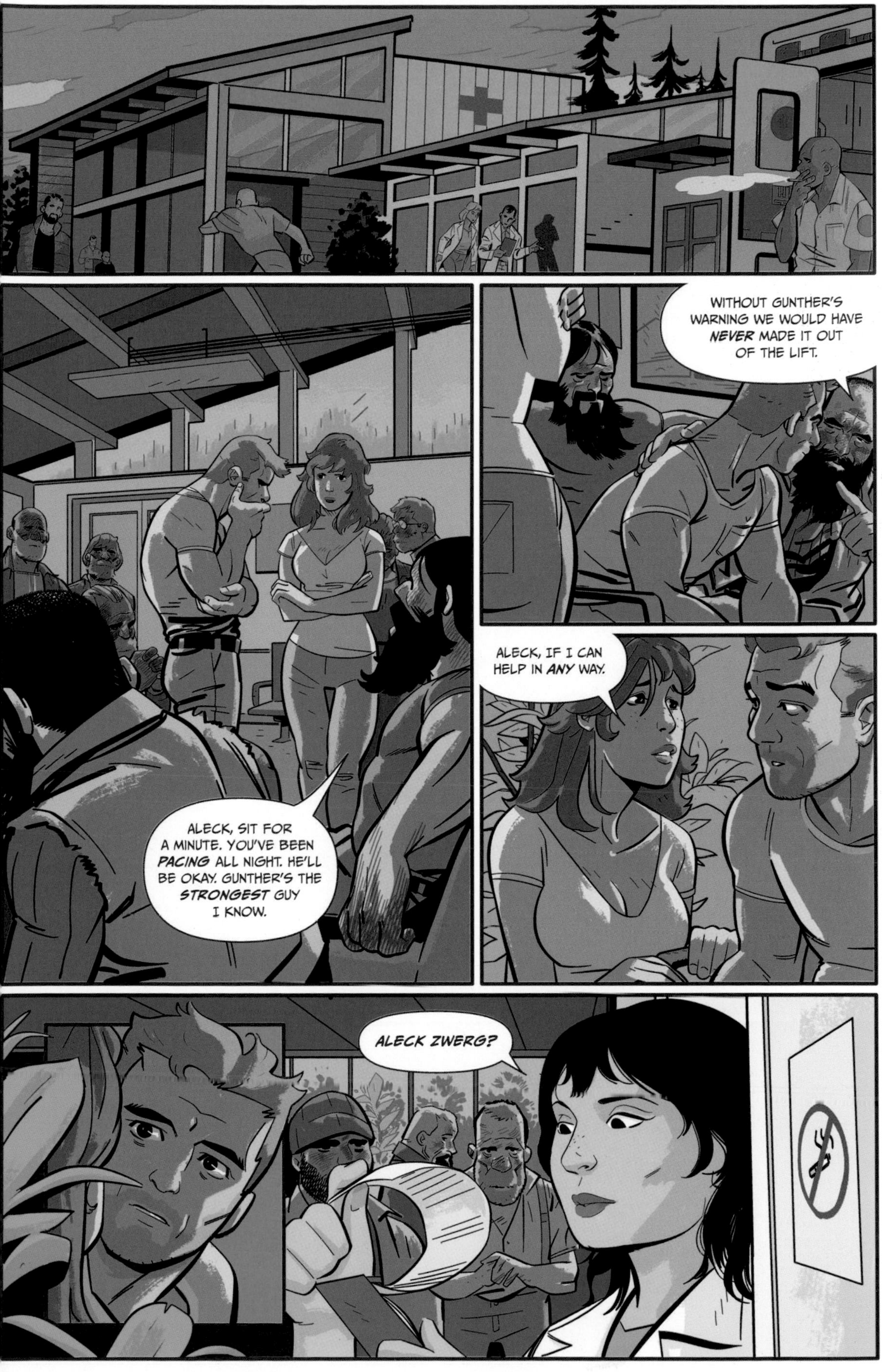
ALECK, SIT FOR A MINUTE. YOU'VE BEEN *PACING* ALL NIGHT. HE'LL BE OKAY. GUNTHER'S THE *STRONGEST* GUY I KNOW.
WITHOUT GUNTHER'S WARNING WE WOULD HAVE *NEVER* MADE IT OUT OF THE LIFT.
ALECK, IF I CAN HELP IN *ANY* WAY.
ALECK ZWERG?

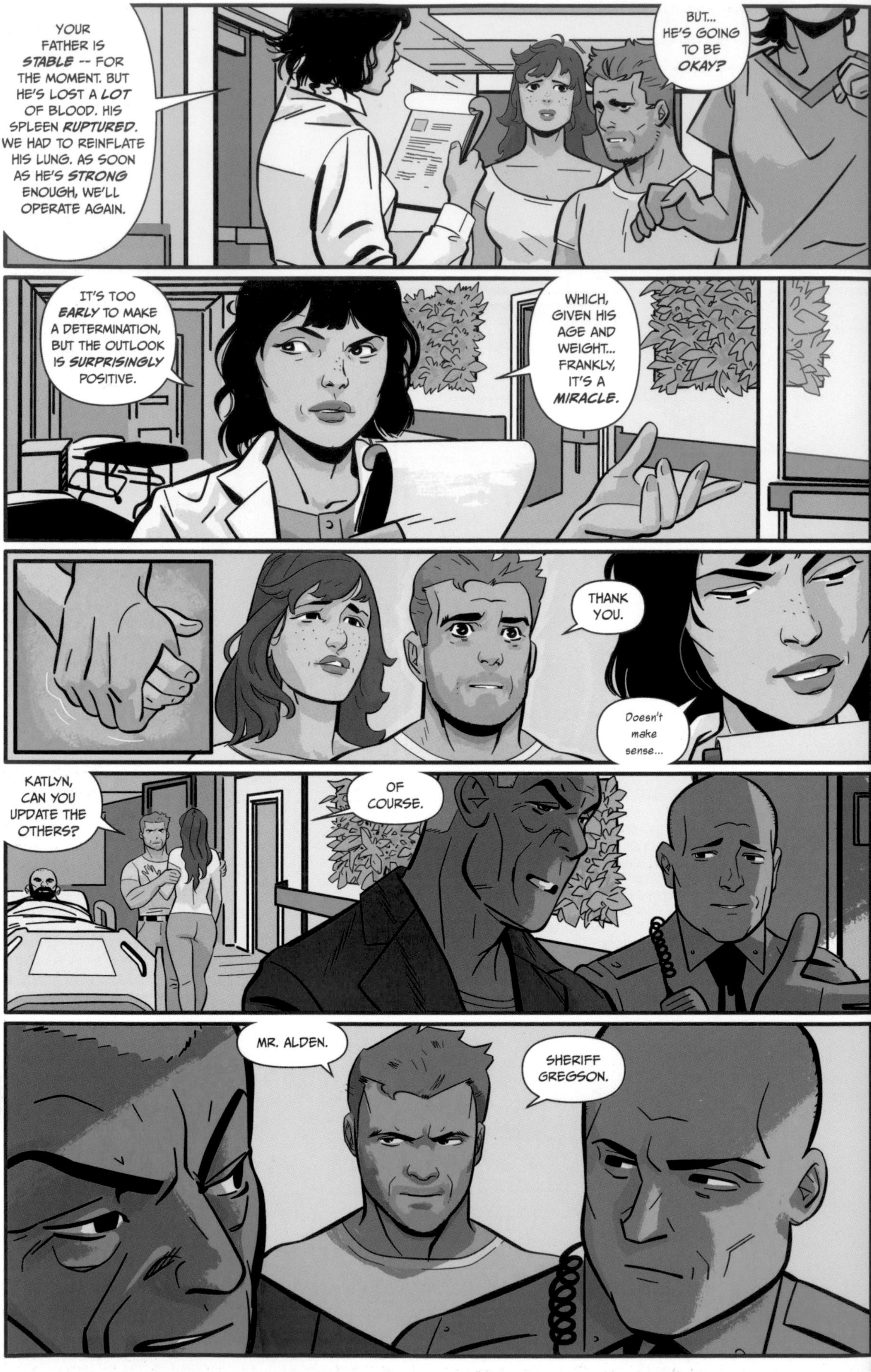
YOUR FATHER IS STABLE -- FOR THE MOMENT. BUT HE'S LOST A LOT OF BLOOD. HIS SPLEEN RUPTURED. WE HAD TO REINFLATE HIS LUNG. AS SOON AS HE'S STRONG ENOUGH, WE'LL OPERATE AGAIN.
BUT... HE'S GOING TO BE OKAY?
IT'S TOO EARLY TO MAKE A DETERMINATION, BUT THE OUTLOOK IS SURPRISINGLY POSITIVE.
WHICH, GIVEN HIS AGE AND WEIGHT... FRANKLY, IT'S A MIRACLE.
THANK YOU.
Doesn't make sense...
KATLYN, CAN YOU UPDATE THE OTHERS?
OF COURSE.
MR. ALDEN.
SHERIFF GREGSON.

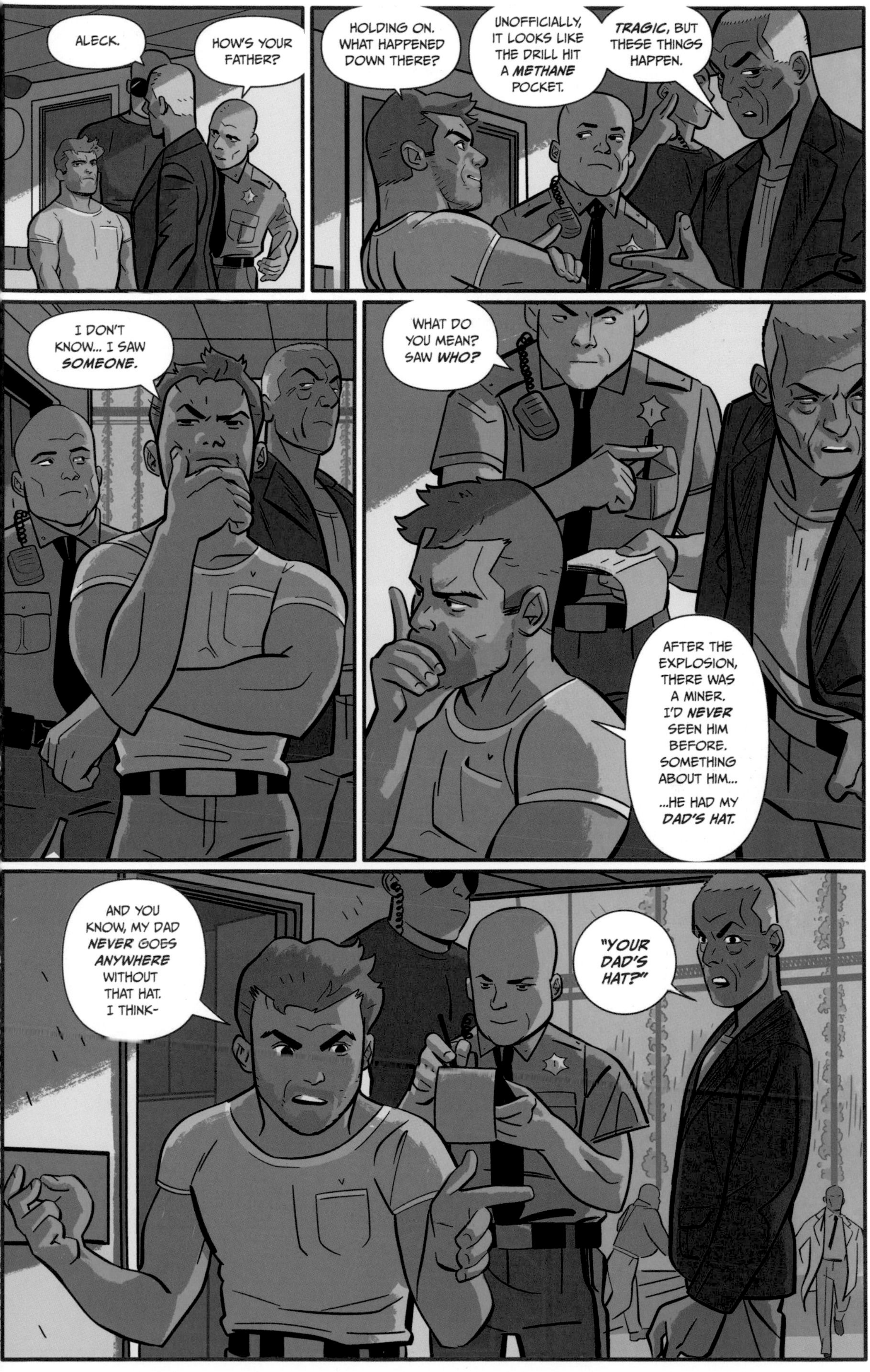
ALECK.
HOW'S YOUR FATHER?
HOLDING ON. WHAT HAPPENED DOWN THERE?
UNOFFICIALLY, IT LOOKS LIKE THE DRILL HIT A *METHANE* POCKET.
TRAGIC, BUT THESE THINGS HAPPEN.
I DON'T KNOW... I SAW *SOMEONE.*
WHAT DO YOU MEAN? SAW *WHO?*
AFTER THE EXPLOSION, THERE WAS A MINER. I'D *NEVER* SEEN HIM BEFORE. SOMETHING ABOUT HIM...
...HE HAD MY *DAD'S HAT.*
AND YOU KNOW, MY DAD *NEVER* GOES *ANYWHERE* WITHOUT THAT HAT. I THINK-
"YOUR DAD'S HAT?"

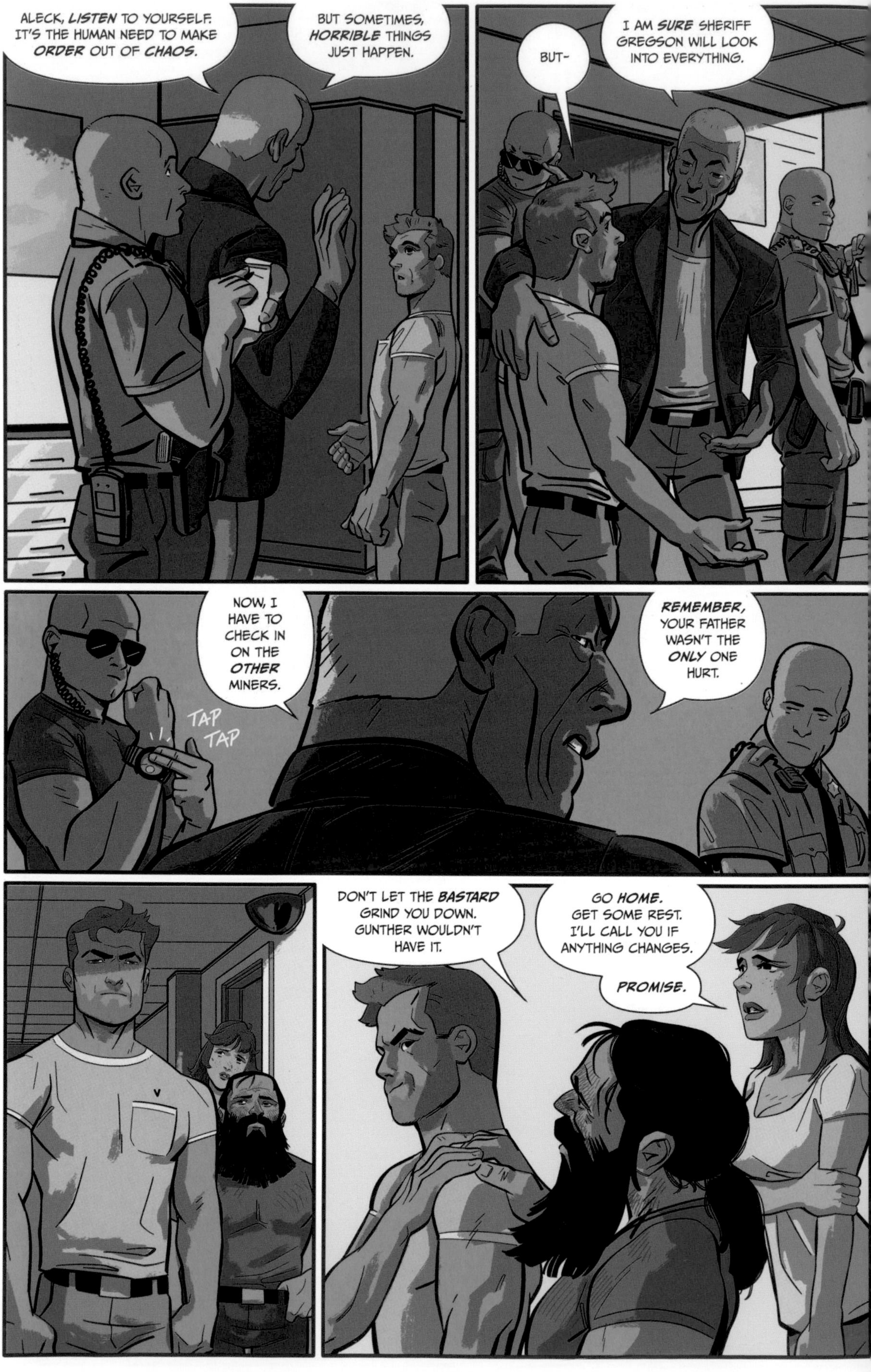

ALECK, **LISTEN** TO YOURSELF. IT'S THE HUMAN NEED TO MAKE **ORDER** OUT OF **CHAOS**.
BUT SOMETIMES, **HORRIBLE** THINGS JUST HAPPEN.
BUT-
I AM **SURE** SHERIFF GREGSON WILL LOOK INTO EVERYTHING.
NOW, I HAVE TO CHECK IN ON THE **OTHER** MINERS.
TAP TAP
REMEMBER, YOUR FATHER WASN'T THE **ONLY** ONE HURT.
DON'T LET THE **BASTARD** GRIND YOU DOWN. GUNTHER WOULDN'T HAVE IT.
GO **HOME**. GET SOME REST. I'LL CALL YOU IF ANYTHING CHANGES.
PROMISE.

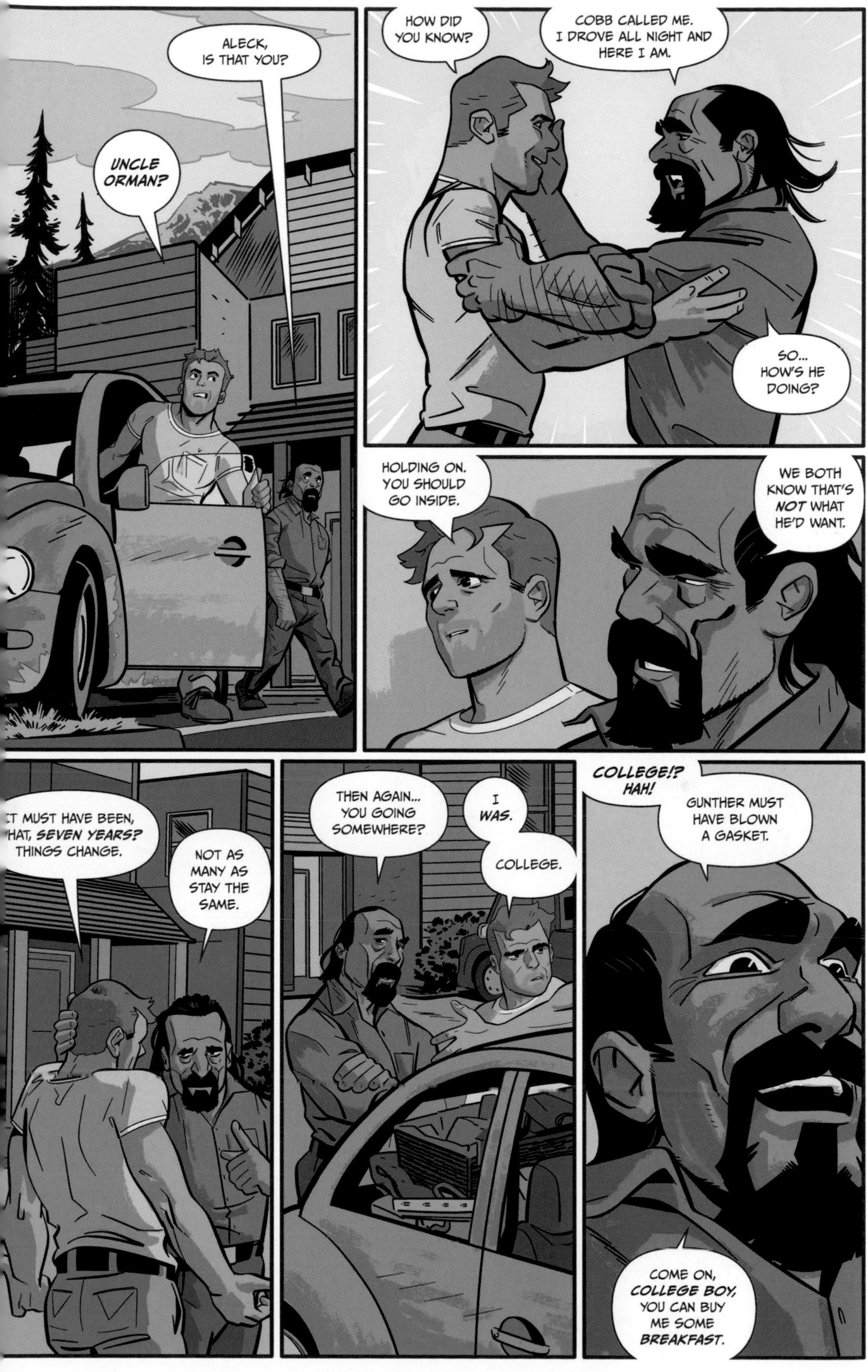
ALECK, IS THAT YOU?
UNCLE ORMAN?
HOW DID YOU KNOW?
COBB CALLED ME. I DROVE ALL NIGHT AND HERE I AM.
SO... HOW'S HE DOING?
HOLDING ON. YOU SHOULD GO INSIDE.
WE BOTH KNOW THAT'S *NOT* WHAT HE'D WANT.
CT MUST HAVE BEEN, HAT, *SEVEN YEARS?* THINGS CHANGE.
NOT AS MANY AS STAY THE SAME.
THEN AGAIN... YOU GOING SOMEWHERE?
I *WAS.*
COLLEGE.
COLLEGE!? HAH!
GUNTHER MUST HAVE BLOWN A GASKET.
COME ON, *COLLEGE BOY,* YOU CAN BUY ME SOME *BREAKFAST.*

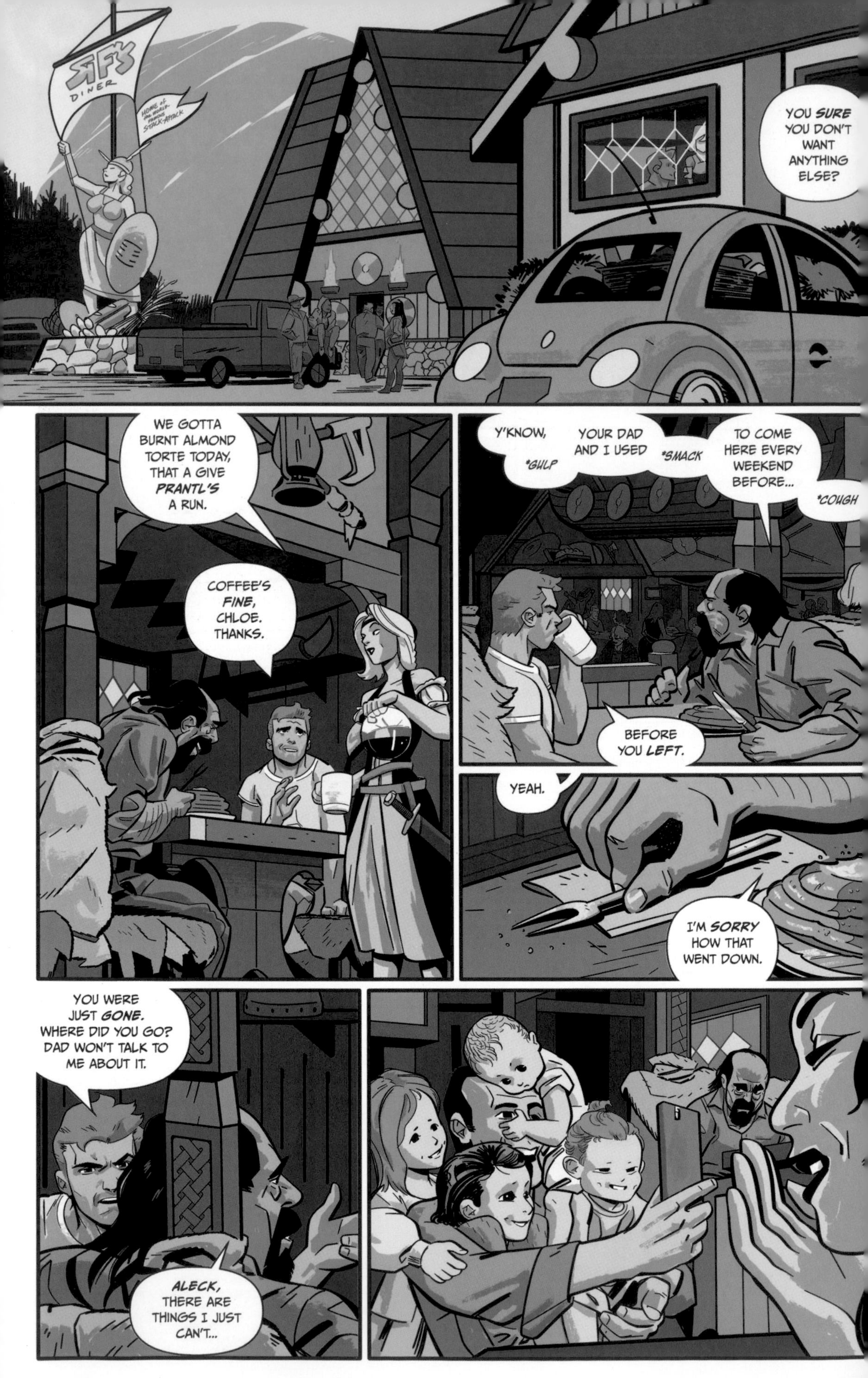
DINER
YOU SURE YOU DON'T WANT ANYTHING ELSE?
WE GOTTA BURNT ALMOND TORTE TODAY, THAT A GIVE PRANTL'S A RUN.
COFFEE'S FINE, CHLOE. THANKS.
Y'KNOW,
*GULP
YOUR DAD AND I USED
*SMACK
TO COME HERE EVERY WEEKEND BEFORE...
*COUGH
BEFORE YOU LEFT.
YEAH.
I'M SORRY HOW THAT WENT DOWN.
YOU WERE JUST GONE. WHERE DID YOU GO? DAD WON'T TALK TO ME ABOUT IT.
ALECK, THERE ARE THINGS I JUST CAN'T...

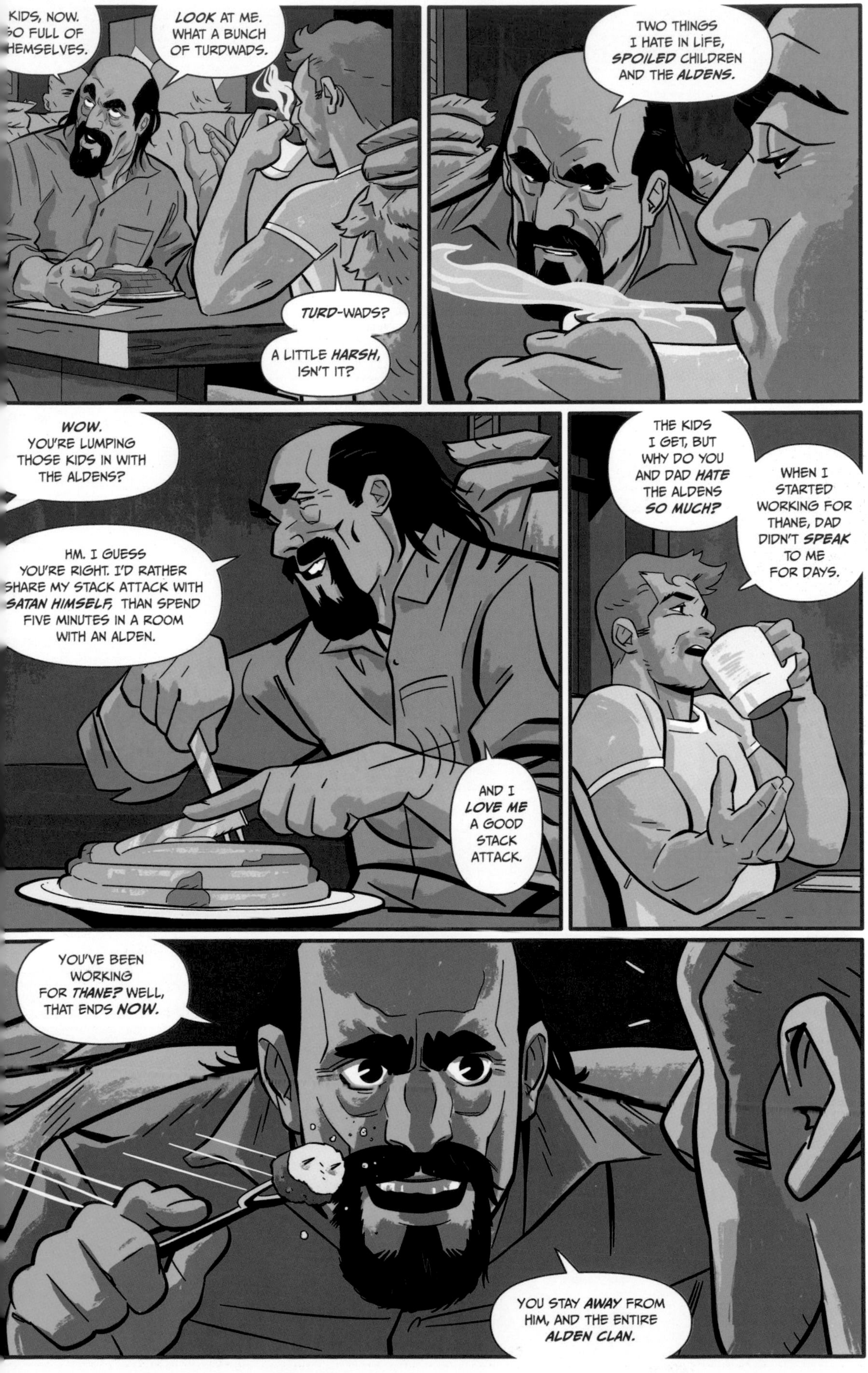
KIDS, NOW. SO FULL OF THEMSELVES.
LOOK AT ME. WHAT A BUNCH OF TURDWADS.
TURD-WADS?
A LITTLE HARSH, ISN'T IT?
TWO THINGS I HATE IN LIFE, SPOILED CHILDREN AND THE ALDENS.
WOW. YOU'RE LUMPING THOSE KIDS IN WITH THE ALDENS?
HM. I GUESS YOU'RE RIGHT. I'D RATHER SHARE MY STACK ATTACK WITH SATAN HIMSELF, THAN SPEND FIVE MINUTES IN A ROOM WITH AN ALDEN.
AND I LOVE ME A GOOD STACK ATTACK.
THE KIDS I GET, BUT WHY DO YOU AND DAD HATE THE ALDENS SO MUCH?
WHEN I STARTED WORKING FOR THANE, DAD DIDN'T SPEAK TO ME FOR DAYS.
YOU'VE BEEN WORKING FOR THANE? WELL, THAT ENDS NOW.
YOU STAY AWAY FROM HIM, AND THE ENTIRE ALDEN CLAN.

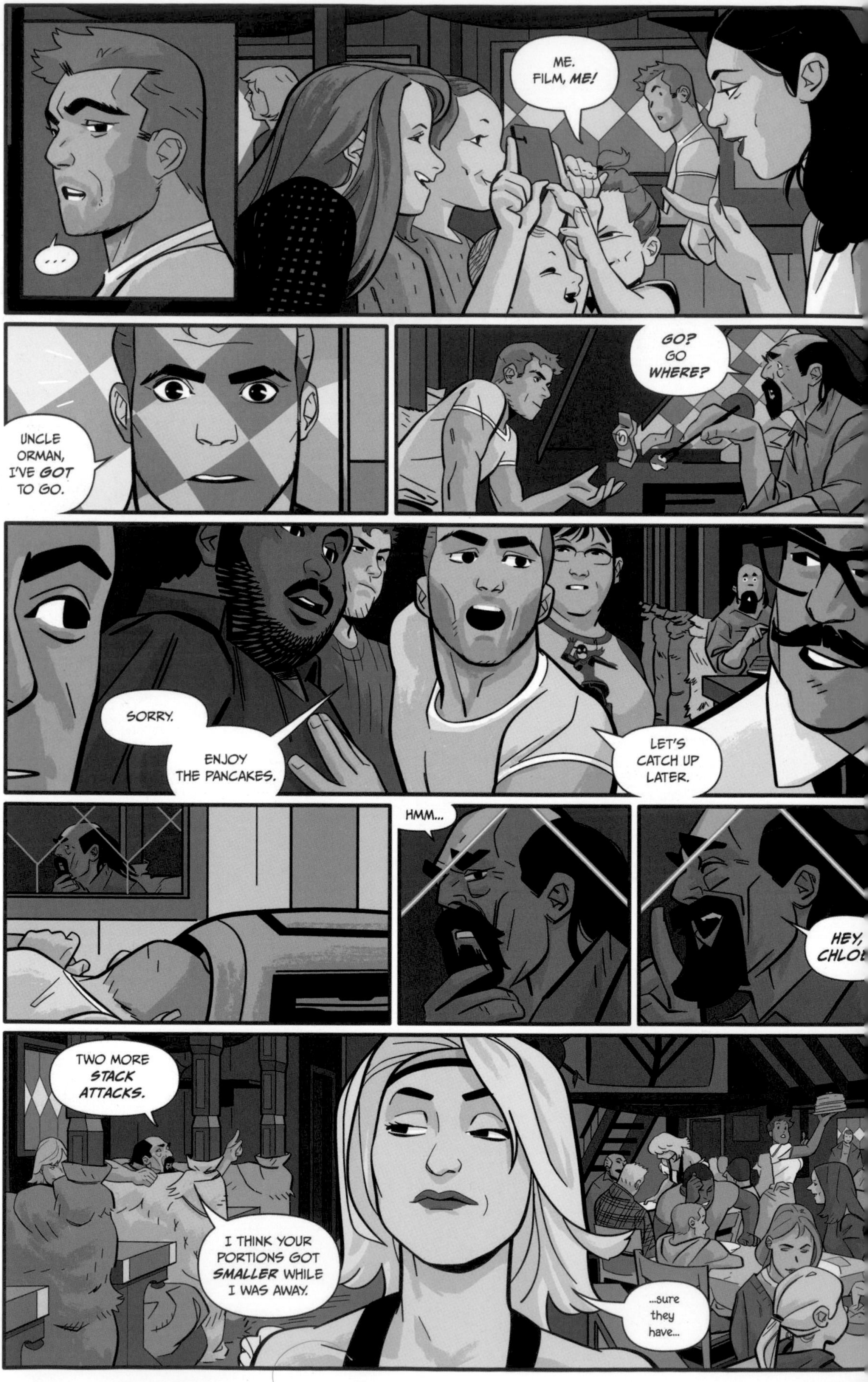
...
ME.
FILM, ME!
UNCLE ORMAN, I'VE GOT TO GO.
GO? GO WHERE?
SORRY.
ENJOY THE PANCAKES.
LET'S CATCH UP LATER.
HMM...
HEY, CHLO
TWO MORE STACK ATTACKS.
I THINK YOUR PORTIONS GOT SMALLER WHILE I WAS AWAY.
...sure they have...

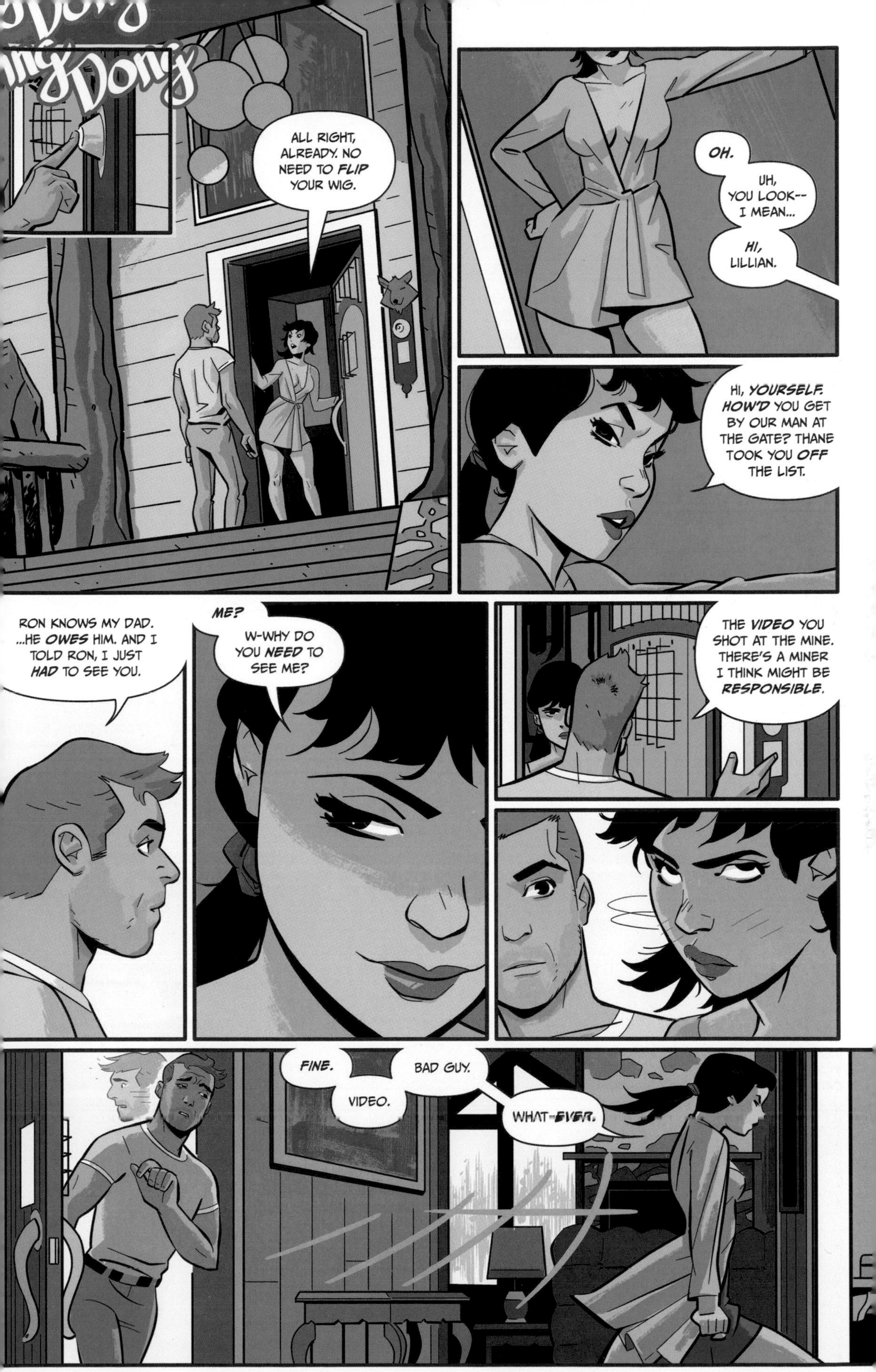
Ding Dong
ALL RIGHT, ALREADY. NO NEED TO FLIP YOUR WIG.
OH.
UH, YOU LOOK-- I MEAN...
HI, LILLIAN.
HI, YOURSELF. HOW'D YOU GET BY OUR MAN AT THE GATE? THANE TOOK YOU OFF THE LIST.
RON KNOWS MY DAD. ...HE OWES HIM. AND I TOLD RON, I JUST HAD TO SEE YOU.
ME?
W-WHY DO YOU NEED TO SEE ME?
THE VIDEO YOU SHOT AT THE MINE. THERE'S A MINER I THINK MIGHT BE RESPONSIBLE.
FINE.
VIDEO.
BAD GUY.
WHAT-EVER.

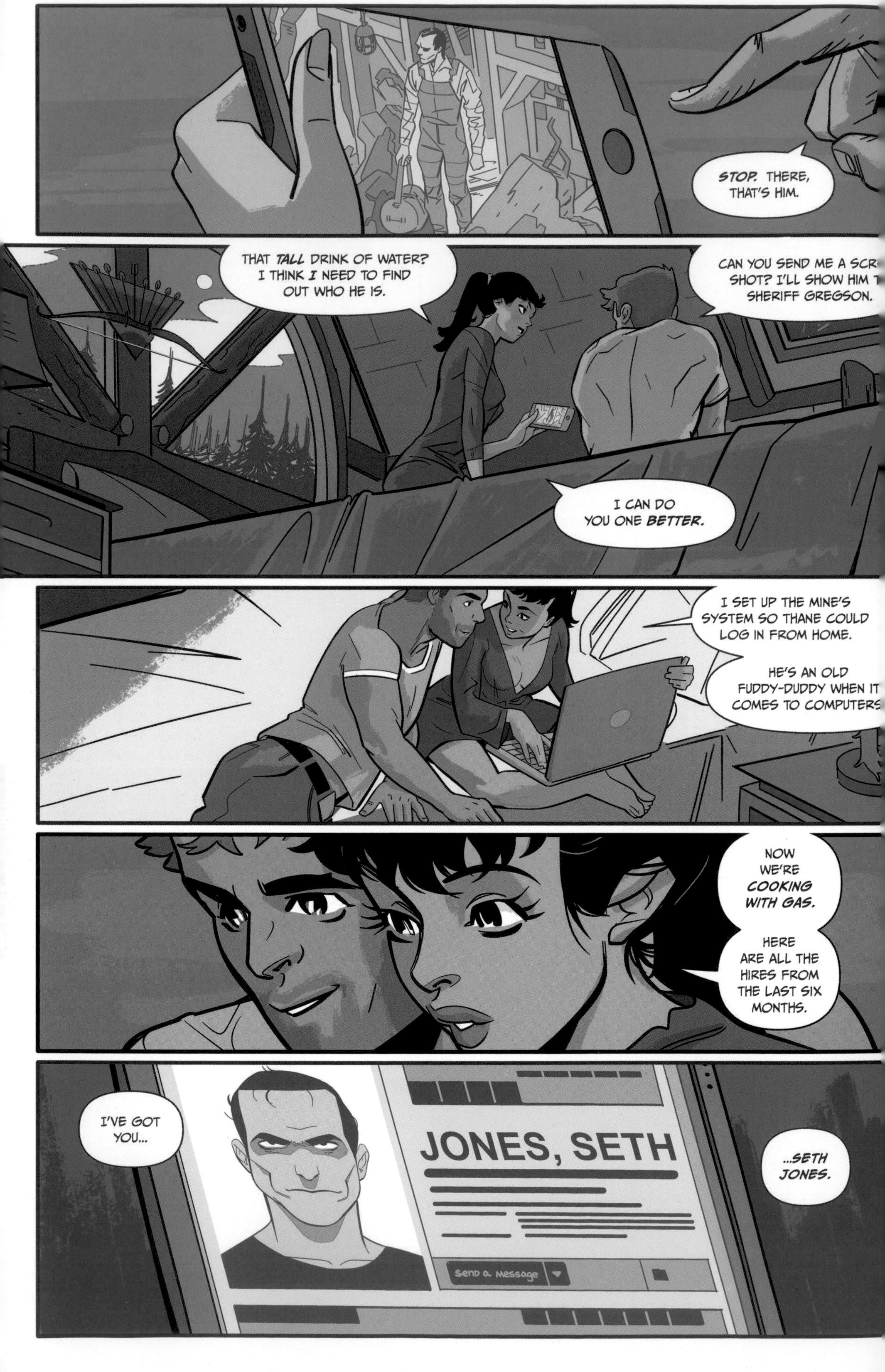
STOP. THERE, THAT'S HIM.
THAT TALL DRINK OF WATER? I THINK I NEED TO FIND OUT WHO HE IS.
CAN YOU SEND ME A SCR SHOT? I'LL SHOW HIM T SHERIFF GREGSON.
I CAN DO YOU ONE BETTER.
I SET UP THE MINE'S SYSTEM SO THANE COULD LOG IN FROM HOME.
HE'S AN OLD FUDDY-DUDDY WHEN IT COMES TO COMPUTERS
NOW WE'RE COOKING WITH GAS.
HERE ARE ALL THE HIRES FROM THE LAST SIX MONTHS.
I'VE GOT YOU...
JONES, SETH
Send a Message
...SETH JONES.

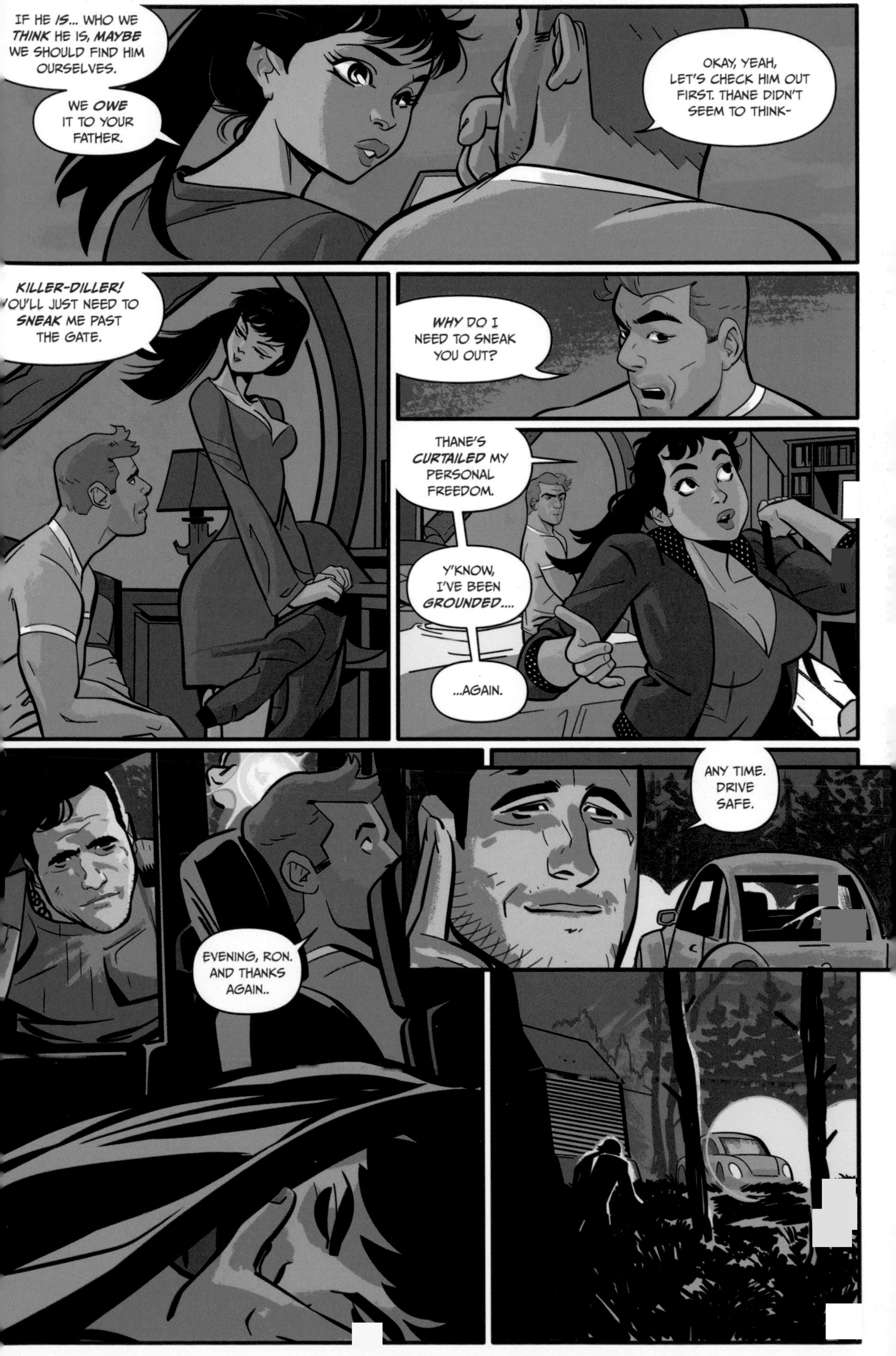
IF HE IS... WHO WE THINK HE IS, MAYBE WE SHOULD FIND HIM OURSELVES.
WE OWE IT TO YOUR FATHER.
OKAY, YEAH, LET'S CHECK HIM OUT FIRST. THANE DIDN'T SEEM TO THINK-
KILLER-DILLER! YOU'LL JUST NEED TO SNEAK ME PAST THE GATE.
WHY DO I NEED TO SNEAK YOU OUT?
THANE'S CURTAILED MY PERSONAL FREEDOM.
Y'KNOW, I'VE BEEN GROUNDED....
...AGAIN.
EVENING, RON. AND THANKS AGAIN..
ANY TIME. DRIVE SAFE.

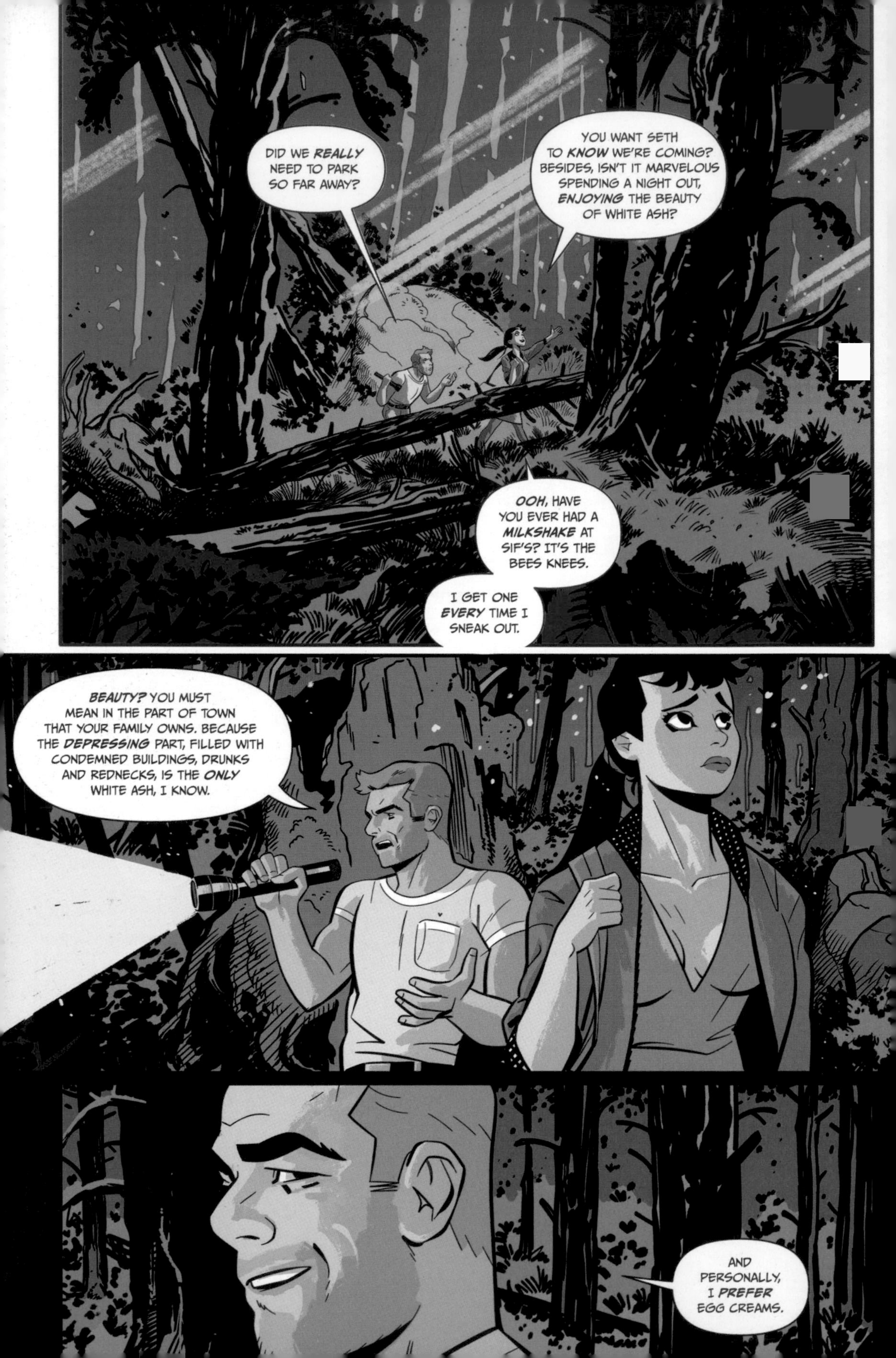
DID WE REALLY NEED TO PARK SO FAR AWAY?
YOU WANT SETH TO KNOW WE'RE COMING? BESIDES, ISN'T IT MARVELOUS SPENDING A NIGHT OUT, ENJOYING THE BEAUTY OF WHITE ASH?
OOH, HAVE YOU EVER HAD A MILKSHAKE AT SIF'S? IT'S THE BEES KNEES.
I GET ONE EVERY TIME I SNEAK OUT.
BEAUTY? YOU MUST MEAN IN THE PART OF TOWN THAT YOUR FAMILY OWNS. BECAUSE THE DEPRESSING PART, FILLED WITH CONDEMNED BUILDINGS, DRUNKS AND REDNECKS, IS THE ONLY WHITE ASH, I KNOW.
AND PERSONALLY, I PREFER EGG CREAMS.

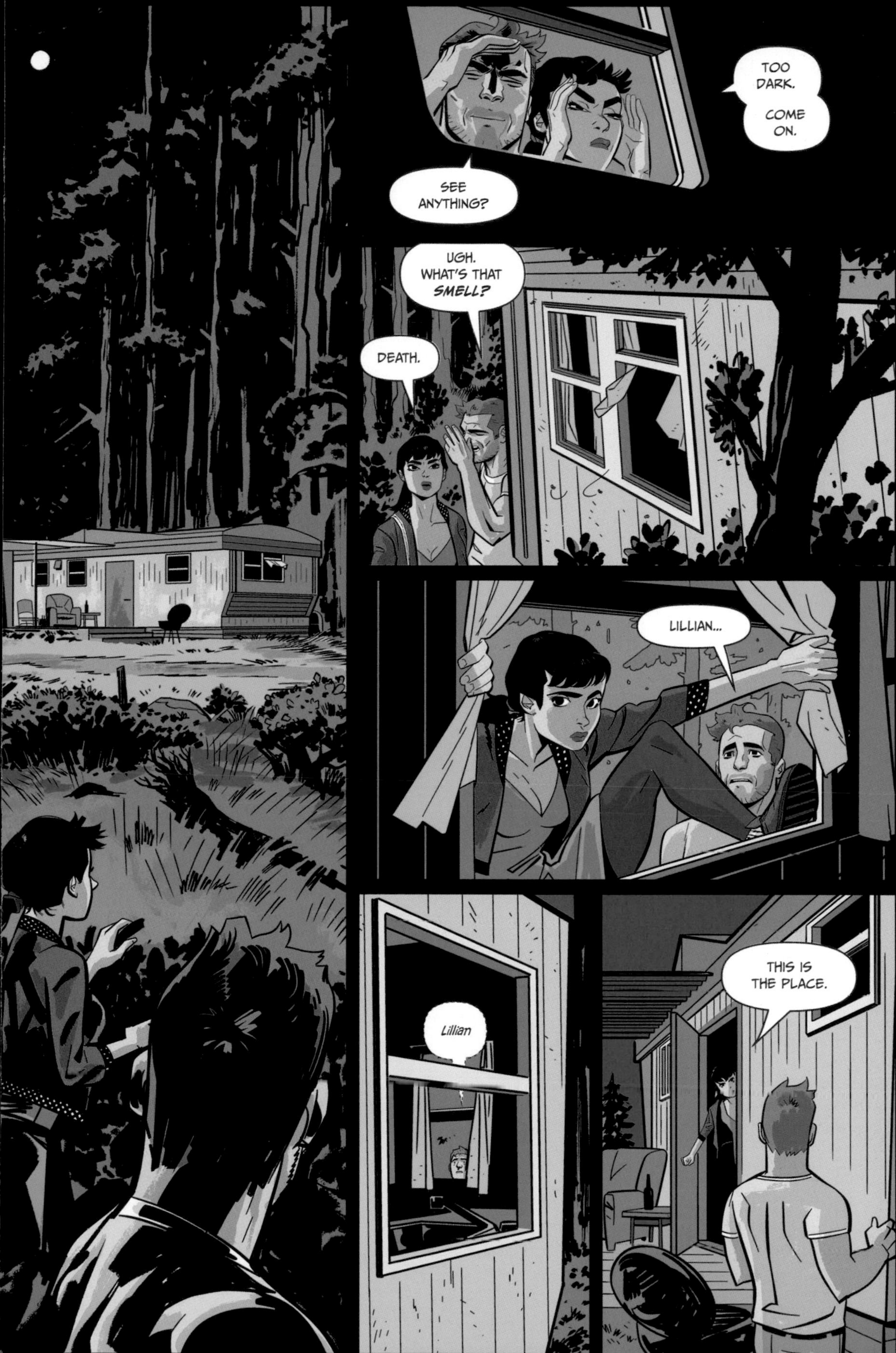
TOO DARK.
COME ON.
SEE ANYTHING?
UGH. WHAT'S THAT SMELL?
DEATH.
LILLIAN...
Lillian
THIS IS THE PLACE.

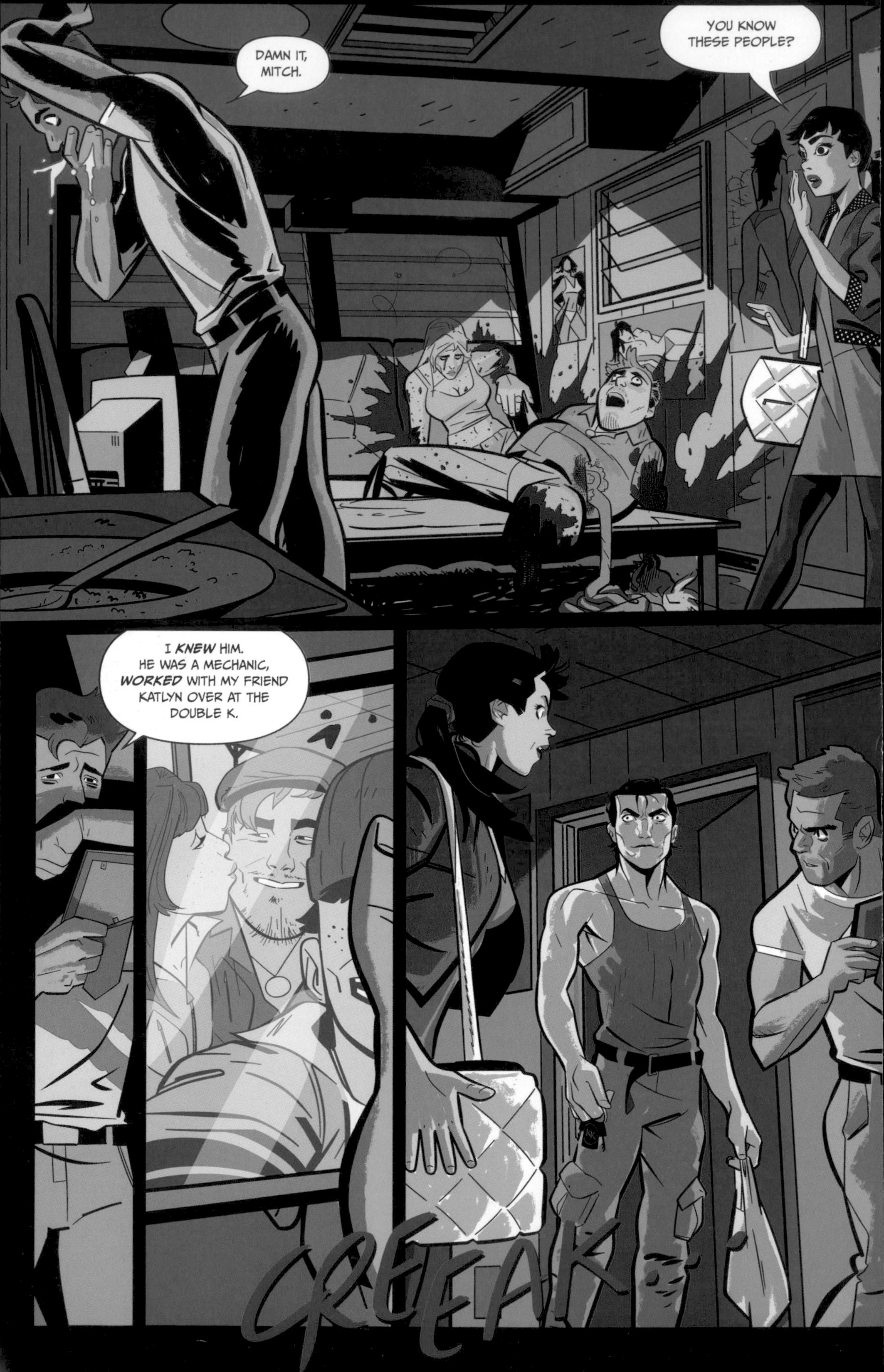
DAMN IT, MITCH.
YOU KNOW THESE PEOPLE?
I KNEW HIM. HE WAS A MECHANIC, WORKED WITH MY FRIEND KATLYN OVER AT THE DOUBLE K.
CREEAK

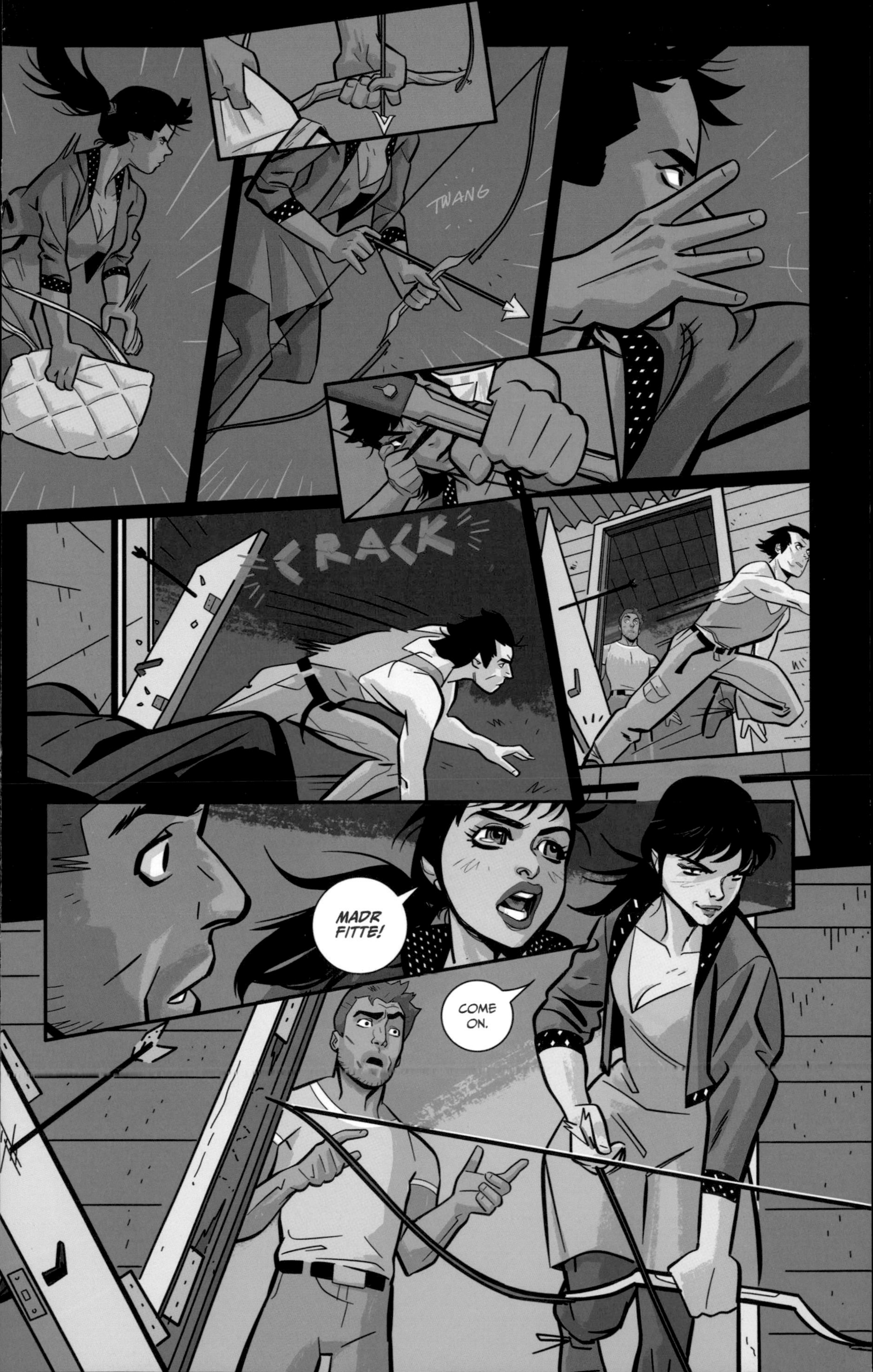

TWANG
CRACK
MADR FITTE!
COME ON.

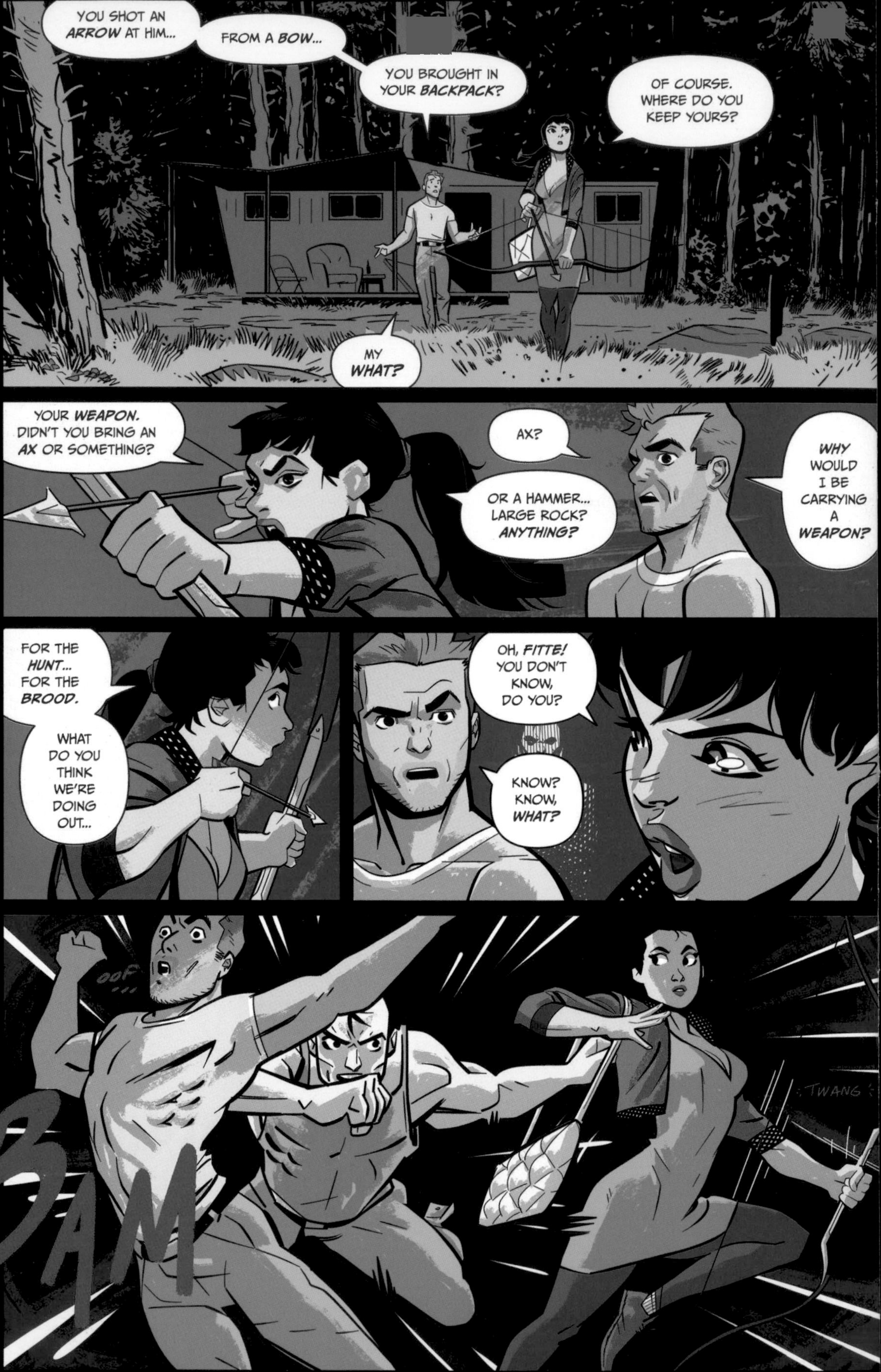
YOU SHOT AN ARROW AT HIM...
FROM A BOW...
YOU BROUGHT IN YOUR BACKPACK?
OF COURSE. WHERE DO YOU KEEP YOURS?
MY WHAT?
YOUR WEAPON. DIDN'T YOU BRING AN AX OR SOMETHING?
AX?
OR A HAMMER... LARGE ROCK? ANYTHING?
WHY WOULD I BE CARRYING A WEAPON?
FOR THE HUNT... FOR THE BROOD.
WHAT DO YOU THINK WE'RE DOING OUT...
OH, FITTE! YOU DON'T KNOW, DO YOU?
KNOW? KNOW, WHAT?
OOF...
TWANG
BAM

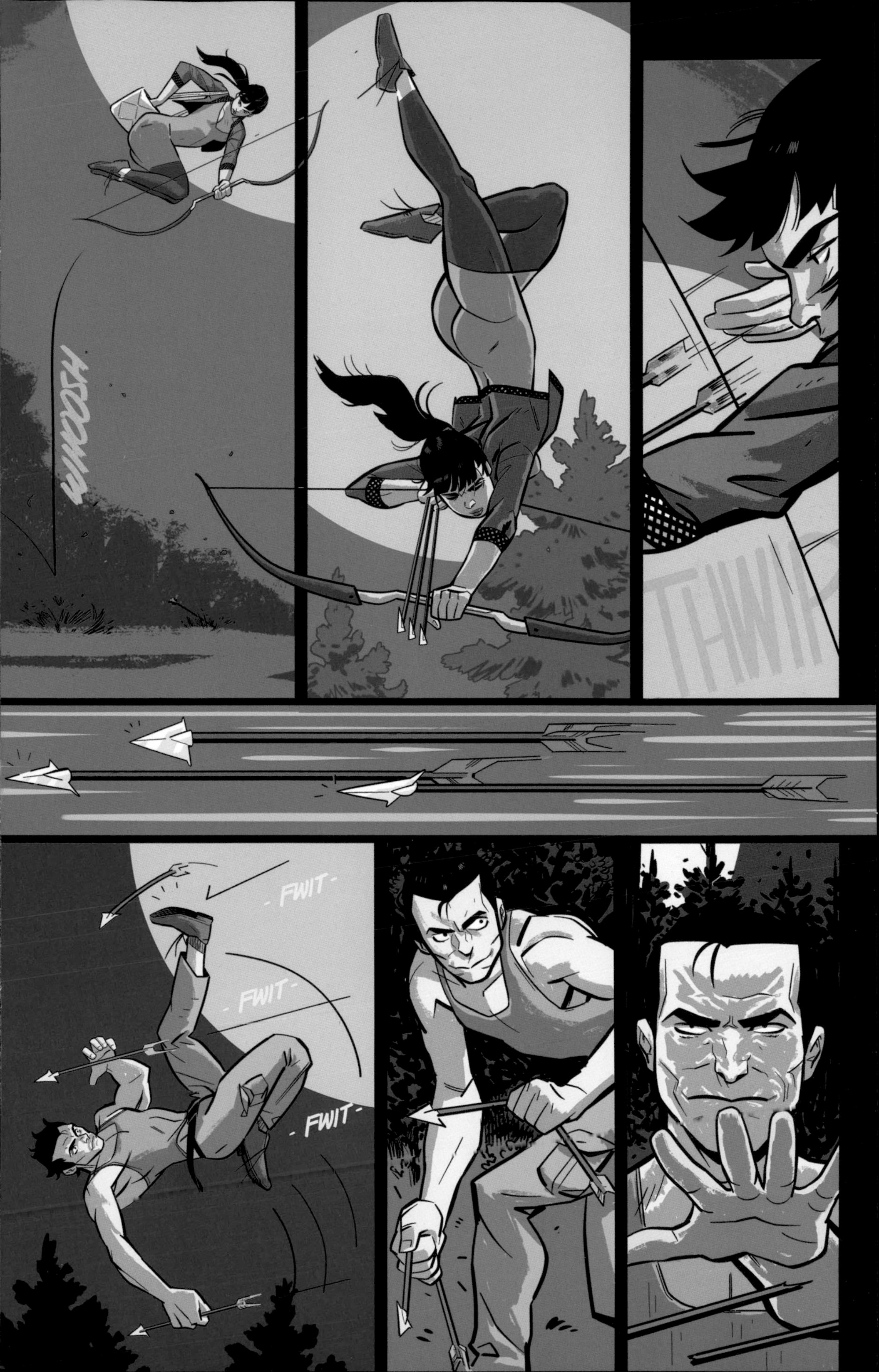
WHOOSH
THWIP
- FWIT -
- FWIT -
- FWIT -

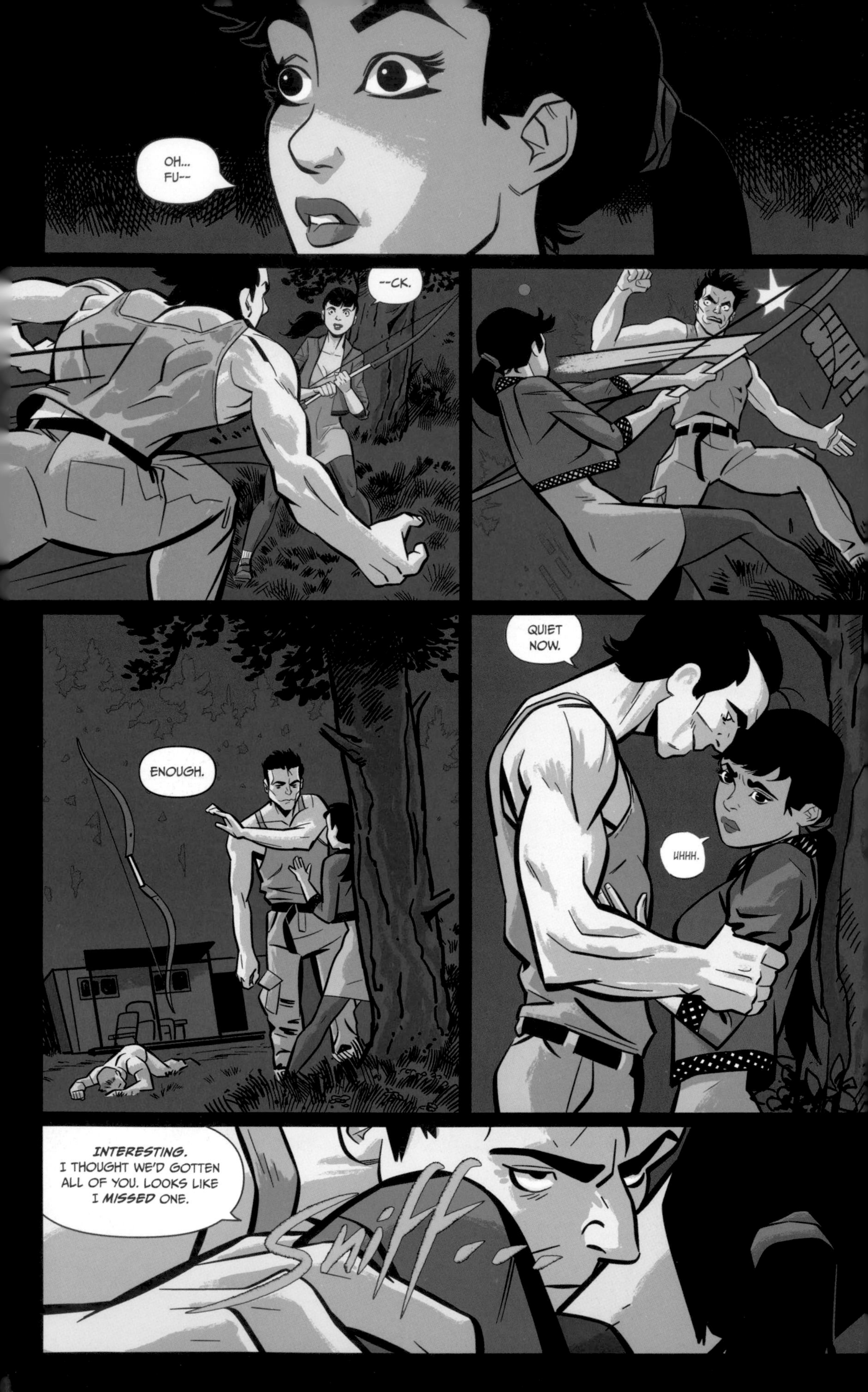
OH...
FU--
--CK.
WHAP!
ENOUGH.
QUIET NOW.
UHHH.
INTERESTING. I THOUGHT WE'D GOTTEN ALL OF YOU. LOOKS LIKE I *MISSED* ONE.
Sniff

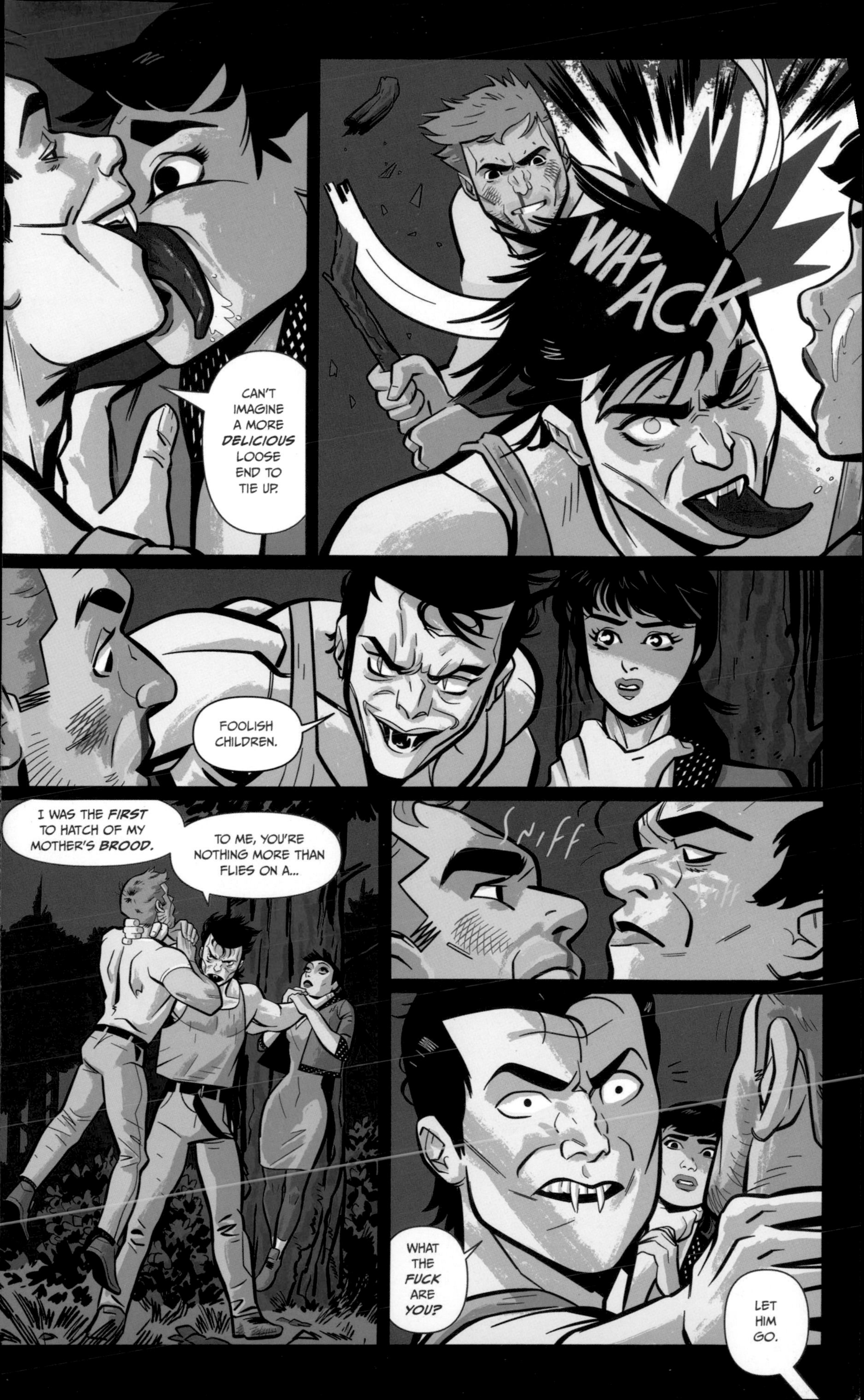
CAN'T IMAGINE A MORE DELICIOUS LOOSE END TO TIE UP.
WHACK
FOOLISH CHILDREN.
I WAS THE FIRST TO HATCH OF MY MOTHER'S BROOD.
TO ME, YOU'RE NOTHING MORE THAN FLIES ON A...
SNIFF
WHAT THE FUCK ARE YOU?
LET HIM GO.

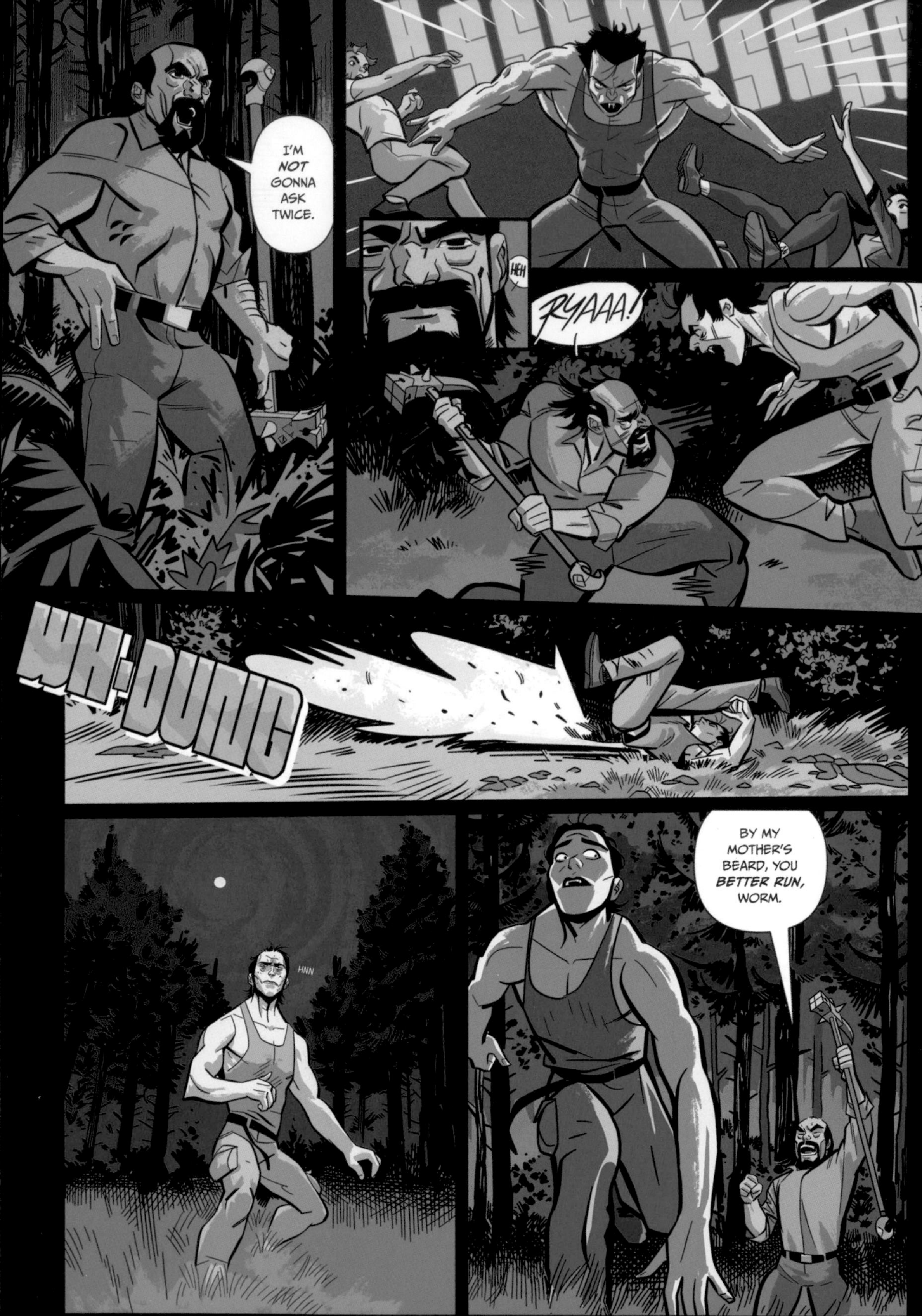
I'M NOT GONNA ASK TWICE.
HEH
RYAAA!
HNN
BY MY MOTHER'S BEARD, YOU BETTER RUN, WORM.

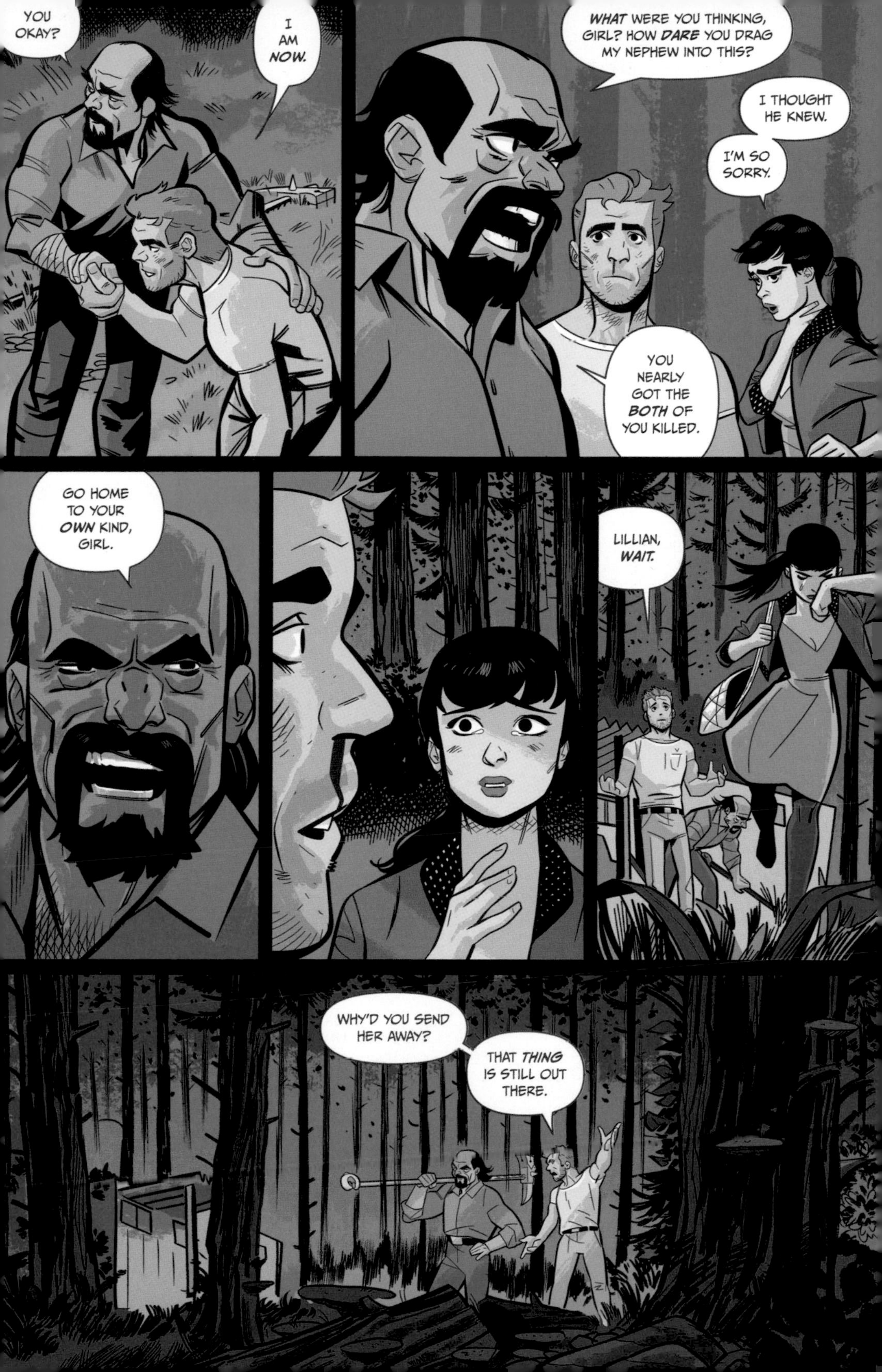
YOU OKAY?
I AM NOW.
WHAT WERE YOU THINKING, GIRL? HOW DARE YOU DRAG MY NEPHEW INTO THIS?
I THOUGHT HE KNEW.
I'M SO SORRY.
YOU NEARLY GOT THE BOTH OF YOU KILLED.
GO HOME TO YOUR OWN KIND, GIRL.
LILLIAN, WAIT.
WHY'D YOU SEND HER AWAY?
THAT THING IS STILL OUT THERE.

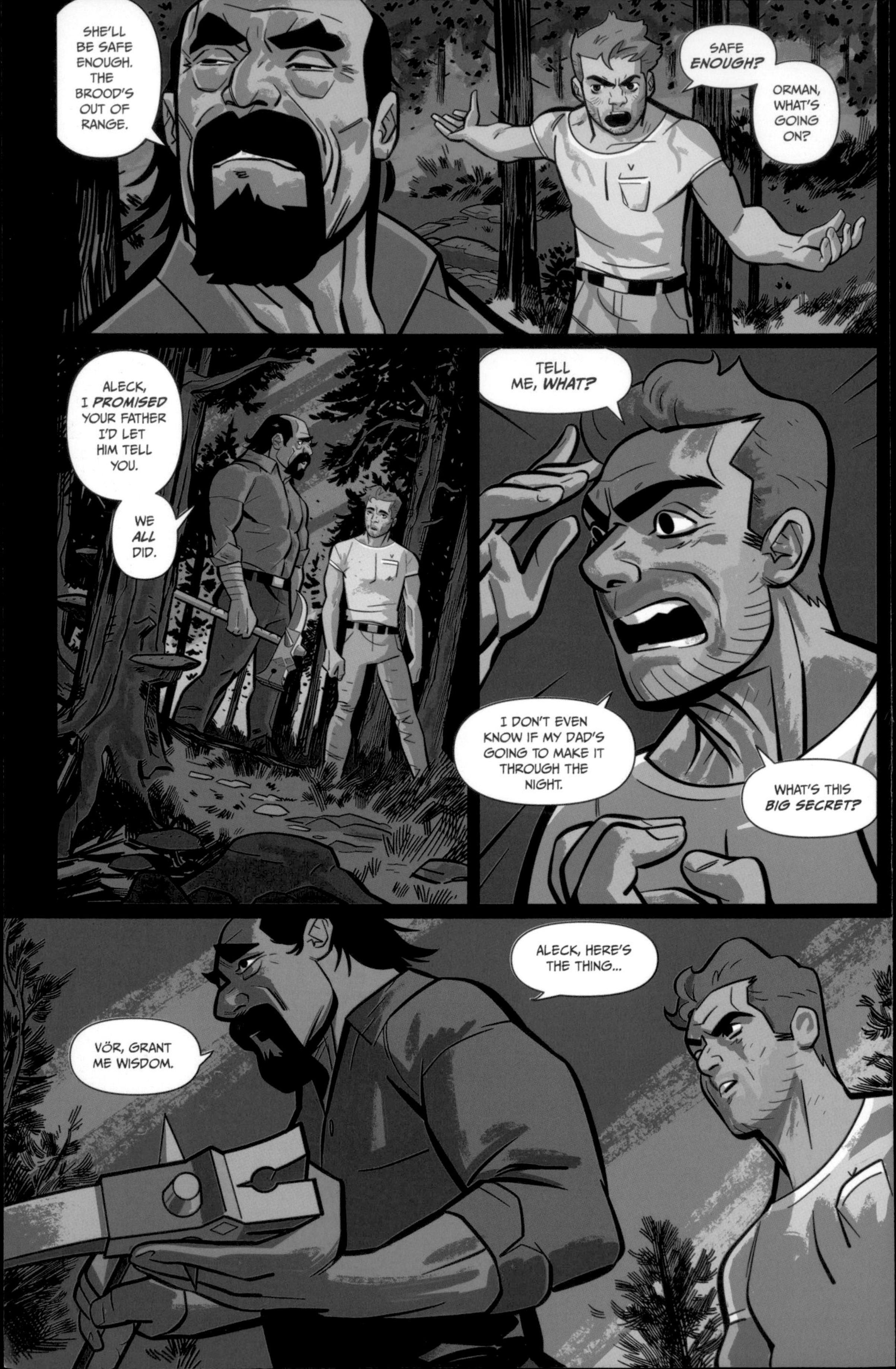
SHE'LL BE SAFE ENOUGH. THE BROOD'S OUT OF RANGE.
SAFE ENOUGH?
ORMAN, WHAT'S GOING ON?
ALECK, I PROMISED YOUR FATHER I'D LET HIM TELL YOU.
WE ALL DID.
TELL ME, WHAT?
I DON'T EVEN KNOW IF MY DAD'S GOING TO MAKE IT THROUGH THE NIGHT.
WHAT'S THIS BIG SECRET?
ALECK, HERE'S THE THING...
VÖR, GRANT ME WISDOM.

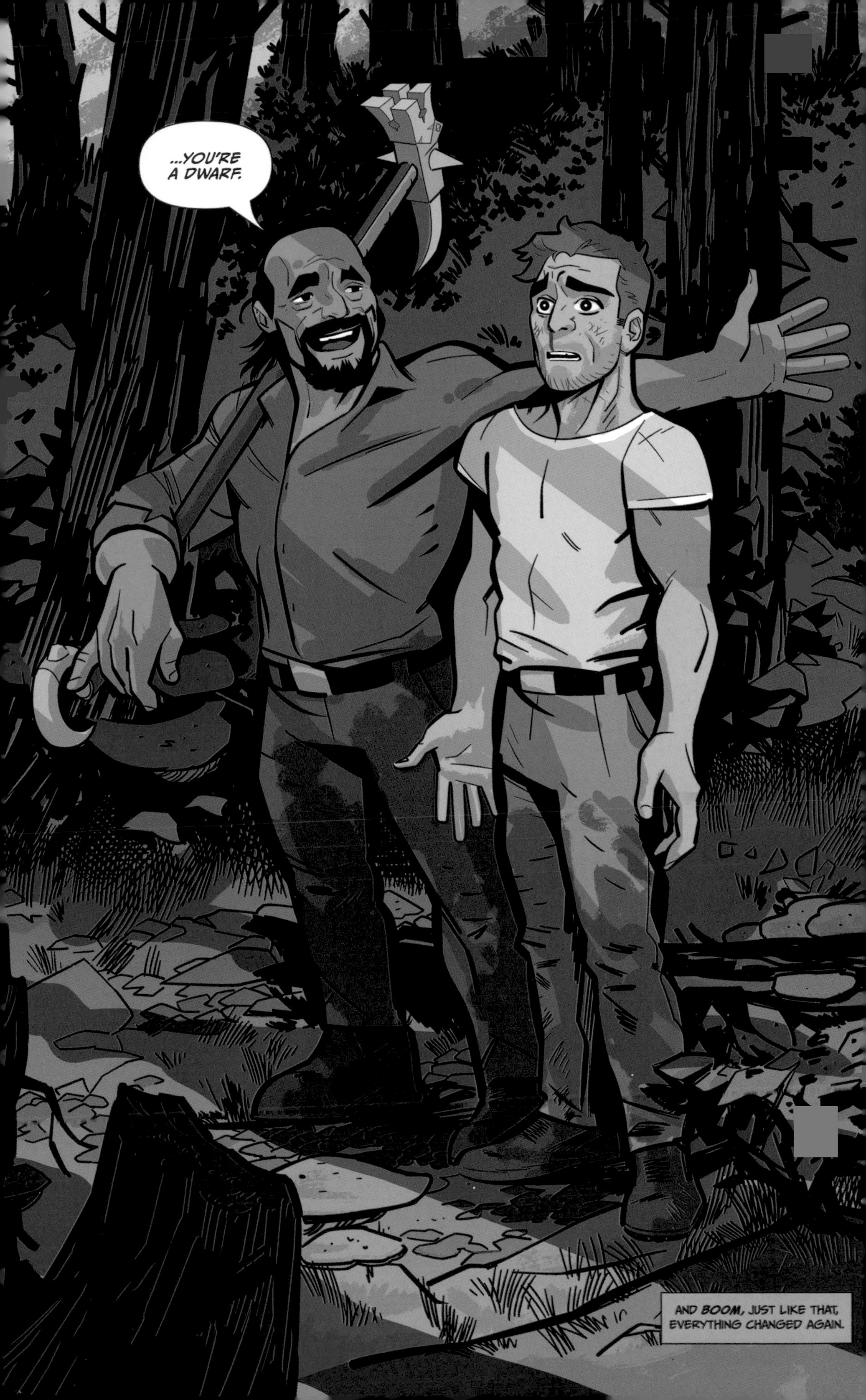
...YOU'RE A DWARF.
AND BOOM, JUST LIKE THAT, EVERYTHING CHANGED AGAIN.

CHAPTER THREE

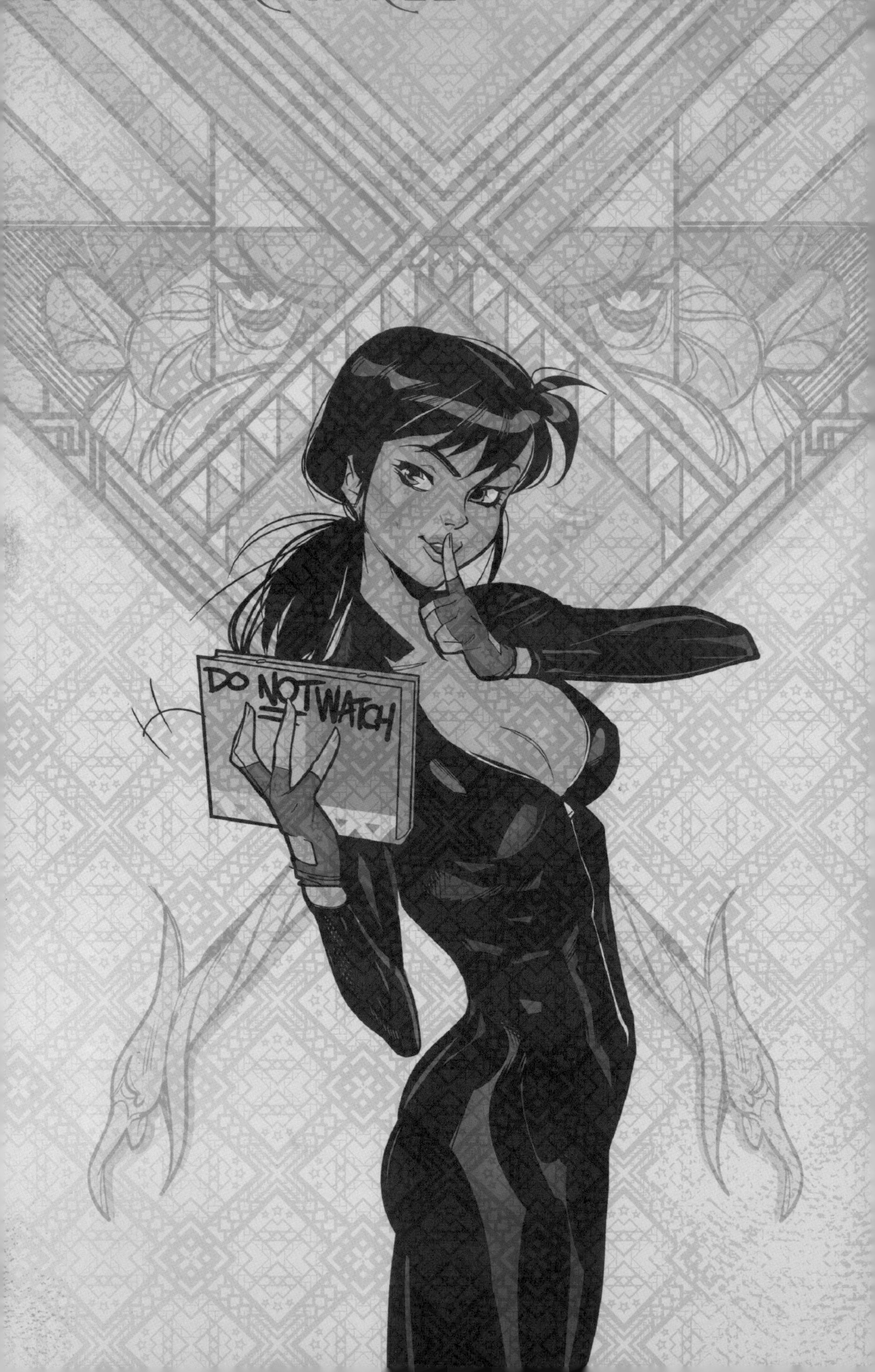
DO NOT WATCH

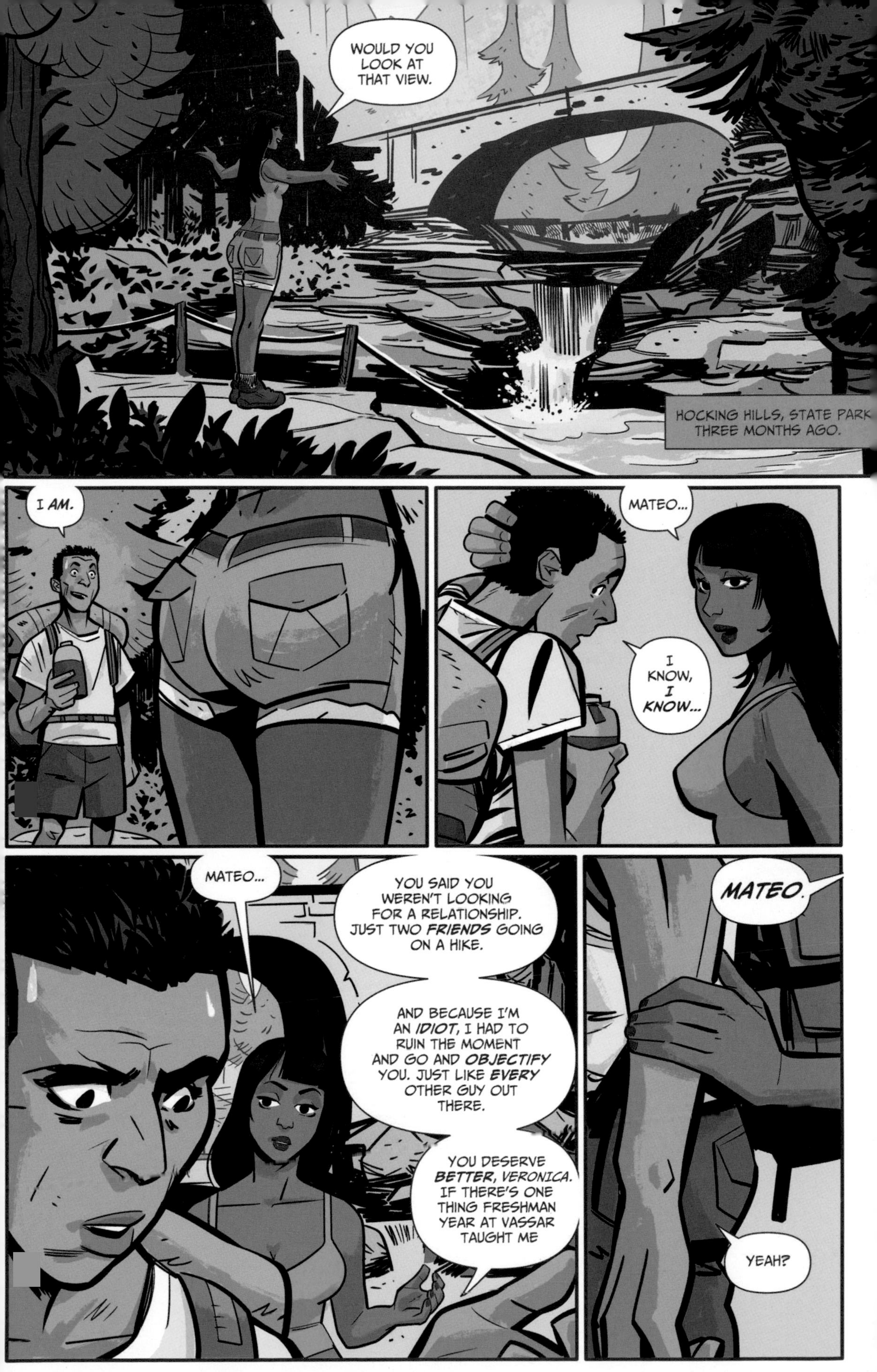
WOULD YOU LOOK AT THAT VIEW.
HOCKING HILLS, STATE PARK THREE MONTHS AGO.
I AM.
MATEO...
I KNOW, I KNOW...
MATEO...
YOU SAID YOU WEREN'T LOOKING FOR A RELATIONSHIP. JUST TWO FRIENDS GOING ON A HIKE.
AND BECAUSE I'M AN IDIOT, I HAD TO RUIN THE MOMENT AND GO AND OBJECTIFY YOU. JUST LIKE EVERY OTHER GUY OUT THERE.
YOU DESERVE BETTER, VERONICA. IF THERE'S ONE THING FRESHMAN YEAR AT VASSAR TAUGHT ME
MATEO.
YEAH?

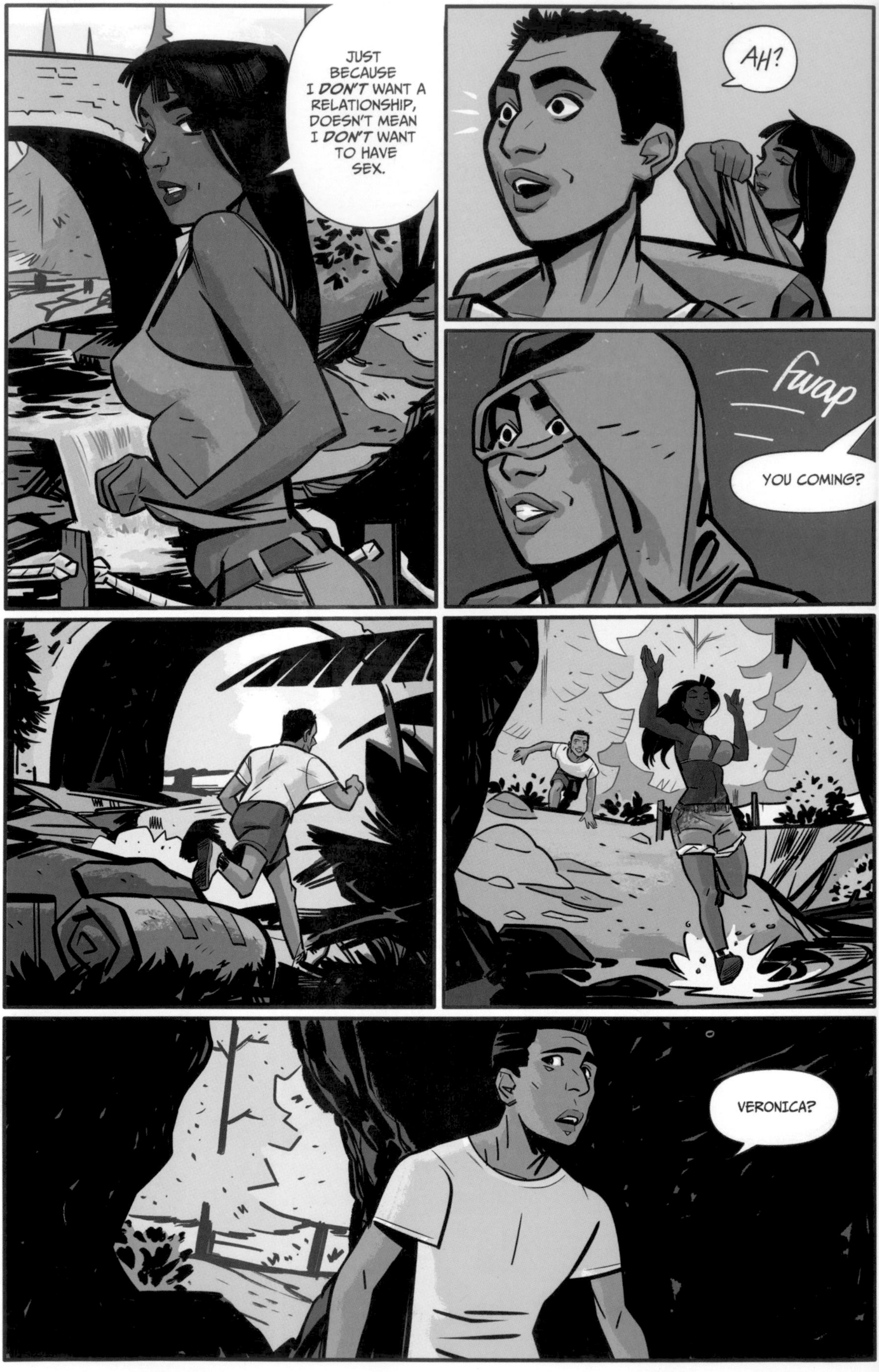
JUST BECAUSE I DON'T WANT A RELATIONSHIP, DOESN'T MEAN I DON'T WANT TO HAVE SEX.
AH?
fwap
YOU COMING?
VERONICA?

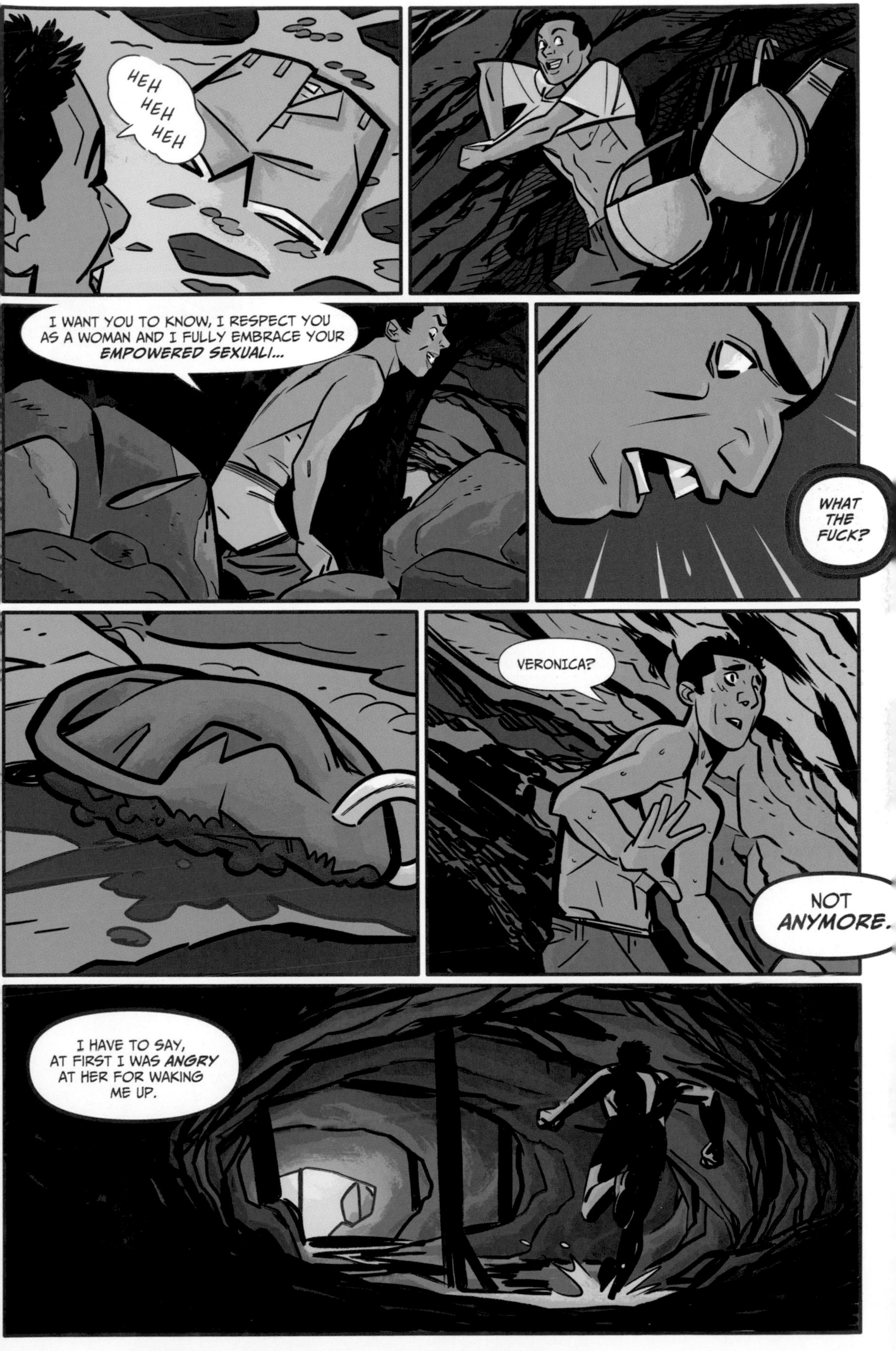
HEH
HEH
HEH
I WANT YOU TO KNOW, I RESPECT YOU AS A WOMAN AND I FULLY EMBRACE YOUR EMPOWERED SEXUALI...
WHAT THE FUCK?
VERONICA?
NOT ANYMORE.
I HAVE TO SAY, AT FIRST I WAS ANGRY AT HER FOR WAKING ME UP.

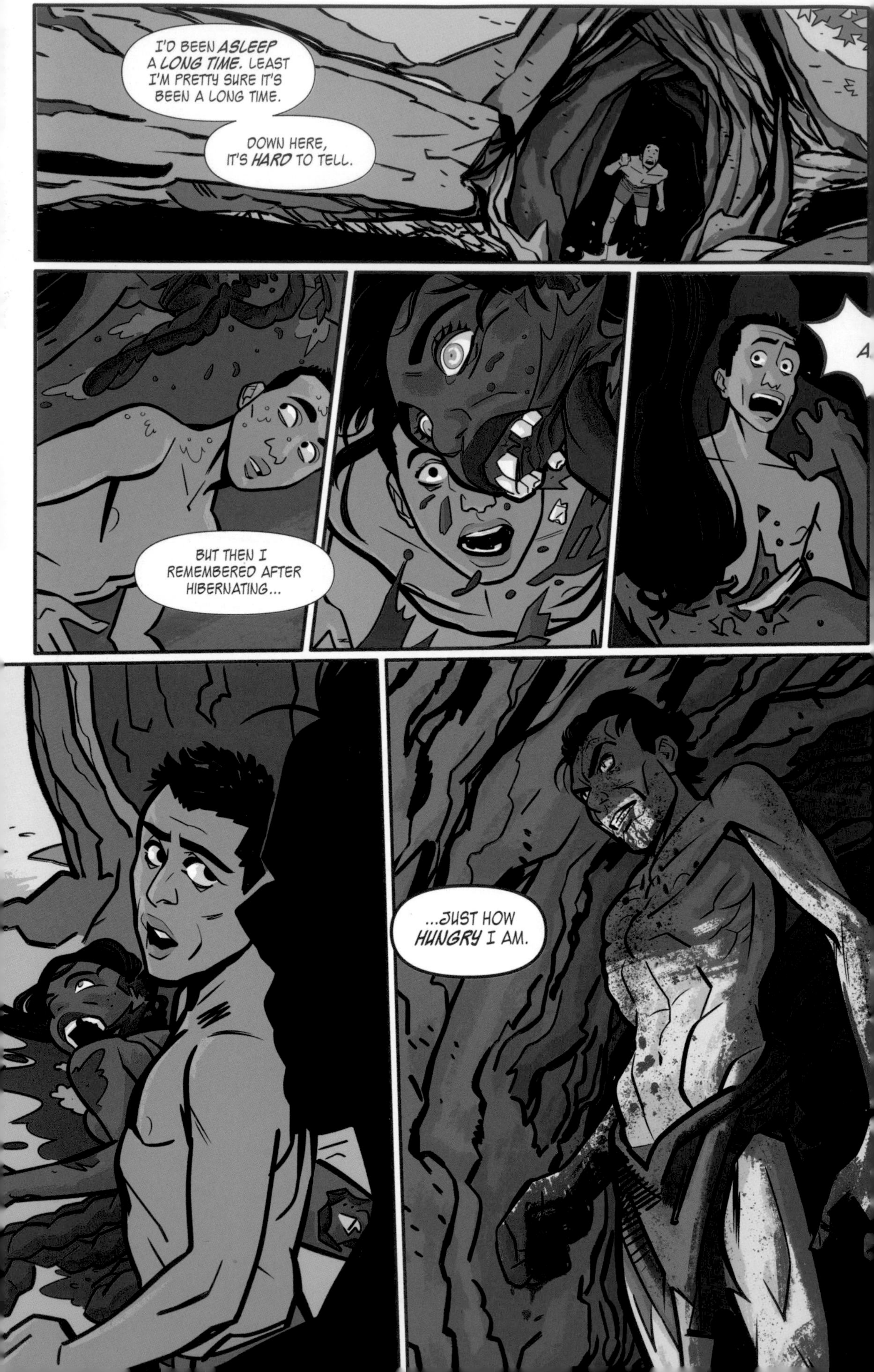
I'D BEEN ASLEEP A LONG TIME. LEAST I'M PRETTY SURE IT'S BEEN A LONG TIME.
DOWN HERE, IT'S HARD TO TELL.
BUT THEN I REMEMBERED AFTER HIBERNATING...
...JUST HOW HUNGRY I AM.

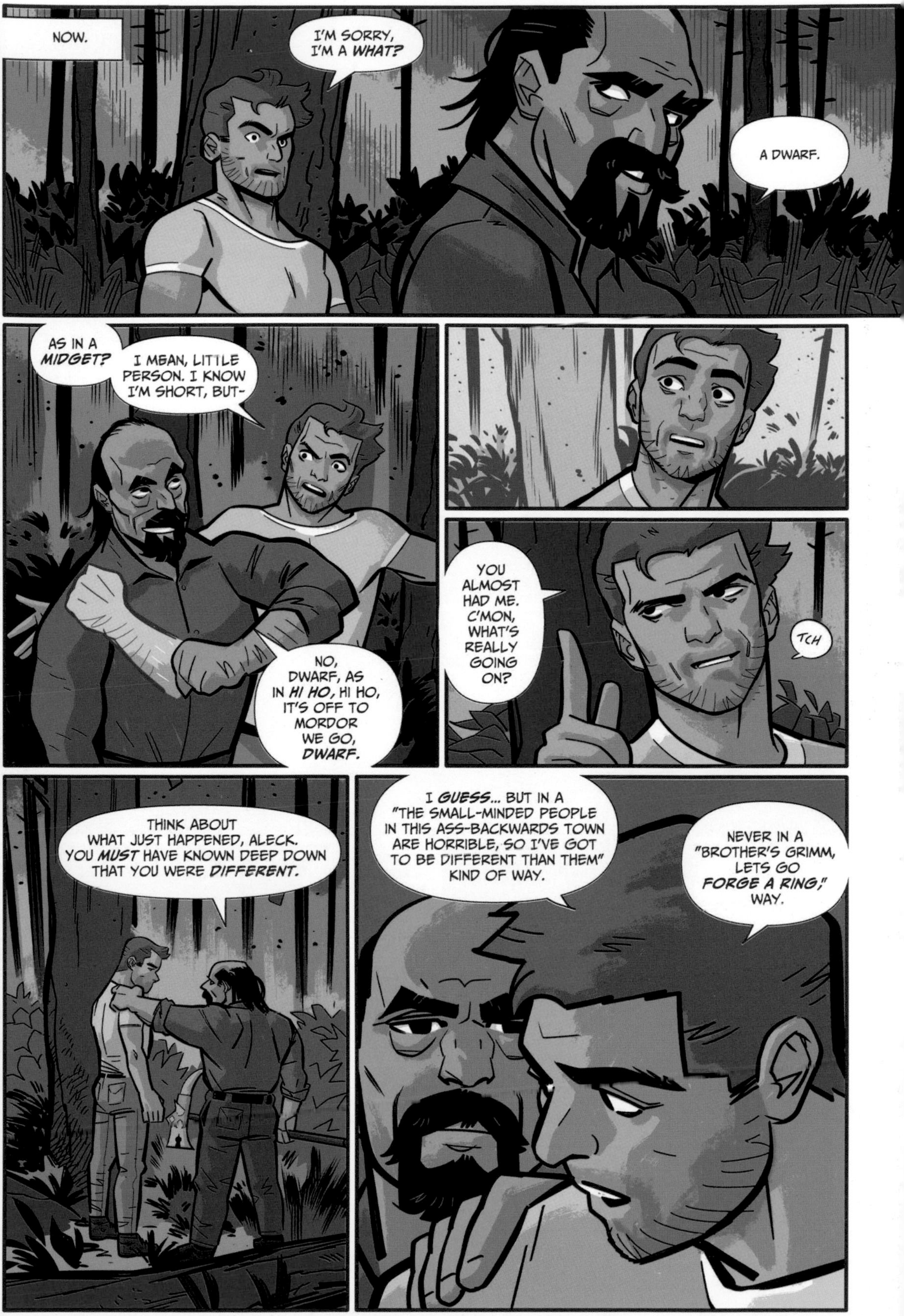
NOW.
I'M SORRY, I'M A WHAT?
A DWARF.
AS IN A MIDGET?
I MEAN, LITTLE PERSON. I KNOW I'M SHORT, BUT-
NO, DWARF, AS IN HI HO, HI HO, IT'S OFF TO MORDOR WE GO, DWARF.
YOU ALMOST HAD ME. C'MON, WHAT'S REALLY GOING ON?
TCH
THINK ABOUT WHAT JUST HAPPENED, ALECK. YOU MUST HAVE KNOWN DEEP DOWN THAT YOU WERE DIFFERENT.
I GUESS... BUT IN A "THE SMALL-MINDED PEOPLE IN THIS ASS-BACKWARDS TOWN ARE HORRIBLE, SO I'VE GOT TO BE DIFFERENT THAN THEM" KIND OF WAY.
NEVER IN A "BROTHER'S GRIMM, LETS GO FORGE A RING," WAY.

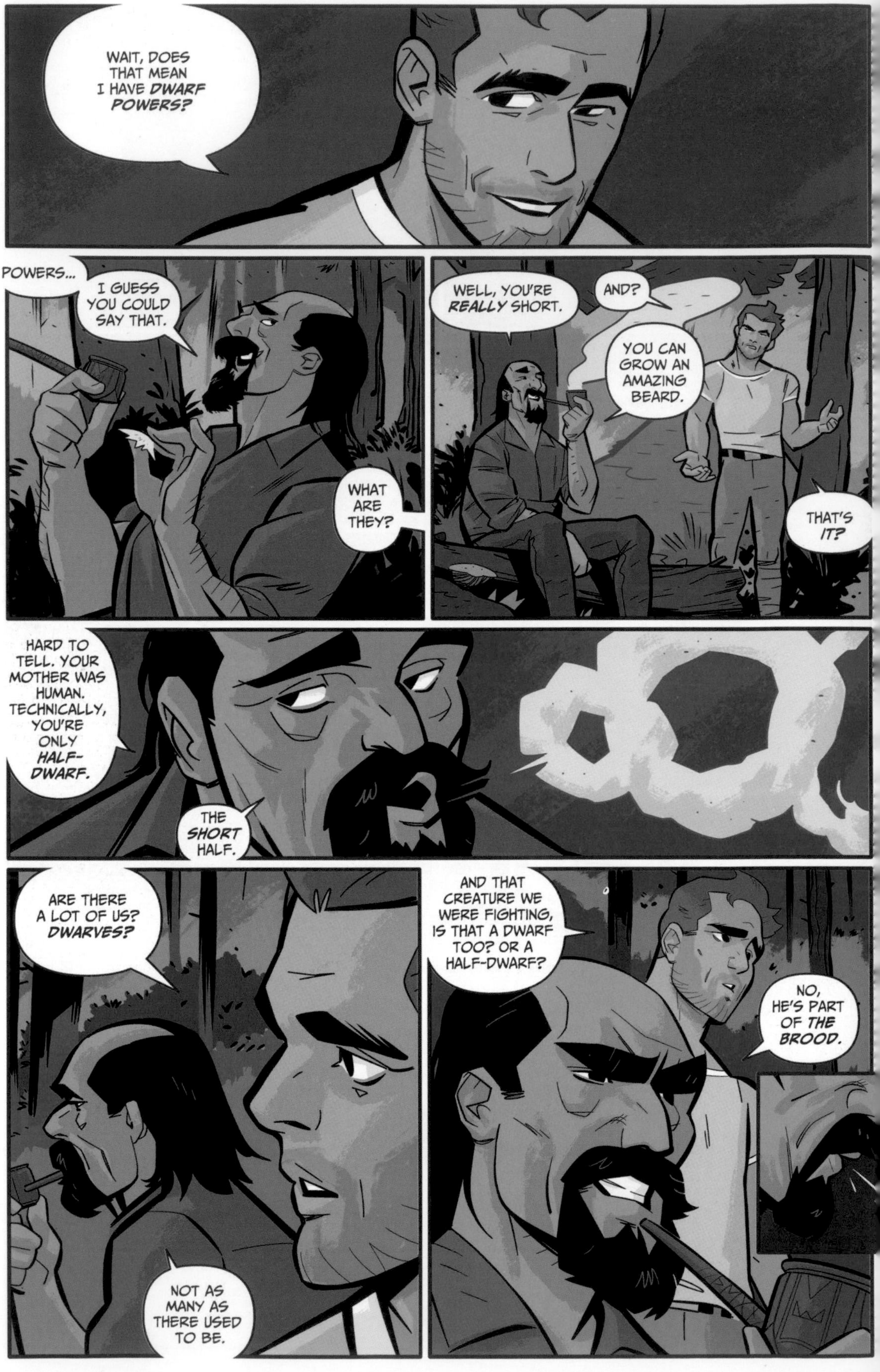

WAIT, DOES THAT MEAN I HAVE DWARF POWERS?
POWERS...
I GUESS YOU COULD SAY THAT.
WHAT ARE THEY?
WELL, YOU'RE REALLY SHORT.
AND?
YOU CAN GROW AN AMAZING BEARD.
THAT'S IT?
HARD TO TELL. YOUR MOTHER WAS HUMAN. TECHNICALLY, YOU'RE ONLY HALF-DWARF.
THE SHORT HALF.
ARE THERE A LOT OF US? DWARVES?
NOT AS MANY AS THERE USED TO BE.
AND THAT CREATURE WE WERE FIGHTING, IS THAT A DWARF TOO? OR A HALF-DWARF?
NO, HE'S PART OF THE BROOD.

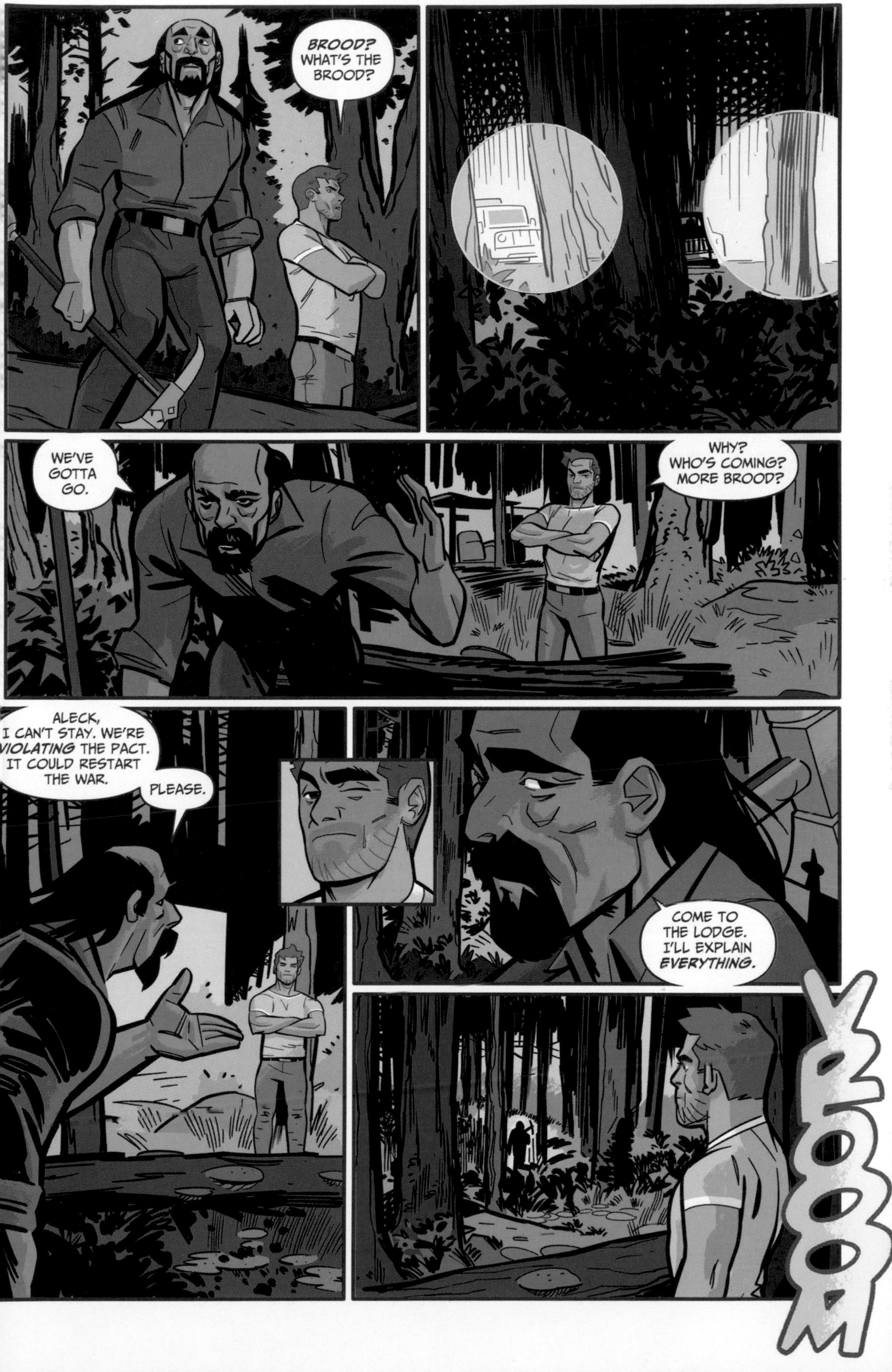
BROOD? WHAT'S THE BROOD?
WE'VE GOTTA GO.
WHY? WHO'S COMING? MORE BROOD?
ALECK, I CAN'T STAY. WE'RE VIOLATING THE PACT. IT COULD RESTART THE WAR.
PLEASE.
COME TO THE LODGE. I'LL EXPLAIN EVERYTHING.
VROOM

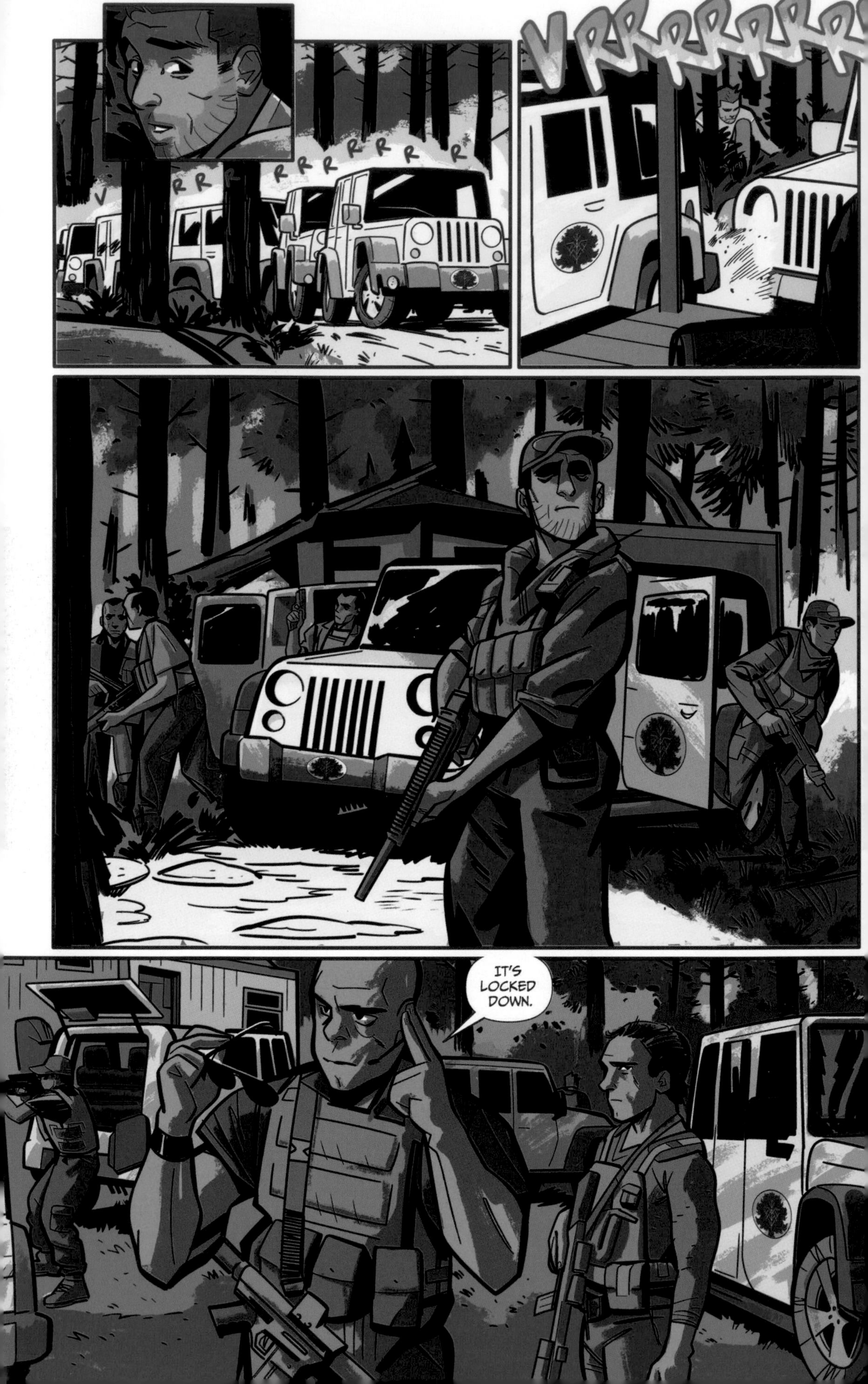
V R R R R R R R R R
VRRRRRRR
IT'S LOCKED DOWN.

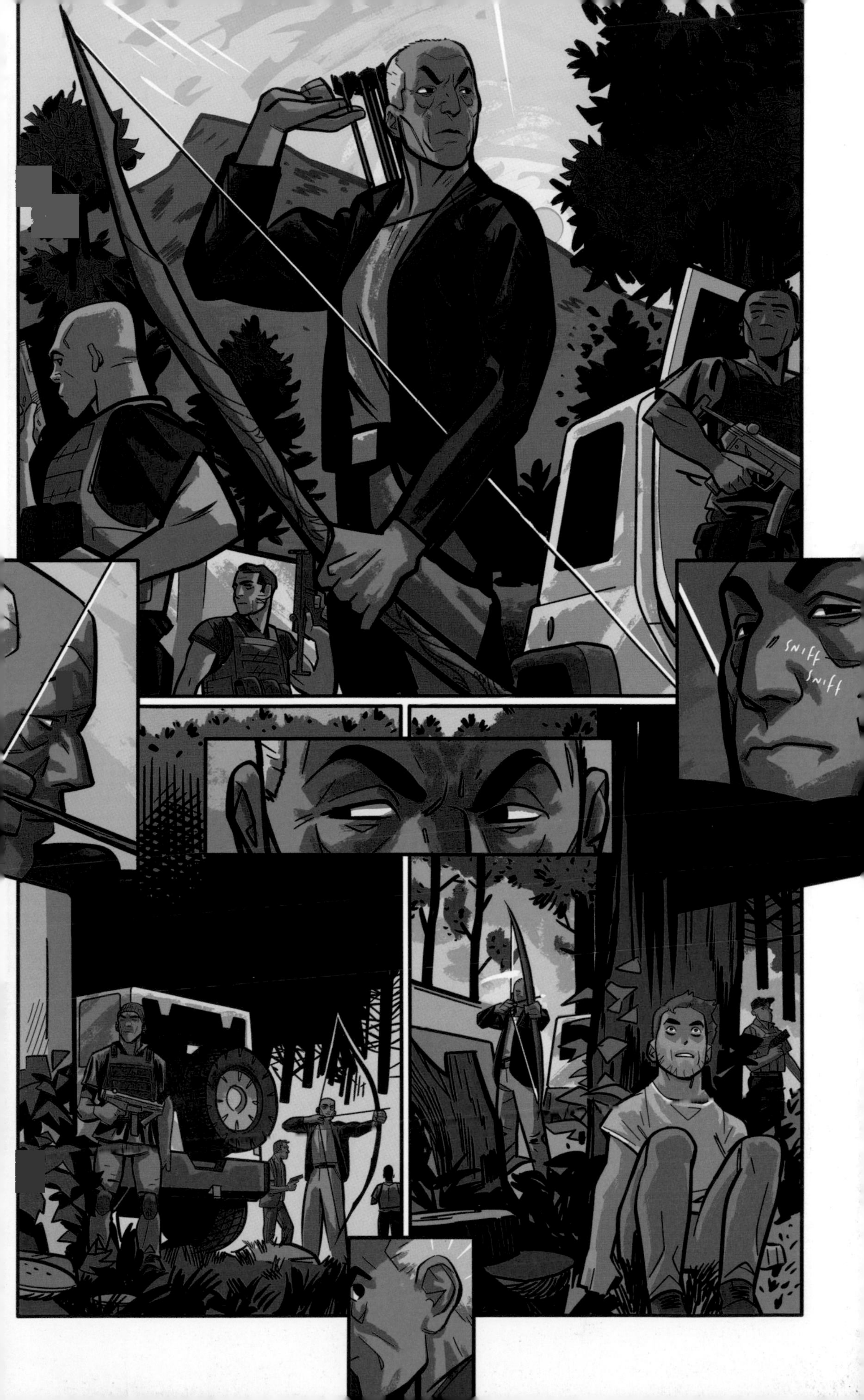
SNIFF
SNIFF

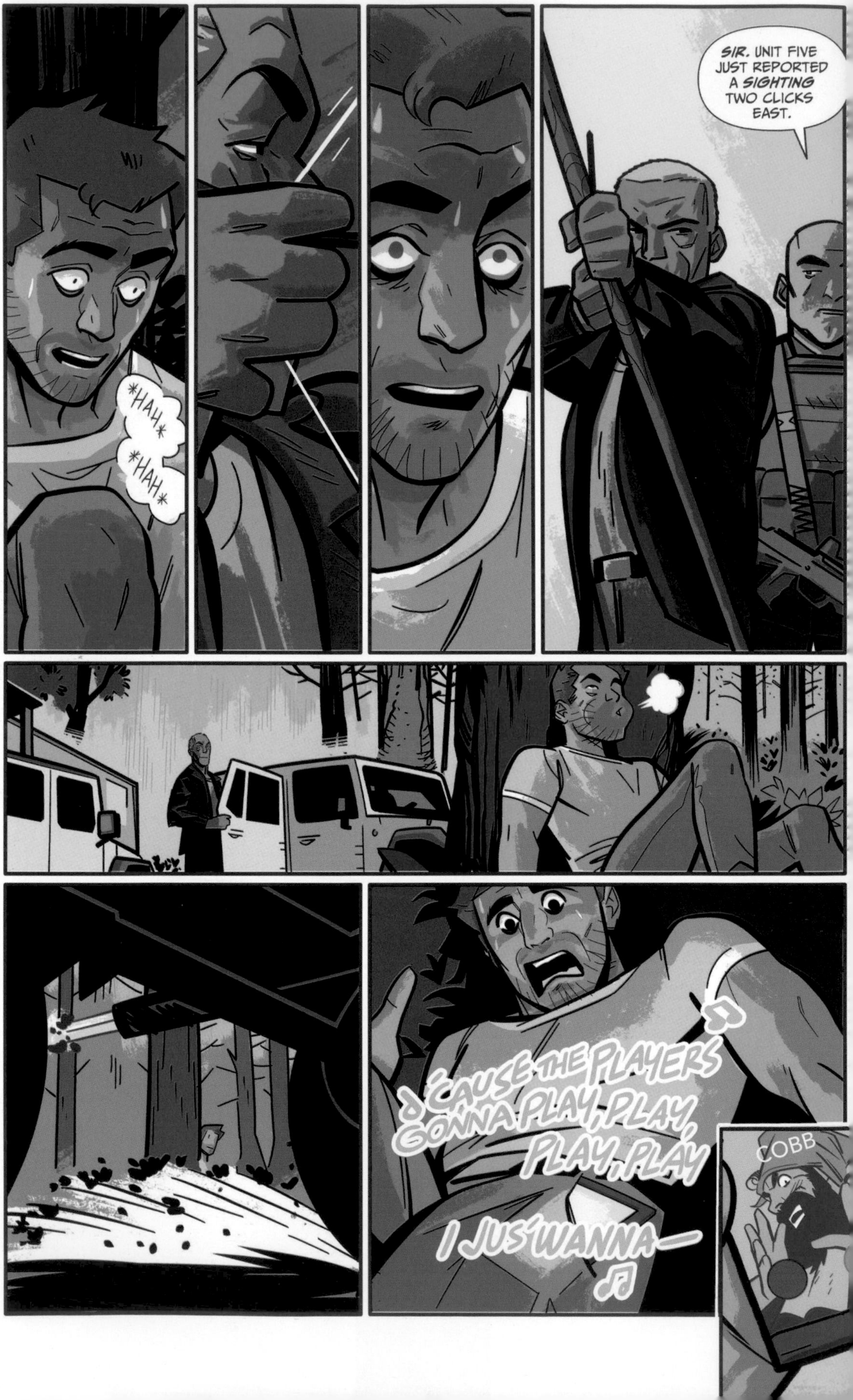
HAH
HAH
SIR. UNIT FIVE JUST REPORTED A SIGHTING TWO CLICKS EAST.
'CAUSE THE PLAYERS GONNA PLAY, PLAY, PLAY, PLAY
I JUS'WANNA—
COBB

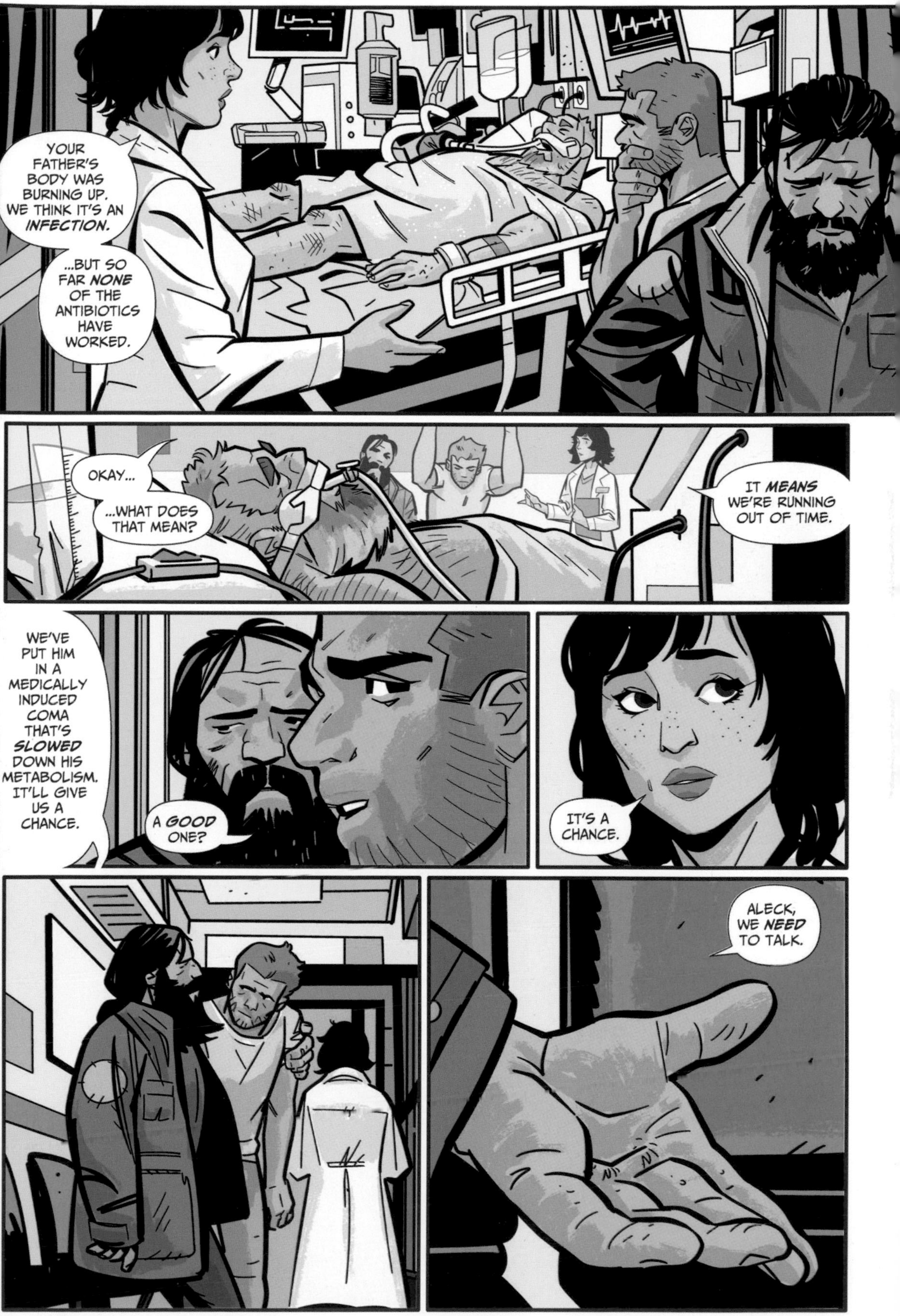
YOUR FATHER'S BODY WAS BURNING UP. WE THINK IT'S AN *INFECTION.*
...BUT SO FAR *NONE* OF THE ANTIBIOTICS HAVE WORKED.
OKAY...
...WHAT DOES THAT MEAN?
IT *MEANS* WE'RE RUNNING OUT OF TIME.
WE'VE PUT HIM IN A MEDICALLY INDUCED COMA THAT'S *SLOWED* DOWN HIS METABOLISM. IT'LL GIVE US A CHANCE.
A *GOOD* ONE?
IT'S A CHANCE.
ALECK, WE *NEED* TO TALK.

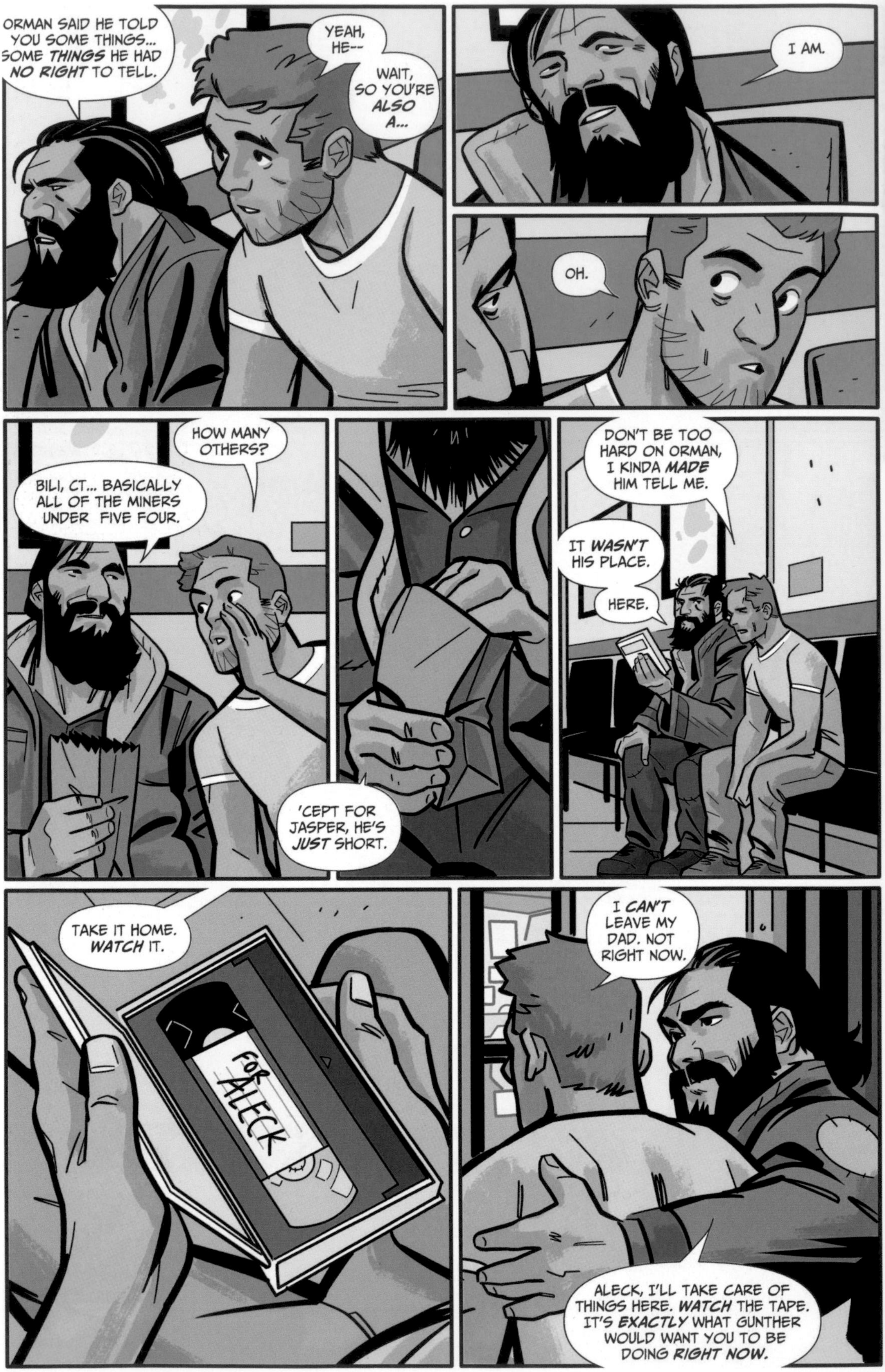
ORMAN SAID HE TOLD YOU SOME THINGS... SOME THINGS HE HAD NO RIGHT TO TELL.
YEAH, HE--
WAIT, SO YOU'RE ALSO A...
I AM.
OH.
HOW MANY OTHERS?
BILI, CT... BASICALLY ALL OF THE MINERS UNDER FIVE FOUR.
'CEPT FOR JASPER, HE'S JUST SHORT.
DON'T BE TOO HARD ON ORMAN, I KINDA MADE HIM TELL ME.
IT WASN'T HIS PLACE.
HERE.
TAKE IT HOME. WATCH IT.
FOR ALECK
I CAN'T LEAVE MY DAD. NOT RIGHT NOW.
ALECK, I'LL TAKE CARE OF THINGS HERE. WATCH THE TAPE. IT'S EXACTLY WHAT GUNTHER WOULD WANT YOU TO BE DOING RIGHT NOW.

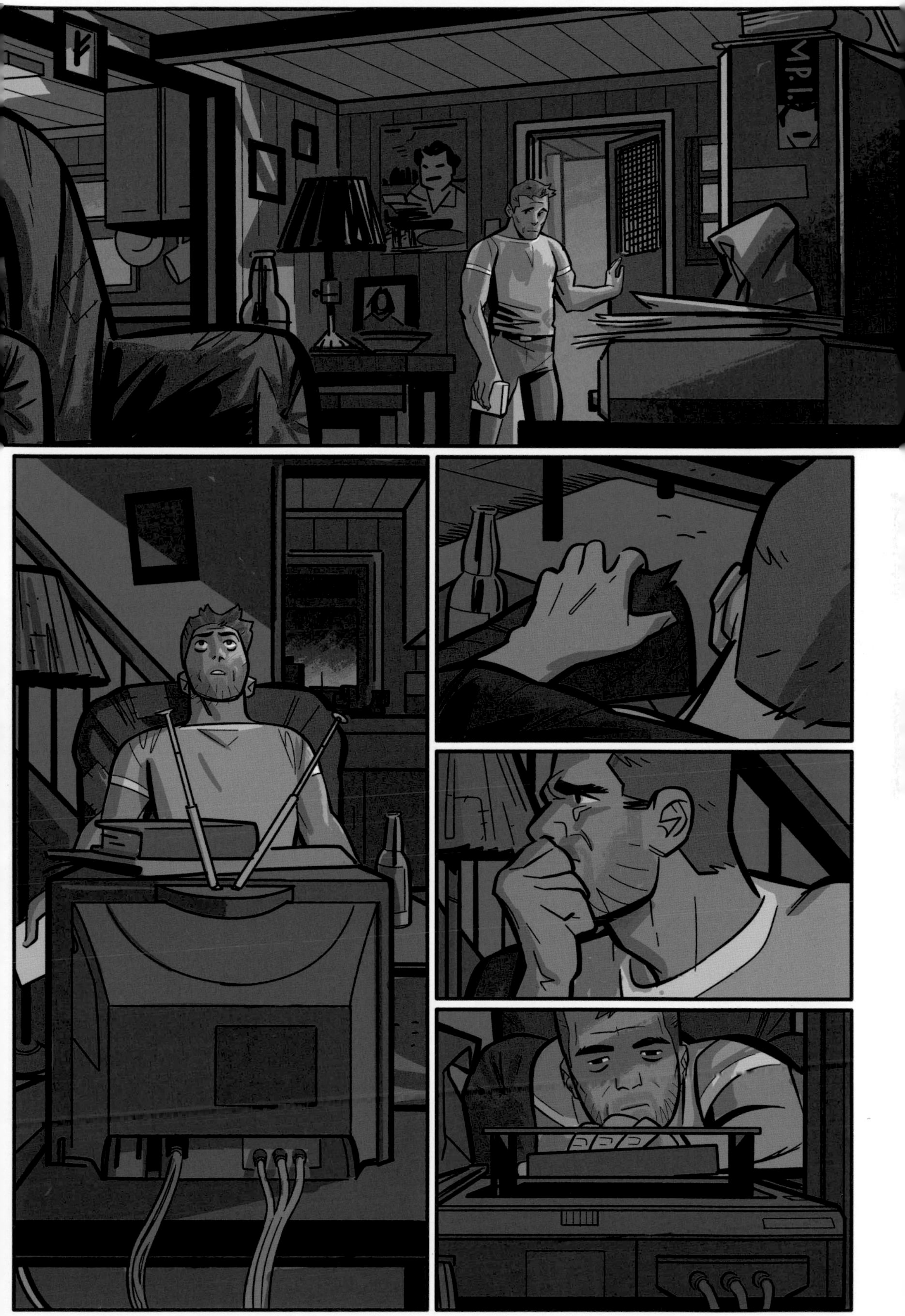

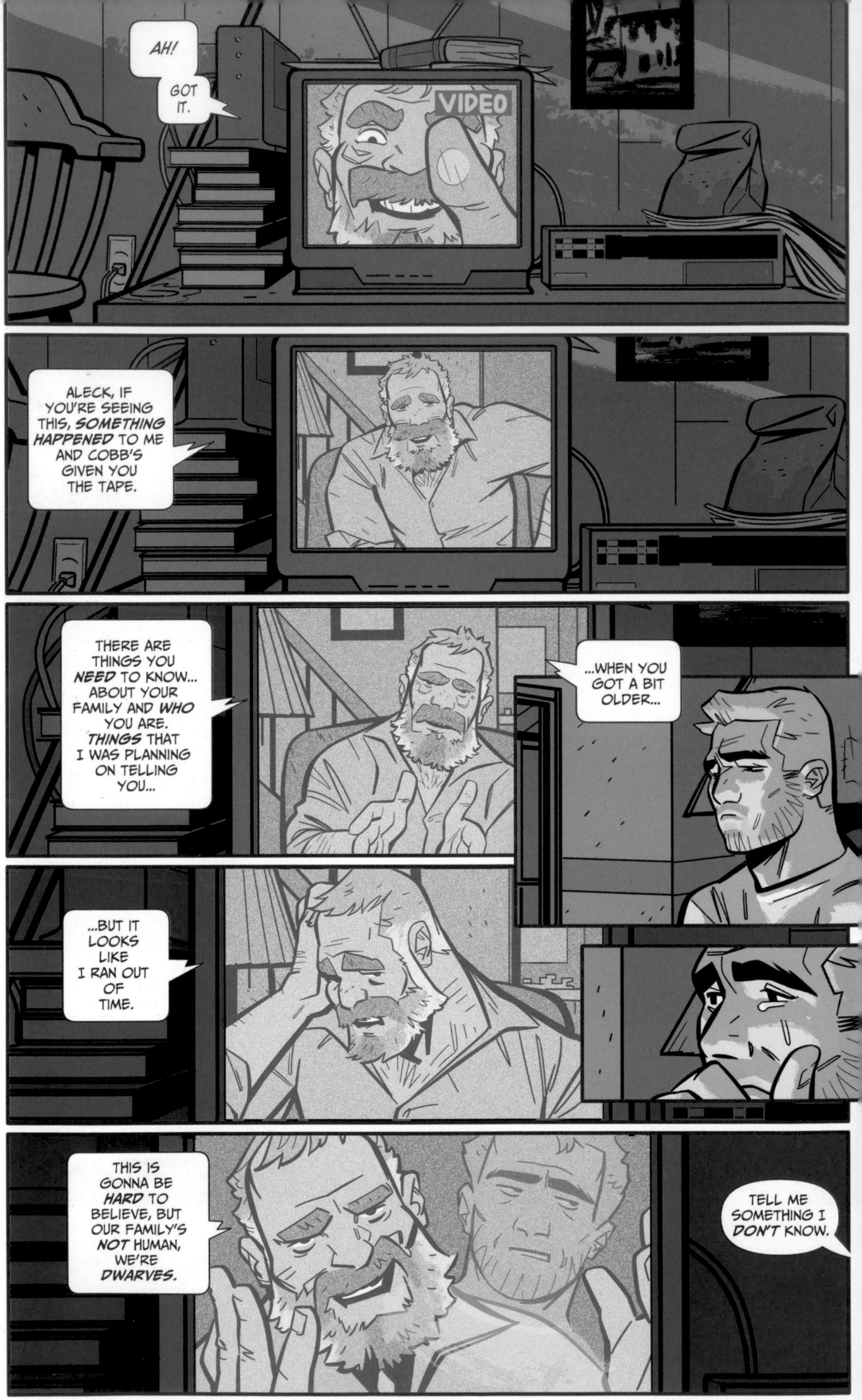
AH!
GOT IT.
VIDEO
ALECK, IF YOU'RE SEEING THIS, SOMETHING HAPPENED TO ME AND COBB'S GIVEN YOU THE TAPE.
THERE ARE THINGS YOU NEED TO KNOW... ABOUT YOUR FAMILY AND WHO YOU ARE. THINGS THAT I WAS PLANNING ON TELLING YOU...
...WHEN YOU GOT A BIT OLDER...
...BUT IT LOOKS LIKE I RAN OUT OF TIME.
THIS IS GONNA BE HARD TO BELIEVE, BUT OUR FAMILY'S NOT HUMAN, WE'RE DWARVES.
TELL ME SOMETHING I DON'T KNOW.

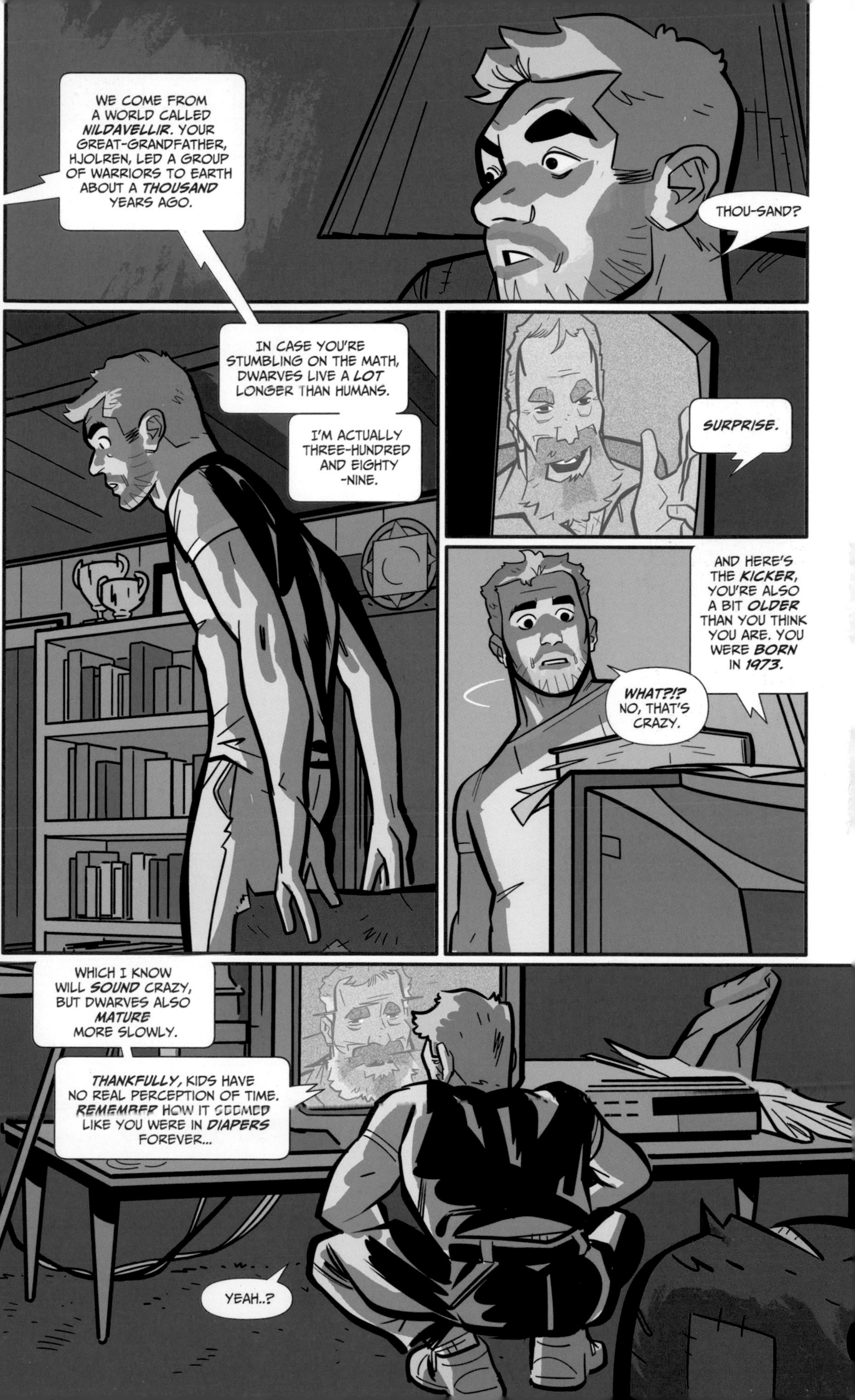
WE COME FROM A WORLD CALLED NILDAVELLIR. YOUR GREAT-GRANDFATHER, HJOLREN, LED A GROUP OF WARRIORS TO EARTH ABOUT A THOUSAND YEARS AGO.
THOU-SAND?
IN CASE YOU'RE STUMBLING ON THE MATH, DWARVES LIVE A LOT LONGER THAN HUMANS.
I'M ACTUALLY THREE-HUNDRED AND EIGHTY -NINE.
SURPRISE.
AND HERE'S THE KICKER, YOU'RE ALSO A BIT OLDER THAN YOU THINK YOU ARE. YOU WERE BORN IN 1973.
WHAT?!? NO, THAT'S CRAZY.
WHICH I KNOW WILL SOUND CRAZY, BUT DWARVES ALSO MATURE MORE SLOWLY.
THANKFULLY, KIDS HAVE NO REAL PERCEPTION OF TIME. REMEMBER HOW IT SEEMED LIKE YOU WERE IN DIAPERS FOREVER...
YEAH..?

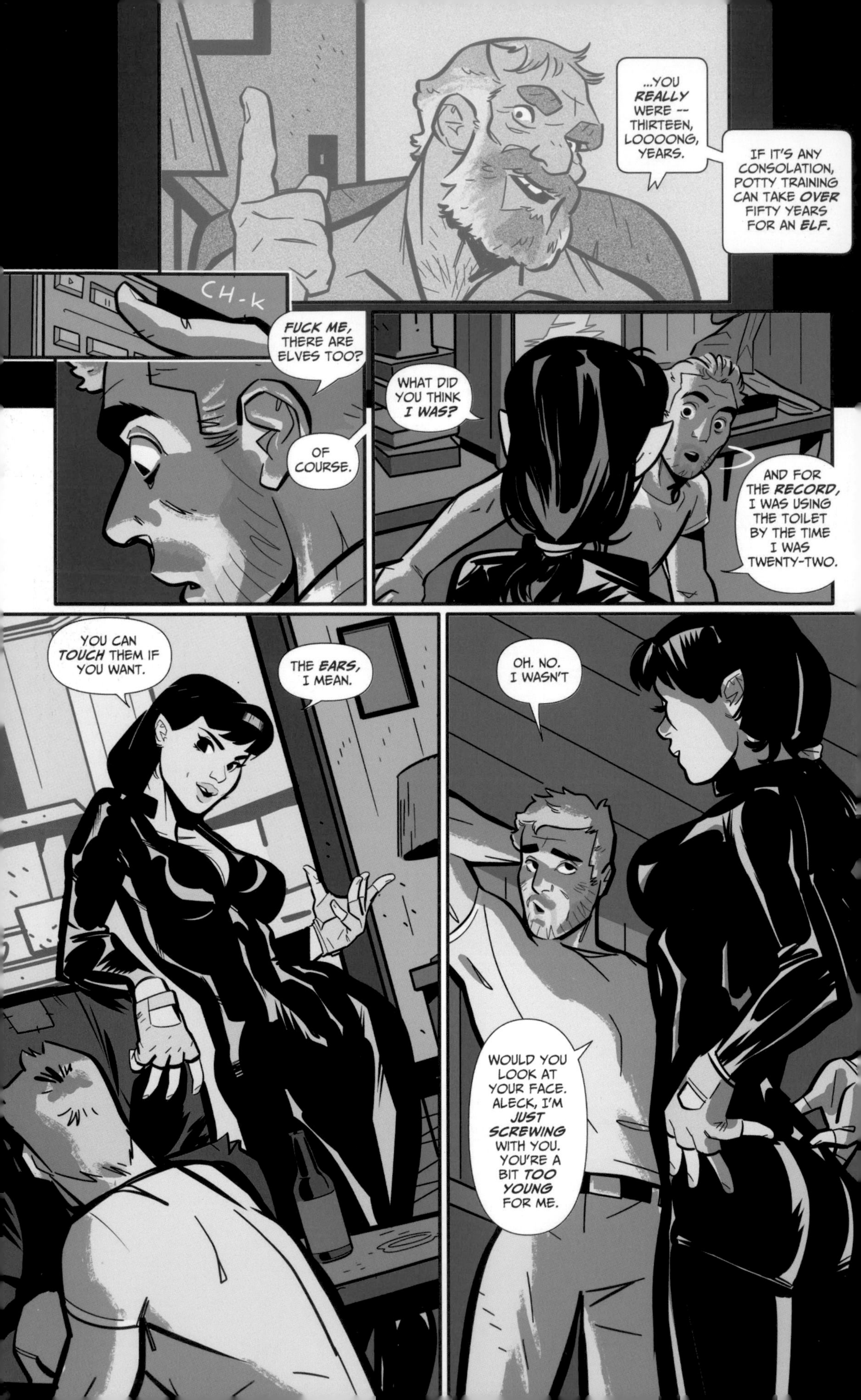
...YOU REALLY WERE -- THIRTEEN, LOOOONG, YEARS.
IF IT'S ANY CONSOLATION, POTTY TRAINING CAN TAKE OVER FIFTY YEARS FOR AN ELF.
CH-K
FUCK ME, THERE ARE ELVES TOO?
OF COURSE.
WHAT DID YOU THINK I WAS?
AND FOR THE RECORD, I WAS USING THE TOILET BY THE TIME I WAS TWENTY-TWO.
YOU CAN TOUCH THEM IF YOU WANT.
THE EARS, I MEAN.
OH. NO. I WASN'T
WOULD YOU LOOK AT YOUR FACE. ALECK, I'M JUST SCREWING WITH YOU. YOU'RE A BIT TOO YOUNG FOR ME.

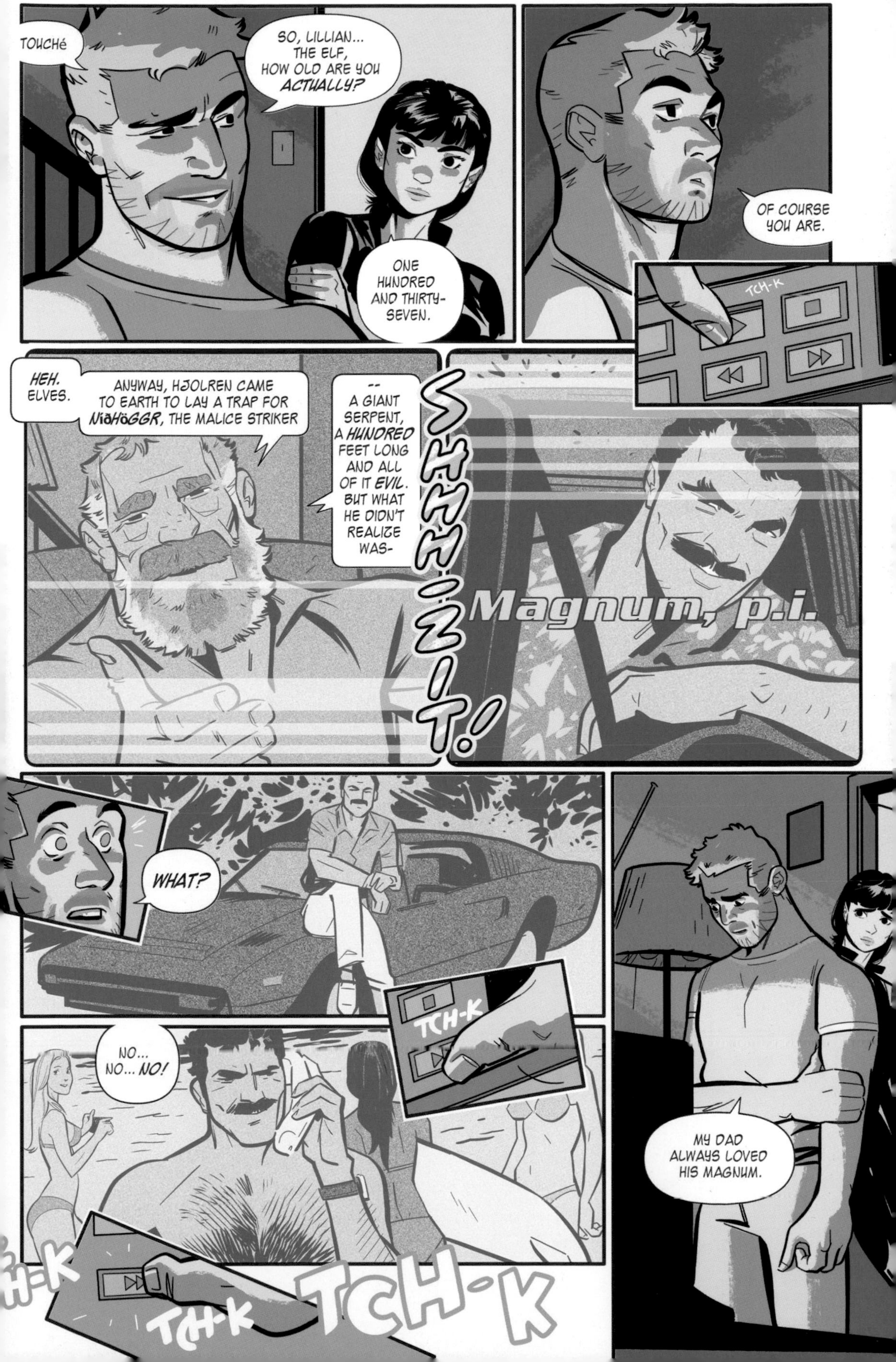
TOUCHé
SO, LILLIAN... THE ELF, HOW OLD ARE YOU ACTUALLY?
ONE HUNDRED AND THIRTY-SEVEN.
OF COURSE YOU ARE.
TCH-K
HEH. ELVES.
ANYWAY, HJOLREN CAME TO EARTH TO LAY A TRAP FOR NIðHöGGR, THE MALICE STRIKER
-- A GIANT SERPENT, A HUNDRED FEET LONG AND ALL OF IT EVIL. BUT WHAT HE DIDN'T REALIZE WAS-
SHHHH-ZZ-I-T!
Magnum, p.i.
WHAT?
NO... NO... NO!
TCH-K
MY DAD ALWAYS LOVED HIS MAGNUM.
TCH-K
TCH-K
TCH-K

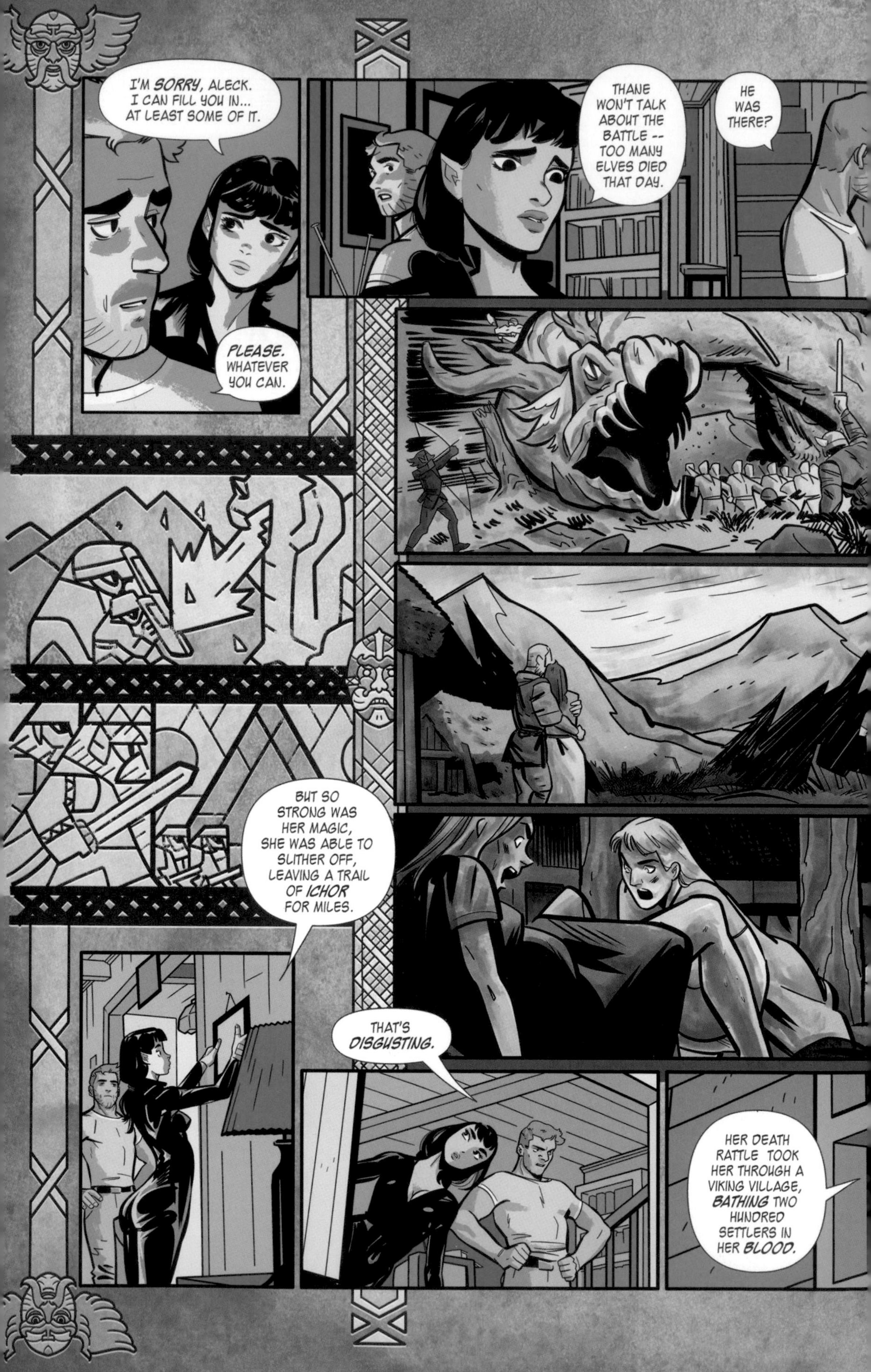
I'M *SORRY*, ALECK. I CAN FILL YOU IN... AT LEAST SOME OF IT.
PLEASE. WHATEVER YOU CAN.
THANE WON'T TALK ABOUT THE BATTLE -- TOO MANY ELVES DIED THAT DAY.
HE WAS THERE?
BUT SO STRONG WAS HER MAGIC, SHE WAS ABLE TO SLITHER OFF, LEAVING A TRAIL OF *ICHOR* FOR MILES.
THAT'S *DISGUSTING.*
HER DEATH RATTLE TOOK HER THROUGH A VIKING VILLAGE, *BATHING* TWO HUNDRED SETTLERS IN HER *BLOOD.*

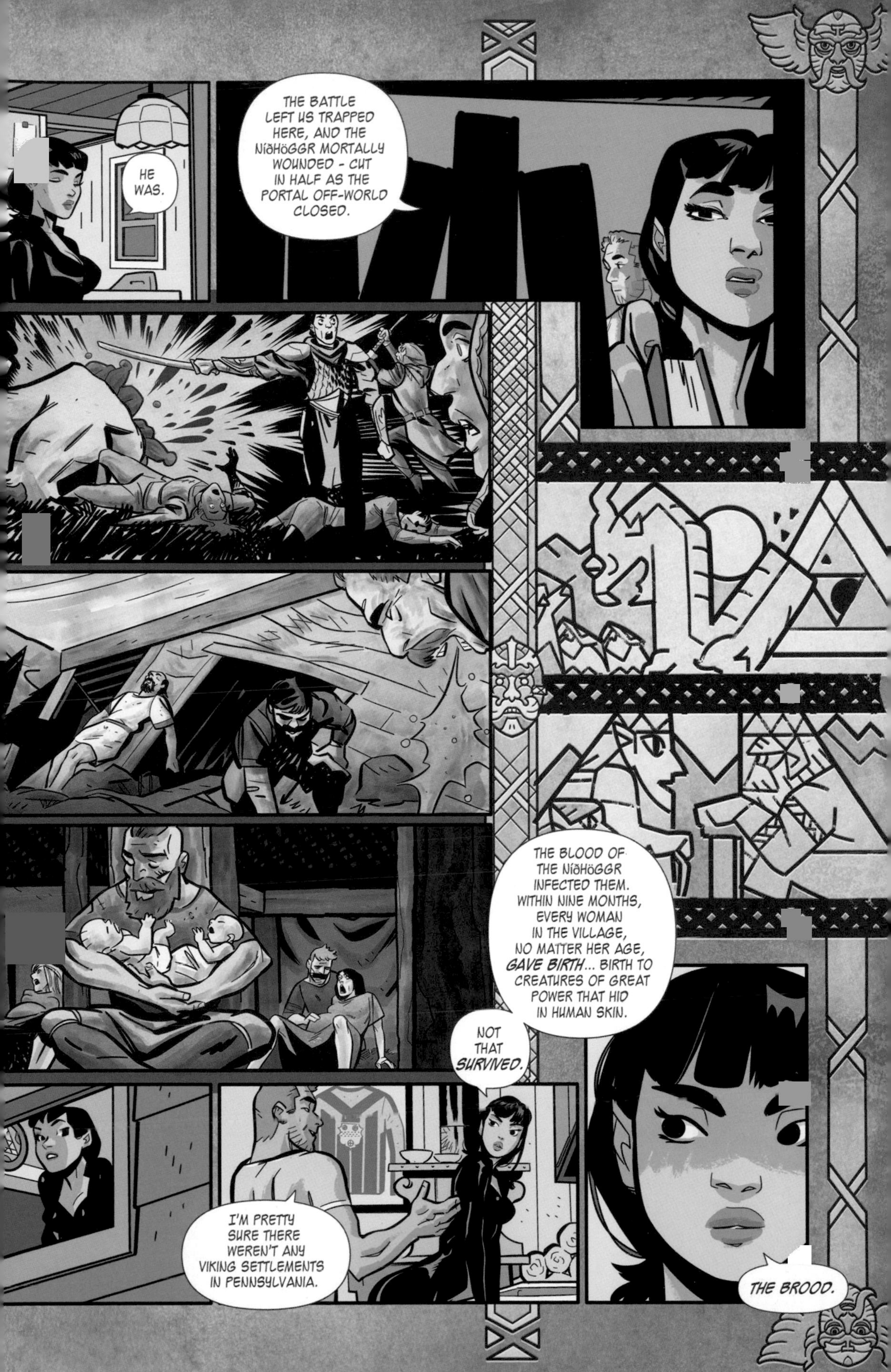
HE WAS.
THE BATTLE LEFT US TRAPPED HERE, AND THE NíðHÖGGR MORTALLY WOUNDED - CUT IN HALF AS THE PORTAL OFF-WORLD CLOSED.
THE BLOOD OF THE NíðHÖGGR INFECTED THEM. WITHIN NINE MONTHS, EVERY WOMAN IN THE VILLAGE, NO MATTER HER AGE, GAVE BIRTH... BIRTH TO CREATURES OF GREAT POWER THAT HID IN HUMAN SKIN.
I'M PRETTY SURE THERE WEREN'T ANY VIKING SETTLEMENTS IN PENNSYLVANIA.
NOT THAT SURVIVED.
THE BROOD.

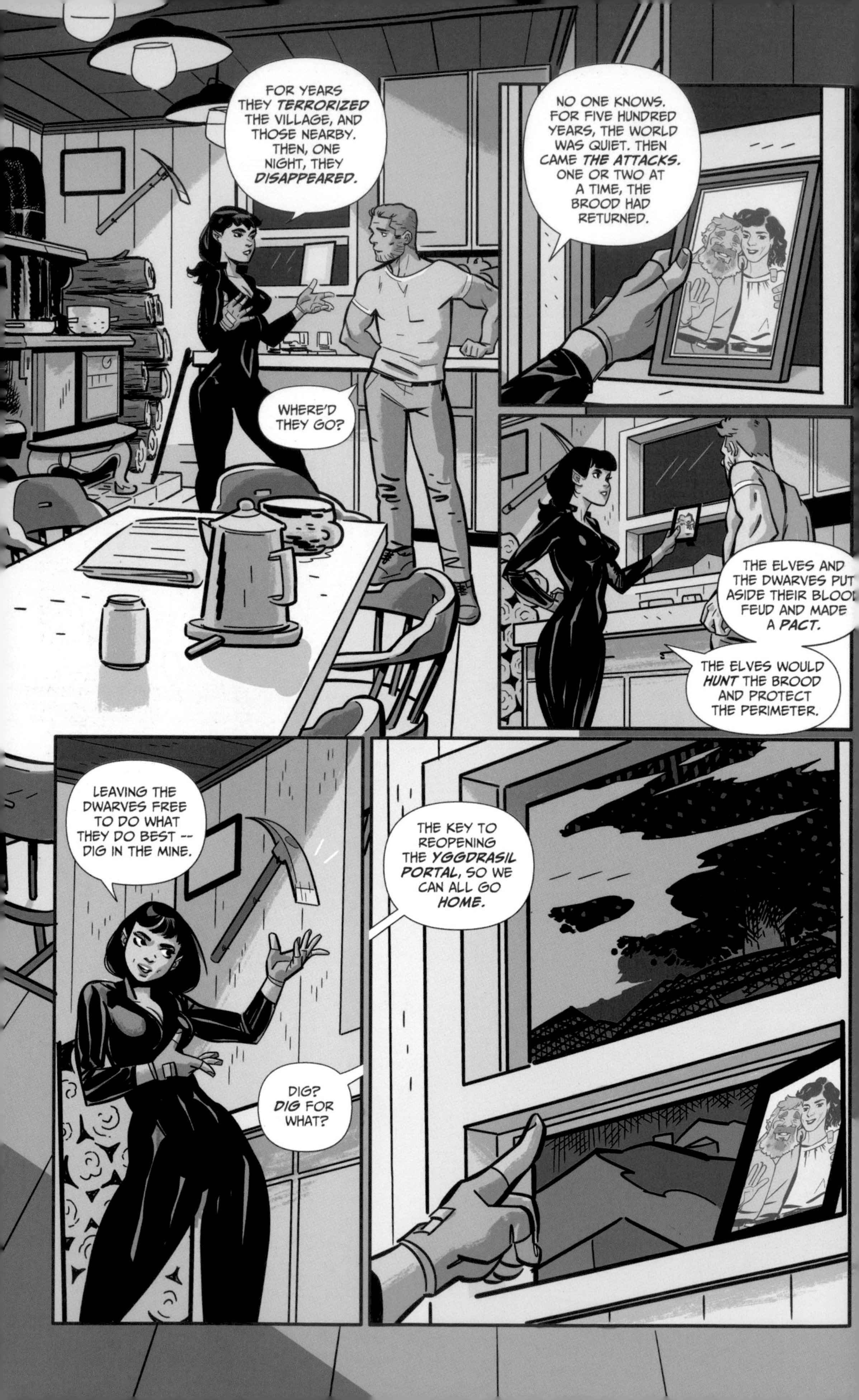
FOR YEARS THEY TERRORIZED THE VILLAGE, AND THOSE NEARBY. THEN, ONE NIGHT, THEY DISAPPEARED.
WHERE'D THEY GO?
NO ONE KNOWS. FOR FIVE HUNDRED YEARS, THE WORLD WAS QUIET. THEN CAME THE ATTACKS. ONE OR TWO AT A TIME, THE BROOD HAD RETURNED.
THE ELVES AND THE DWARVES PUT ASIDE THEIR BLOOD FEUD AND MADE A PACT.
THE ELVES WOULD HUNT THE BROOD AND PROTECT THE PERIMETER.
LEAVING THE DWARVES FREE TO DO WHAT THEY DO BEST -- DIG IN THE MINE.
DIG? DIG FOR WHAT?
THE KEY TO REOPENING THE YGGDRASIL PORTAL, SO WE CAN ALL GO HOME.

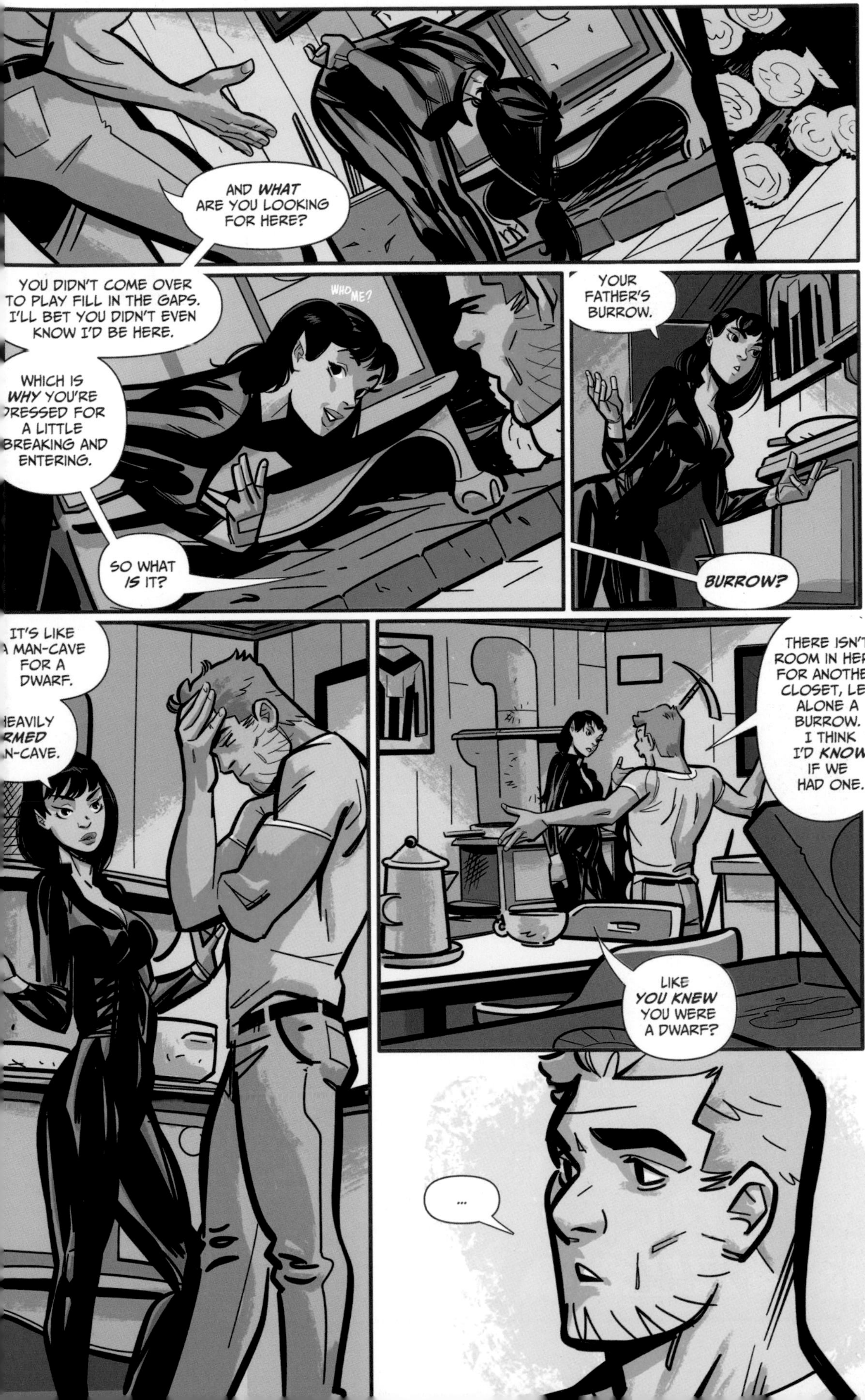
AND *WHAT* ARE YOU LOOKING FOR HERE?
YOU DIDN'T COME OVER TO PLAY FILL IN THE GAPS. I'LL BET YOU DIDN'T EVEN KNOW I'D BE HERE.
WHO ME?
WHICH IS *WHY* YOU'RE RESSED FOR A LITTLE BREAKING AND ENTERING.
SO WHAT *IS* IT?
YOUR FATHER'S BURROW.
BURROW?
IT'S LIKE A MAN-CAVE FOR A DWARF.
EAVILY RMED N-CAVE.
THERE ISN'T ROOM IN HERE FOR ANOTHER CLOSET, LET ALONE A BURROW. I THINK I'D *KNOW* IF WE HAD ONE.
LIKE *YOU KNEW* YOU WERE A DWARF?
...

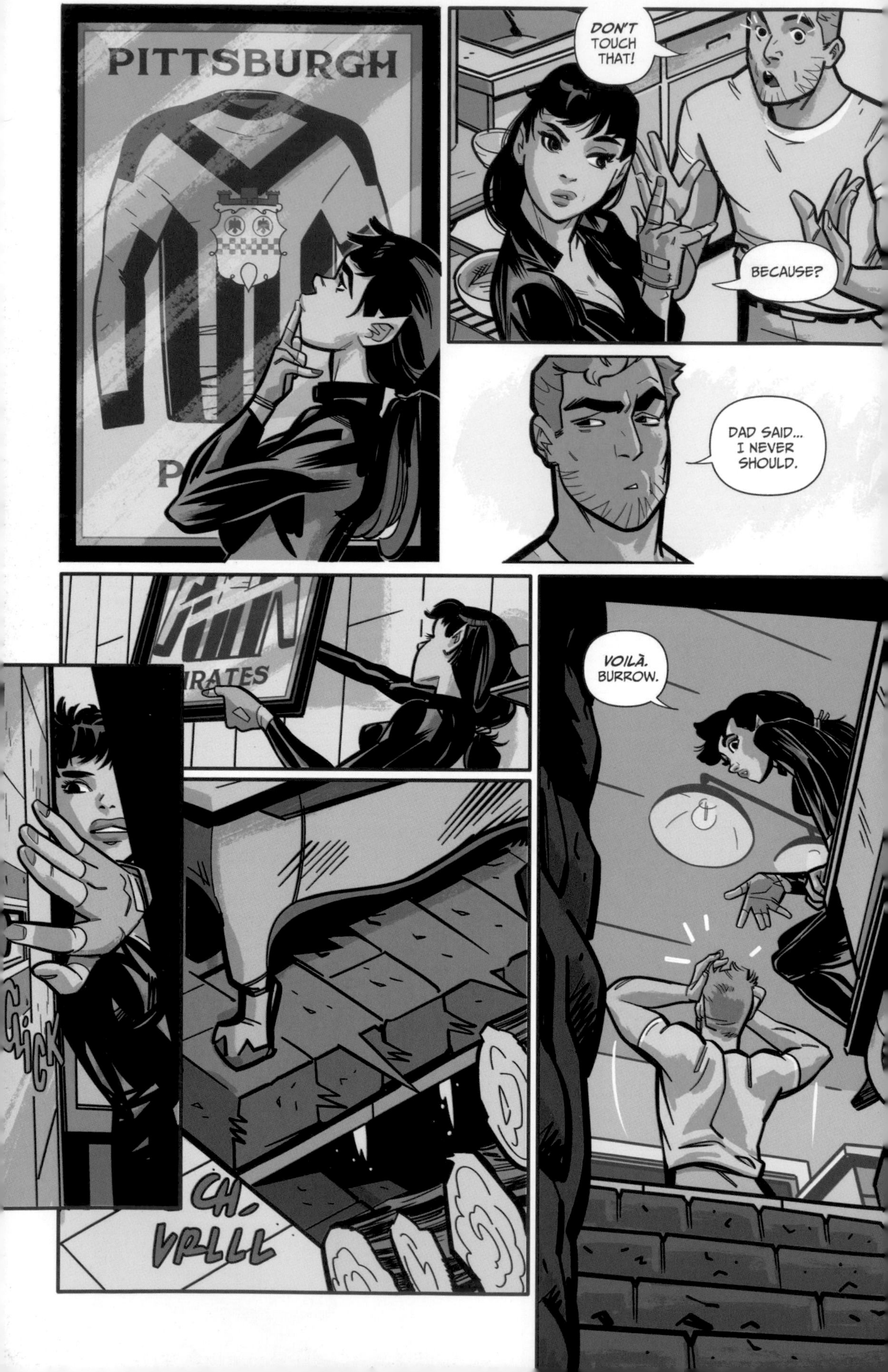

PITTSBURGH
DON'T TOUCH THAT!
BECAUSE?
DAD SAID... I NEVER SHOULD.
IRATES
CHICK
CH-
VRLLL
VOILÀ. BURROW.

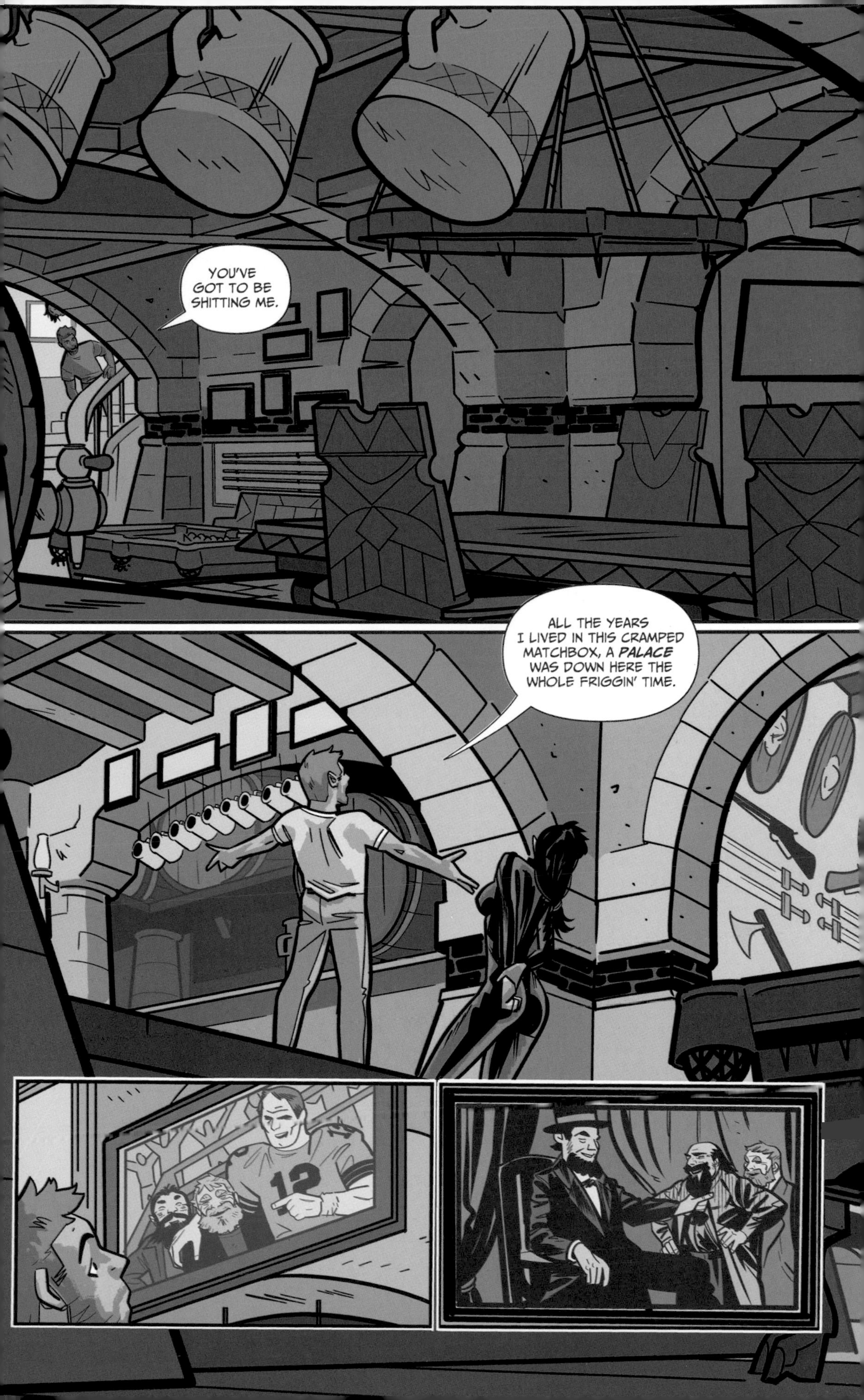
YOU'VE GOT TO BE SHITTING ME.
ALL THE YEARS I LIVED IN THIS CRAMPED MATCHBOX, A *PALACE* WAS DOWN HERE THE WHOLE FRIGGIN' TIME.
12

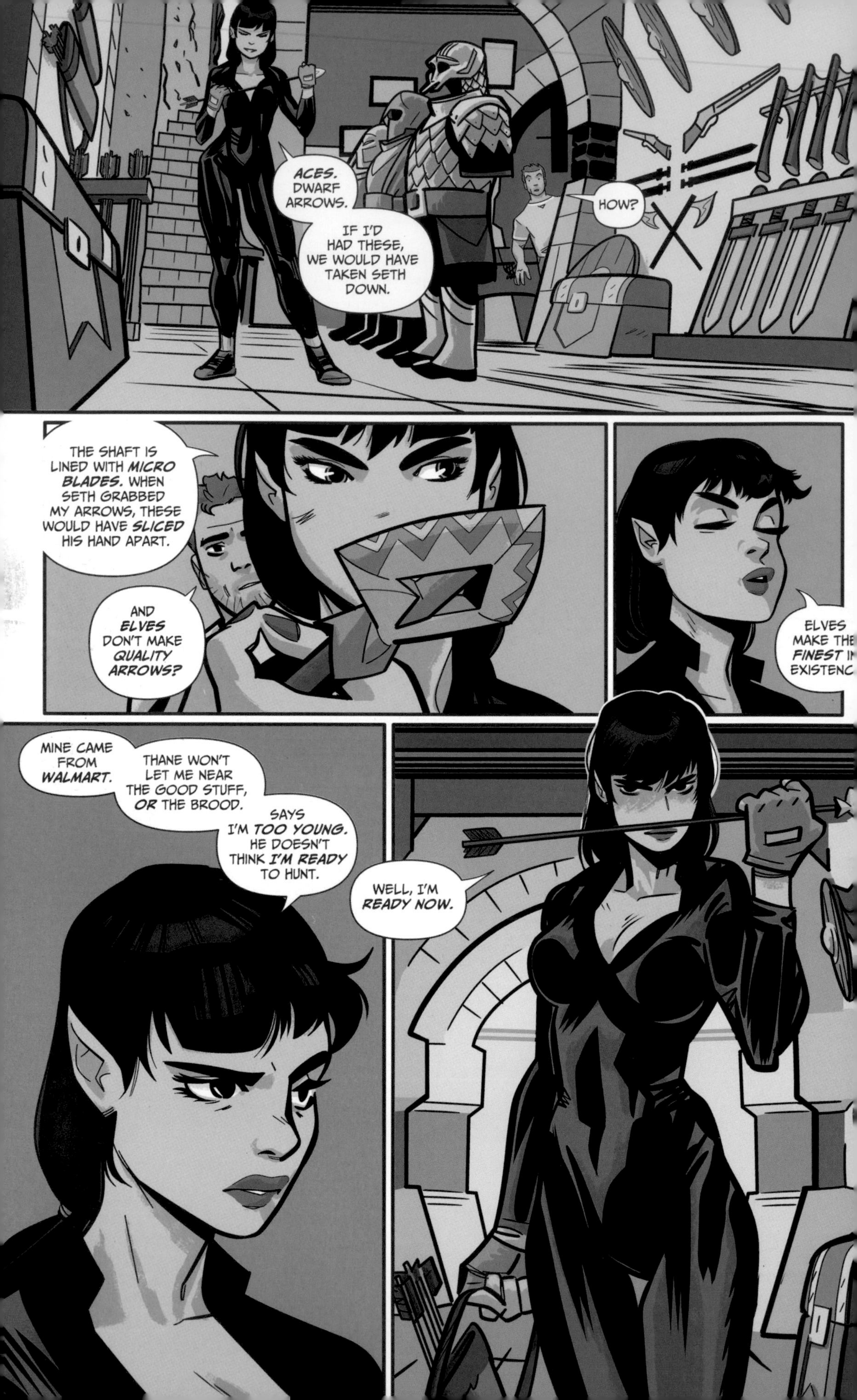
ACES. DWARF ARROWS.
IF I'D HAD THESE, WE WOULD HAVE TAKEN SETH DOWN.
HOW?
THE SHAFT IS LINED WITH MICRO BLADES. WHEN SETH GRABBED MY ARROWS, THESE WOULD HAVE SLICED HIS HAND APART.
AND ELVES DON'T MAKE QUALITY ARROWS?
ELVES MAKE THE FINEST I EXISTENC
MINE CAME FROM WALMART.
THANE WON'T LET ME NEAR THE GOOD STUFF, OR THE BROOD.
SAYS I'M TOO YOUNG. HE DOESN'T THINK I'M READY TO HUNT.
WELL, I'M READY NOW.

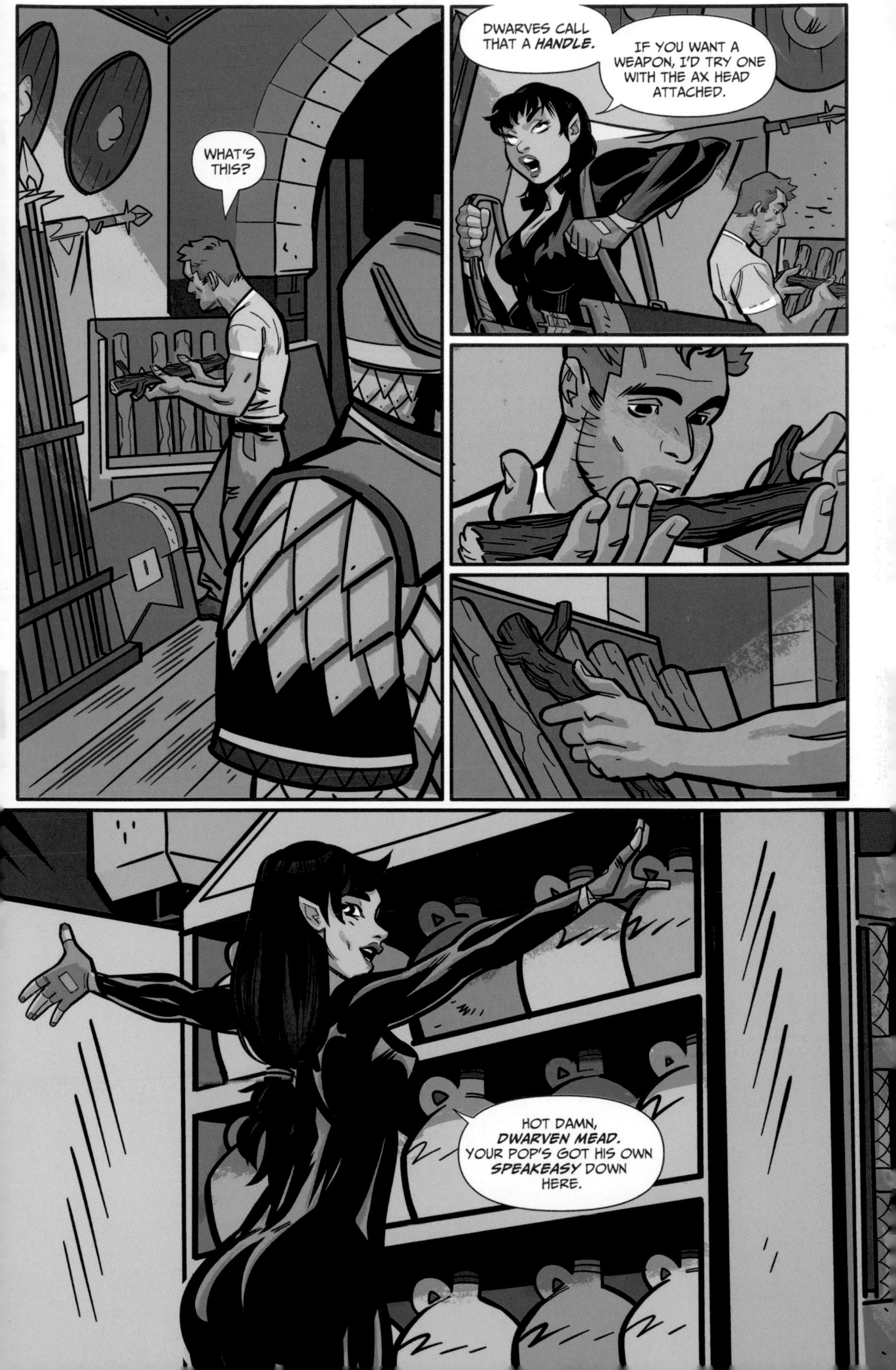
WHAT'S THIS?
DWARVES CALL THAT A HANDLE.
IF YOU WANT A WEAPON, I'D TRY ONE WITH THE AX HEAD ATTACHED.
HOT DAMN, DWARVEN MEAD. YOUR POP'S GOT HIS OWN SPEAKEASY DOWN HERE.

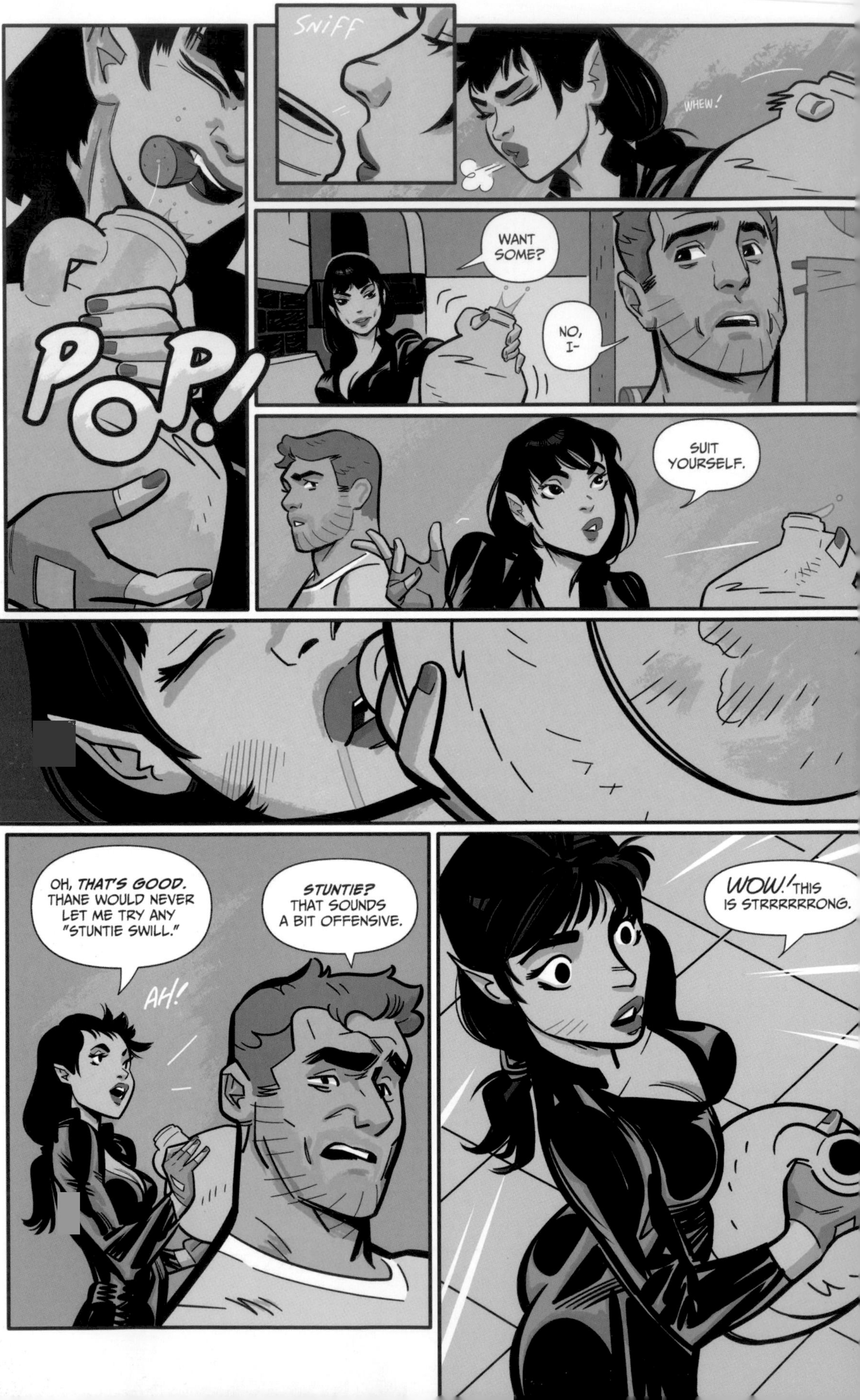
POP!
SNIFF
WHEW!
WANT SOME?
NO, I-
SUIT YOURSELF.
OH, THAT'S GOOD. THANE WOULD NEVER LET ME TRY ANY "STUNTIE SWILL."
AH!
STUNTIE? THAT SOUNDS A BIT OFFENSIVE.
WOW! THIS IS STRRRRRRONG.

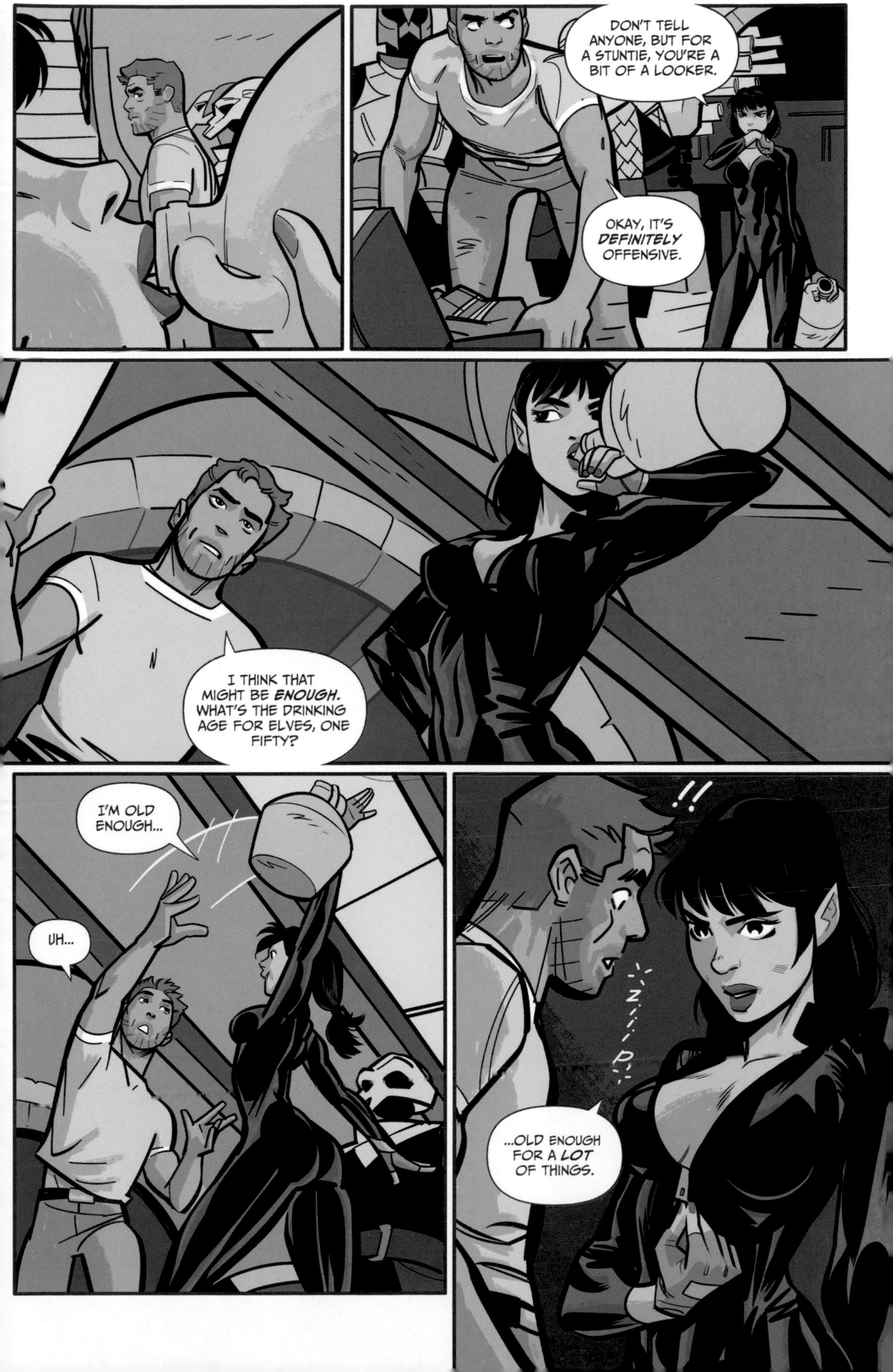
DON'T TELL ANYONE, BUT FOR A STUNTIE, YOU'RE A BIT OF A LOOKER.
OKAY, IT'S DEFINITELY OFFENSIVE.
I THINK THAT MIGHT BE ENOUGH. WHAT'S THE DRINKING AGE FOR ELVES, ONE FIFTY?
I'M OLD ENOUGH...
UH...
!!
ZIP
...OLD ENOUGH FOR A LOT OF THINGS.

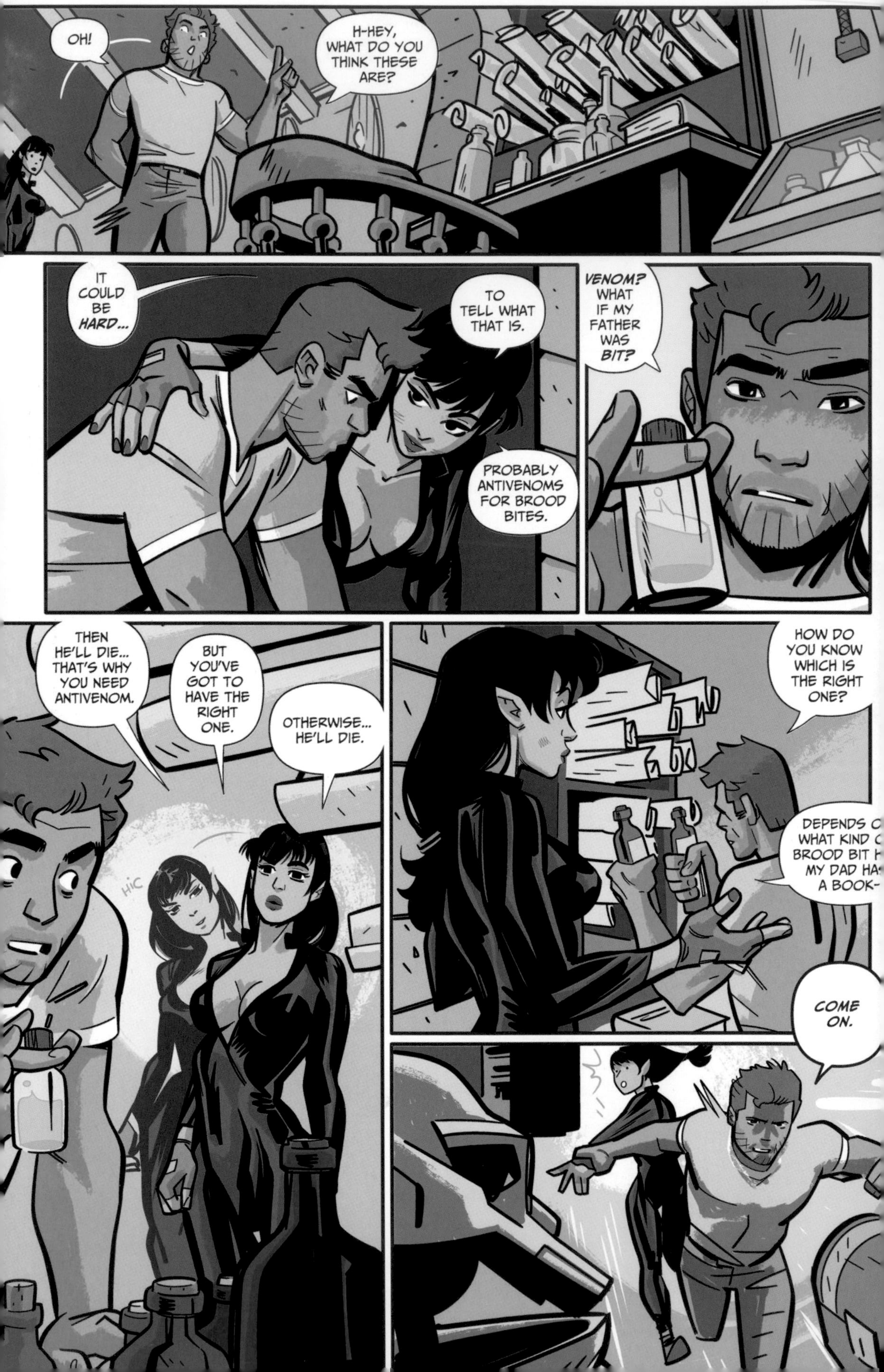
OH!
H-HEY, WHAT DO YOU THINK THESE ARE?
IT COULD BE HARD...
TO TELL WHAT THAT IS.
PROBABLY ANTIVENOMS FOR BROOD BITES.
VENOM? WHAT IF MY FATHER WAS BIT?
THEN HE'LL DIE... THAT'S WHY YOU NEED ANTIVENOM.
BUT YOU'VE GOT TO HAVE THE RIGHT ONE.
OTHERWISE... HE'LL DIE.
HIC
HOW DO YOU KNOW WHICH IS THE RIGHT ONE?
DEPENDS O
WHAT KIND O
BROOD BIT H
MY DAD HA
A BOOK-
COME ON.

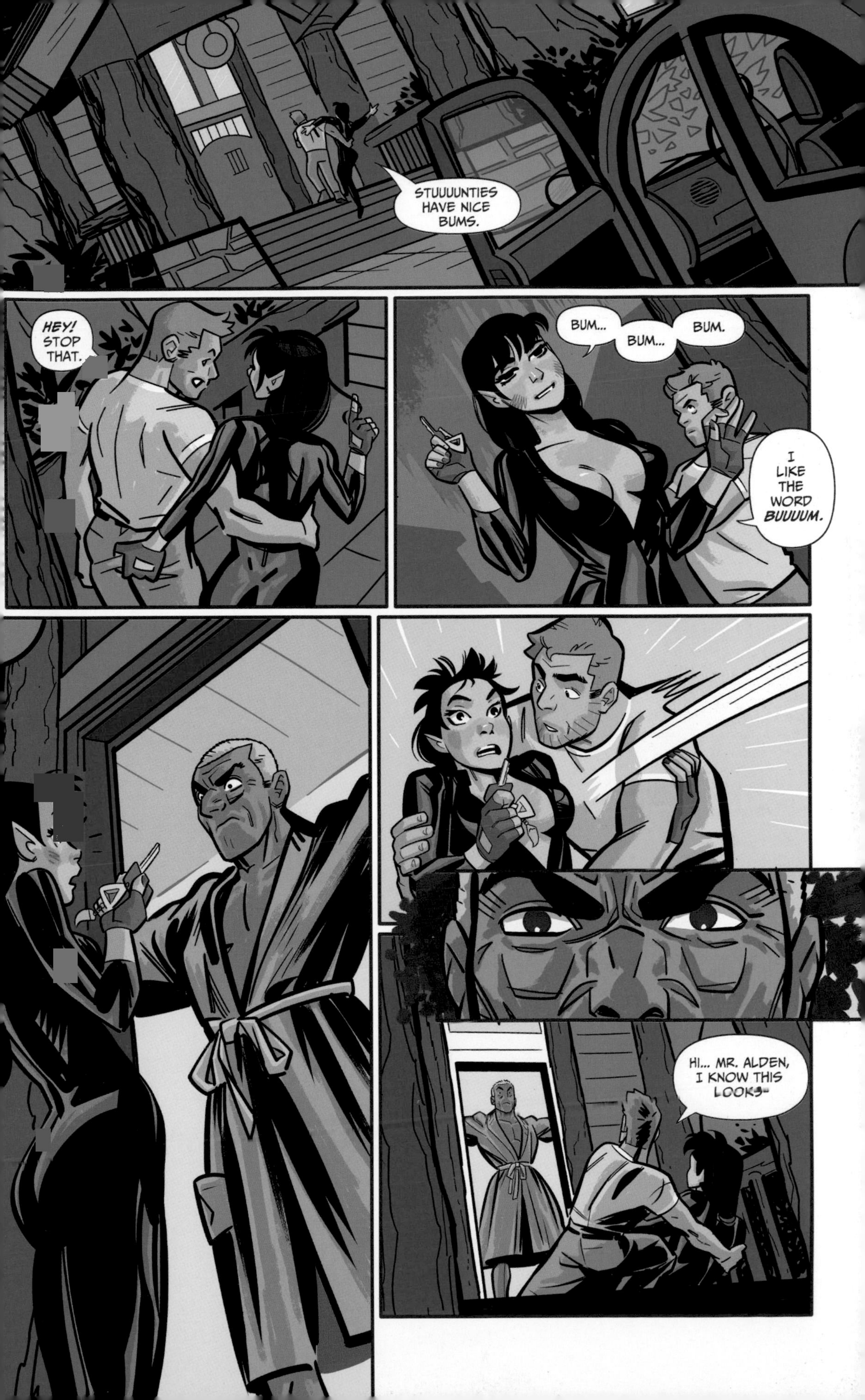
STUUUUNTIES HAVE NICE BUMS.
HEY! STOP THAT.
BUM...
BUM...
BUM.
I LIKE THE WORD BUUUUM.
HI... MR. ALDEN, I KNOW THIS LOOKS—

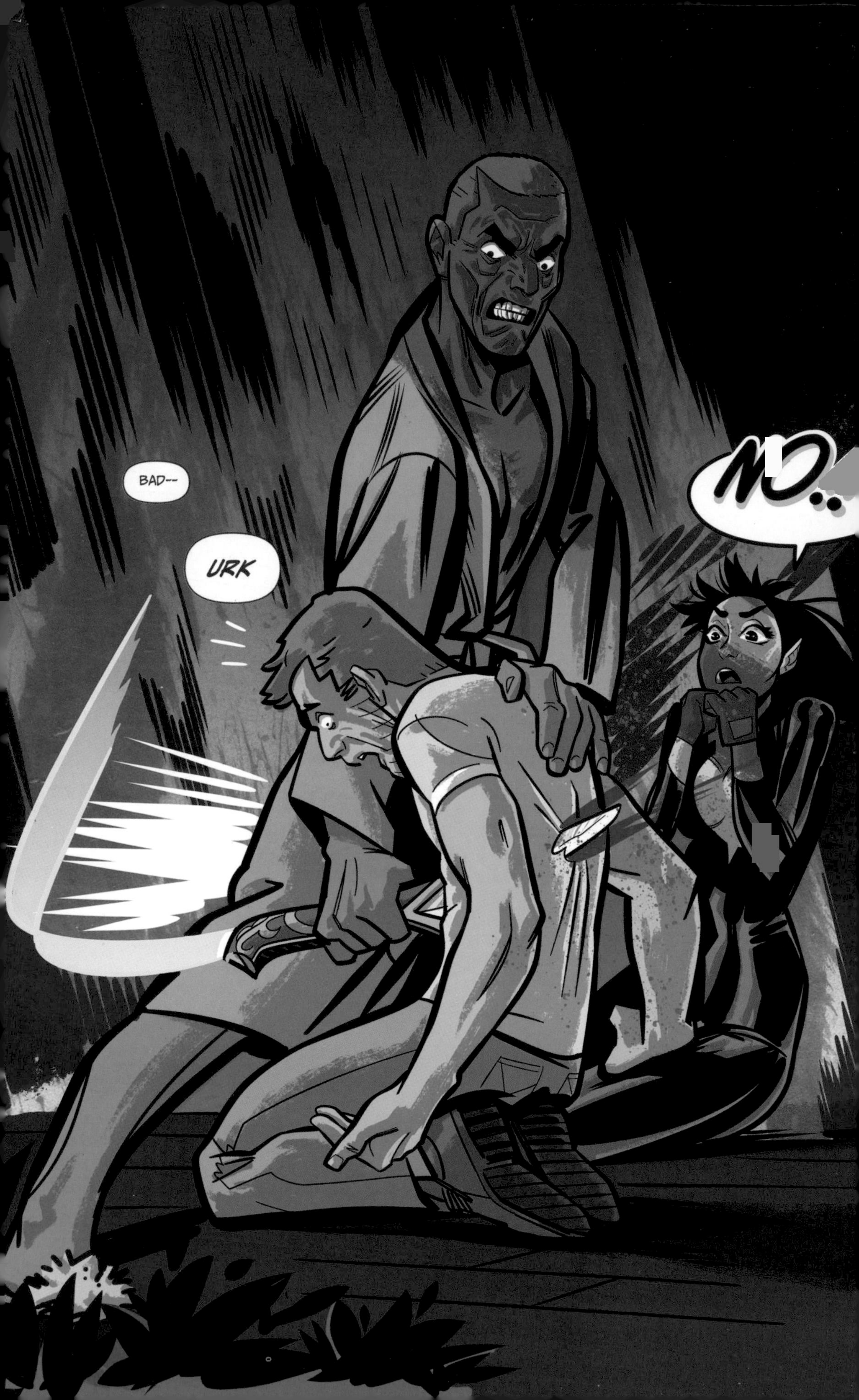
BAD--
URK
NO...

CHAPTER FOUR

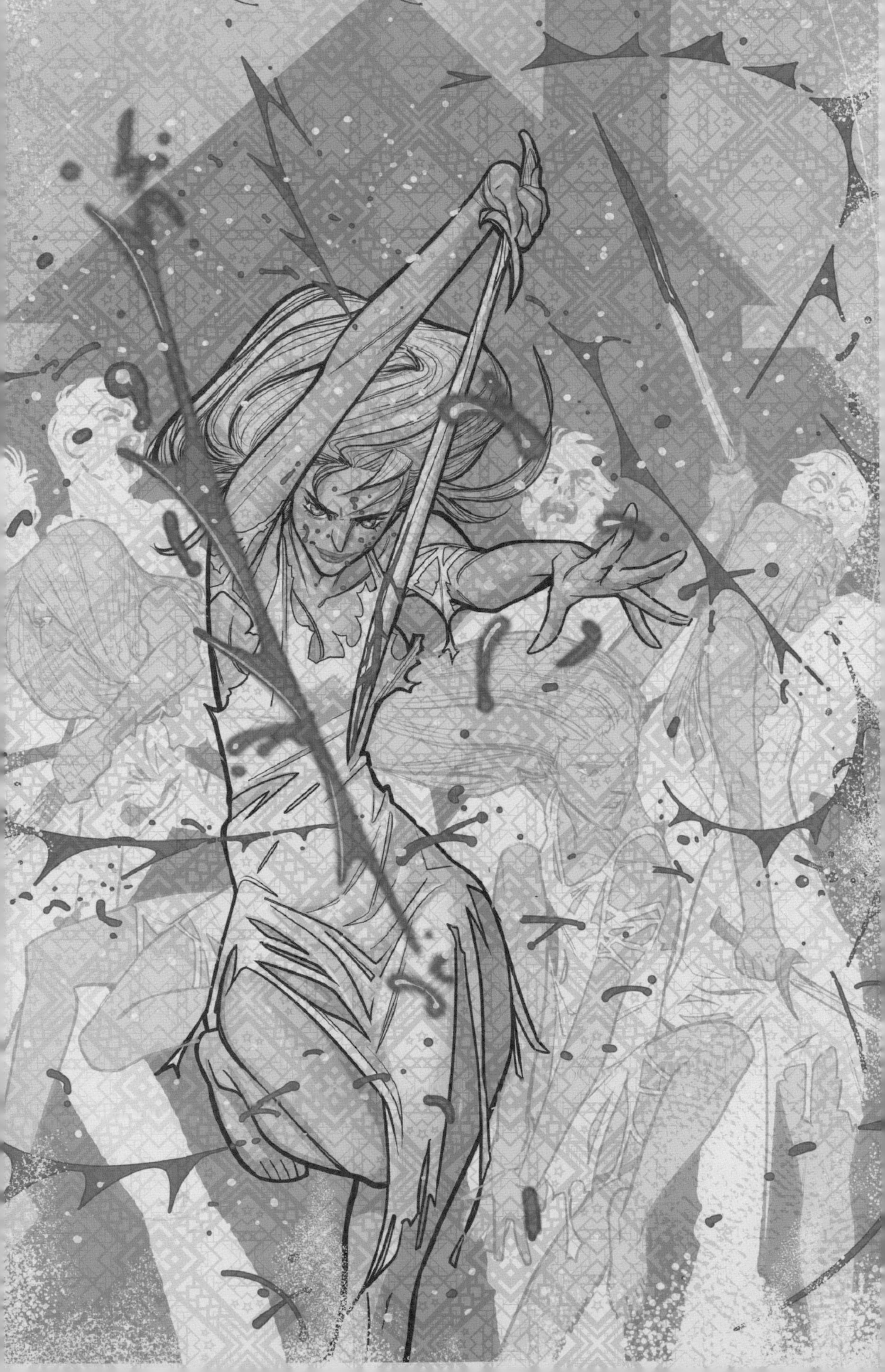

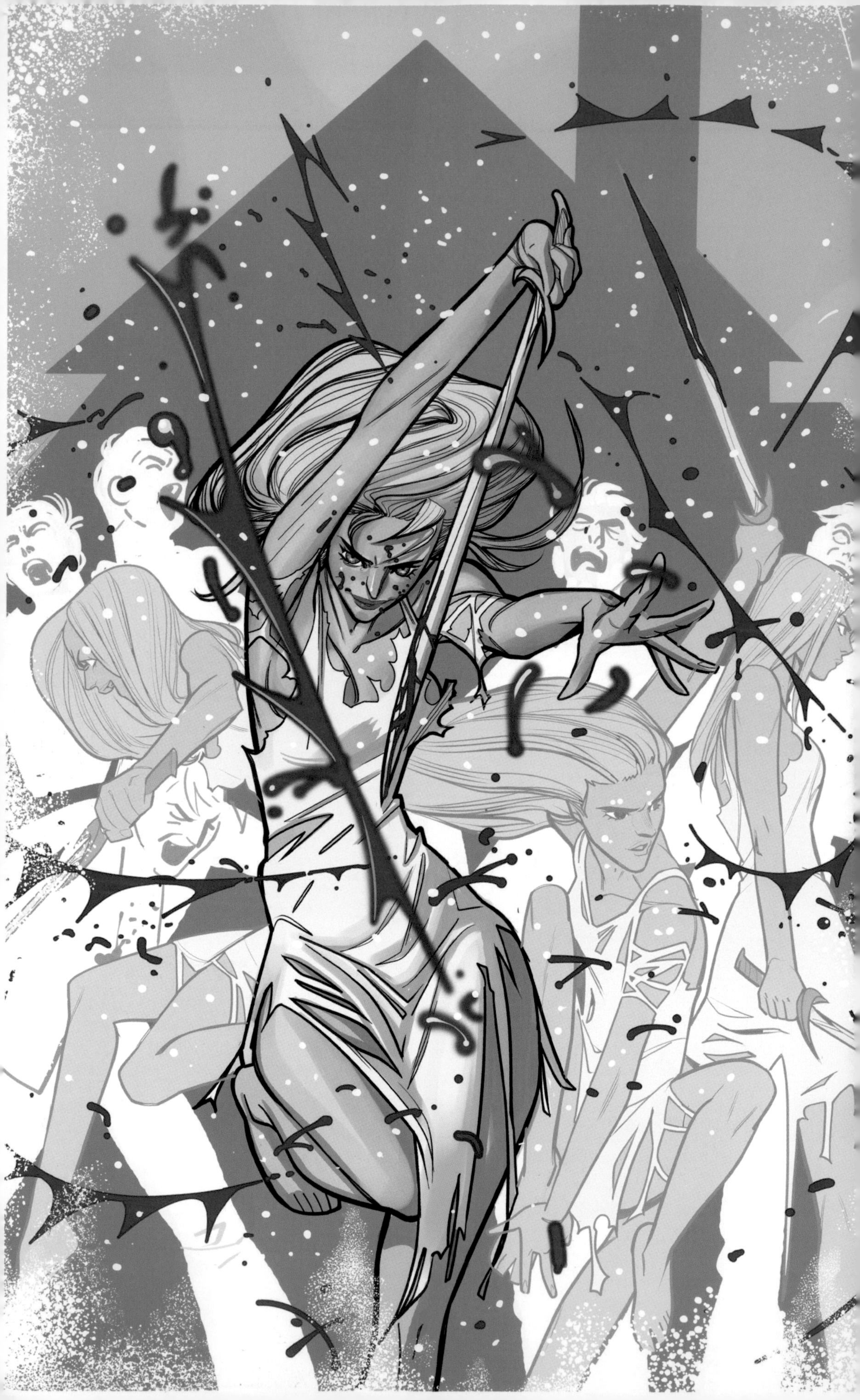

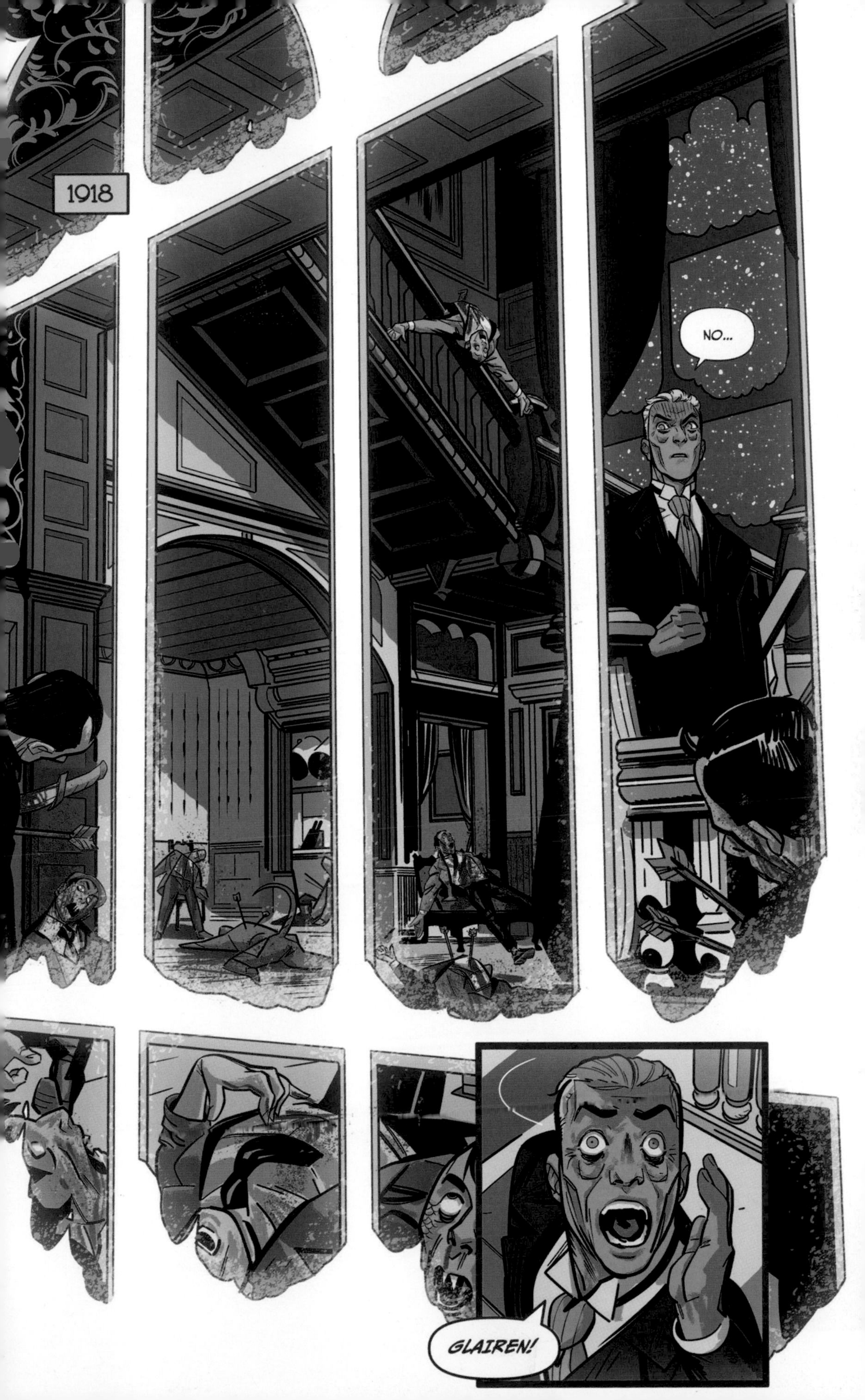
1918
NO...
GLAIREN!

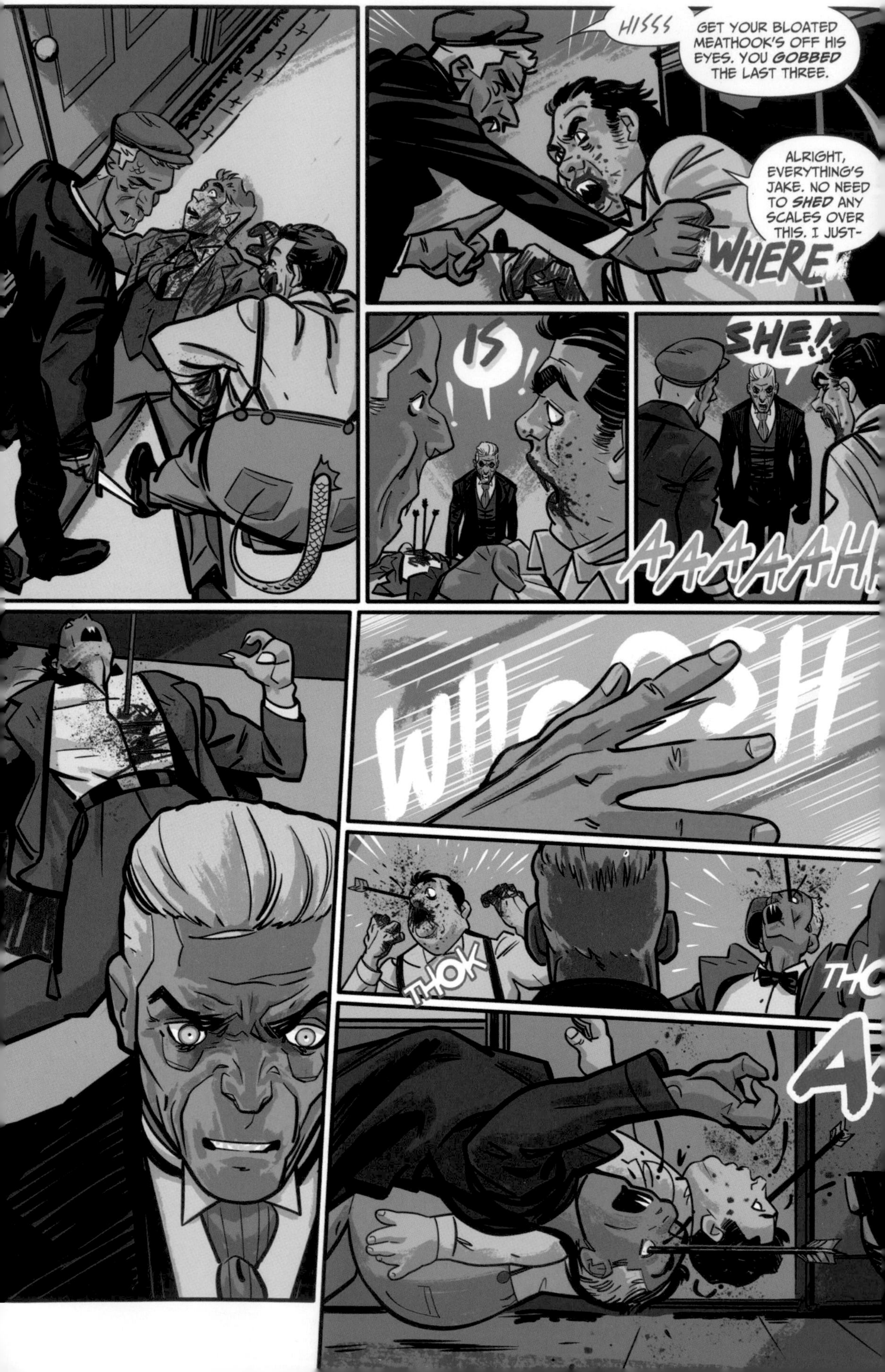
HISSS
GET YOUR BLOATED MEATHOOK'S OFF HIS EYES. YOU GOBBED THE LAST THREE.
ALRIGHT, EVERYTHING'S JAKE. NO NEED TO SHED ANY SCALES OVER THIS. I JUST-
WHERE
IS
SHE!?
AAAAAAH
WHOOSH
THOK
THO
A

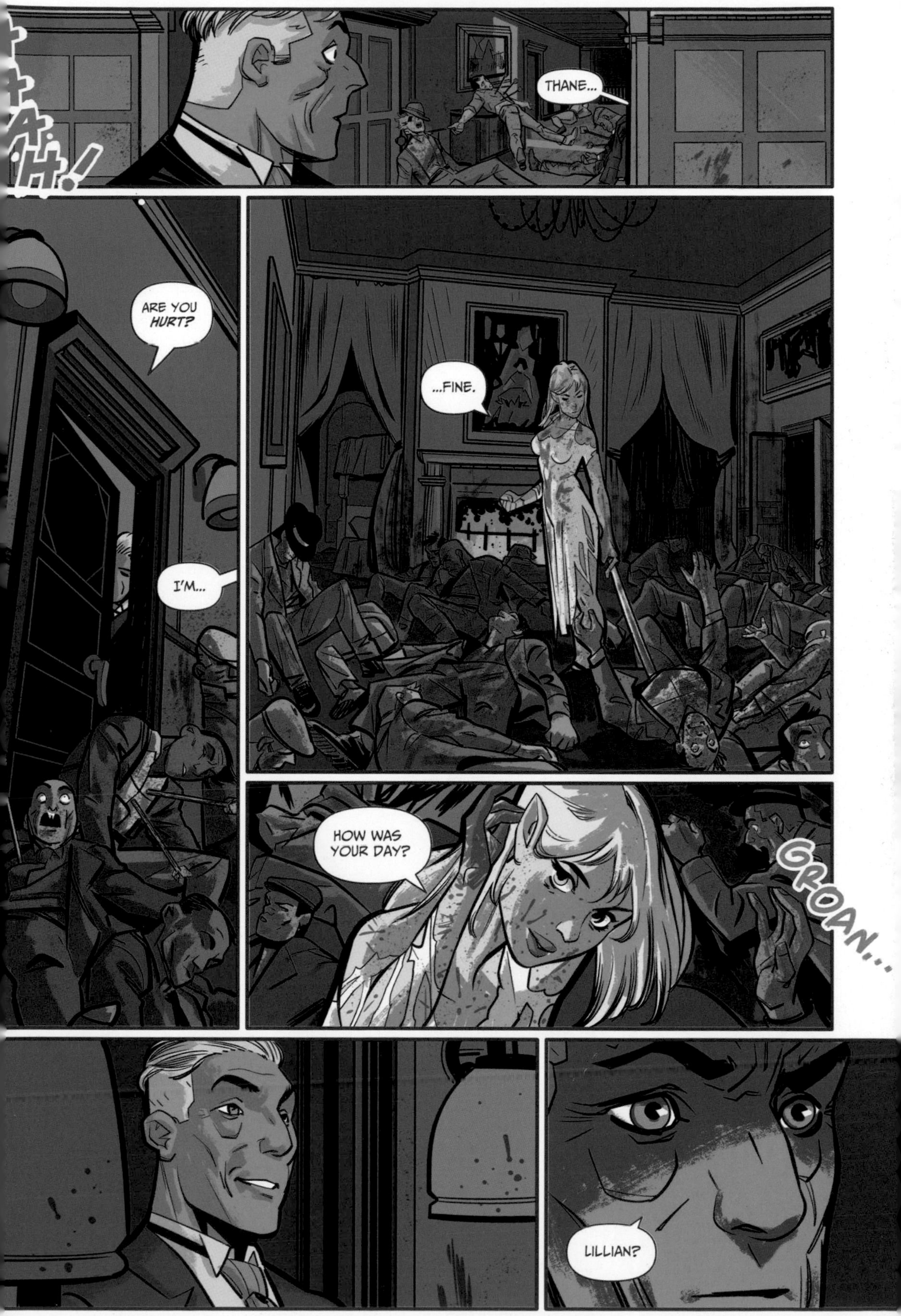
THANE...
ARE YOU HURT?
I'M...
...FINE.
HOW WAS YOUR DAY?
GROAN...
LILLIAN?

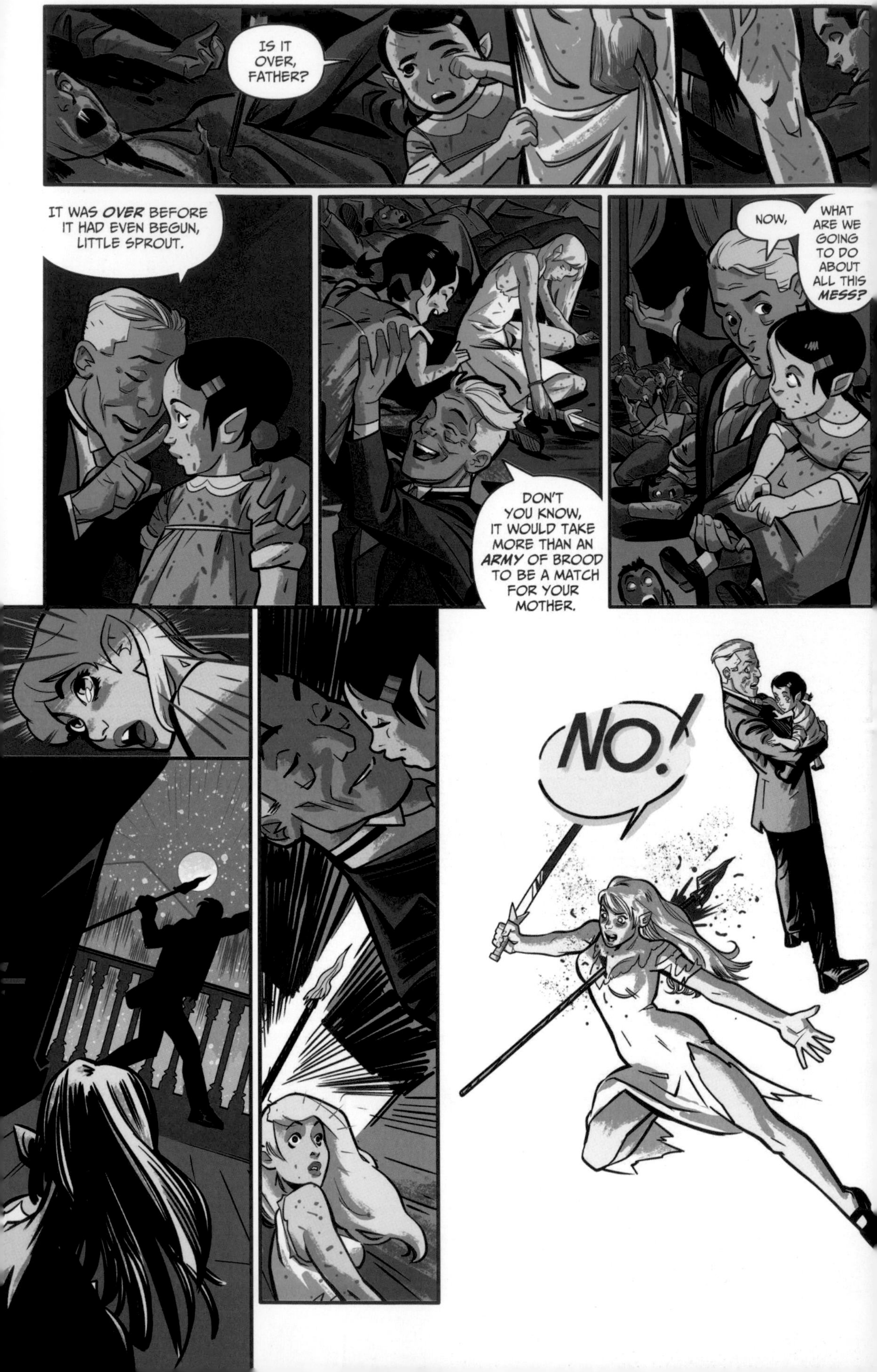
IS IT OVER, FATHER?
IT WAS *OVER* BEFORE IT HAD EVEN BEGUN, LITTLE SPROUT.
DON'T YOU KNOW, IT WOULD TAKE MORE THAN AN *ARMY* OF BROOD TO BE A MATCH FOR YOUR MOTHER.
NOW,
WHAT ARE WE GOING TO DO ABOUT ALL THIS *MESS?*
NO!

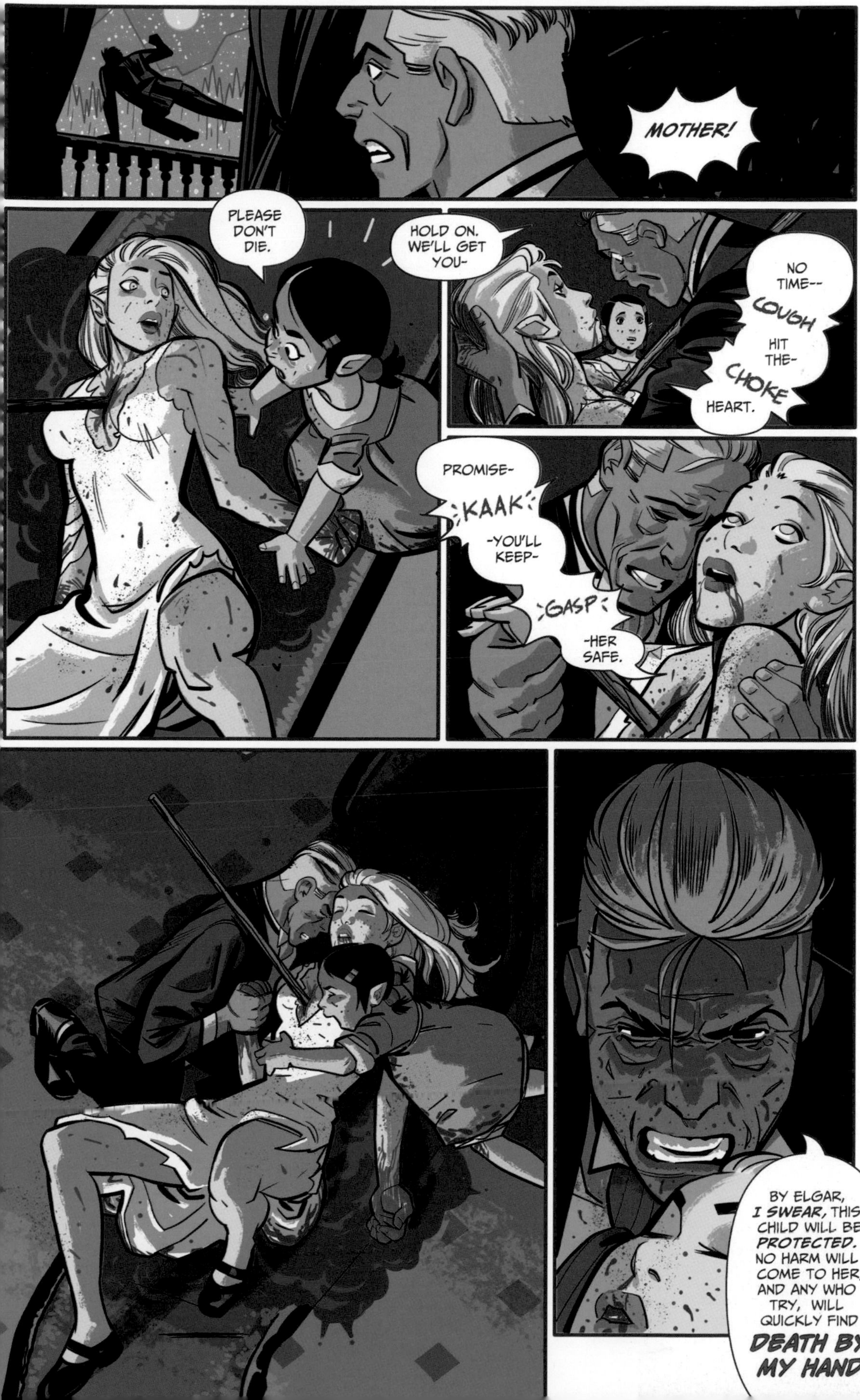

MOTHER!
PLEASE DON'T DIE.
HOLD ON. WE'LL GET YOU-
NO TIME--
COUGH
HIT THE-
CHOKE
HEART.
PROMISE-
KAAK
-YOU'LL KEEP-
GASP
-HER SAFE.
BY ELGAR, I SWEAR, THIS CHILD WILL BE PROTECTED. NO HARM WILL COME TO HER, AND ANY WHO TRY, WILL QUICKLY FIND DEATH BY MY HAND.

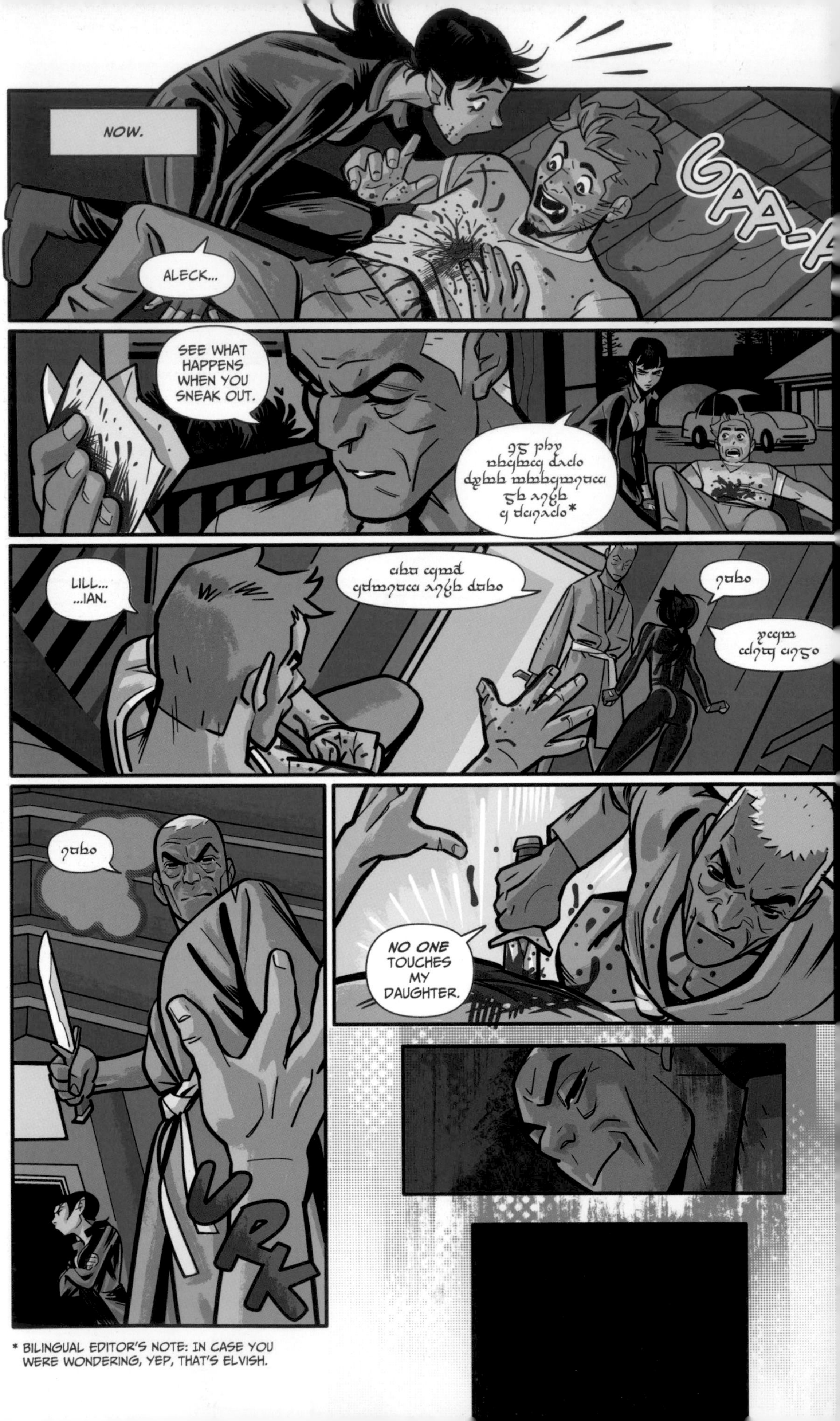
NOW.
GAA-A
ALECK...
SEE WHAT HAPPENS WHEN YOU SNEAK OUT.
LILL... ...IAN.
NO ONE TOUCHES MY DAUGHTER.
VRK

* BILINGUAL EDITOR'S NOTE: IN CASE YOU WERE WONDERING, YEP, THAT'S ELVISH.

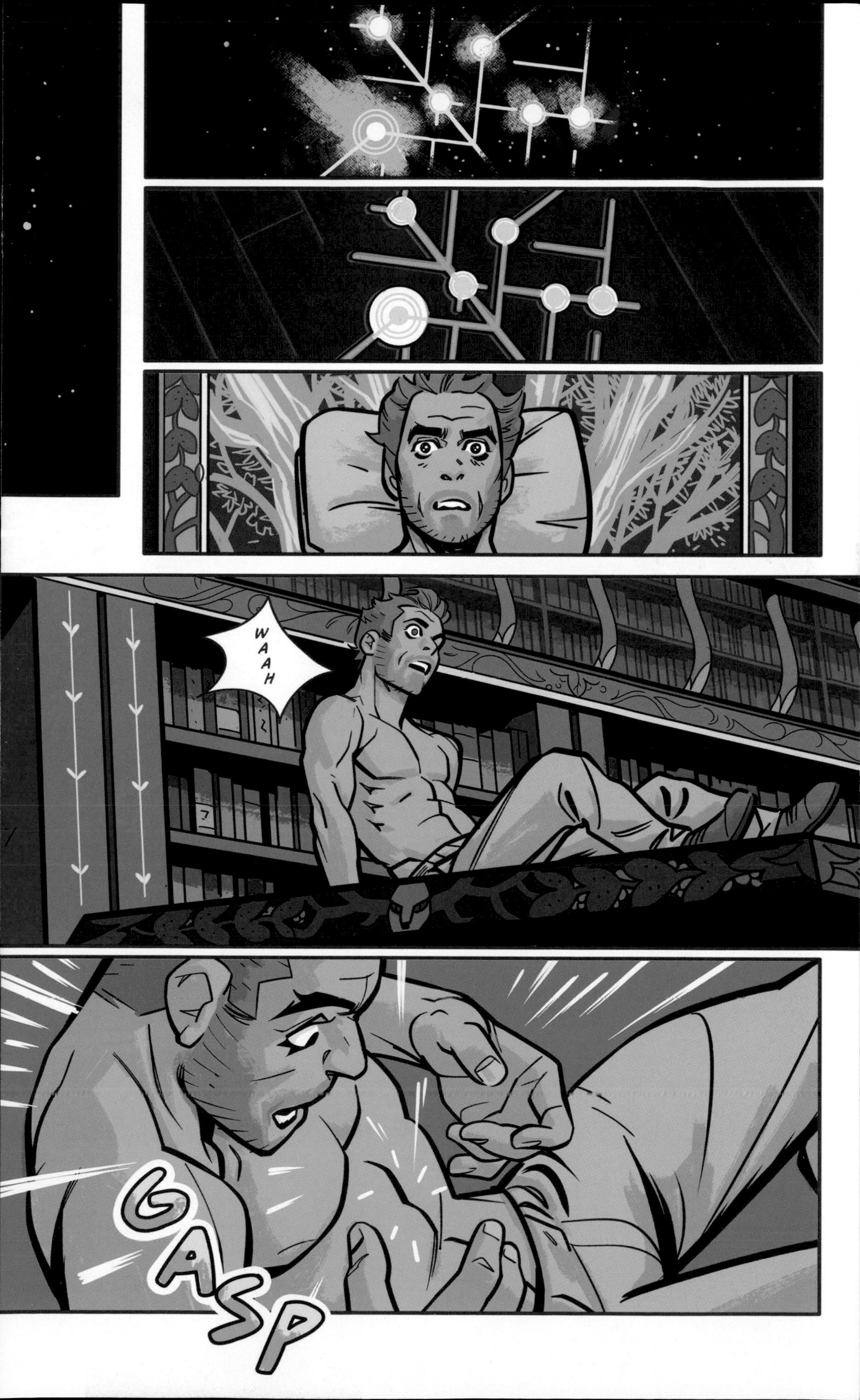
WAAAH
GASP

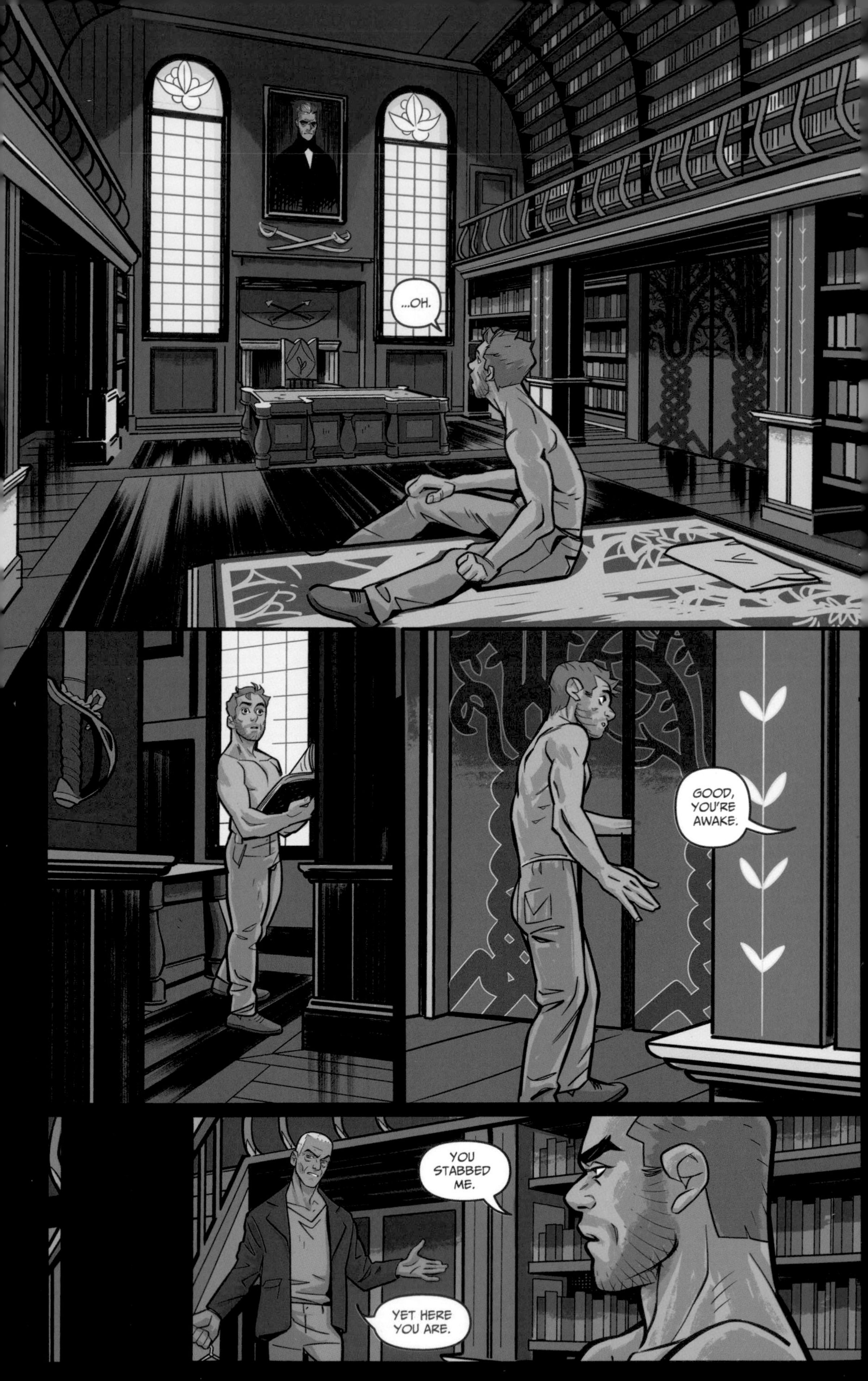
...OH.
GOOD, YOU'RE AWAKE.
YOU STABBED ME.
YET HERE YOU ARE.

THERE'S NO WOUND... NO SCAR... IT'S LIKE...

...MAGIC

HOW *PERCEPTIVE.* NO WONDER THEY SNATCHED YOU UP AT CARNEGIE MELLON.

...

IT'S THE ELVEN VERSION OF A *BOKKEN* -- AN ENCHANTED PRACTICE WEAPON. IF A MISHAP OCCURS--

LIKE IF SOMEONE *STABBED* YOU?

-- YOU HAVE TWO MINUTES TO *RECTIFY* BEFORE IT BECOMES PERMANENT.

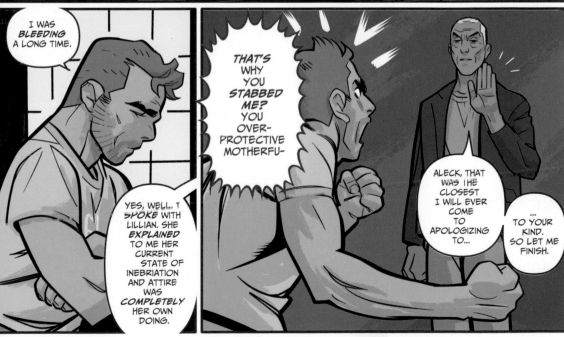

I WAS *BLEEDING* A LONG TIME.

THAT'S WHY YOU *STABBED ME?* YOU OVER-PROTECTIVE MOTHERFU-

YES, WELL, I *SPOKE* WITH LILLIAN. SHE *EXPLAINED* TO ME HER CURRENT STATE OF INEBRIATION AND ATTIRE WAS *COMPLETELY* HER OWN DOING.

ALECK, THAT WAS THE CLOSEST I WILL EVER COME TO APOLOGIZING TO...

...TO YOUR KIND. SO LET ME FINISH.

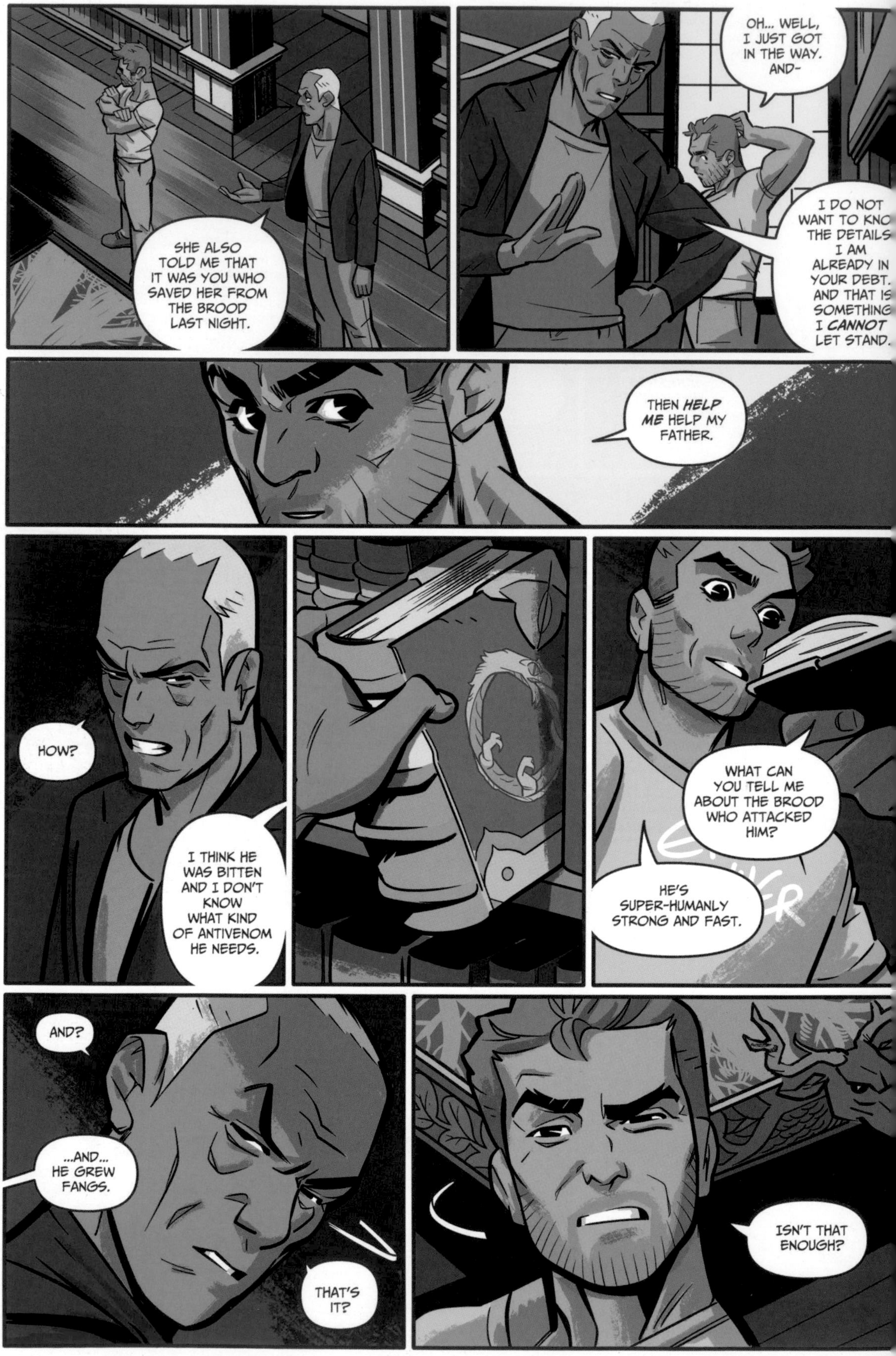
SHE ALSO TOLD ME THAT IT WAS YOU WHO SAVED HER FROM THE BROOD LAST NIGHT.
OH... WELL, I JUST GOT IN THE WAY. AND-
I DO NOT WANT TO KNO THE DETAILS I AM ALREADY IN YOUR DEBT. AND THAT IS SOMETHING I CANNOT LET STAND.
THEN HELP ME HELP MY FATHER.
HOW?
I THINK HE WAS BITTEN AND I DON'T KNOW WHAT KIND OF ANTIVENOM HE NEEDS.
WHAT CAN YOU TELL ME ABOUT THE BROOD WHO ATTACKED HIM?
HE'S SUPER-HUMANLY STRONG AND FAST.
AND?
...AND... HE GREW FANGS.
THAT'S IT?
ISN'T THAT ENOUGH?

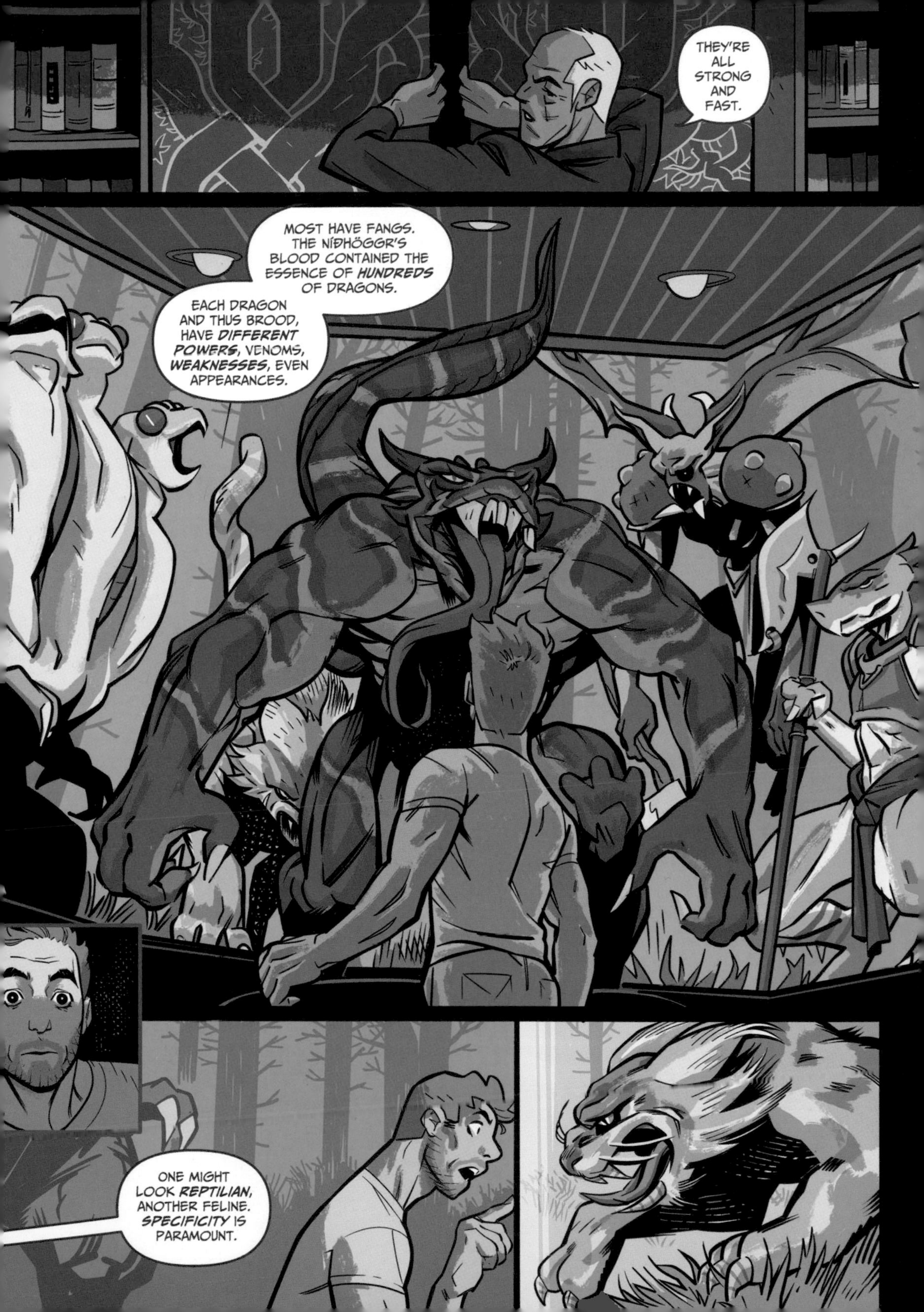
THEY'RE ALL STRONG AND FAST.
MOST HAVE FANGS. THE NÍÐHÖGGR'S BLOOD CONTAINED THE ESSENCE OF HUNDREDS OF DRAGONS.
EACH DRAGON AND THUS BROOD, HAVE DIFFERENT POWERS, VENOMS, WEAKNESSES, EVEN APPEARANCES.
ONE MIGHT LOOK REPTILIAN, ANOTHER FELINE. SPECIFICITY IS PARAMOUNT.

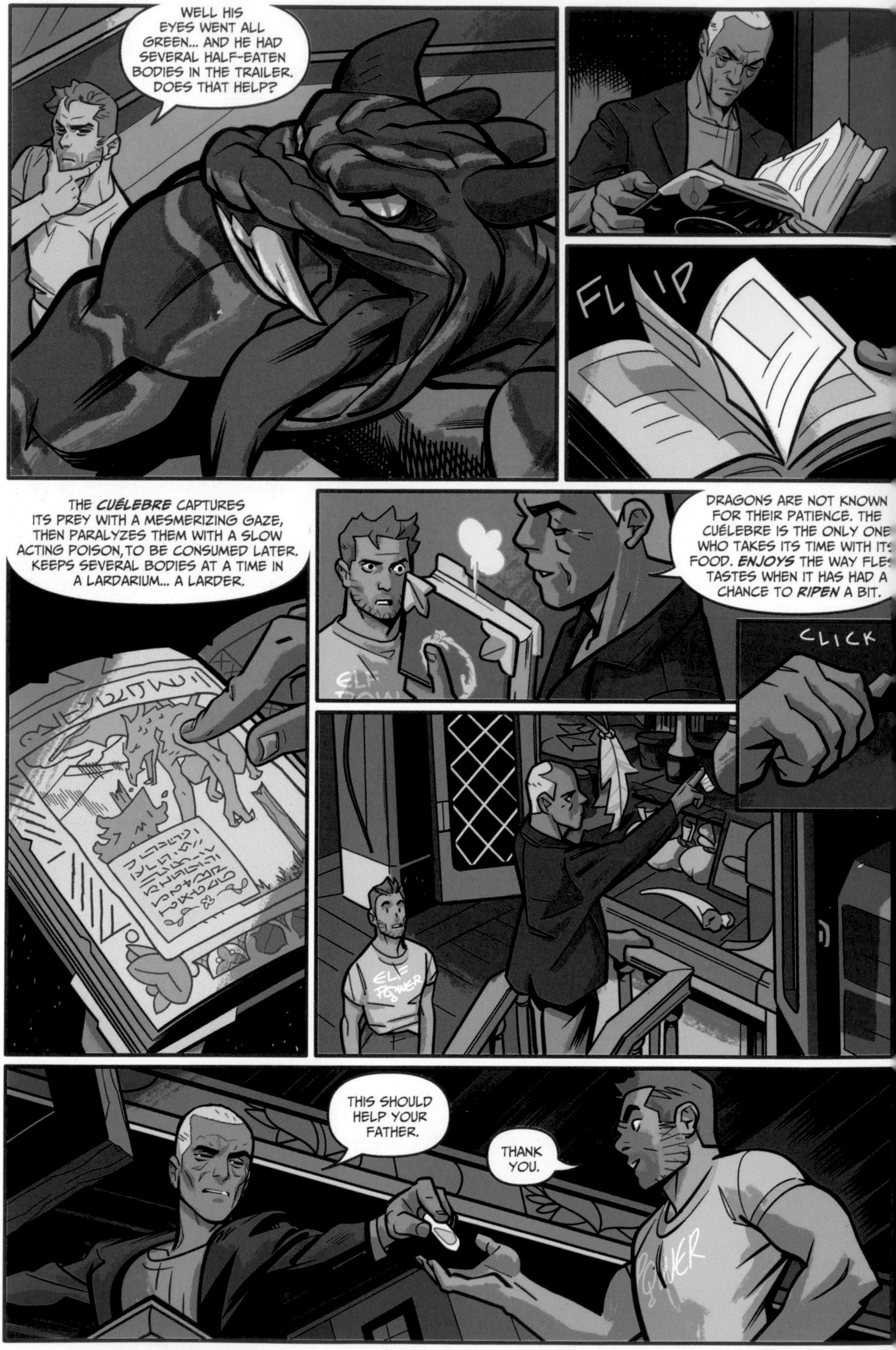
WELL HIS EYES WENT ALL GREEN... AND HE HAD SEVERAL HALF-EATEN BODIES IN THE TRAILER. DOES THAT HELP?
FLIP
THE *CUÉLEBRE* CAPTURES ITS PREY WITH A MESMERIZING GAZE, THEN PARALYZES THEM WITH A SLOW ACTING POISON, TO BE CONSUMED LATER. KEEPS SEVERAL BODIES AT A TIME IN A LARDARIUM... A LARDER.
DRAGONS ARE NOT KNOWN FOR THEIR PATIENCE. THE CUÉLEBRE IS THE ONLY ONE WHO TAKES ITS TIME WITH ITS FOOD. *ENJOYS* THE WAY FLES TASTES WHEN IT HAS HAD A CHANCE TO *RIPEN* A BIT.
CLICK
THIS SHOULD HELP YOUR FATHER.
THANK YOU.

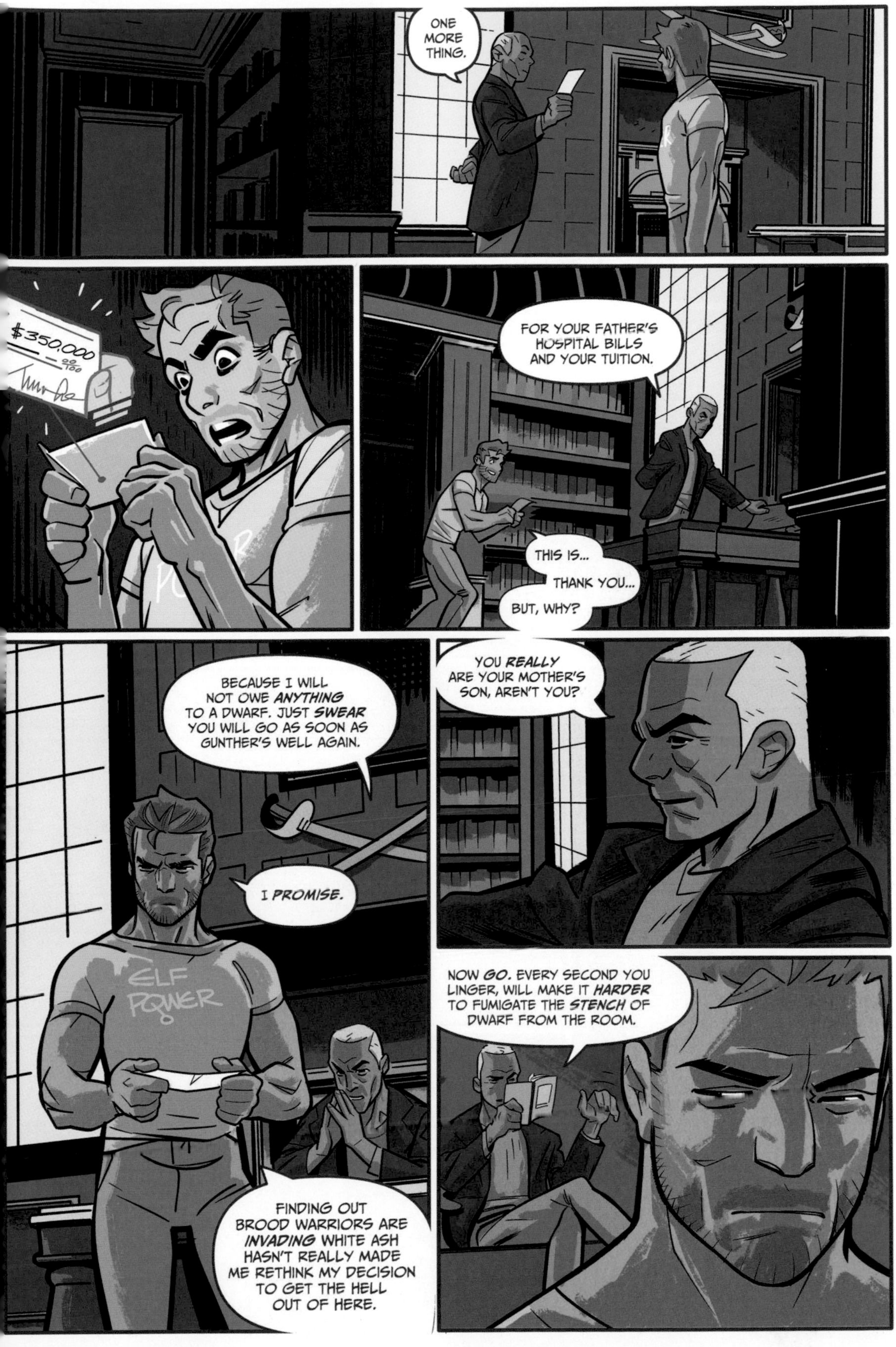
ONE MORE THING.
$350,000
FOR YOUR FATHER'S HOSPITAL BILLS AND YOUR TUITION.
THIS IS...
THANK YOU...
BUT, WHY?
BECAUSE I WILL NOT OWE ANYTHING TO A DWARF. JUST SWEAR YOU WILL GO AS SOON AS GUNTHER'S WELL AGAIN.
I PROMISE.
ELF POWER
FINDING OUT BROOD WARRIORS ARE INVADING WHITE ASH HASN'T REALLY MADE ME RETHINK MY DECISION TO GET THE HELL OUT OF HERE.
YOU REALLY ARE YOUR MOTHER'S SON, AREN'T YOU?
NOW GO. EVERY SECOND YOU LINGER, WILL MAKE IT HARDER TO FUMIGATE THE STENCH OF DWARF FROM THE ROOM.

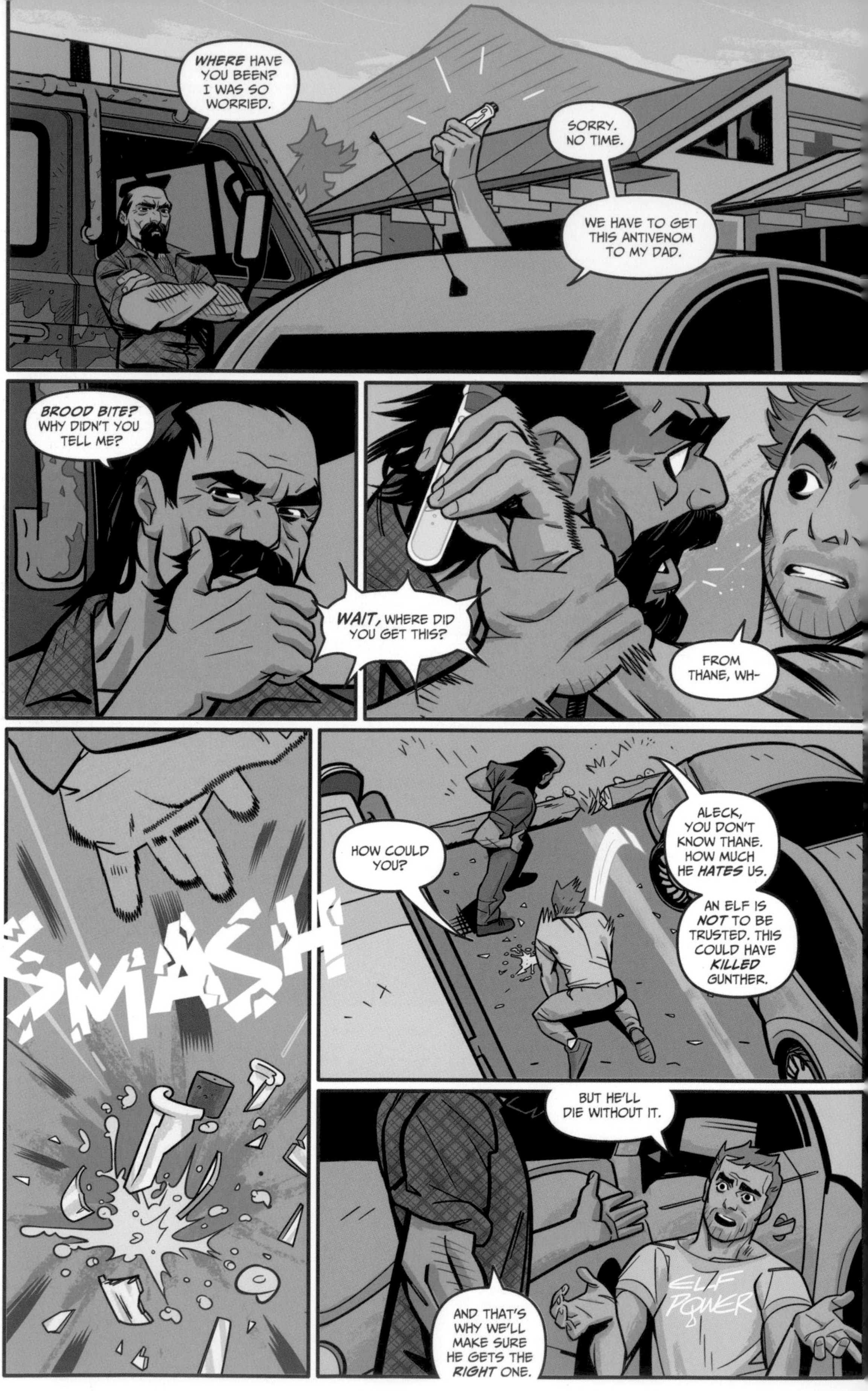
WHERE HAVE YOU BEEN? I WAS SO WORRIED.
SORRY. NO TIME.
WE HAVE TO GET THIS ANTIVENOM TO MY DAD.
BROOD BITE? WHY DIDN'T YOU TELL ME?
WAIT, WHERE DID YOU GET THIS?
FROM THANE, WH-
SMASH!
HOW COULD YOU?
ALECK, YOU DON'T KNOW THANE. HOW MUCH HE HATES US.
AN ELF IS NOT TO BE TRUSTED. THIS COULD HAVE KILLED GUNTHER.
BUT HE'LL DIE WITHOUT IT.
AND THAT'S WHY WE'LL MAKE SURE HE GETS THE RIGHT ONE.
ELF POWER

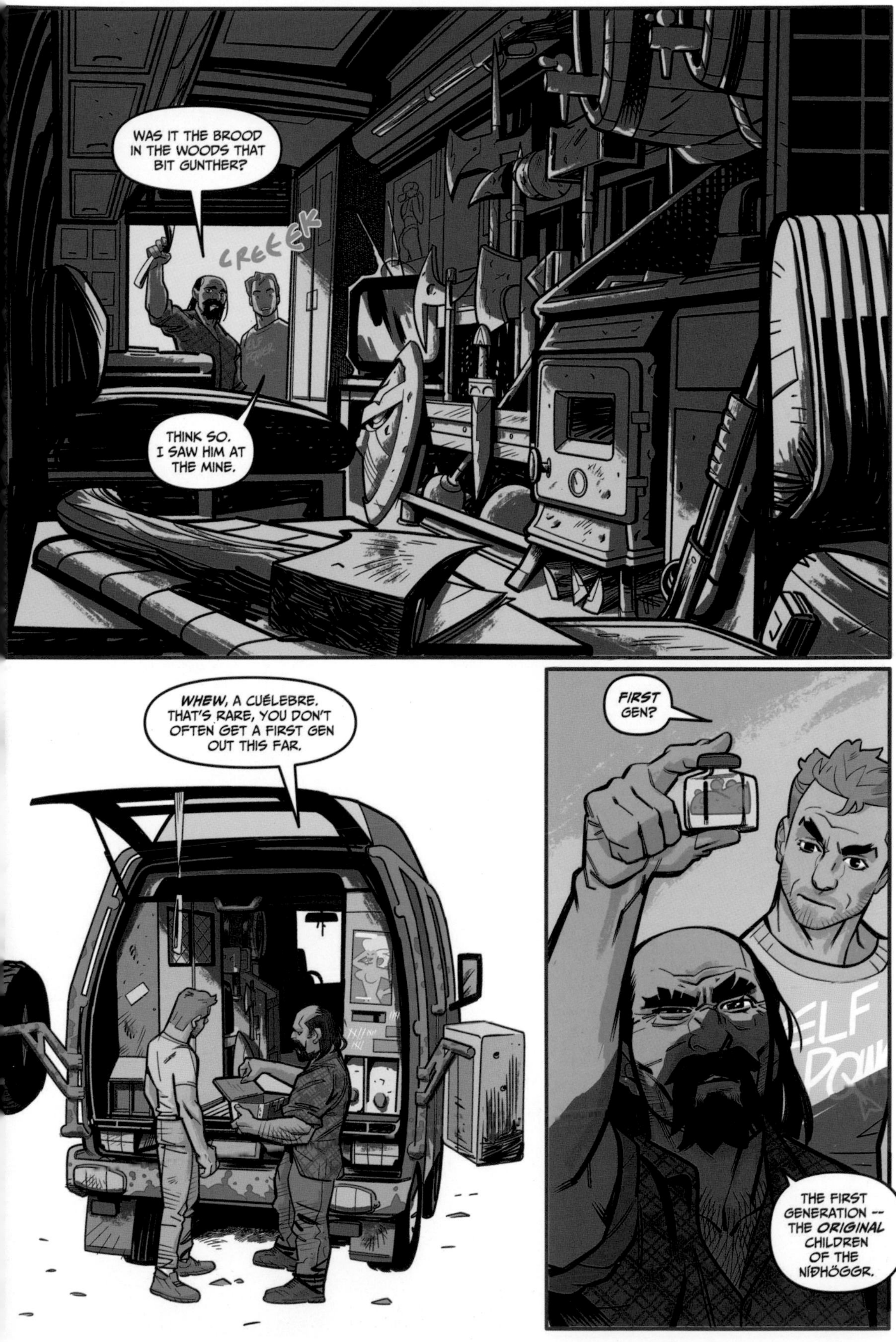
WAS IT THE BROOD IN THE WOODS THAT BIT GUNTHER?
CREEEK
THINK SO. I SAW HIM AT THE MINE.
WHEW, A CUÉLEBRE. THAT'S RARE, YOU DON'T OFTEN GET A FIRST GEN OUT THIS FAR.
FIRST GEN?
THE FIRST GENERATION -- THE ORIGINAL CHILDREN OF THE NÍÐHÖGGR.

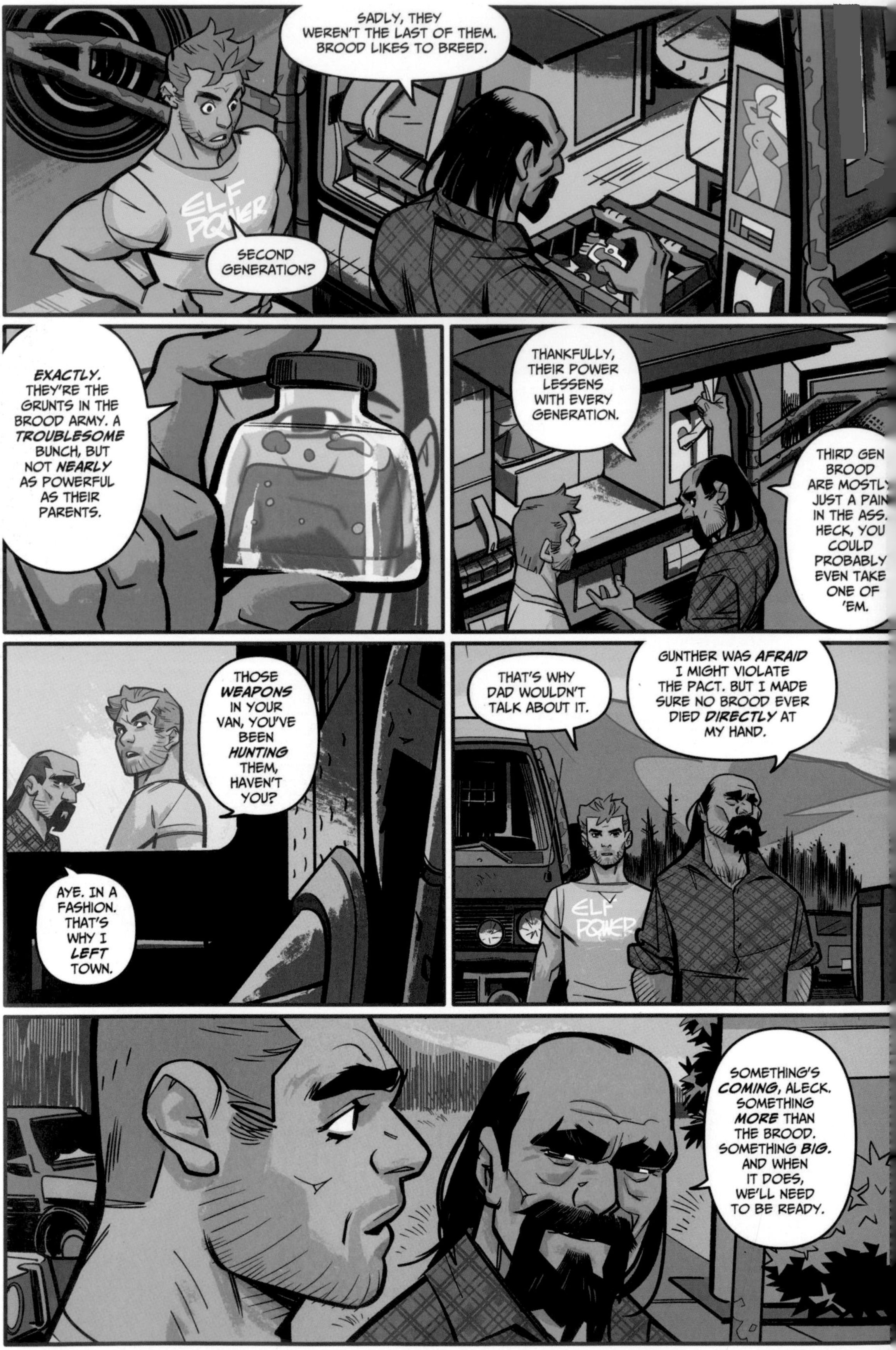
SADLY, THEY WEREN'T THE LAST OF THEM. BROOD LIKES TO BREED.
SECOND GENERATION?
EXACTLY. THEY'RE THE GRUNTS IN THE BROOD ARMY. A TROUBLESOME BUNCH, BUT NOT NEARLY AS POWERFUL AS THEIR PARENTS.
THANKFULLY, THEIR POWER LESSENS WITH EVERY GENERATION.
THIRD GEN BROOD ARE MOSTLY JUST A PAIN IN THE ASS. HECK, YOU COULD PROBABLY EVEN TAKE ONE OF 'EM.
THOSE WEAPONS IN YOUR VAN, YOU'VE BEEN HUNTING THEM, HAVEN'T YOU?
AYE. IN A FASHION. THAT'S WHY I LEFT TOWN.
THAT'S WHY DAD WOULDN'T TALK ABOUT IT.
GUNTHER WAS AFRAID I MIGHT VIOLATE THE PACT. BUT I MADE SURE NO BROOD EVER DIED DIRECTLY AT MY HAND.
SOMETHING'S COMING, ALECK. SOMETHING MORE THAN THE BROOD. SOMETHING BIG. AND WHEN IT DOES, WE'LL NEED TO BE READY.

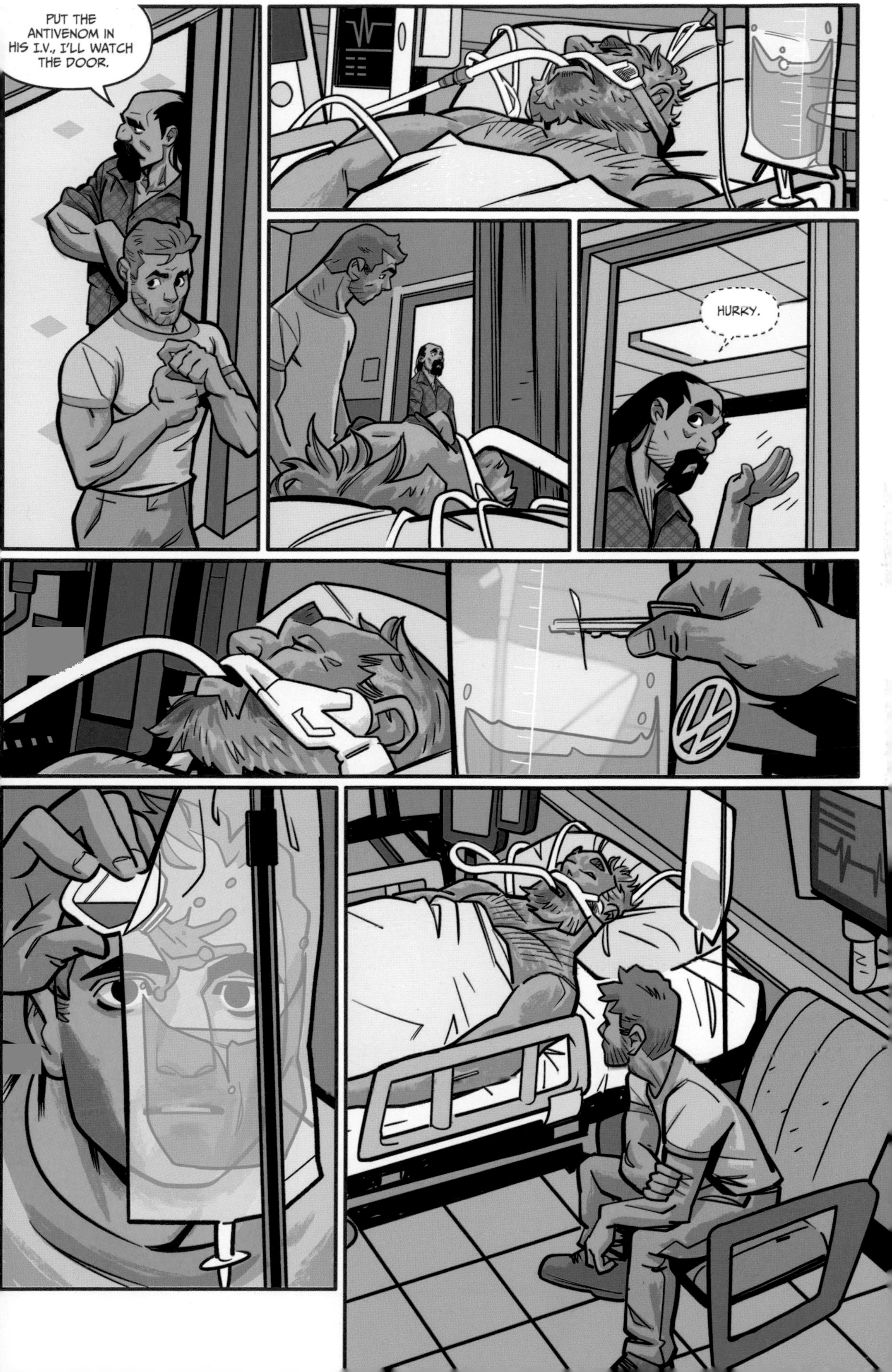
PUT THE ANTIVENOM IN HIS I.V., I'LL WATCH THE DOOR.
HURRY.

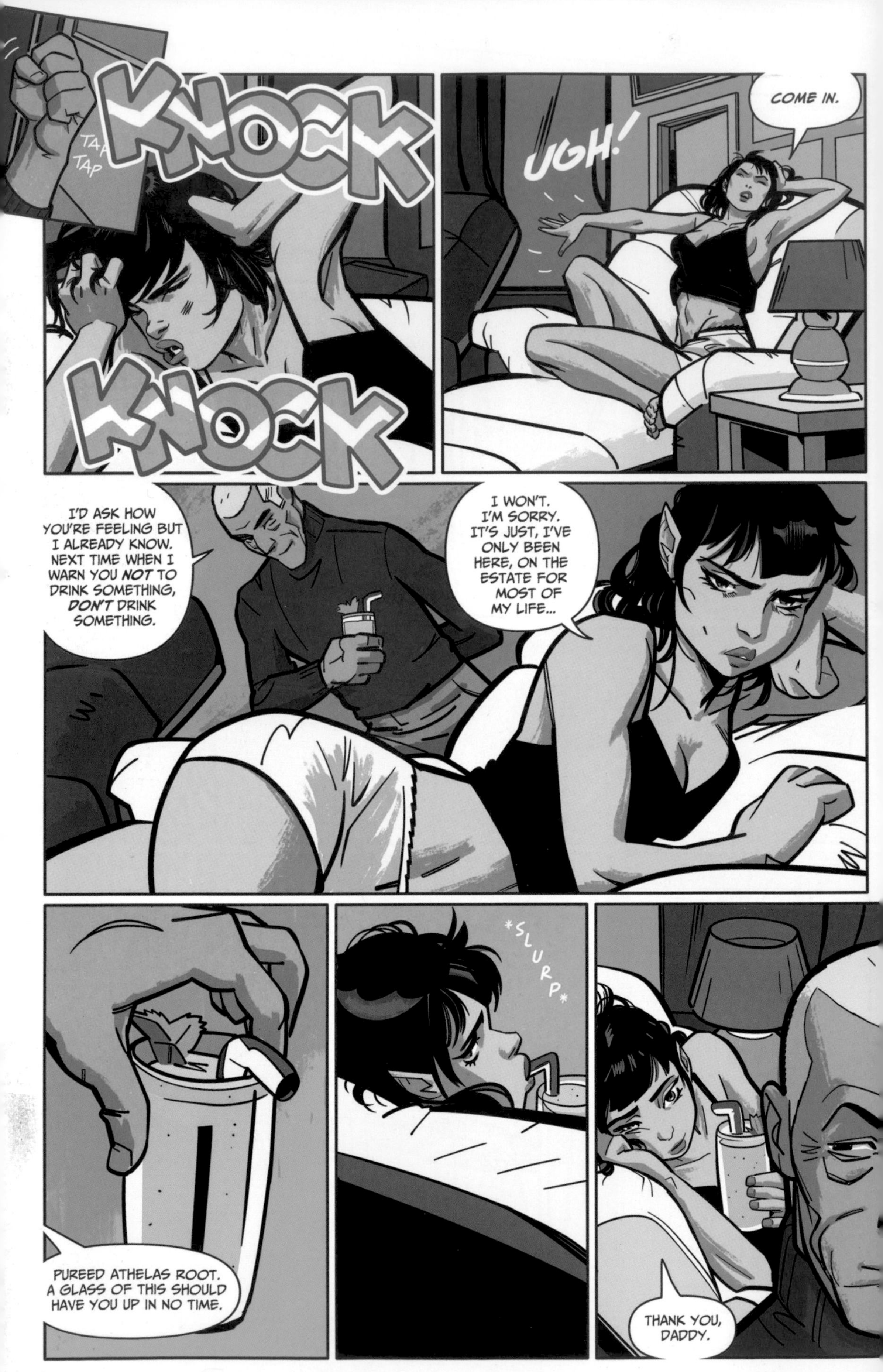
TAP TAP
KNOCK
KNOCK
UGH!
COME IN.
I'D ASK HOW YOU'RE FEELING BUT I ALREADY KNOW. NEXT TIME WHEN I WARN YOU NOT TO DRINK SOMETHING, DON'T DRINK SOMETHING.
I WON'T. I'M SORRY. IT'S JUST, I'VE ONLY BEEN HERE, ON THE ESTATE FOR MOST OF MY LIFE...
PUREED ATHELAS ROOT. A GLASS OF THIS SHOULD HAVE YOU UP IN NO TIME.
SLURP
THANK YOU, DADDY.

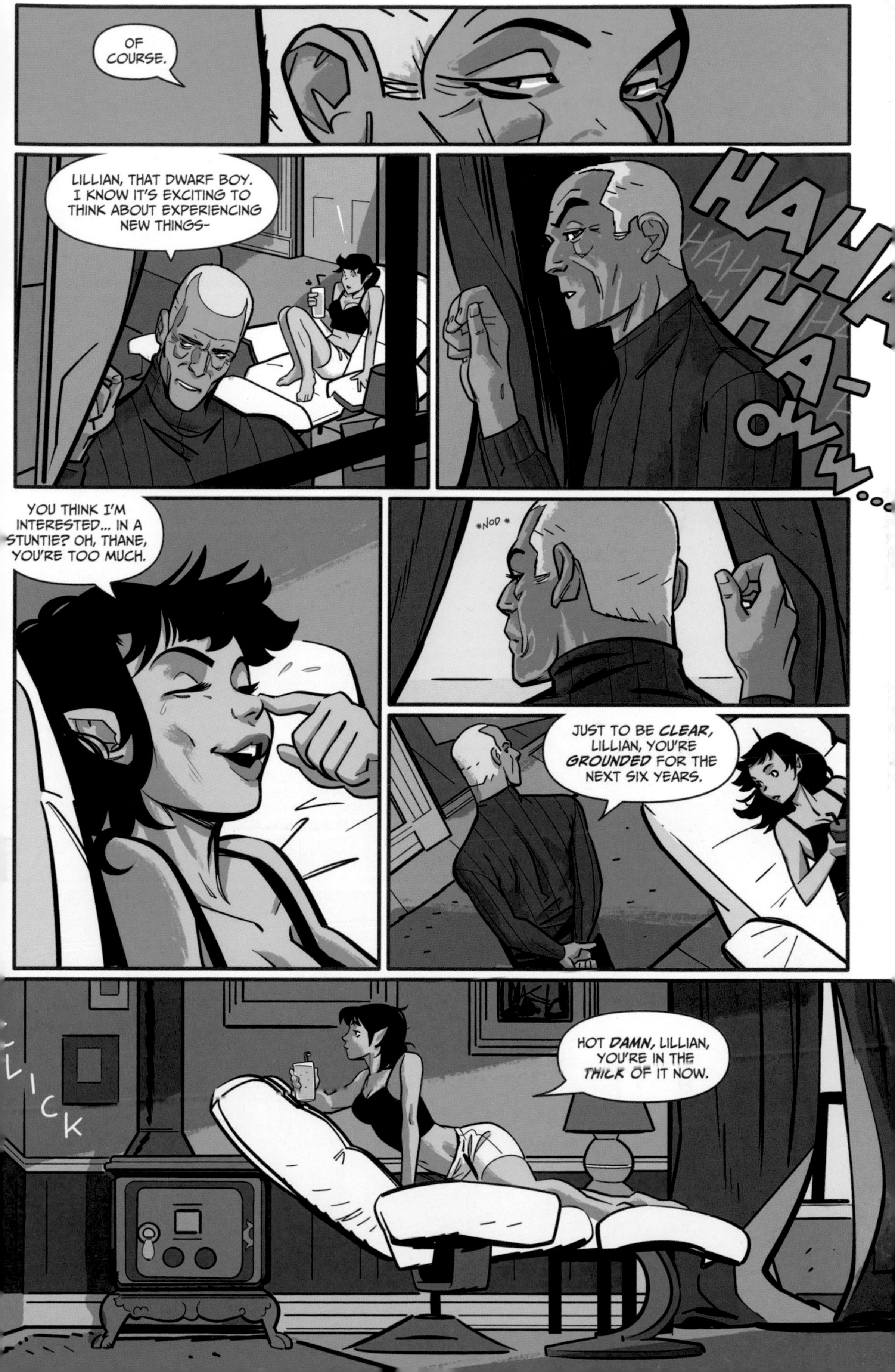
OF COURSE.
LILLIAN, THAT DWARF BOY. I KNOW IT'S EXCITING TO THINK ABOUT EXPERIENCING NEW THINGS-
HAHAHA HA-OWW...
YOU THINK I'M INTERESTED... IN A STUNTIE? OH, THANE, YOU'RE TOO MUCH.
NOD
JUST TO BE CLEAR, LILLIAN, YOU'RE GROUNDED FOR THE NEXT SIX YEARS.
CLICK
HOT DAMN, LILLIAN, YOU'RE IN THE THICK OF IT NOW.

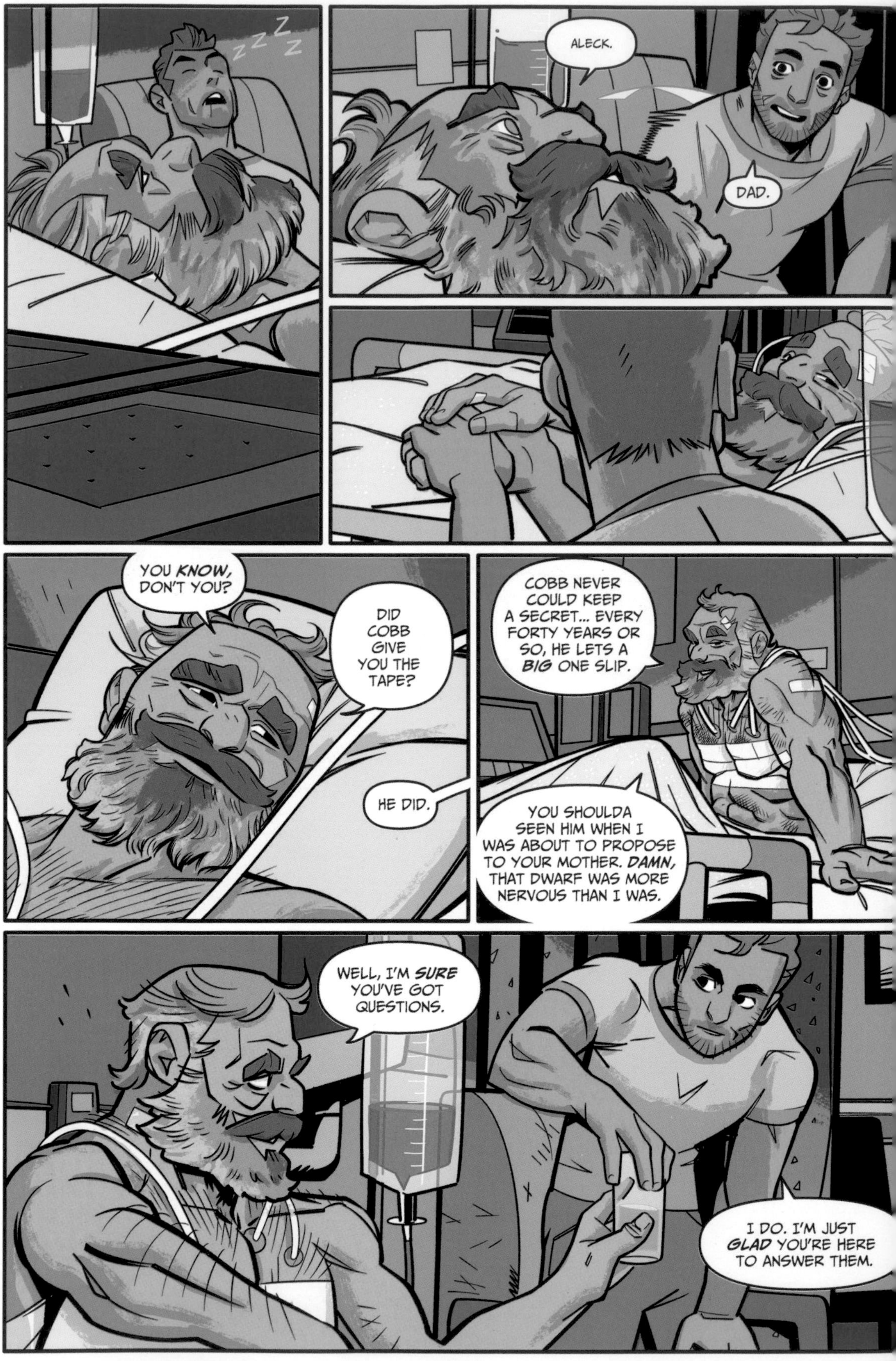

ZZZZ
ALECK.
DAD.
YOU KNOW, DON'T YOU?
DID COBB GIVE YOU THE TAPE?
HE DID.
COBB NEVER COULD KEEP A SECRET... EVERY FORTY YEARS OR SO, HE LETS A BIG ONE SLIP.
YOU SHOULDA SEEN HIM WHEN I WAS ABOUT TO PROPOSE TO YOUR MOTHER. DAMN, THAT DWARF WAS MORE NERVOUS THAN I WAS.
WELL, I'M SURE YOU'VE GOT QUESTIONS.
I DO. I'M JUST GLAD YOU'RE HERE TO ANSWER THEM.

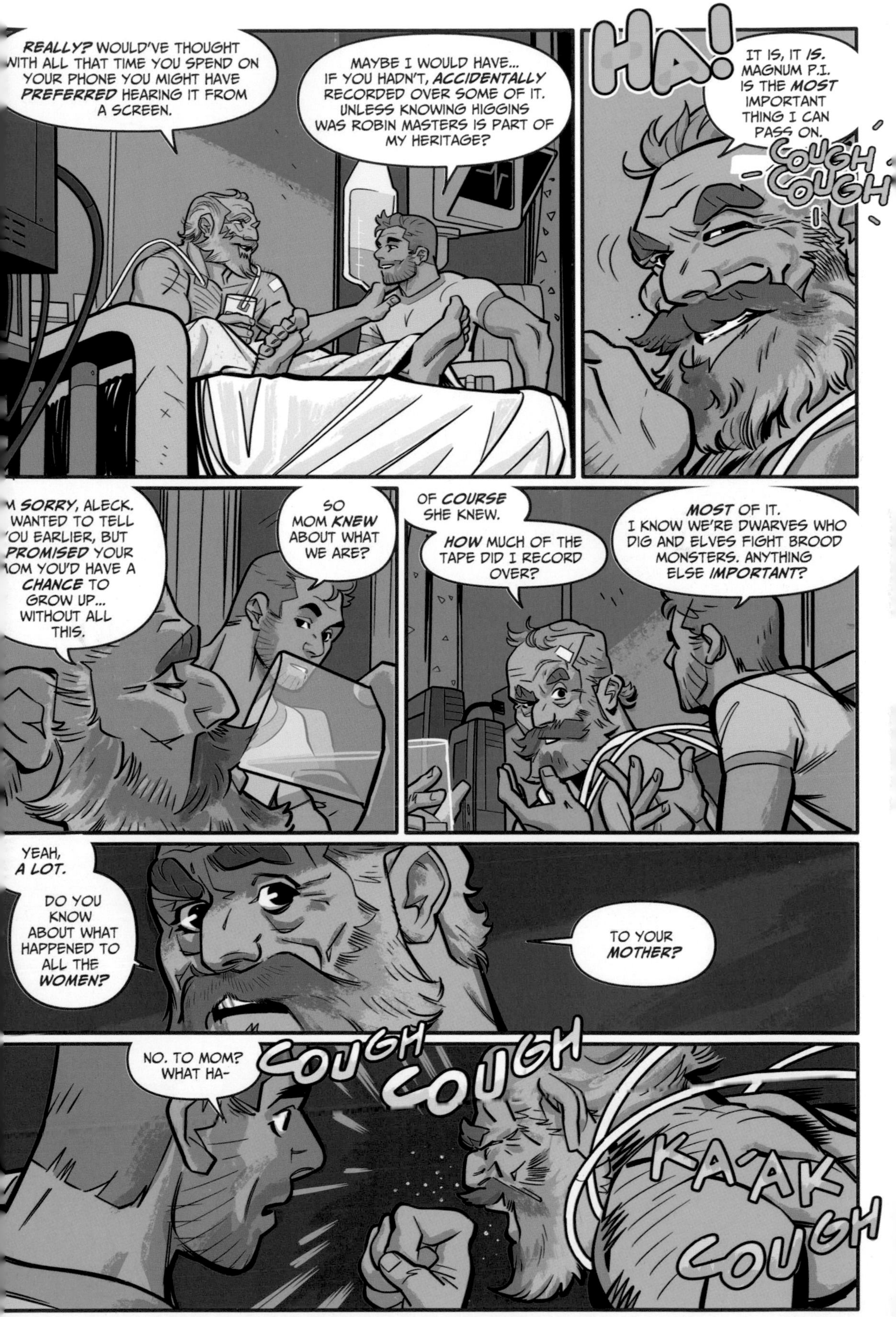
REALLY? WOULD'VE THOUGHT WITH ALL THAT TIME YOU SPEND ON YOUR PHONE YOU MIGHT HAVE PREFERRED HEARING IT FROM A SCREEN.
MAYBE I WOULD HAVE... IF YOU HADN'T, ACCIDENTALLY RECORDED OVER SOME OF IT. UNLESS KNOWING HIGGINS WAS ROBIN MASTERS IS PART OF MY HERITAGE?
HA!
IT IS, IT IS. MAGNUM P.I. IS THE MOST IMPORTANT THING I CAN PASS ON.
COUGH COUGH
M SORRY, ALECK. WANTED TO TELL YOU EARLIER, BUT PROMISED YOUR MOM YOU'D HAVE A CHANCE TO GROW UP... WITHOUT ALL THIS.
SO MOM KNEW ABOUT WHAT WE ARE?
OF COURSE SHE KNEW.
HOW MUCH OF THE TAPE DID I RECORD OVER?
MOST OF IT. I KNOW WE'RE DWARVES WHO DIG AND ELVES FIGHT BROOD MONSTERS. ANYTHING ELSE IMPORTANT?
YEAH, A LOT.
DO YOU KNOW ABOUT WHAT HAPPENED TO ALL THE WOMEN?
TO YOUR MOTHER?
NO. TO MOM? WHAT HA-
COUGH COUGH
KA'AK
COUGH

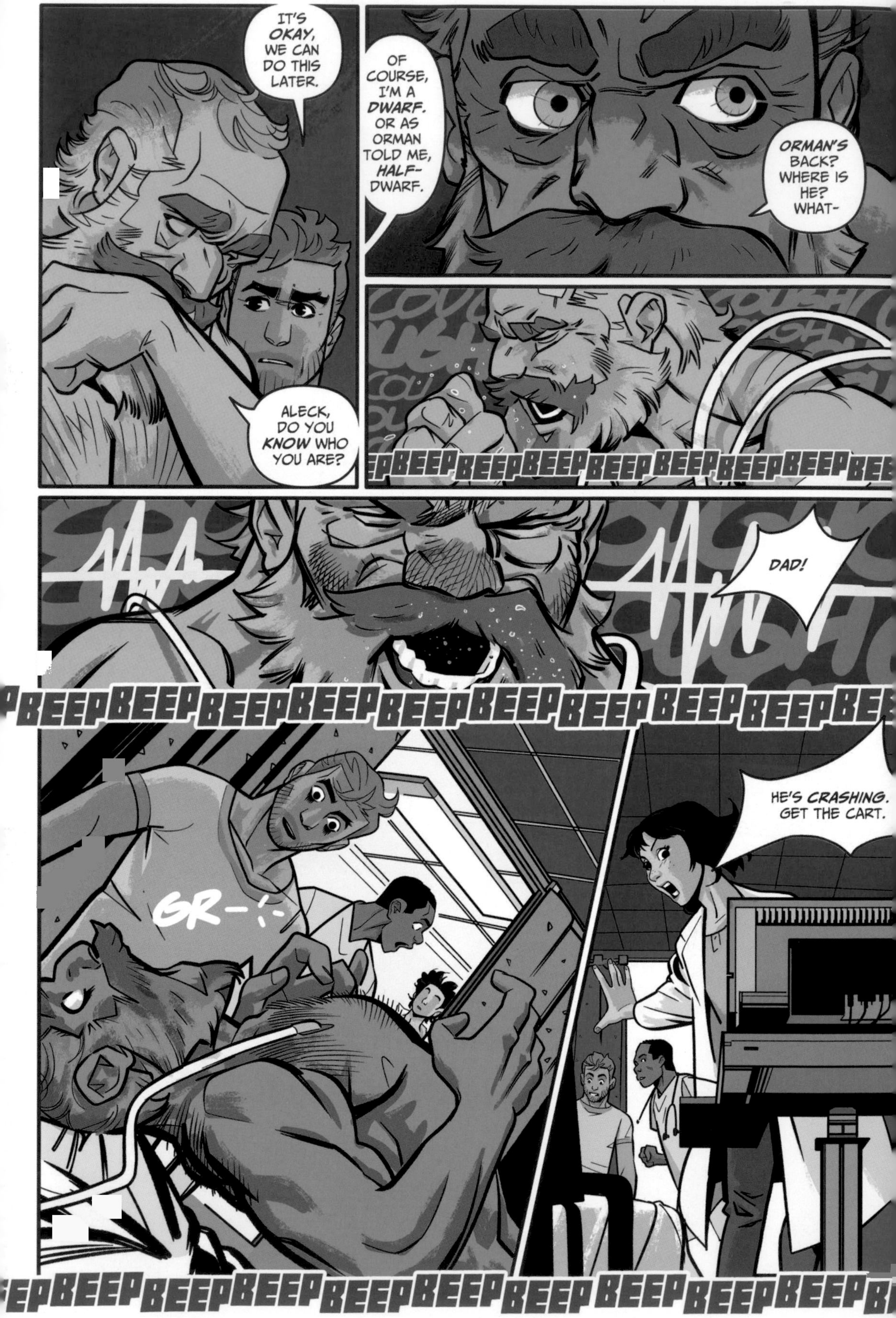
IT'S OKAY, WE CAN DO THIS LATER.
ALECK, DO YOU KNOW WHO YOU ARE?
OF COURSE, I'M A DWARF. OR AS ORMAN TOLD ME, HALF-DWARF.
ORMAN'S BACK? WHERE IS HE? WHAT-
BEEPBEEPBEEPBEEPBEEPBEEPBEEP
DAD!
BEEPBEEPBEEPBEEPBEEPBEEPBEEPBEEPBEEP
GR-
HE'S CRASHING. GET THE CART.
BEEPBEEPBEEPBEEPBEEPBEEPBEEPBEEPBEEP

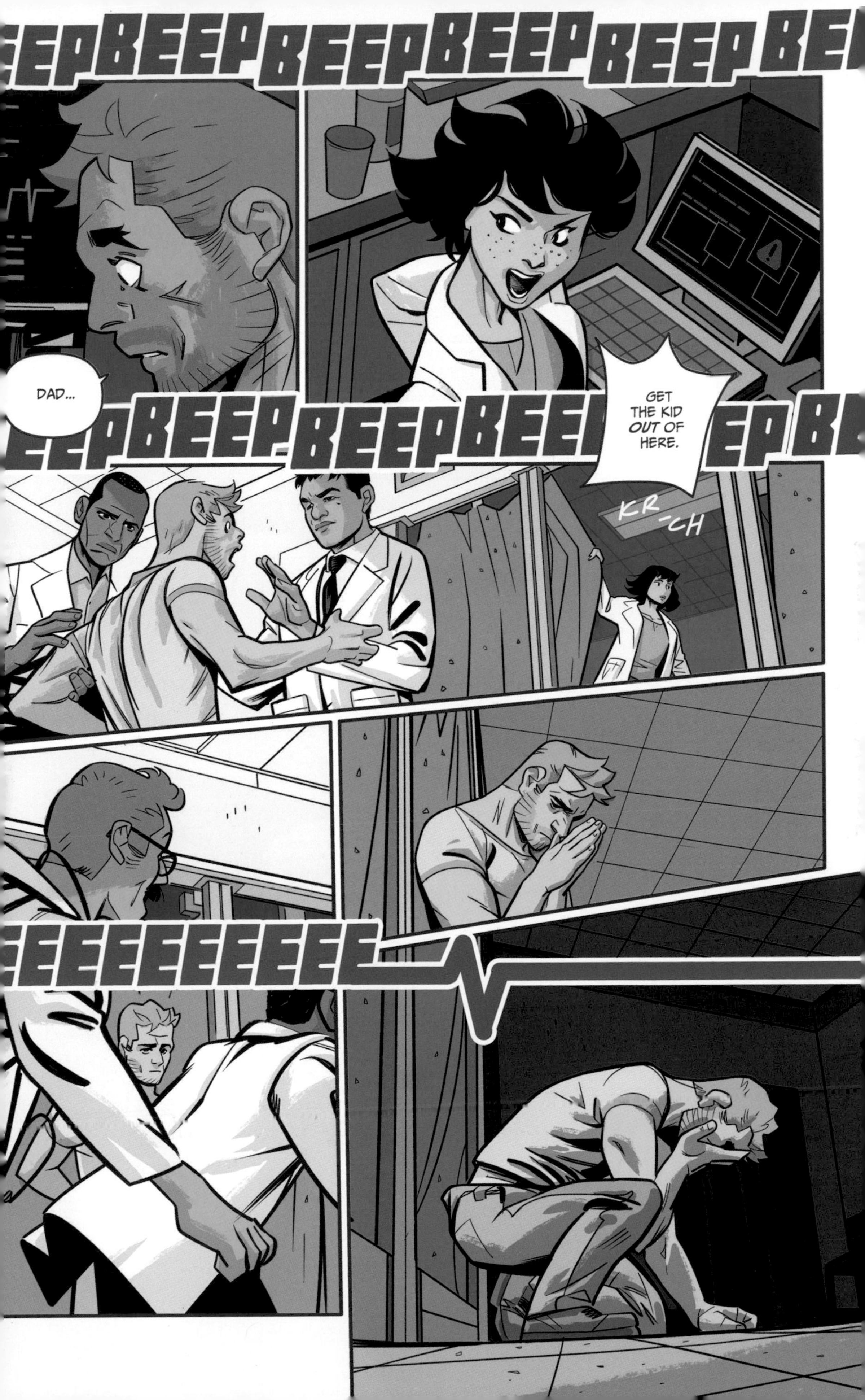
BEEP BEEP BEEP
DAD...
BEEP BEEP
GET THE KID OUT OF HERE.
KR-CH
EEEEEEEEEE

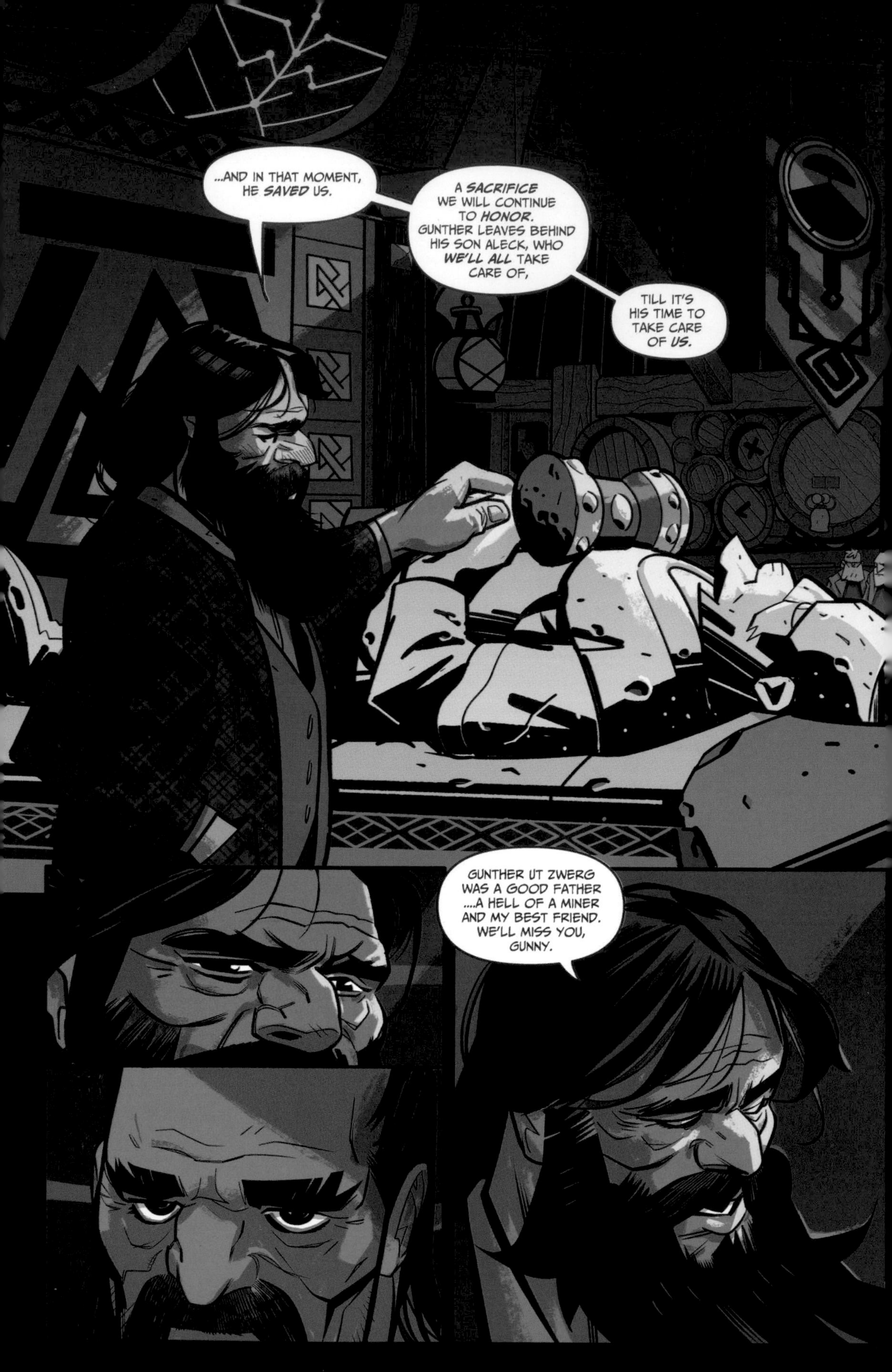
...AND IN THAT MOMENT, HE *SAVED* US.
A *SACRIFICE* WE WILL CONTINUE TO *HONOR*. GUNTHER LEAVES BEHIND HIS SON ALECK, WHO *WE'LL ALL* TAKE CARE OF,
TILL IT'S HIS TIME TO TAKE CARE OF *US*.
GUNTHER UT ZWERG WAS A GOOD FATHER ....A HELL OF A MINER AND MY BEST FRIEND. WE'LL MISS YOU, GUNNY.

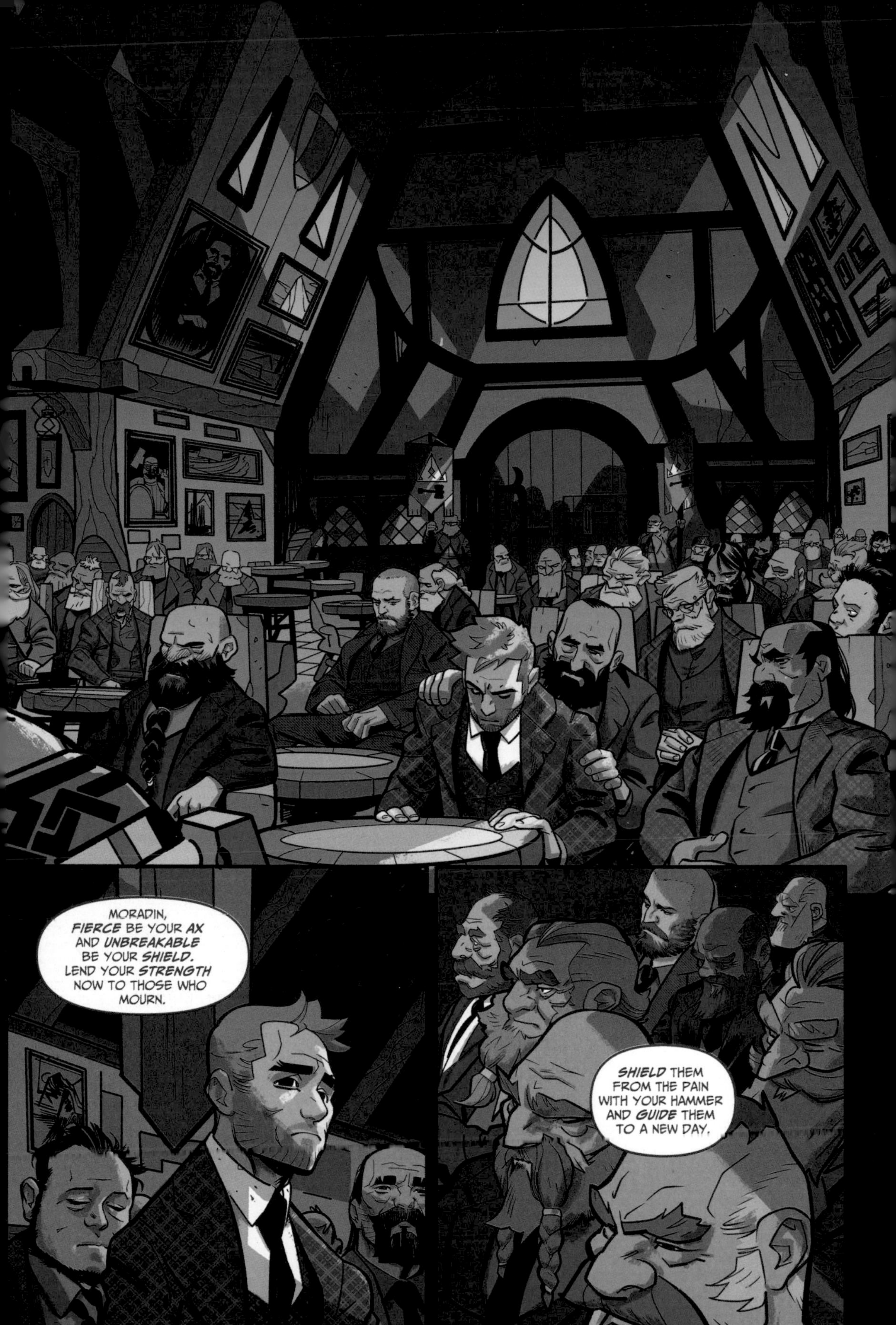
MORADIN, FIERCE BE YOUR AX AND UNBREAKABLE BE YOUR SHIELD. LEND YOUR STRENGTH NOW TO THOSE WHO MOURN.
SHIELD THEM FROM THE PAIN WITH YOUR HAMMER AND GUIDE THEM TO A NEW DAY.

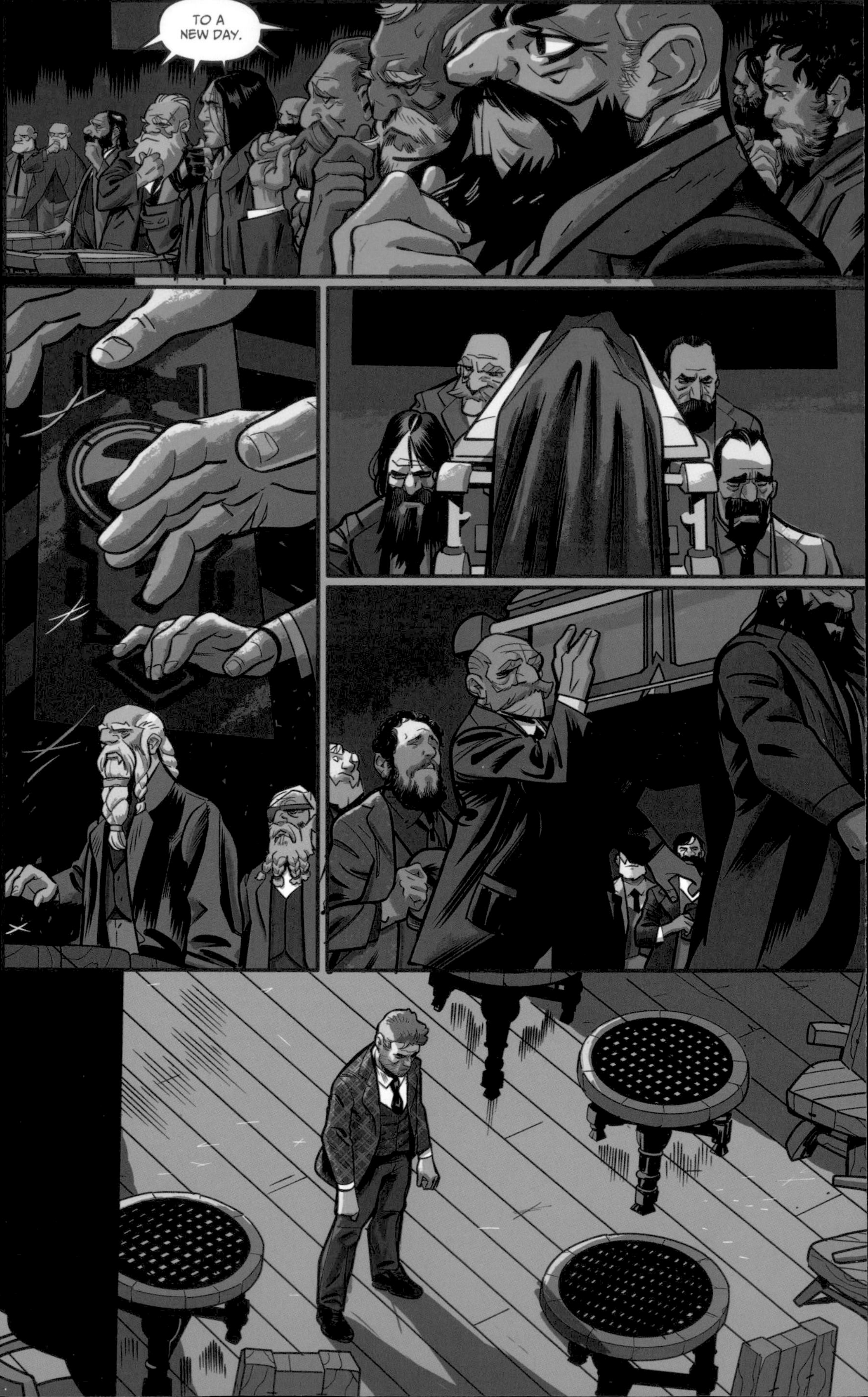
TO A NEW DAY.

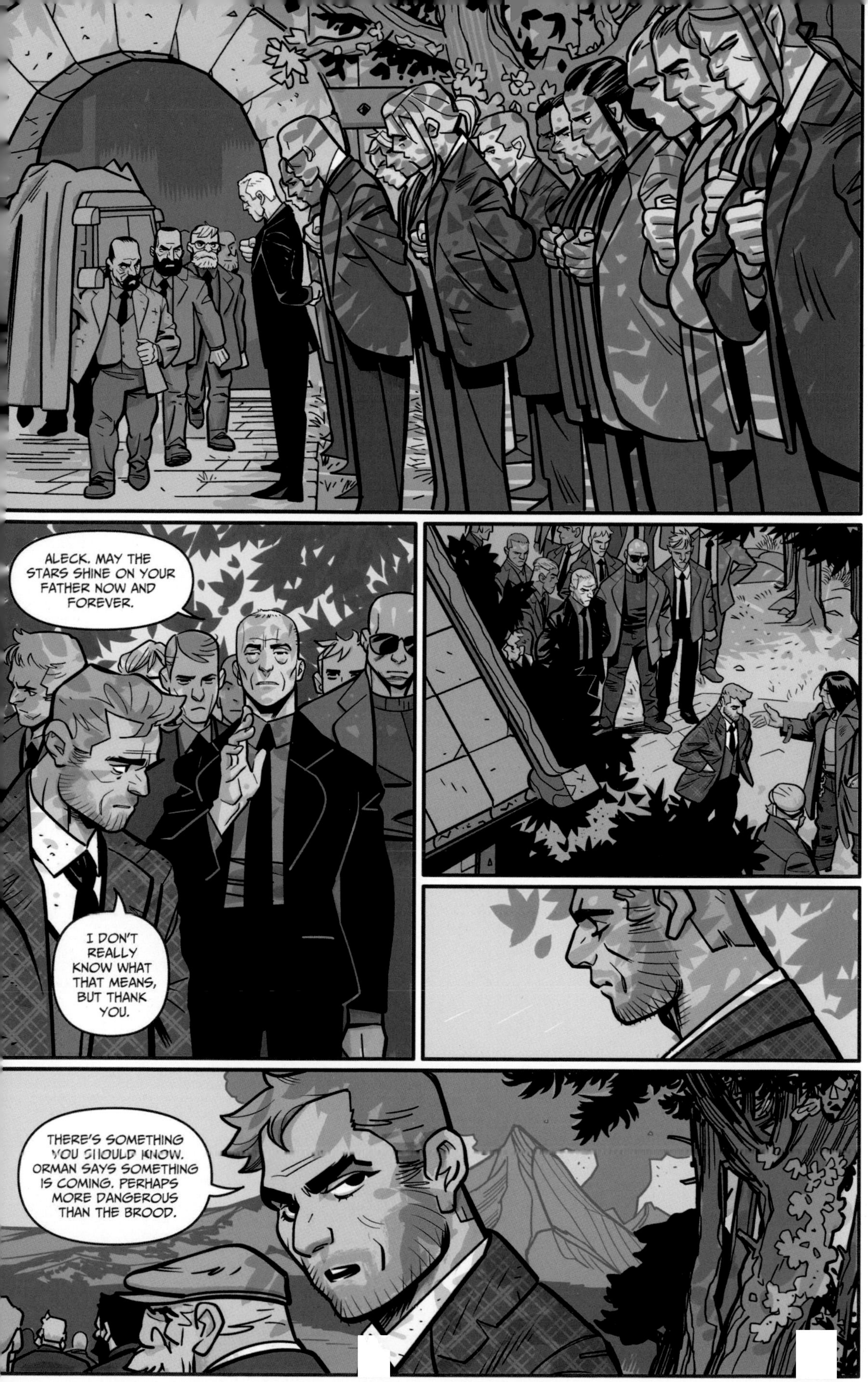
ALECK. MAY THE STARS SHINE ON YOUR FATHER NOW AND FOREVER.
I DON'T REALLY KNOW WHAT THAT MEANS, BUT THANK YOU.
THERE'S SOMETHING YOU SHOULD KNOW. ORMAN SAYS SOMETHING IS COMING. PERHAPS MORE DANGEROUS THAN THE BROOD.

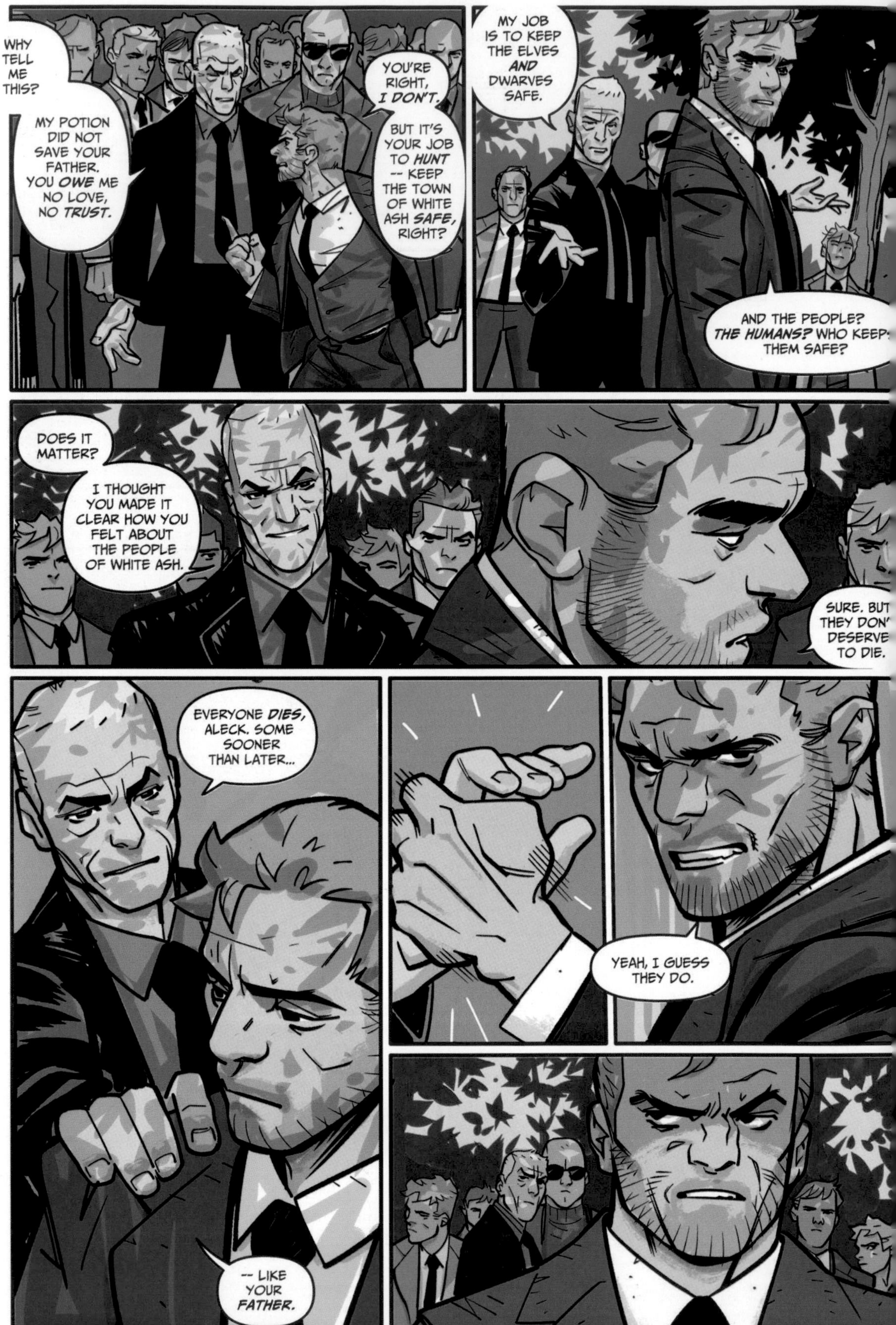
WHY TELL ME THIS?
MY POTION DID NOT SAVE YOUR FATHER. YOU *OWE* ME NO LOVE, NO *TRUST*.
YOU'RE RIGHT, *I DON'T*.
BUT IT'S YOUR JOB TO *HUNT* -- KEEP THE TOWN OF WHITE ASH *SAFE*, RIGHT?
MY JOB IS TO KEEP THE ELVES *AND* DWARVES SAFE.
AND THE PEOPLE? *THE HUMANS?* WHO KEEPS THEM SAFE?
DOES IT MATTER?
I THOUGHT YOU MADE IT CLEAR HOW YOU FELT ABOUT THE PEOPLE OF WHITE ASH.
SURE. BUT THEY DON'T DESERVE TO DIE.
EVERYONE *DIES*, ALECK. SOME SOONER THAN LATER...
-- LIKE YOUR *FATHER*.
YEAH, I GUESS THEY DO.

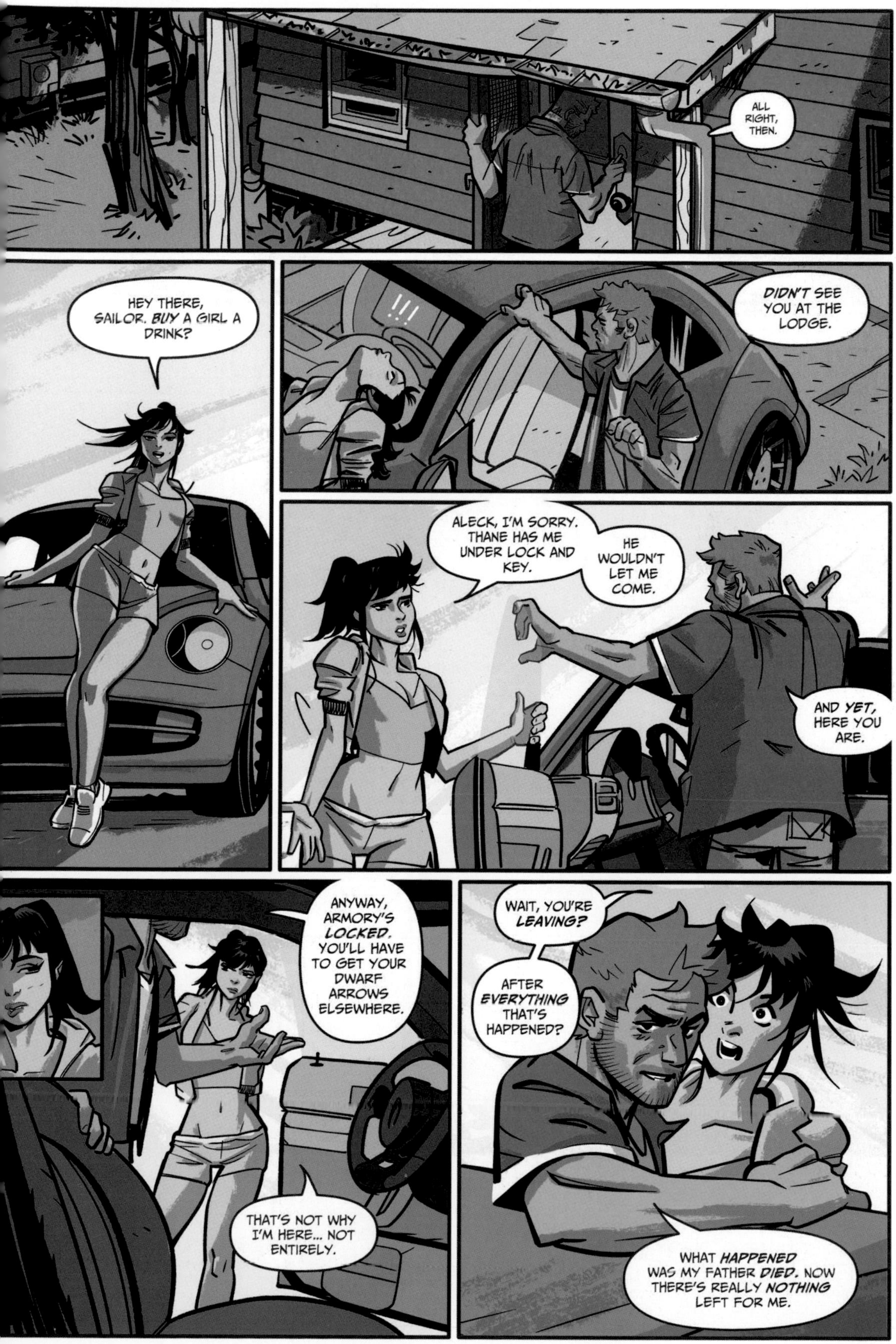
ALL RIGHT, THEN.
HEY THERE, SAILOR. BUY A GIRL A DRINK?
!!!
DIDN'T SEE YOU AT THE LODGE.
ALECK, I'M SORRY. THANE HAS ME UNDER LOCK AND KEY.
HE WOULDN'T LET ME COME.
AND YET, HERE YOU ARE.
ANYWAY, ARMORY'S LOCKED. YOU'LL HAVE TO GET YOUR DWARF ARROWS ELSEWHERE.
THAT'S NOT WHY I'M HERE... NOT ENTIRELY.
WAIT, YOU'RE LEAVING?
AFTER EVERYTHING THAT'S HAPPENED?
WHAT HAPPENED WAS MY FATHER DIED. NOW THERE'S REALLY NOTHING LEFT FOR ME.

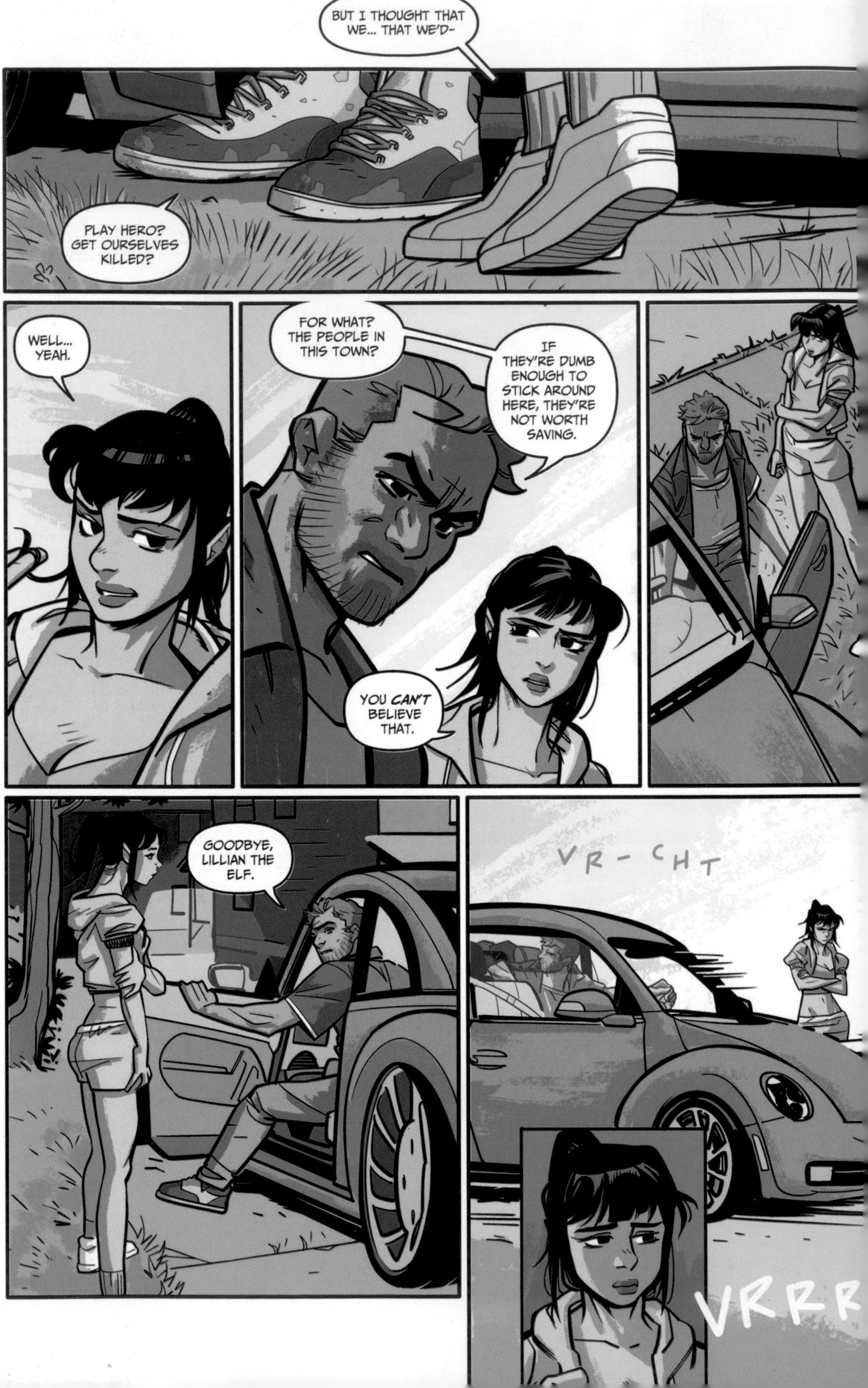
BUT I THOUGHT THAT WE... THAT WE'D-
PLAY HERO? GET OURSELVES KILLED?
WELL... YEAH.
FOR WHAT? THE PEOPLE IN THIS TOWN?
IF THEY'RE DUMB ENOUGH TO STICK AROUND HERE, THEY'RE NOT WORTH SAVING.
YOU CAN'T BELIEVE THAT.
GOODBYE, LILLIAN THE ELF.
VR-CHT
VRRR

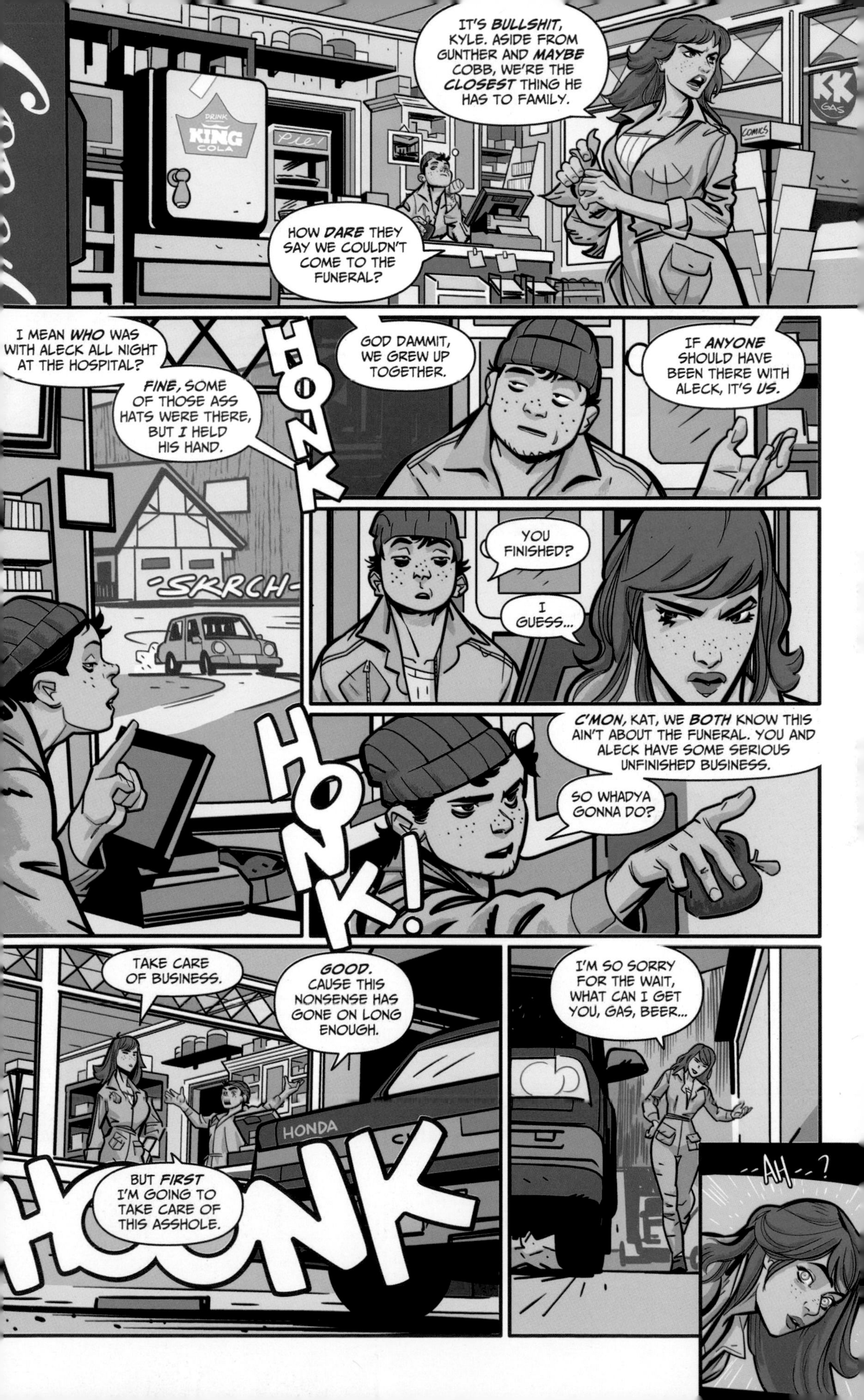
DRINK KING COLA
PIE!
KK GAS
COMICS
IT'S BULLSHIT, KYLE. ASIDE FROM GUNTHER AND MAYBE COBB, WE'RE THE CLOSEST THING HE HAS TO FAMILY.
HOW DARE THEY SAY WE COULDN'T COME TO THE FUNERAL?
I MEAN WHO WAS WITH ALECK ALL NIGHT AT THE HOSPITAL?
FINE, SOME OF THOSE ASS HATS WERE THERE, BUT I HELD HIS HAND.
HONK
GOD DAMMIT, WE GREW UP TOGETHER.
IF ANYONE SHOULD HAVE BEEN THERE WITH ALECK, IT'S US.
-SKRCH-
YOU FINISHED?
I GUESS...
HONK!
C'MON, KAT, WE BOTH KNOW THIS AIN'T ABOUT THE FUNERAL. YOU AND ALECK HAVE SOME SERIOUS UNFINISHED BUSINESS.
SO WHADYA GONNA DO?
TAKE CARE OF BUSINESS.
GOOD. CAUSE THIS NONSENSE HAS GONE ON LONG ENOUGH.
HONDA
HOONK
BUT FIRST I'M GOING TO TAKE CARE OF THIS ASSHOLE.
I'M SO SORRY FOR THE WAIT, WHAT CAN I GET YOU, GAS, BEER...
--AH--?

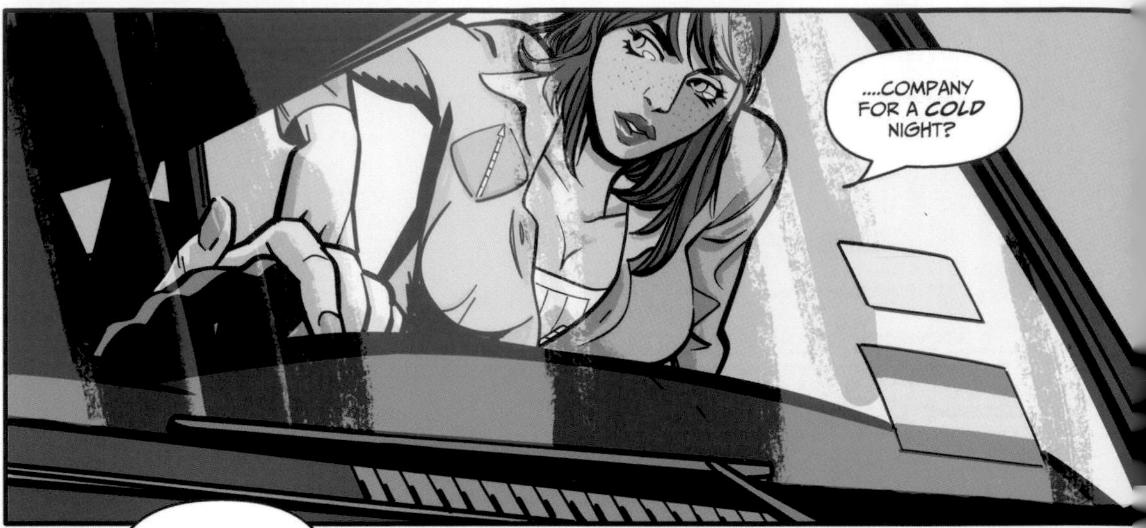
....COMPANY FOR A COLD NIGHT?

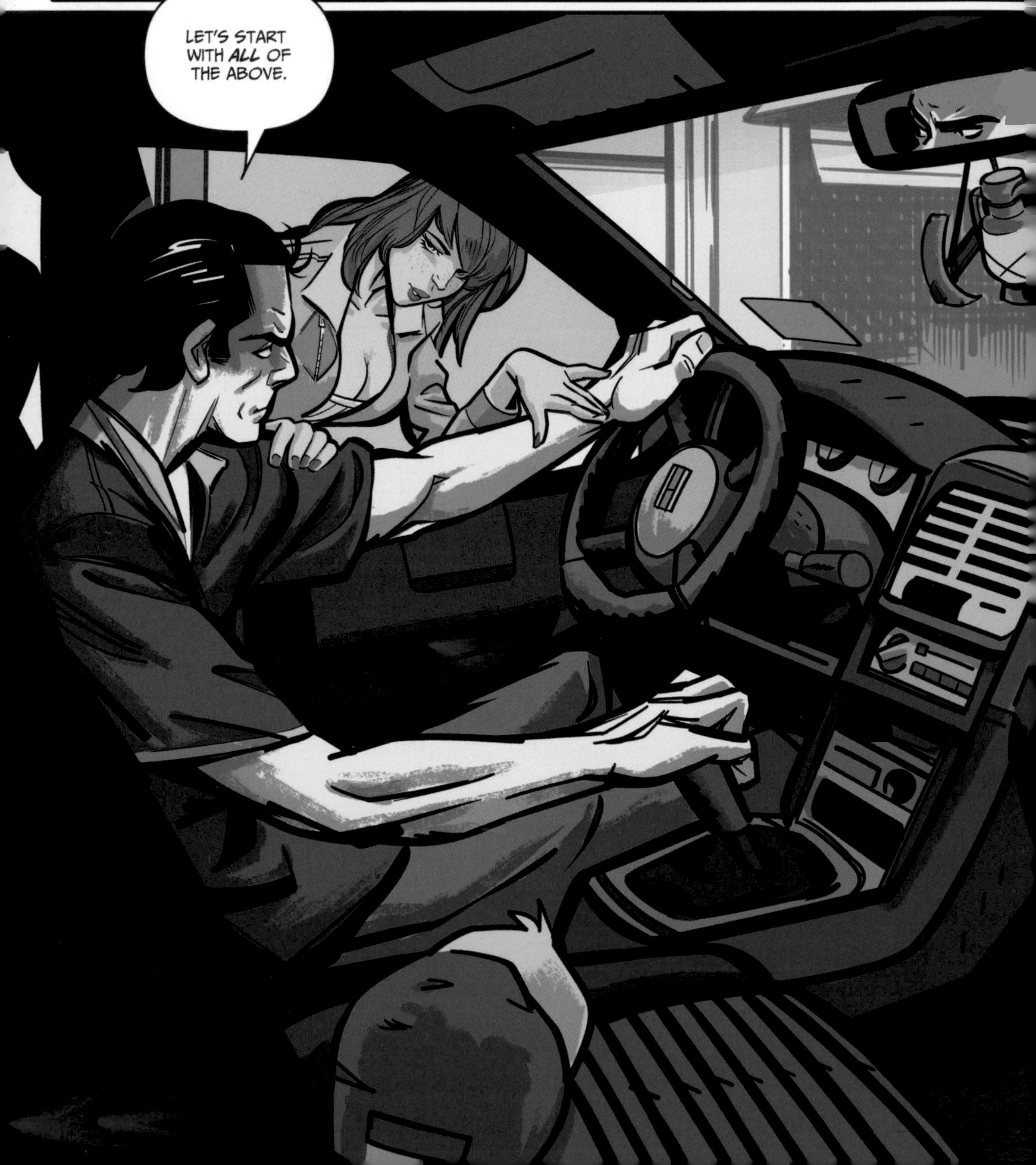
LET'S START WITH ALL OF THE ABOVE.

CHAPTER FIVE

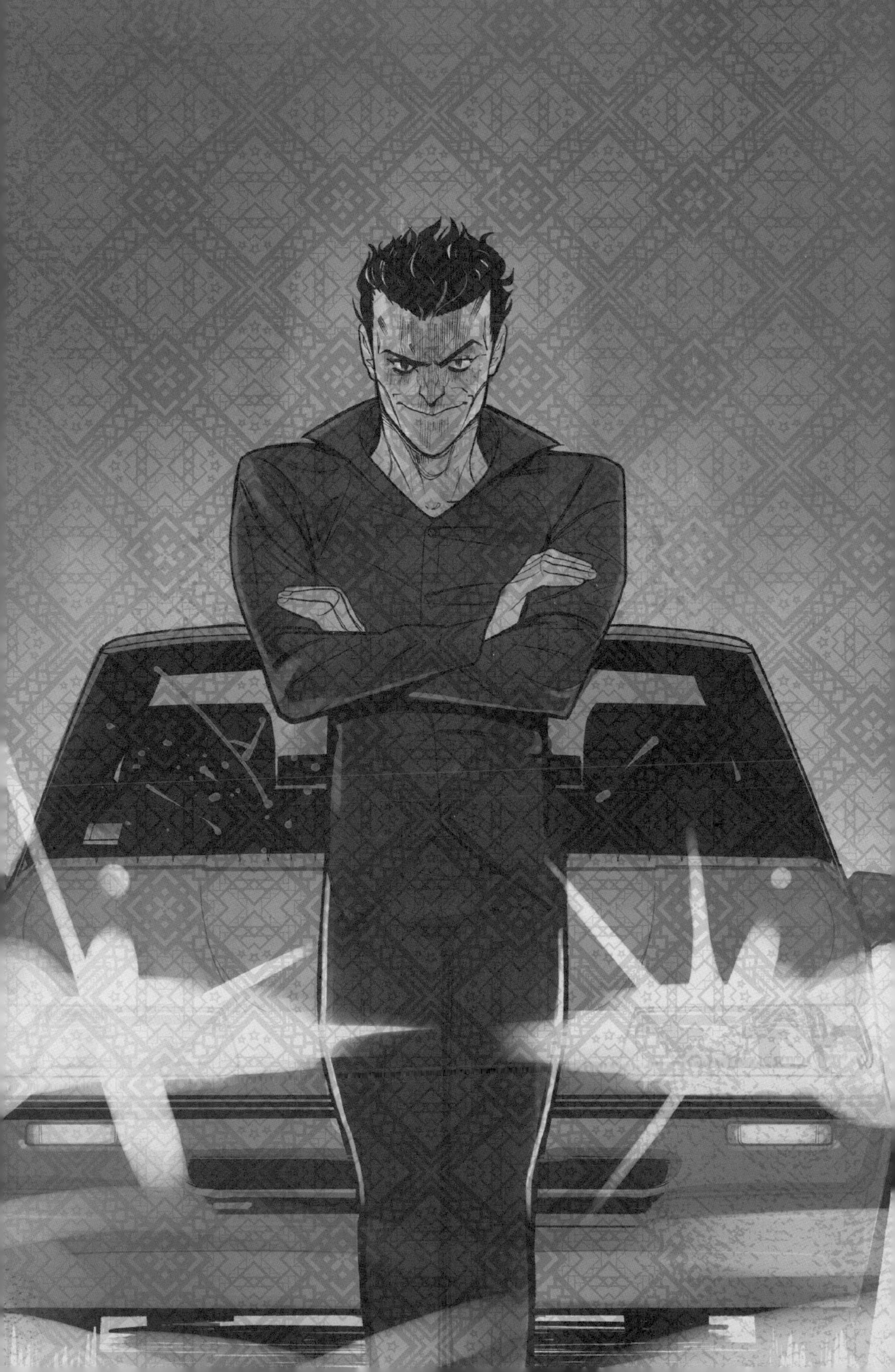

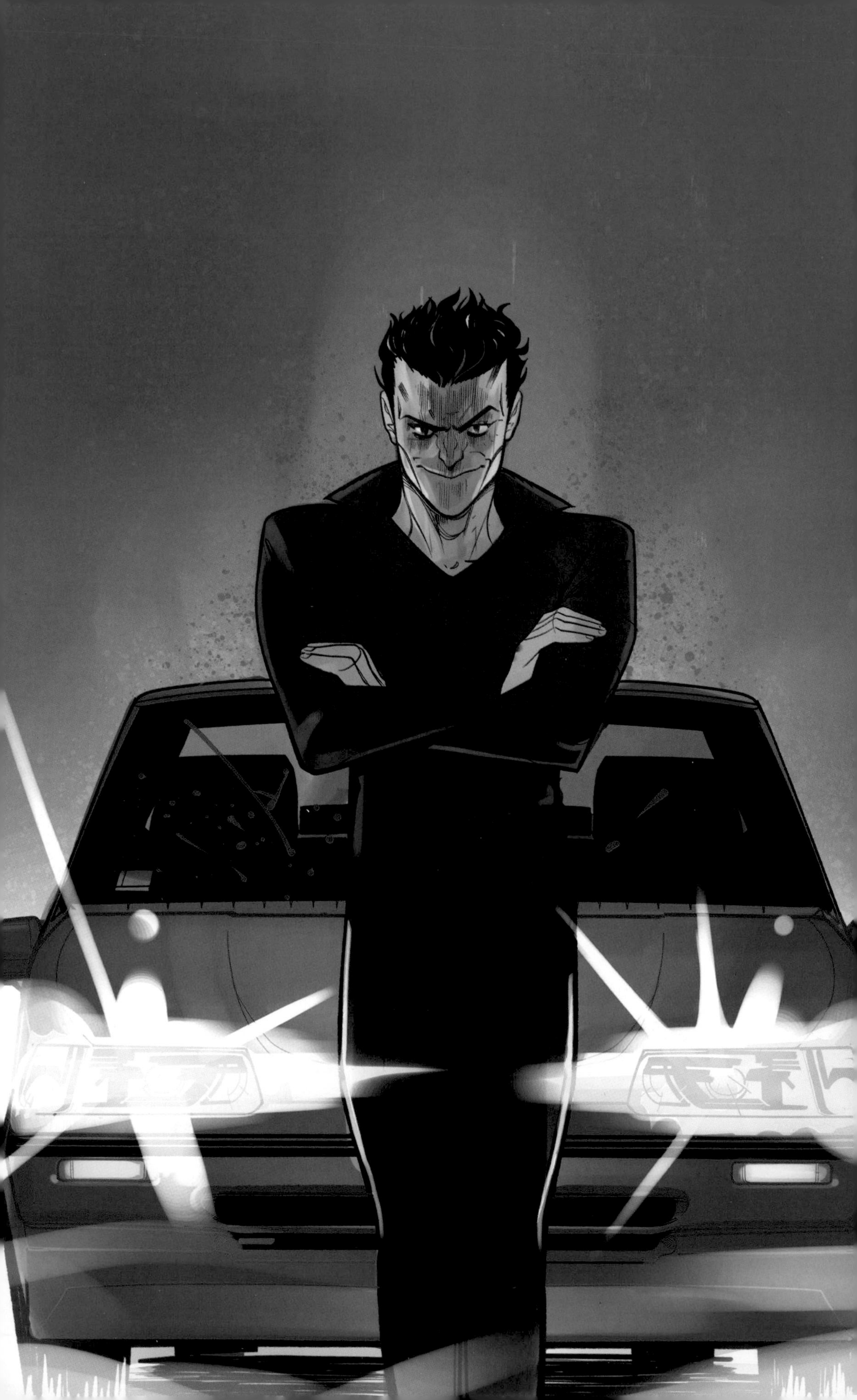

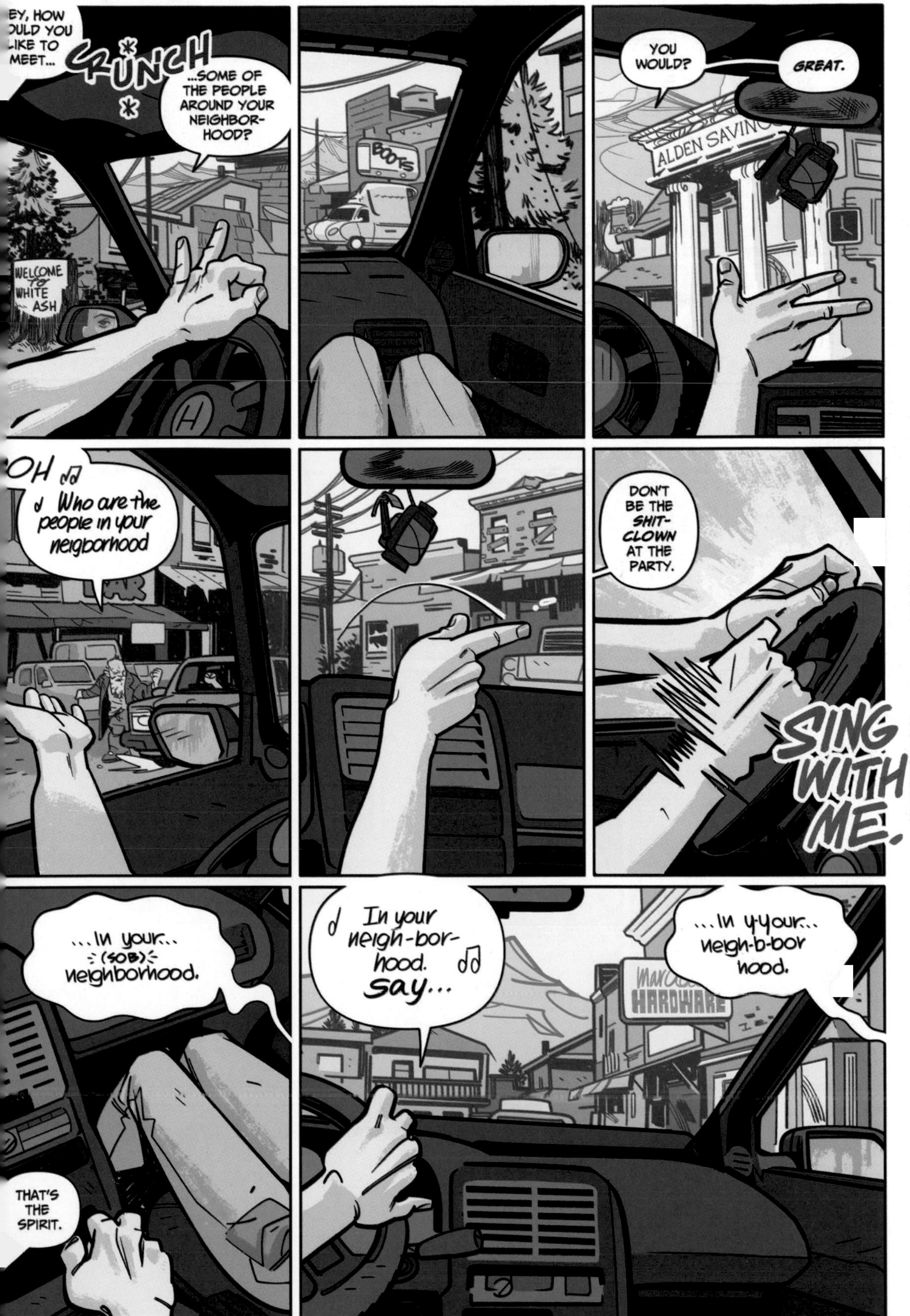
EY, HOW
OULD YOU
LIKE TO
MEET...
CRUNCH
...SOME OF THE PEOPLE AROUND YOUR NEIGHBOR-HOOD?
WELCOME TO WHITE ASH
BOOTS
YOU WOULD?
GREAT.
ALDEN SAVIN
OH
Who are the people in your neigborhood
DON'T BE THE SHIT-CLOWN AT THE PARTY.
SING WITH ME.
...In your... (SOB) neighborhood.
In your neigh-bor-hood. Say...
HARDWARE
...In y-your... neigh-b-bor hood.
THAT'S THE SPIRIT.

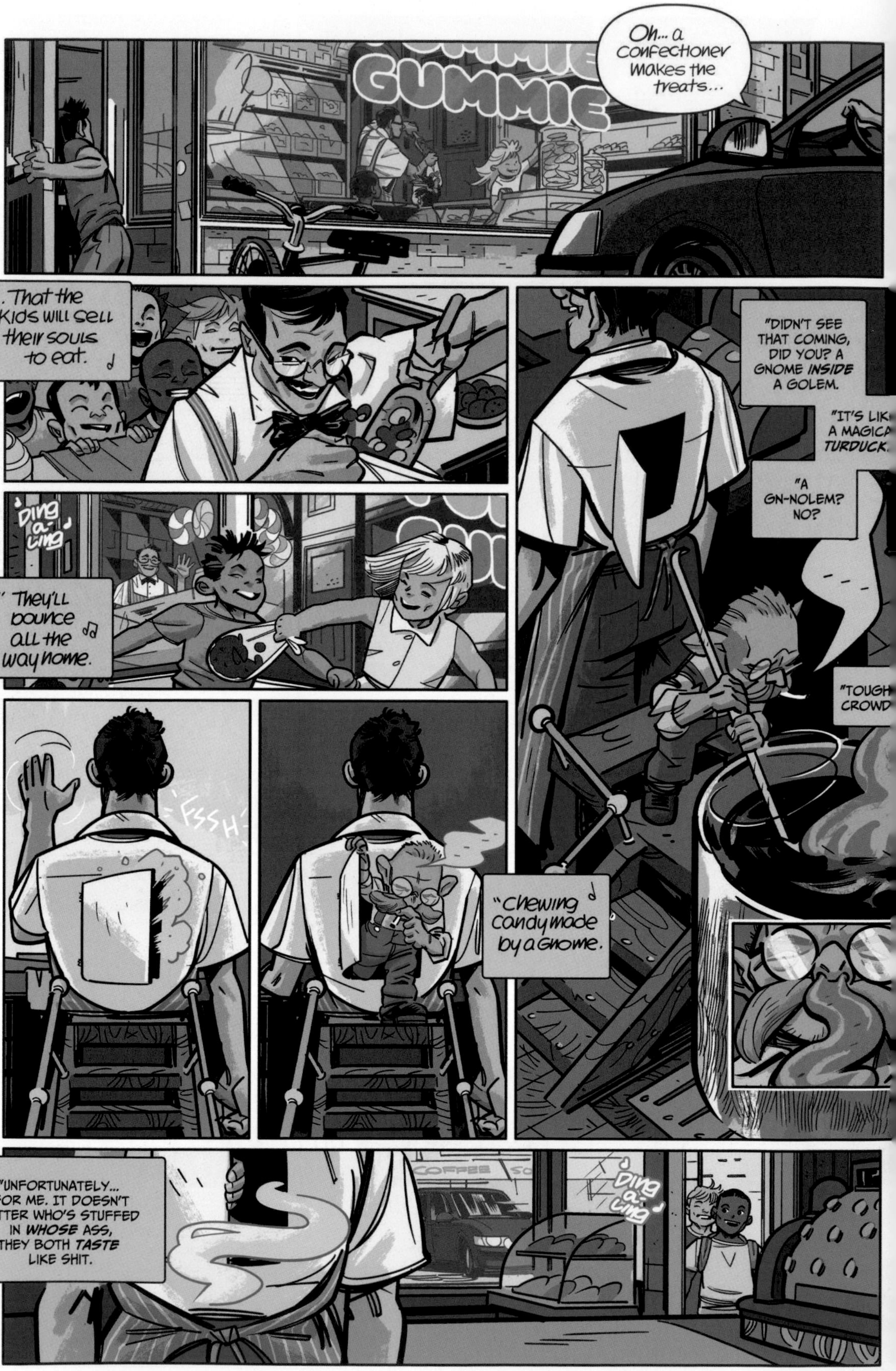
GUMMIE
Oh... a confectioner makes the treats...
"...That the kids will sell their souls to eat.
"Didn't see that coming, did you? A gnome *inside* a golem.
"It's lik
a magica
turduck
"A Gn-nolem? No?
Ding a-ling
" They'll bounce all the way home.
"Tough
crowd
FSSH
"Chewing candy made by a gnome.
"Unfortunately... for me, it doesn't matter who's stuffed in *whose* ass, they both *taste* like shit.
COFFEE
Ding a-ling

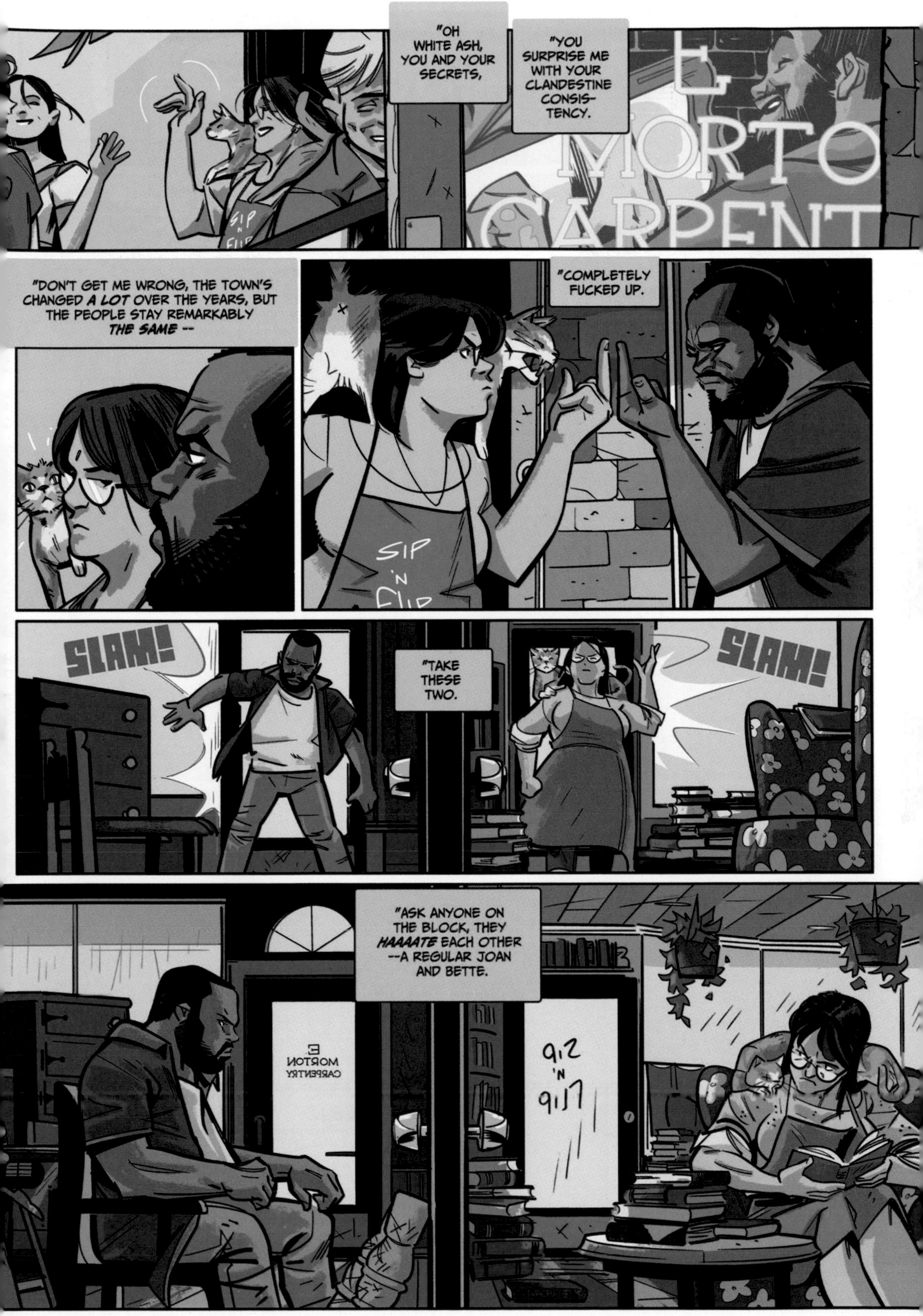

"OH WHITE ASH, YOU AND YOUR SECRETS,
"YOU SURPRISE ME WITH YOUR CLANDESTINE CONSIS-TENCY.
"DON'T GET ME WRONG, THE TOWN'S CHANGED *A LOT* OVER THE YEARS, BUT THE PEOPLE STAY REMARKABLY *THE SAME* --
"COMPLETELY FUCKED UP.
SIP 'N
SLAM!
"TAKE THESE TWO.
SLAM!
"ASK ANYONE ON THE BLOCK, THEY *HAAAATE* EACH OTHER --A REGULAR JOAN AND BETTE.
E. MORTON CARPENTRY
Sip 'n Flip

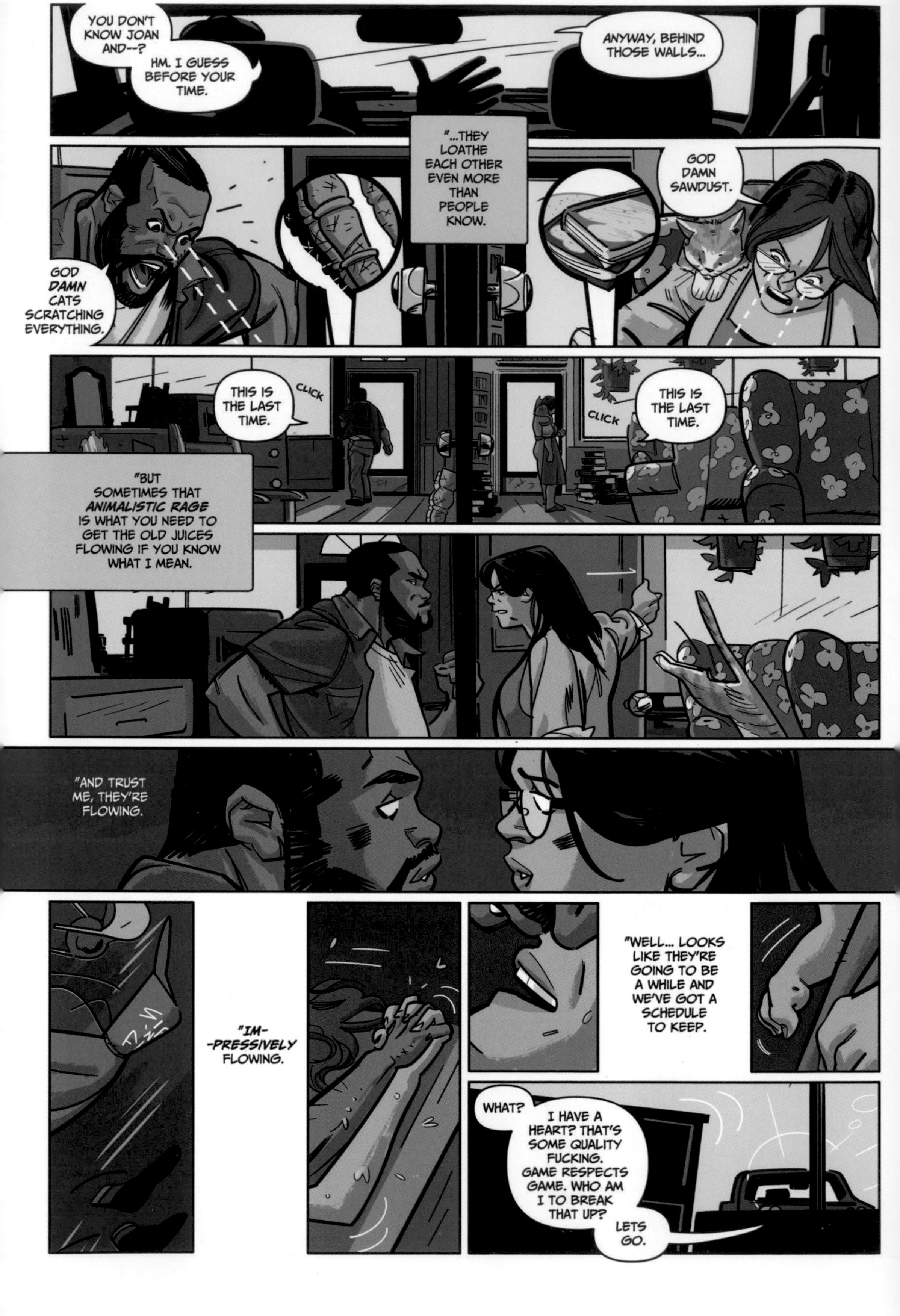
YOU DON'T KNOW JOAN AND--?
HM. I GUESS BEFORE YOUR TIME.
ANYWAY, BEHIND THOSE WALLS...
"...THEY LOATHE EACH OTHER EVEN MORE THAN PEOPLE KNOW.
GOD *DAMN* CATS SCRATCHING EVERYTHING.
GOD DAMN SAWDUST.
THIS IS THE LAST TIME.
CLICK
CLICK
THIS IS THE LAST TIME.
"BUT SOMETIMES THAT *ANIMALISTIC RAGE* IS WHAT YOU NEED TO GET THE OLD JUICES FLOWING IF YOU KNOW WHAT I MEAN.
"AND TRUST ME, THEY'RE FLOWING.
"*IM- -PRESSIVELY* FLOWING.
"WELL... LOOKS LIKE THEY'RE GOING TO BE A WHILE AND WE'VE GOT A SCHEDULE TO KEEP.
WHAT?
I HAVE A HEART? THAT'S SOME QUALITY FUCKING. GAME RESPECTS GAME. WHO AM I TO BREAK THAT UP?
LETS GO.

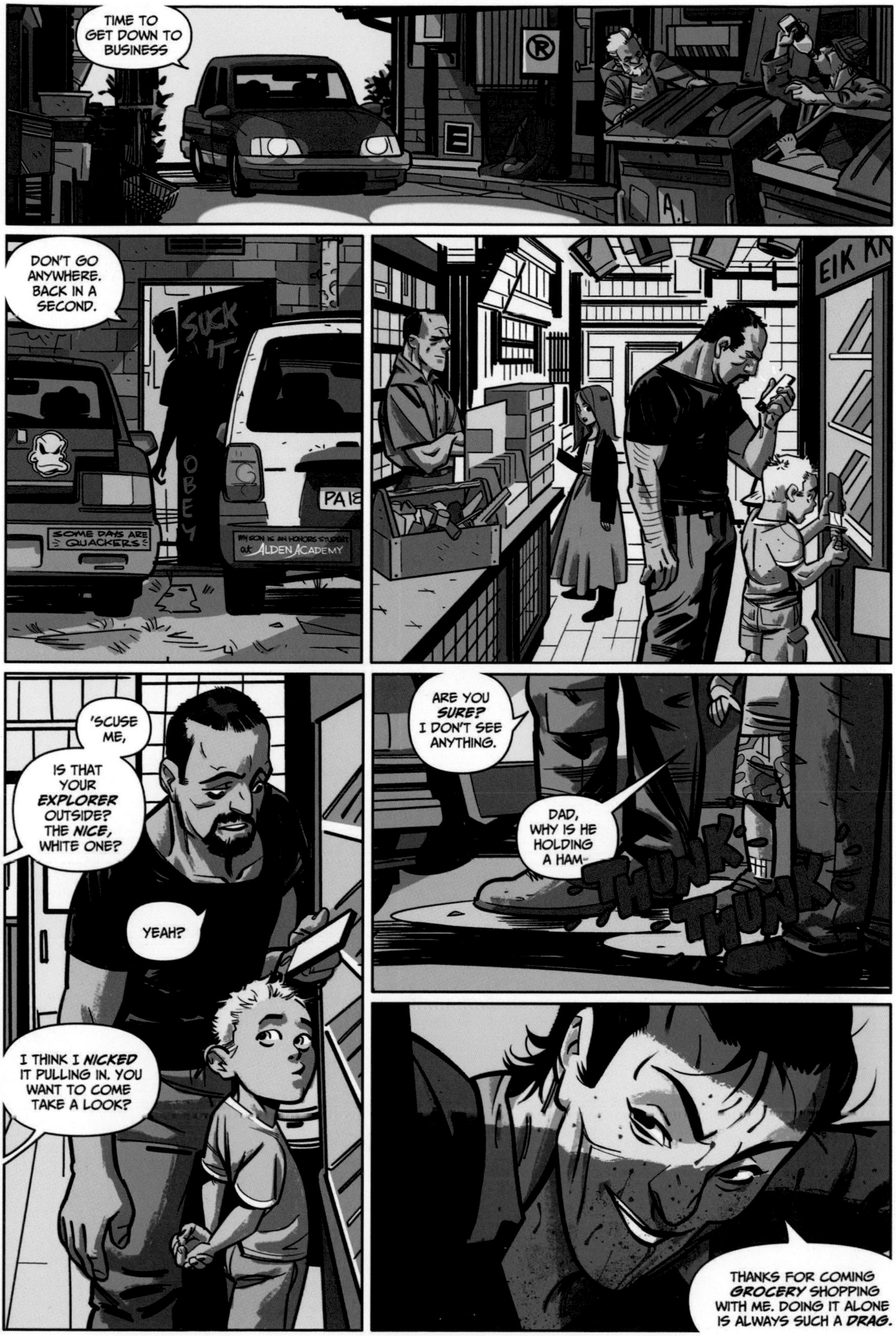
TIME TO GET DOWN TO BUSINESS
A.L.
DON'T GO ANYWHERE. BACK IN A SECOND.
SUCK IT
OBEY
SOME DAYS ARE QUACKERS
PA18
MY SON IS AN HONORS STUDENT at ALDEN ACADEMY
EIK KN
'SCUSE ME,
IS THAT YOUR EXPLORER OUTSIDE? THE NICE, WHITE ONE?
YEAH?
I THINK I NICKED IT PULLING IN. YOU WANT TO COME TAKE A LOOK?
ARE YOU SURE? I DON'T SEE ANYTHING.
DAD, WHY IS HE HOLDING A HAM-
THUNK
THUNK
THANKS FOR COMING GROCERY SHOPPING WITH ME. DOING IT ALONE IS ALWAYS SUCH A DRAG.

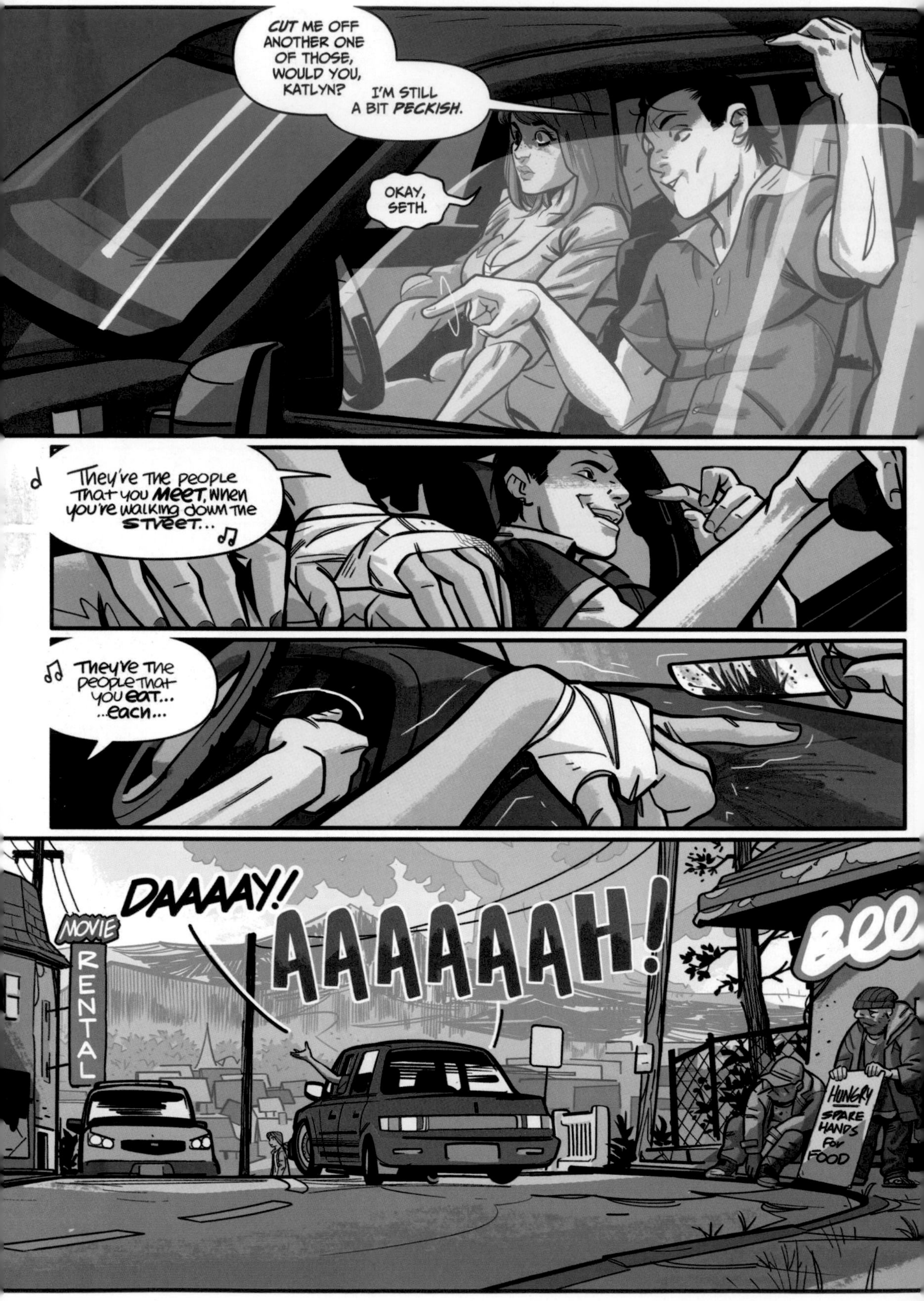
CUT ME OFF ANOTHER ONE OF THOSE, WOULD YOU, KATLYN? I'M STILL A BIT PECKISH.
OKAY, SETH.
They're the people that you meet, when you're walking down the street...
They're the people that you eat... ...each...
DAAAAY!
AAAAAAH!
MOVIE RENTAL
HUNGRY SPARE HANDS FOR FOOD

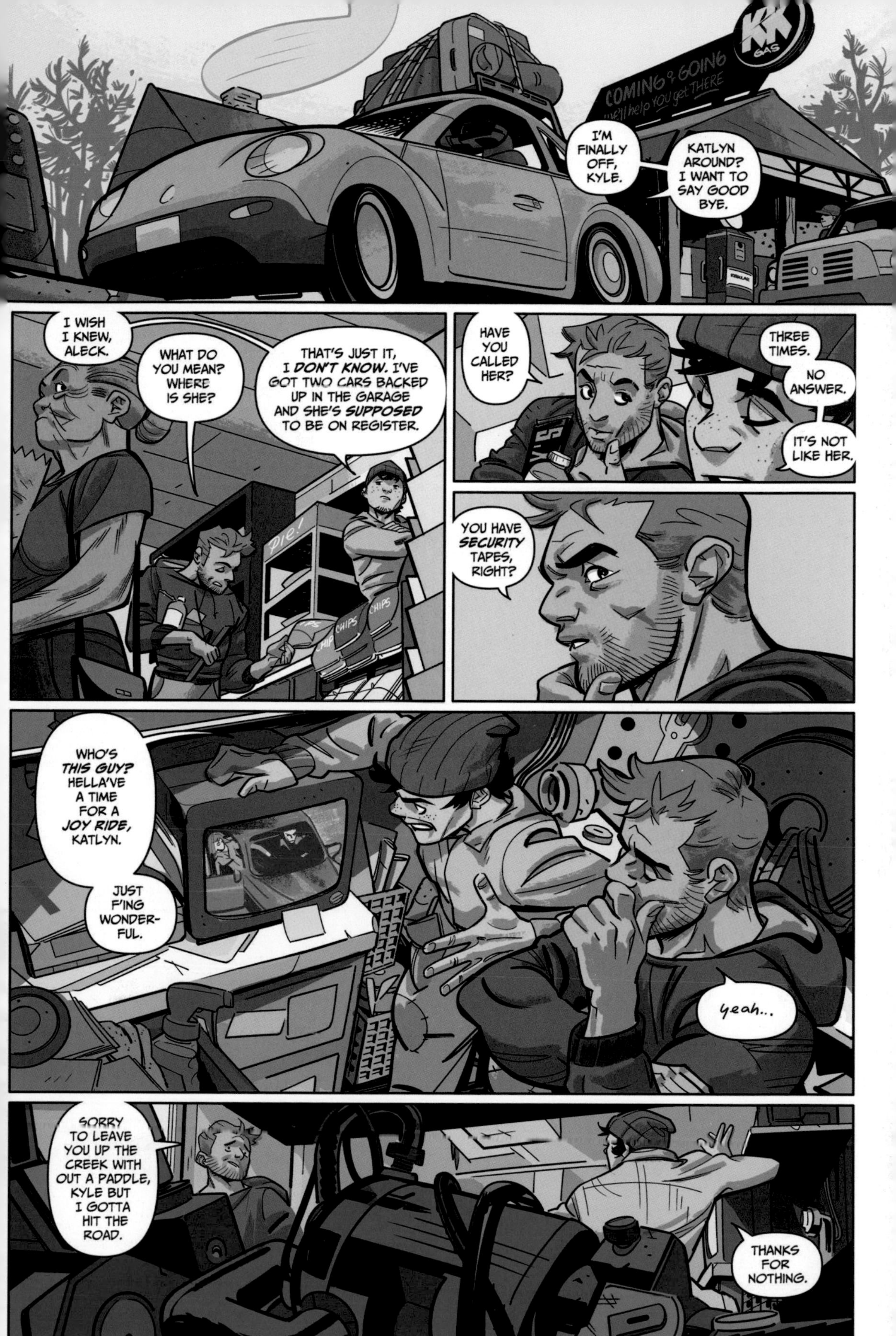
COMING & GOING
we'll help YOU get THERE
I'M FINALLY OFF, KYLE.
KATLYN AROUND? I WANT TO SAY GOOD BYE.
I WISH I KNEW, ALECK.
WHAT DO YOU MEAN? WHERE IS SHE?
THAT'S JUST IT, I DON'T KNOW. I'VE GOT TWO CARS BACKED UP IN THE GARAGE AND SHE'S SUPPOSED TO BE ON REGISTER.
Pie!
CHIPS
HAVE YOU CALLED HER?
THREE TIMES.
NO ANSWER.
IT'S NOT LIKE HER.
YOU HAVE SECURITY TAPES, RIGHT?
WHO'S THIS GUY? HELLA'VE A TIME FOR A JOY RIDE, KATLYN.
JUST F'ING WONDER-FUL.
yeah...
SORRY TO LEAVE YOU UP THE CREEK WITH OUT A PADDLE, KYLE BUT I GOTTA HIT THE ROAD.
THANKS FOR NOTHING.

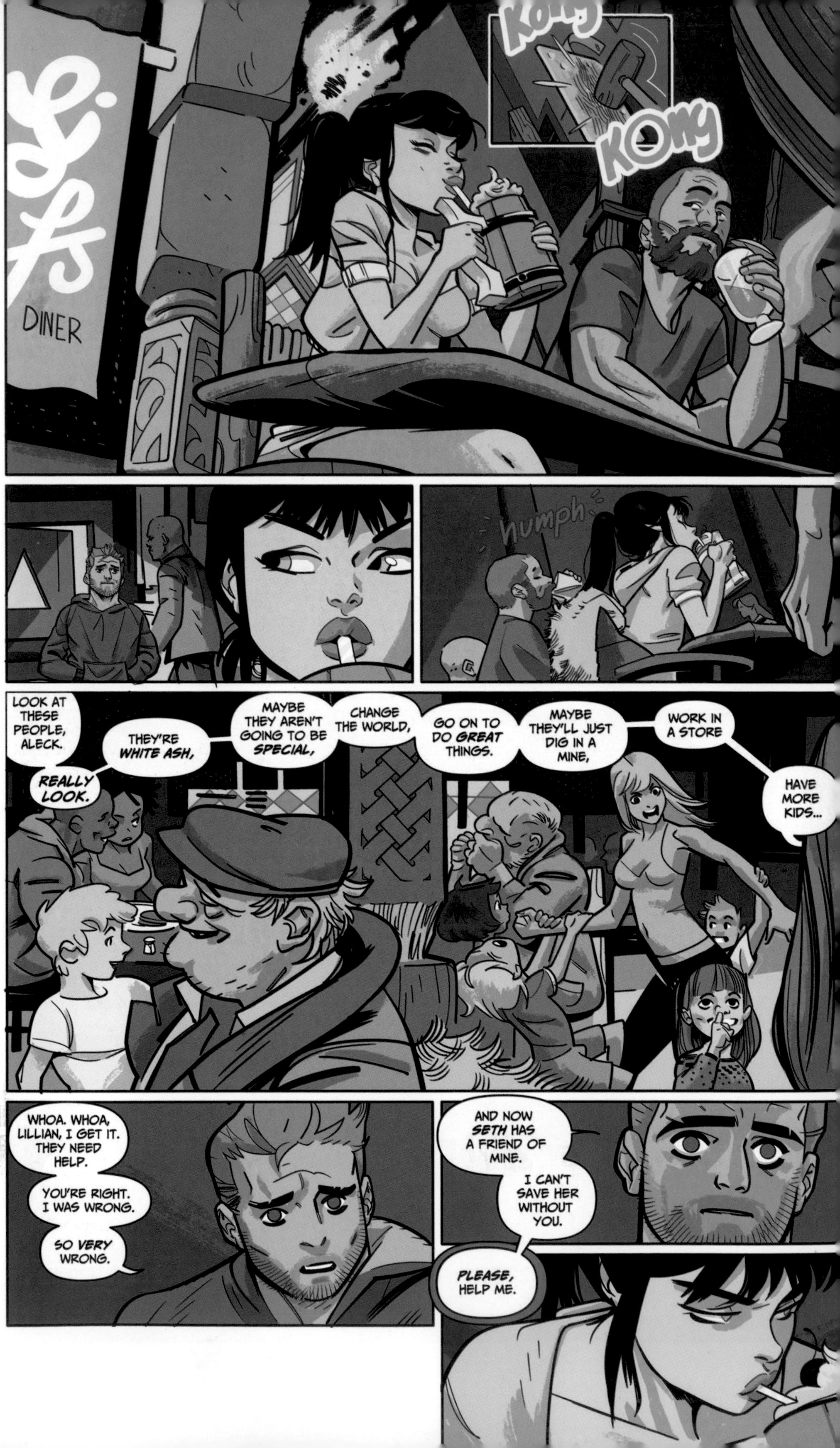
Lil's
DINER
KONG
KONG
humph
LOOK AT THESE PEOPLE, ALECK.
REALLY LOOK.
THEY'RE WHITE ASH,
MAYBE THEY AREN'T GOING TO BE SPECIAL,
CHANGE THE WORLD,
GO ON TO DO GREAT THINGS.
MAYBE THEY'LL JUST DIG IN A MINE,
WORK IN A STORE
HAVE MORE KIDS...
WHOA. WHOA, LILLIAN, I GET IT. THEY NEED HELP.
YOU'RE RIGHT. I WAS WRONG.
SO VERY WRONG.
AND NOW SETH HAS A FRIEND OF MINE.
I CAN'T SAVE HER WITHOUT YOU.
PLEASE, HELP ME.

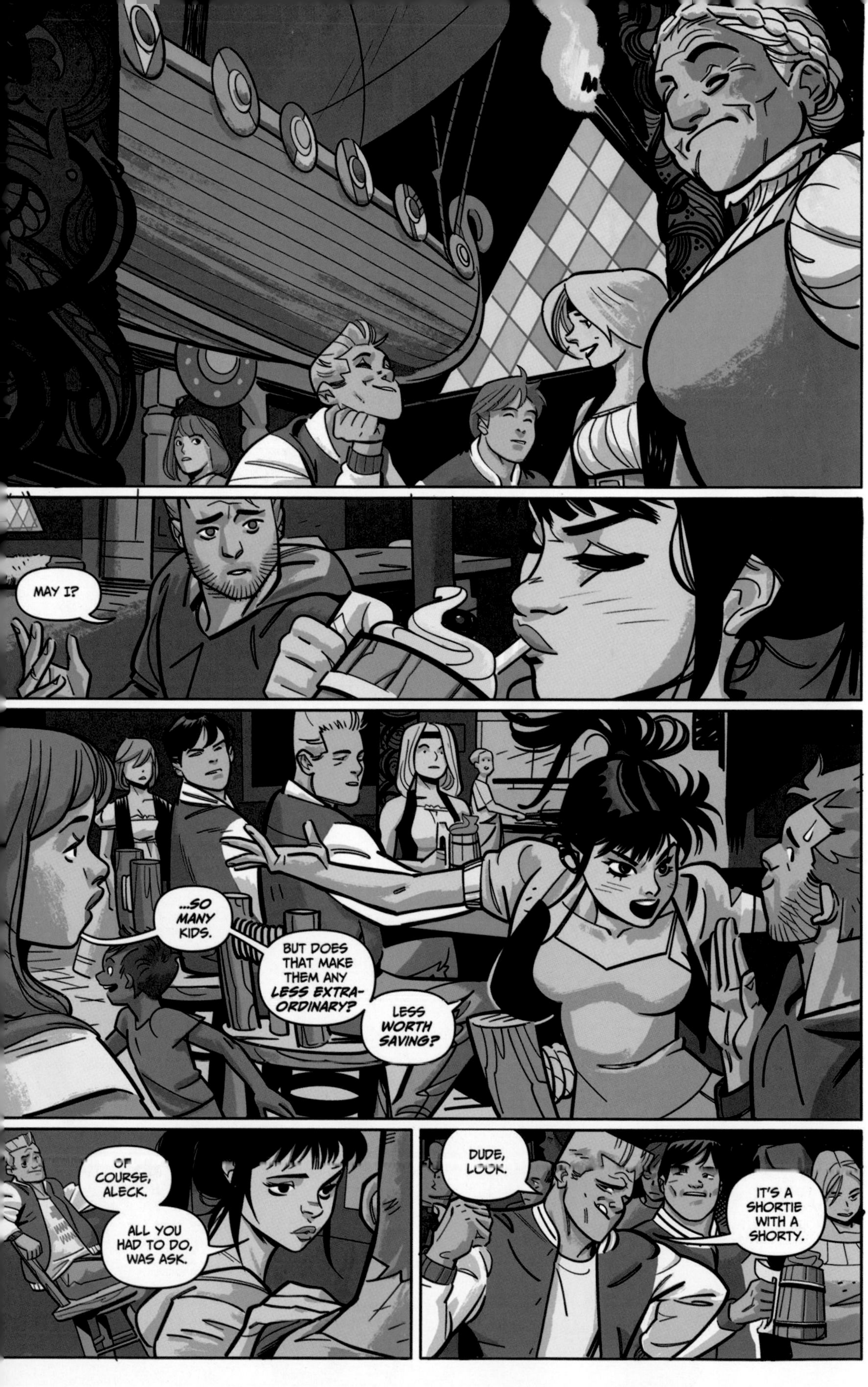
MAY I?
...SO MANY KIDS.
BUT DOES THAT MAKE THEM ANY LESS EXTRA-ORDINARY?
LESS WORTH SAVING?
OF COURSE, ALECK.
ALL YOU HAD TO DO, WAS ASK.
DUDE, LOOK.
IT'S A SHORTIE WITH A SHORTY.

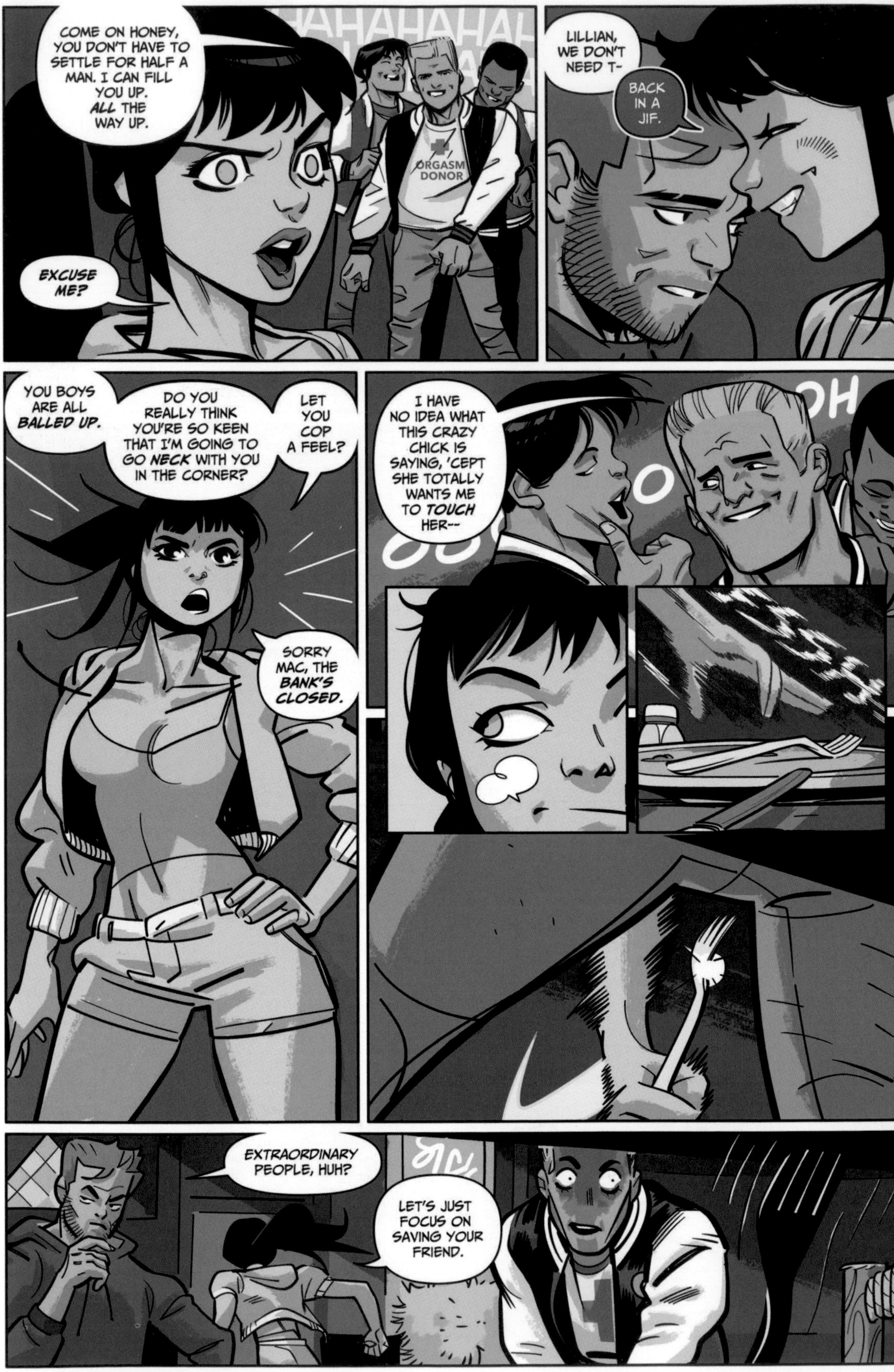
HAHAHAHAH
COME ON HONEY, YOU DON'T HAVE TO SETTLE FOR HALF A MAN. I CAN FILL YOU UP. ALL THE WAY UP.
ORGASM DONOR
EXCUSE ME?
LILLIAN, WE DON'T NEED T-
BACK IN A JIF.
YOU BOYS ARE ALL BALLED UP.
DO YOU REALLY THINK YOU'RE SO KEEN THAT I'M GOING TO GO NECK WITH YOU IN THE CORNER?
LET YOU COP A FEEL?
SORRY MAC, THE BANK'S CLOSED.
I HAVE NO IDEA WHAT THIS CRAZY CHICK IS SAYING, 'CEPT SHE TOTALLY WANTS ME TO TOUCH HER--
EXTRAORDINARY PEOPLE, HUH?
LET'S JUST FOCUS ON SAVING YOUR FRIEND.

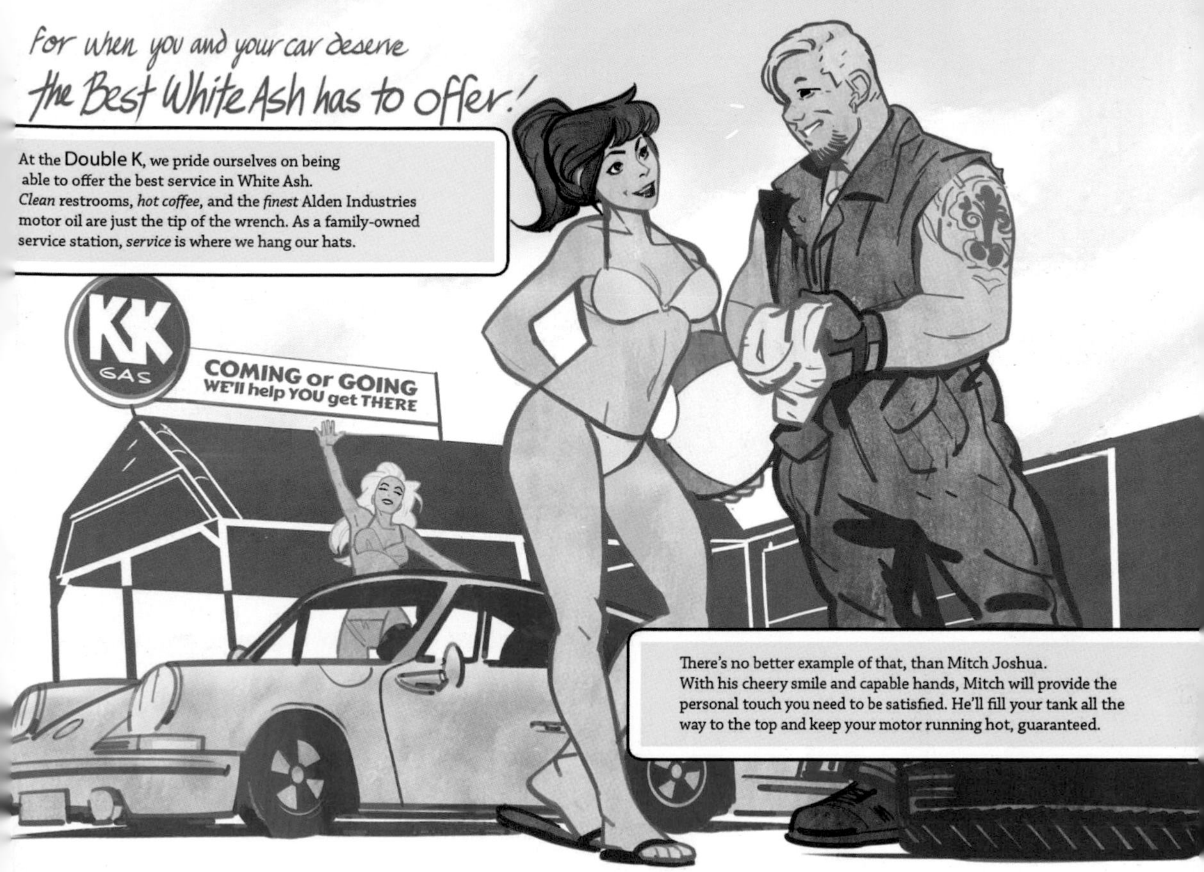

For when you and your car deserve
the Best White Ash has to offer!
At the Double K, we pride ourselves on being able to offer the best service in White Ash. *Clean* restrooms, *hot coffee*, and the *finest* Alden Industries motor oil are just the tip of the wrench. As a family-owned service station, *service* is where we hang our hats.
KK GAS
COMING or GOING
WE'll help YOU get THERE
There's no better example of that, than Mitch Joshua. With his cheery smile and capable hands, Mitch will provide the personal touch you need to be satisfied. He'll fill your tank all the way to the top and keep your motor running hot, guaranteed.

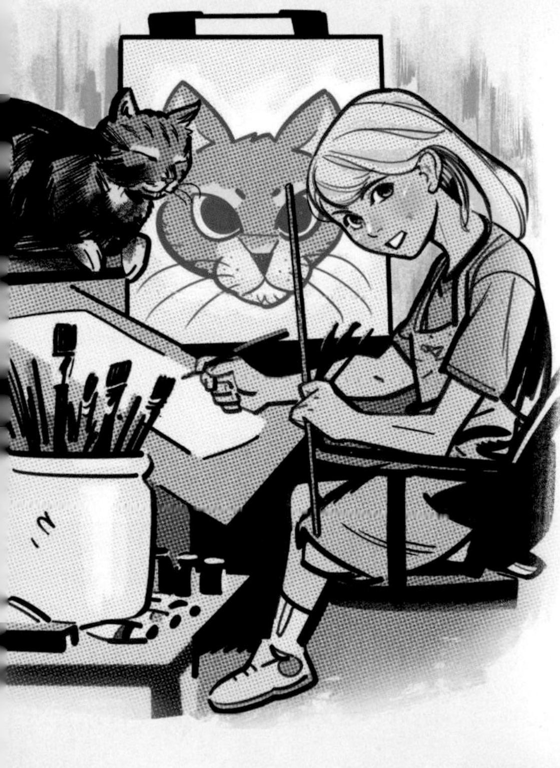

"We're looking for people who like to draw cats" says Taegan Kelley

Today, hundreds of men and women who never thought they could be artists are drawing pictures of cats. From calendars to mugs, to the occasional internet meme, they're sketching the felines and getting well paid for it. They all can thank a group of famous artists brought together by child prodigy Taegan Kelley, who have devoted much of their time and talent to helping others find success in cat art.

Some of the people the Famous Cat Artists have helped

Jon Webb was 44 year old computer programer slogging his way though arrays and files when he enrolled. Today he's responsible for some of the grumpiest cat-related online content.

Chad Gervich of Iowa took The Course while being a stay-at-home dad. Now his exhibits are some of the most sought out on the Venice Boardwalk.

Before her Famous Cat Artists training, Ashley Russell was trapped in a dead-end job manufacturing alarm clock parts. Now her paintings of Siamese Cats are the sixth most popular cat-related art on etsy.

A plan to help others make cats

It started over two years ago when Taegan asked her father, "Why aren't more people drawing cats?" Teagan envisioned a new kind of school with coursework devoted to whiskers, paws, and various expressions of aloof disinterest. She reached out to some of the most famous cat artists in the business and they all agreed, the world needed more cat illustrations.

Famous Cat Artists Talent Test

To find others with Cat Art talent worth developing, the Famous Cat Artists created a 16-page Talent Test. Millions have paid to take this test, but now The School offers and grades it for free. Men and women who do well on the test… or well enough/ just have the money, may enroll in The School. But there is no obligation. Simply mail the coupon.

Founding Faculty of the Famous Cat Artists School

Taegan Kelley
Norman Rockwell
Bill Watterson
George Gately
Jim Davis

Famous Cat Artists School
Studio A 666
White Ash, PA 15091

I would like to find out whether I have cat art talent worth developing. Please send me, without obligation, your Famous Cat Artist Talent Test and information about your courses.

Mr.
Ms.
Street__________________Apt. #_____
City________
State________________
Age________ Zip_________

Accredited by the Accrediting Commission.

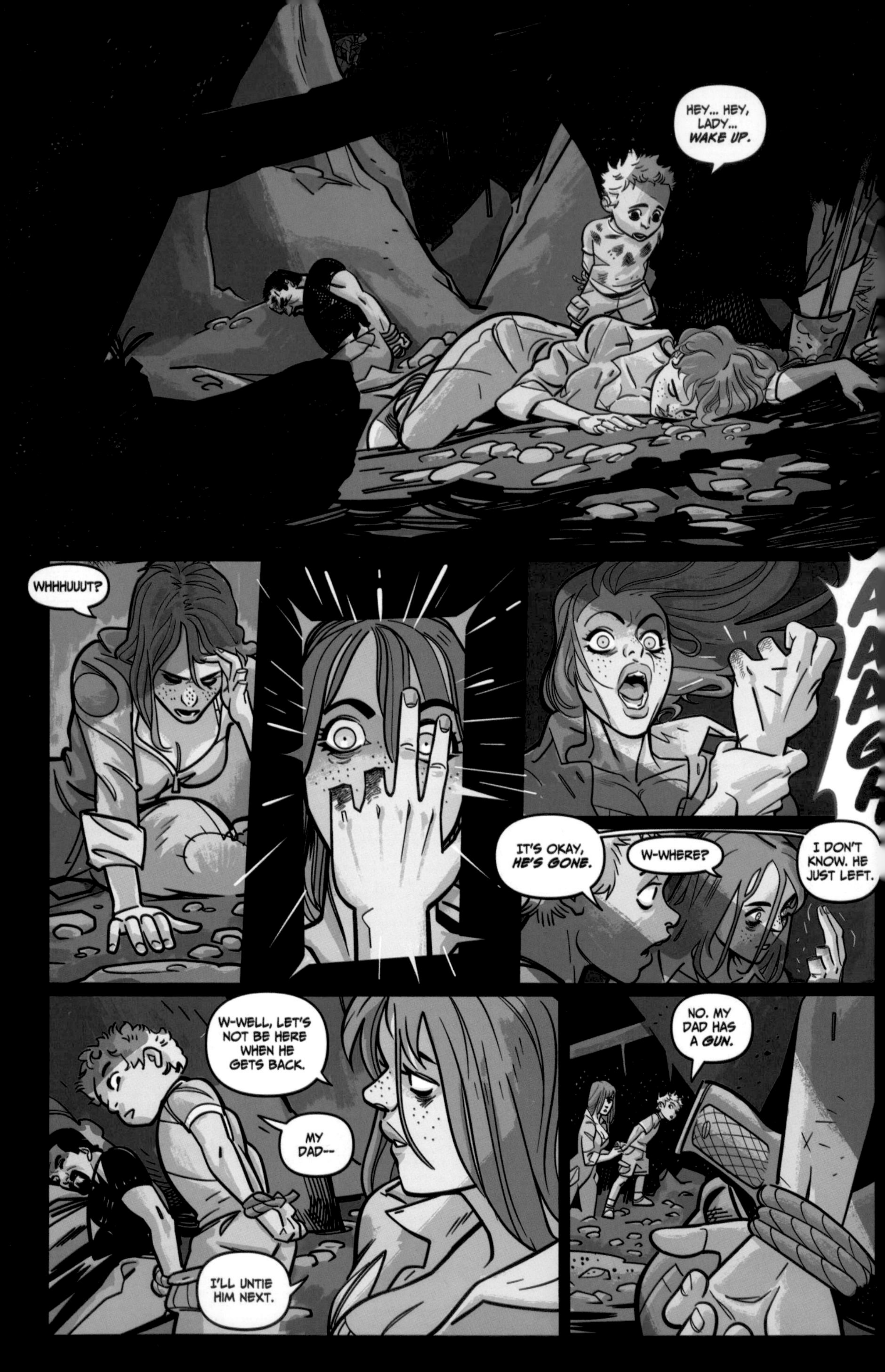
HEY... HEY, LADY... WAKE UP.
WHHHUUUT?
AAAGH
IT'S OKAY, HE'S GONE.
W-WHERE?
I DON'T KNOW. HE JUST LEFT.
W-WELL, LET'S NOT BE HERE WHEN HE GETS BACK.
MY DAD--
I'LL UNTIE HIM NEXT.
NO. MY DAD HAS A GUN.

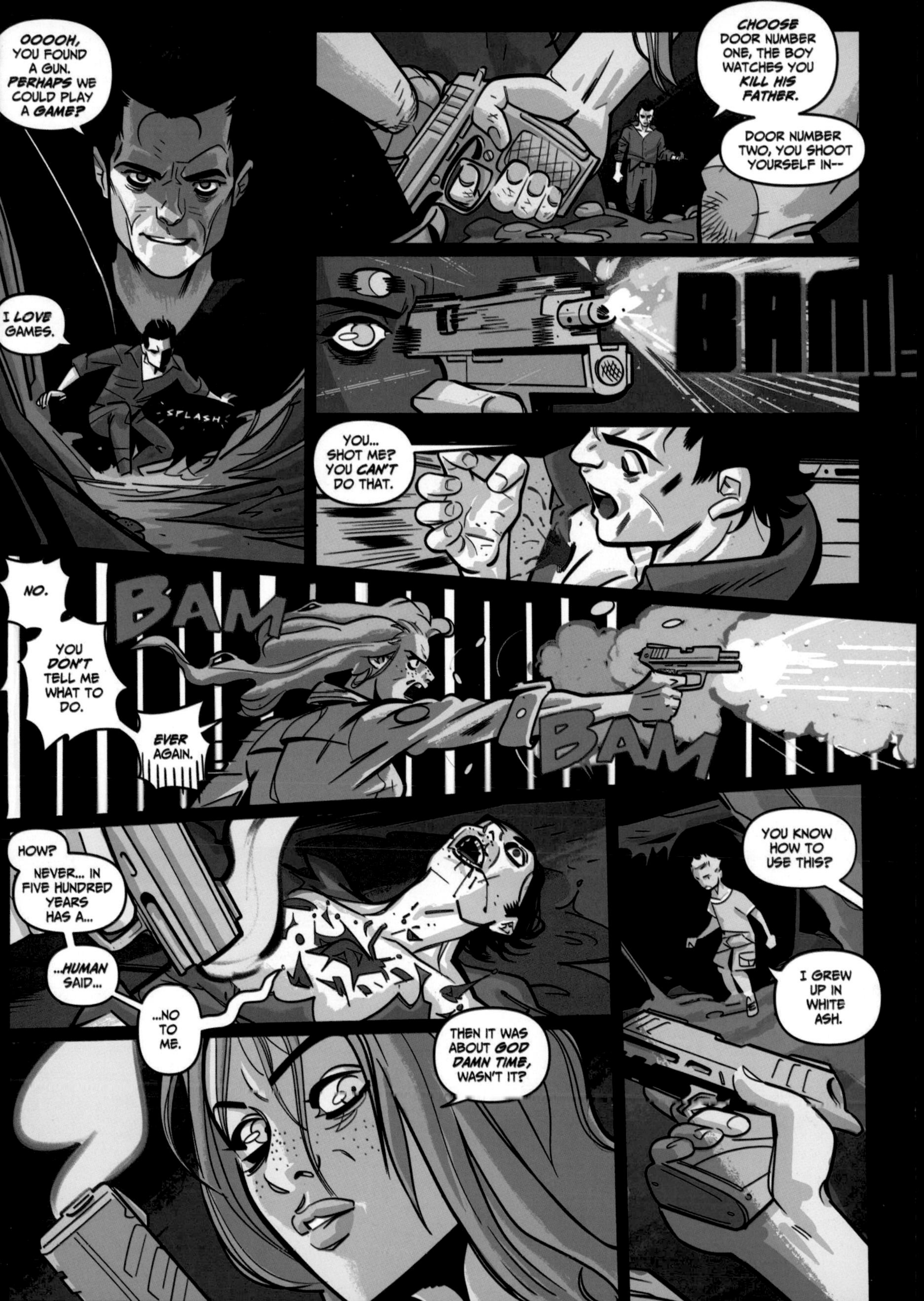
OOOOH, YOU FOUND A GUN. PERHAPS WE COULD PLAY A GAME?
I LOVE GAMES.
SPLASH
CHOOSE DOOR NUMBER ONE, THE BOY WATCHES YOU KILL HIS FATHER.
DOOR NUMBER TWO, YOU SHOOT YOURSELF IN--
BAM
YOU... SHOT ME? YOU CAN'T DO THAT.
NO.
BAM
YOU DON'T TELL ME WHAT TO DO.
EVER AGAIN.
BAM
HOW?
NEVER... IN FIVE HUNDRED YEARS HAS A...
...HUMAN SAID...
...NO TO ME.
THEN IT WAS ABOUT GOD DAMN TIME, WASN'T IT?
YOU KNOW HOW TO USE THIS?
I GREW UP IN WHITE ASH.

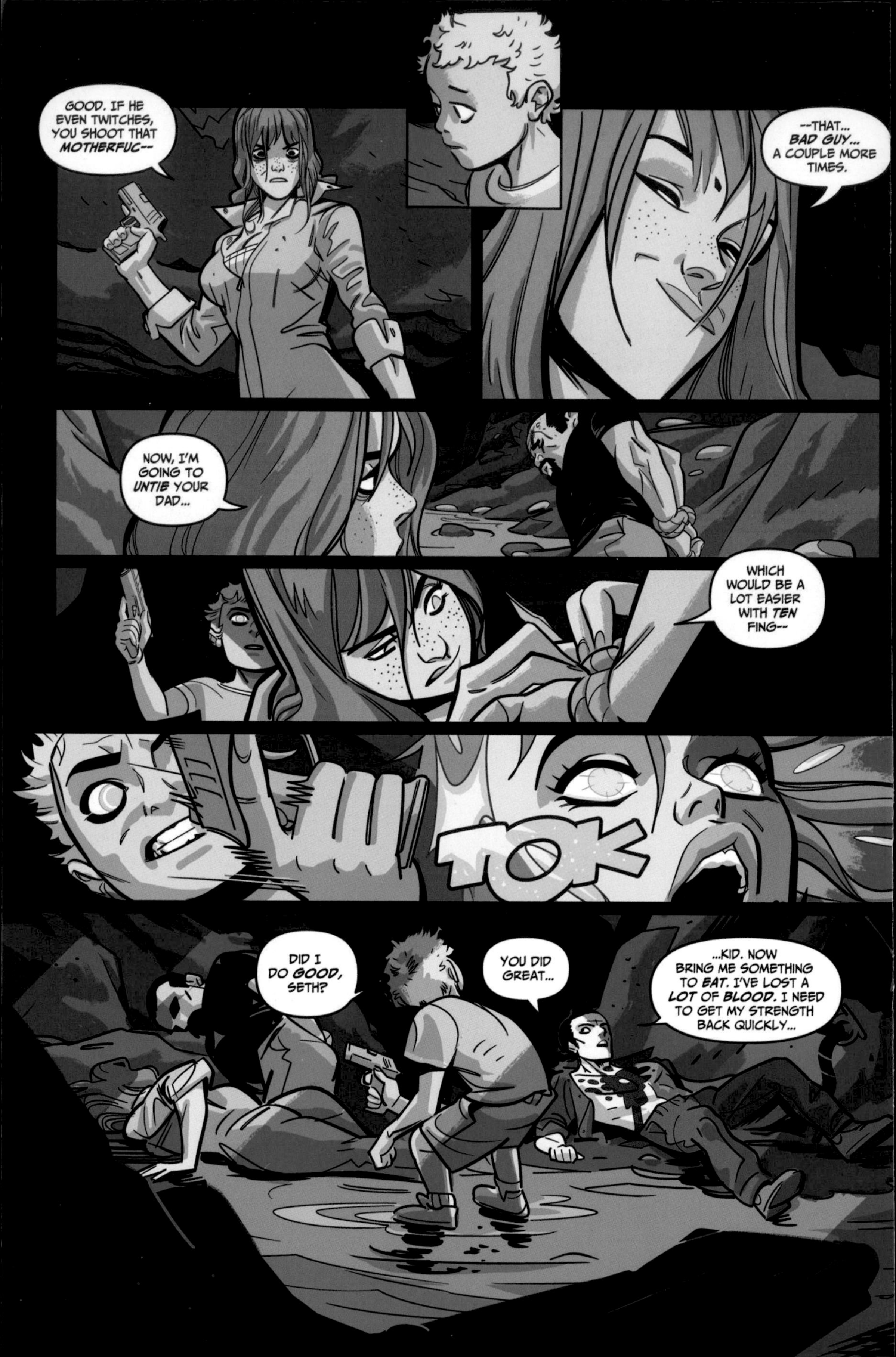
GOOD. IF HE EVEN TWITCHES, YOU SHOOT THAT *MOTHERFUC--*
--THAT... *BAD GUY...* A COUPLE MORE TIMES.
NOW, I'M GOING TO *UNTIE* YOUR DAD...
WHICH WOULD BE A LOT EASIER WITH *TEN* FING--
TOK
DID I DO *GOOD,* SETH?
YOU DID GREAT...
...KID. NOW BRING ME SOMETHING TO *EAT.* I'VE LOST A *LOT OF BLOOD.* I NEED TO GET MY STRENGTH BACK QUICKLY...

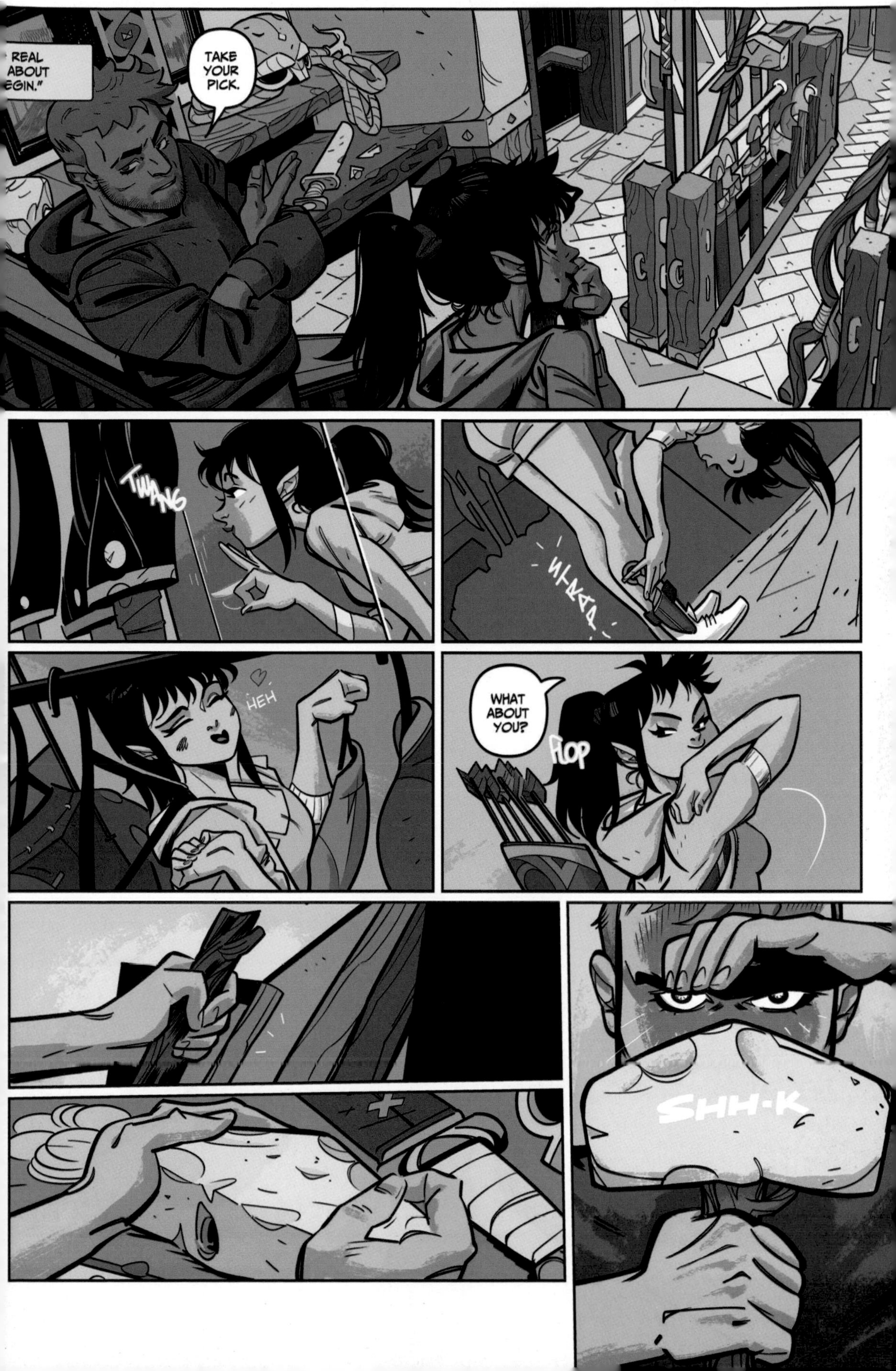

REAL ABOUT EGIN."
TAKE YOUR PICK.
TWANG
HEH
WHAT ABOUT YOU?
FLOP
SHH-K

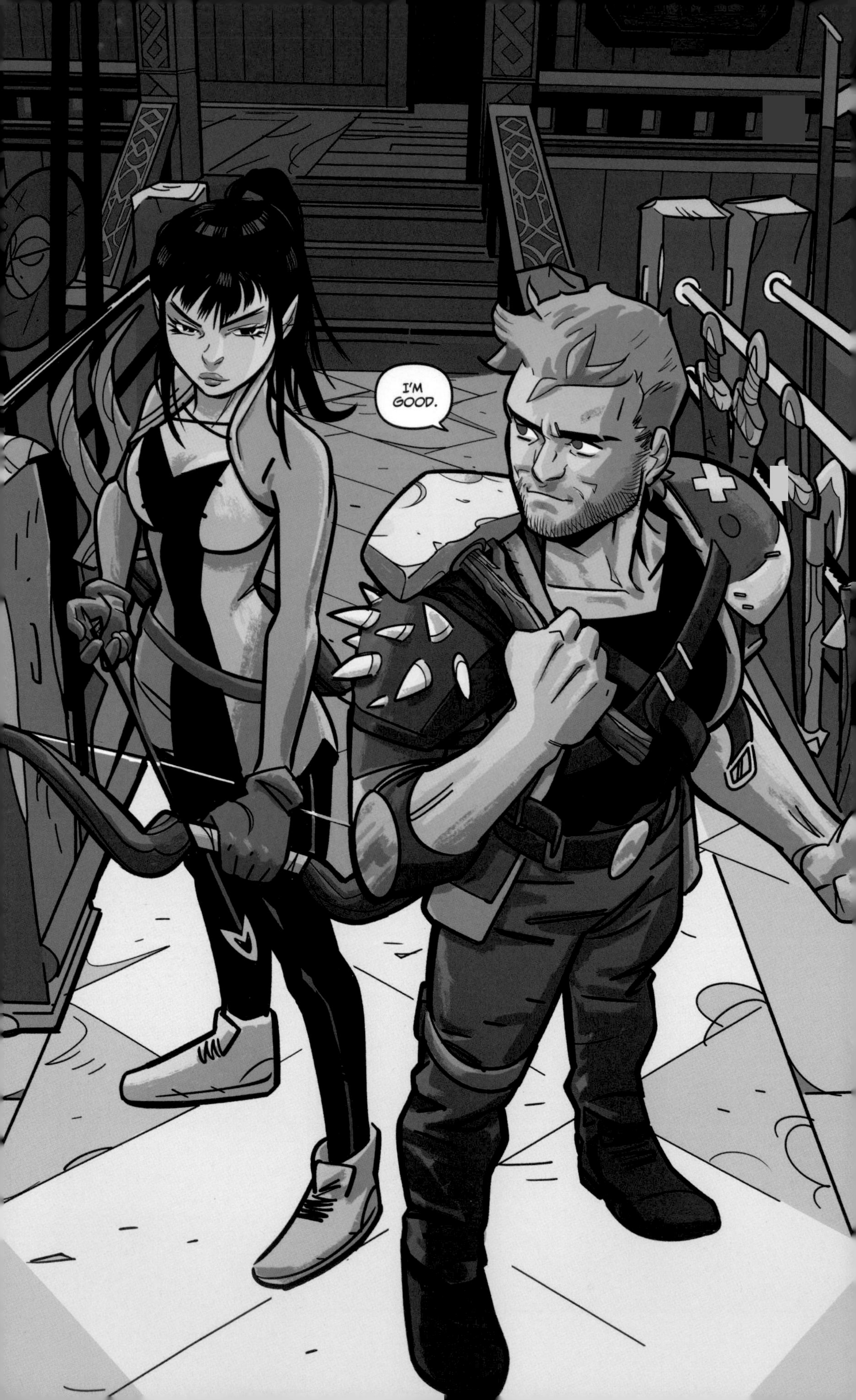
I'M GOOD.

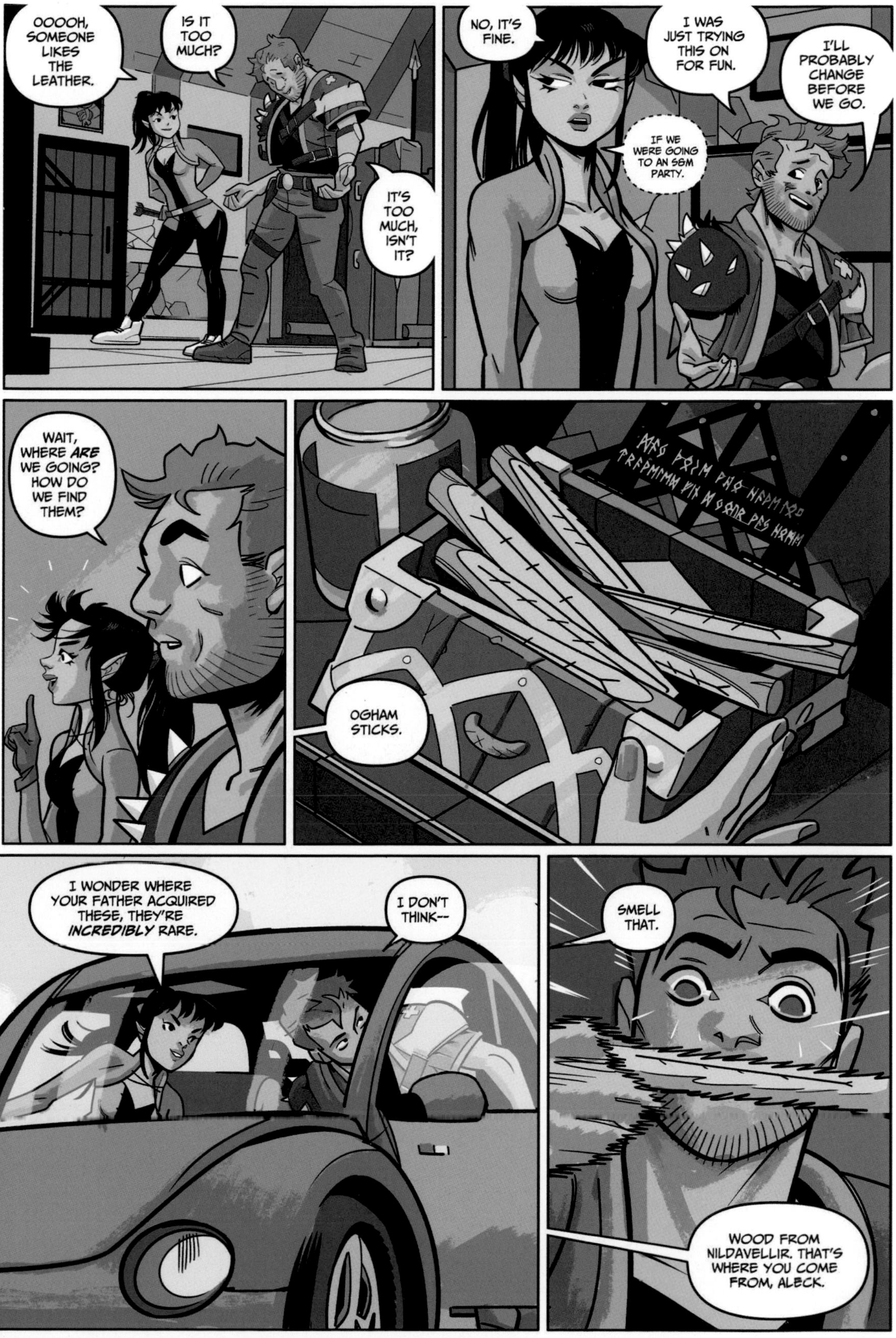
OOOOH, SOMEONE LIKES THE LEATHER.
IS IT TOO MUCH?
IT'S TOO MUCH, ISN'T IT?
NO, IT'S FINE.
IF WE WERE GOING TO AN S&M PARTY.
I WAS JUST TRYING THIS ON FOR FUN.
I'LL PROBABLY CHANGE BEFORE WE GO.
WAIT, WHERE *ARE* WE GOING? HOW DO WE FIND THEM?
OGHAM STICKS.
I WONDER WHERE YOUR FATHER ACQUIRED THESE, THEY'RE *INCREDIBLY* RARE.
I DON'T THINK--
SMELL THAT.
WOOD FROM NILDAVELLIR. THAT'S WHERE YOU COME FROM, ALECK.

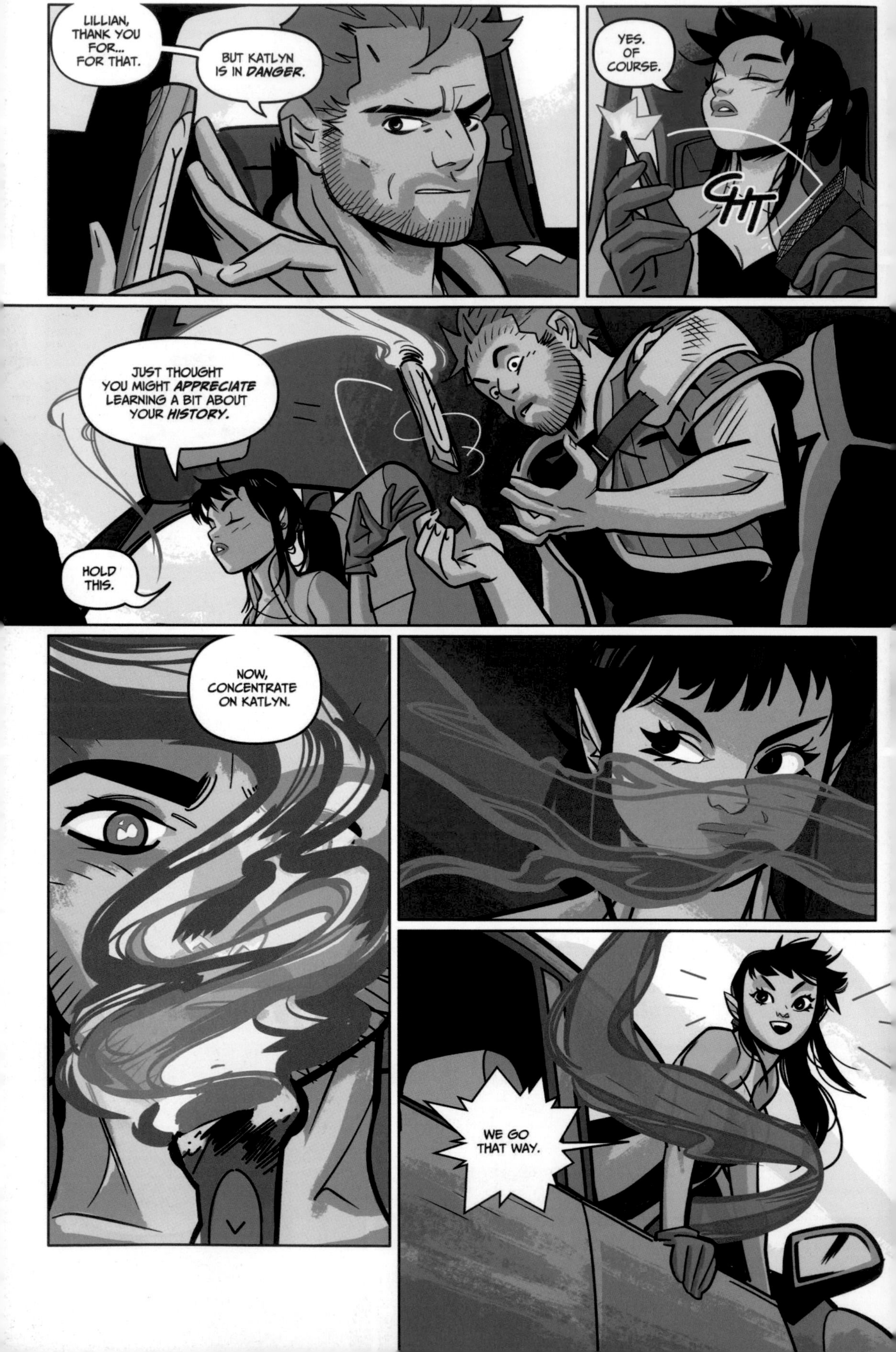
LILLIAN, THANK YOU FOR... FOR THAT.
BUT KATLYN IS IN *DANGER*.
YES. OF COURSE.
CHT
JUST THOUGHT YOU MIGHT *APPRECIATE* LEARNING A BIT ABOUT YOUR *HISTORY*.
HOLD THIS.
NOW, CONCENTRATE ON KATLYN.
WE GO THAT WAY.

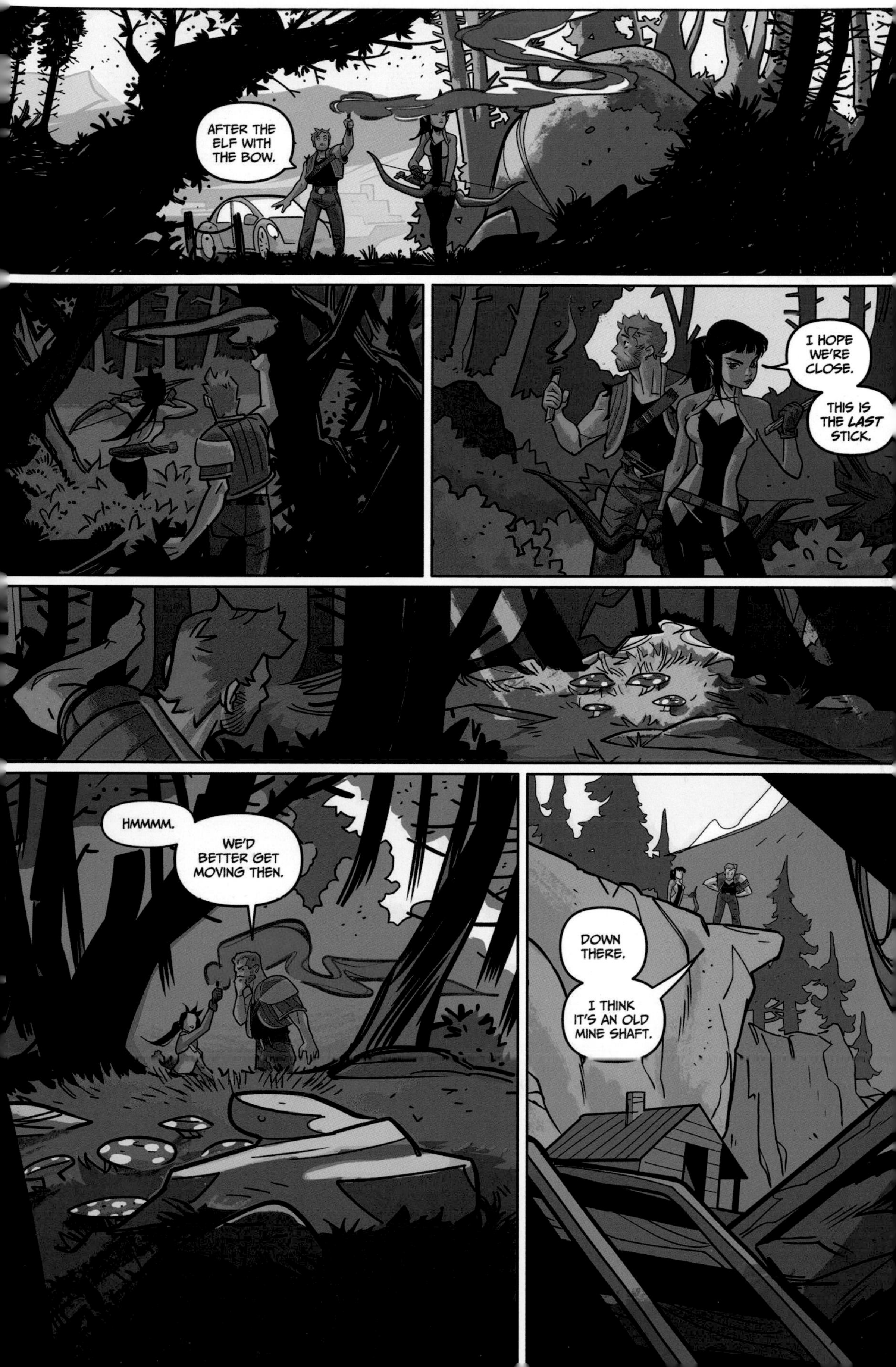
AFTER THE ELF WITH THE BOW.
I HOPE WE'RE CLOSE.
THIS IS THE *LAST* STICK.
HMMMM.
WE'D BETTER GET MOVING THEN.
DOWN THERE.
I THINK IT'S AN OLD MINE SHAFT.

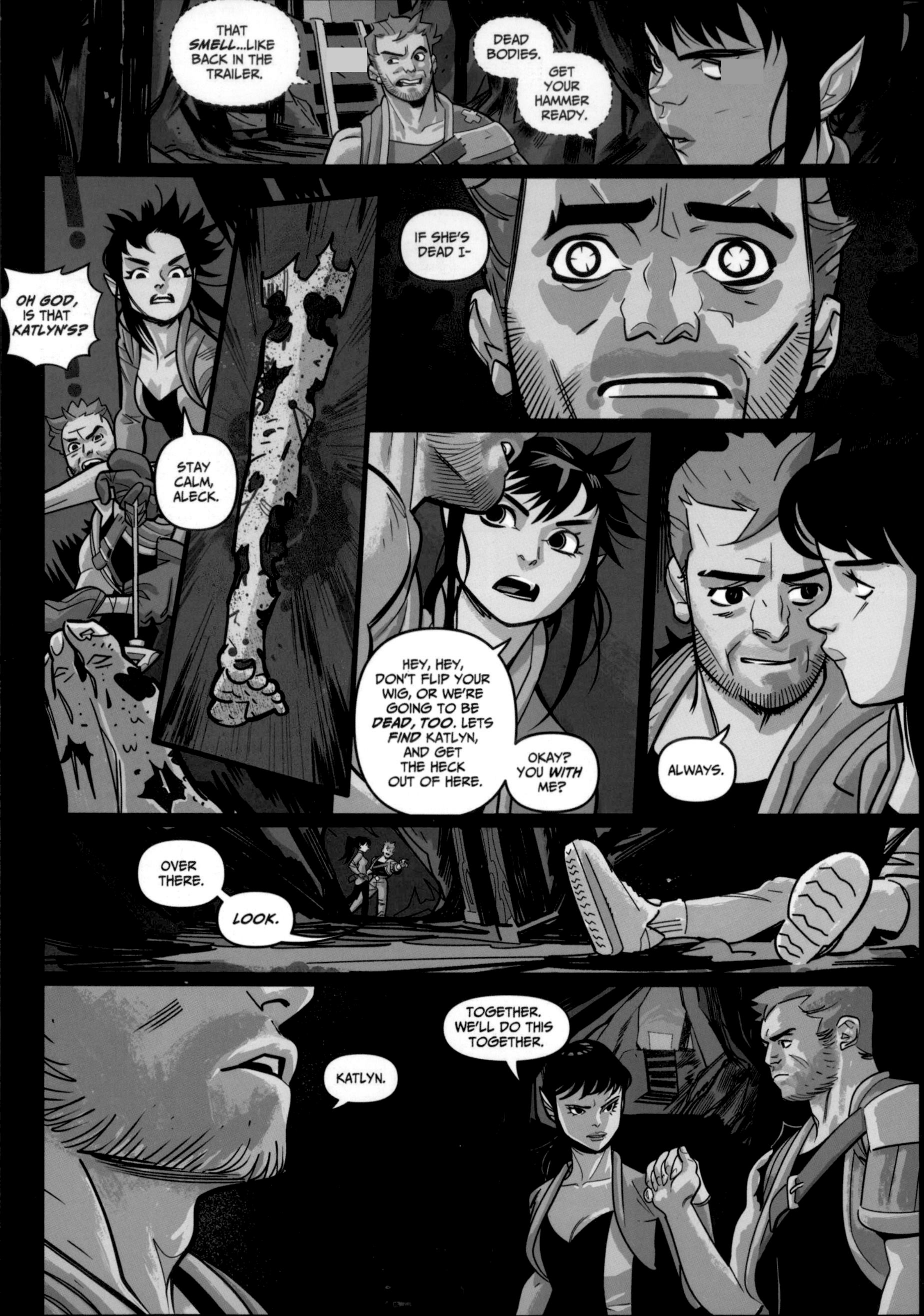
THAT SMELL...LIKE BACK IN THE TRAILER.
DEAD BODIES.
GET YOUR HAMMER READY.
OH GOD, IS THAT KATLYN'S?
STAY CALM, ALECK.
IF SHE'S DEAD I-
HEY, HEY, DON'T FLIP YOUR WIG, OR WE'RE GOING TO BE DEAD, TOO. LETS FIND KATLYN, AND GET THE HECK OUT OF HERE.
OKAY? YOU WITH ME?
ALWAYS.
OVER THERE.
LOOK.
KATLYN.
TOGETHER. WE'LL DO THIS TOGETHER.

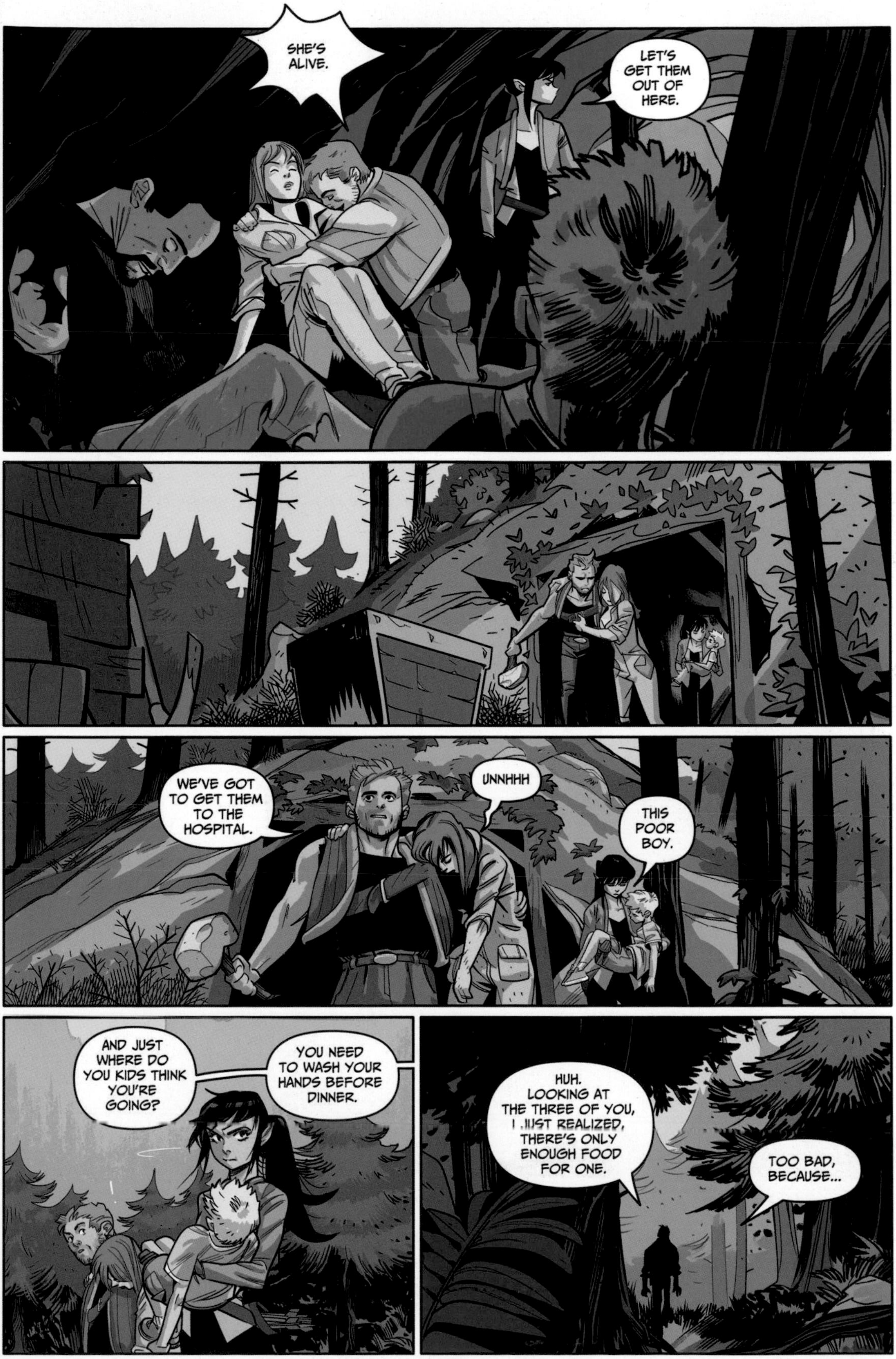
SHE'S ALIVE.
LET'S GET THEM OUT OF HERE.
WE'VE GOT TO GET THEM TO THE HOSPITAL.
UNNHHH
THIS POOR BOY.
AND JUST WHERE DO YOU KIDS THINK YOU'RE GOING?
YOU NEED TO WASH YOUR HANDS BEFORE DINNER.
HUH. LOOKING AT THE THREE OF YOU, I JUST REALIZED, THERE'S ONLY ENOUGH FOOD FOR ONE.
TOO BAD, BECAUSE...

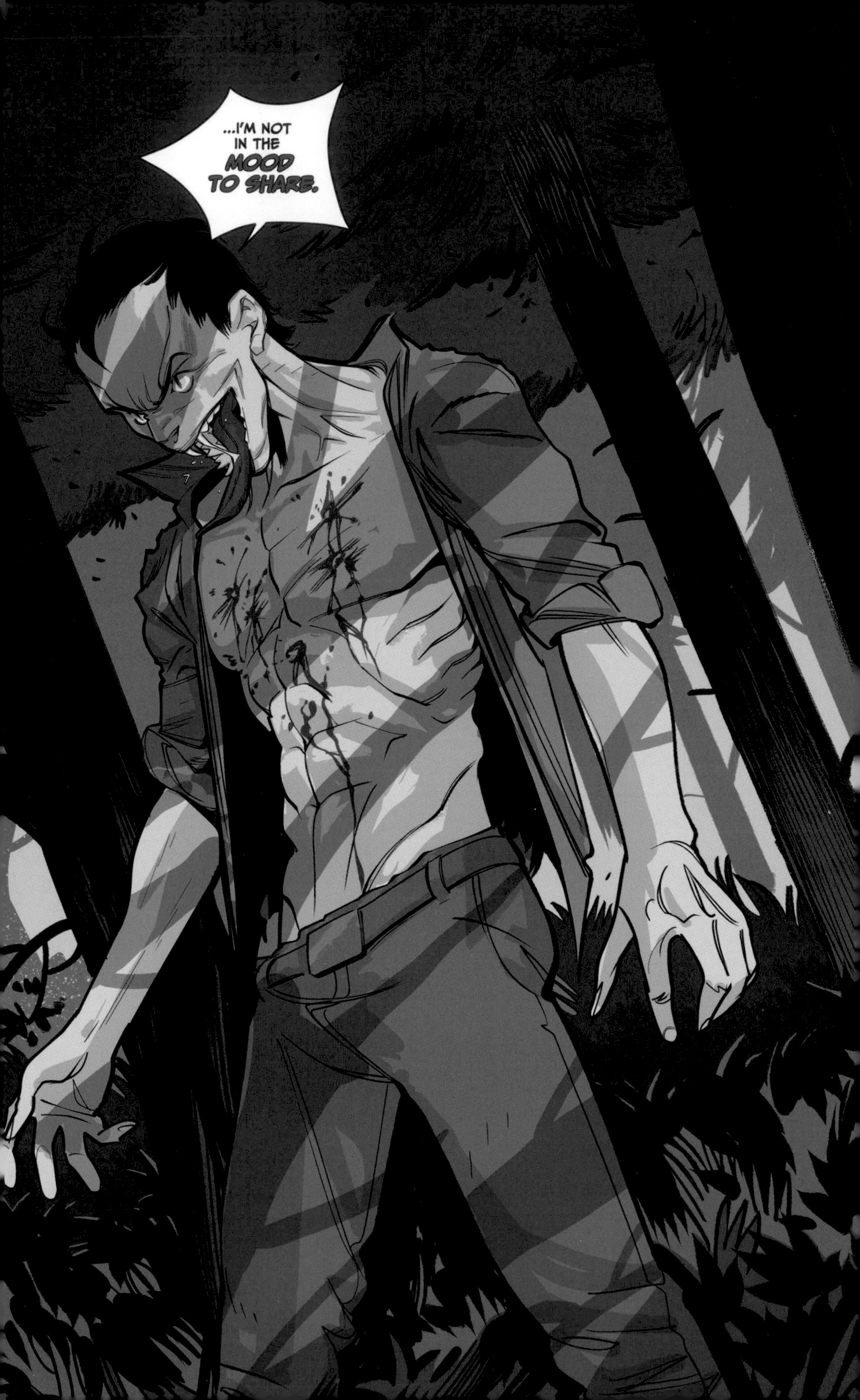
...I'M NOT IN THE MOOD TO SHARE.

CHAPTER SIX

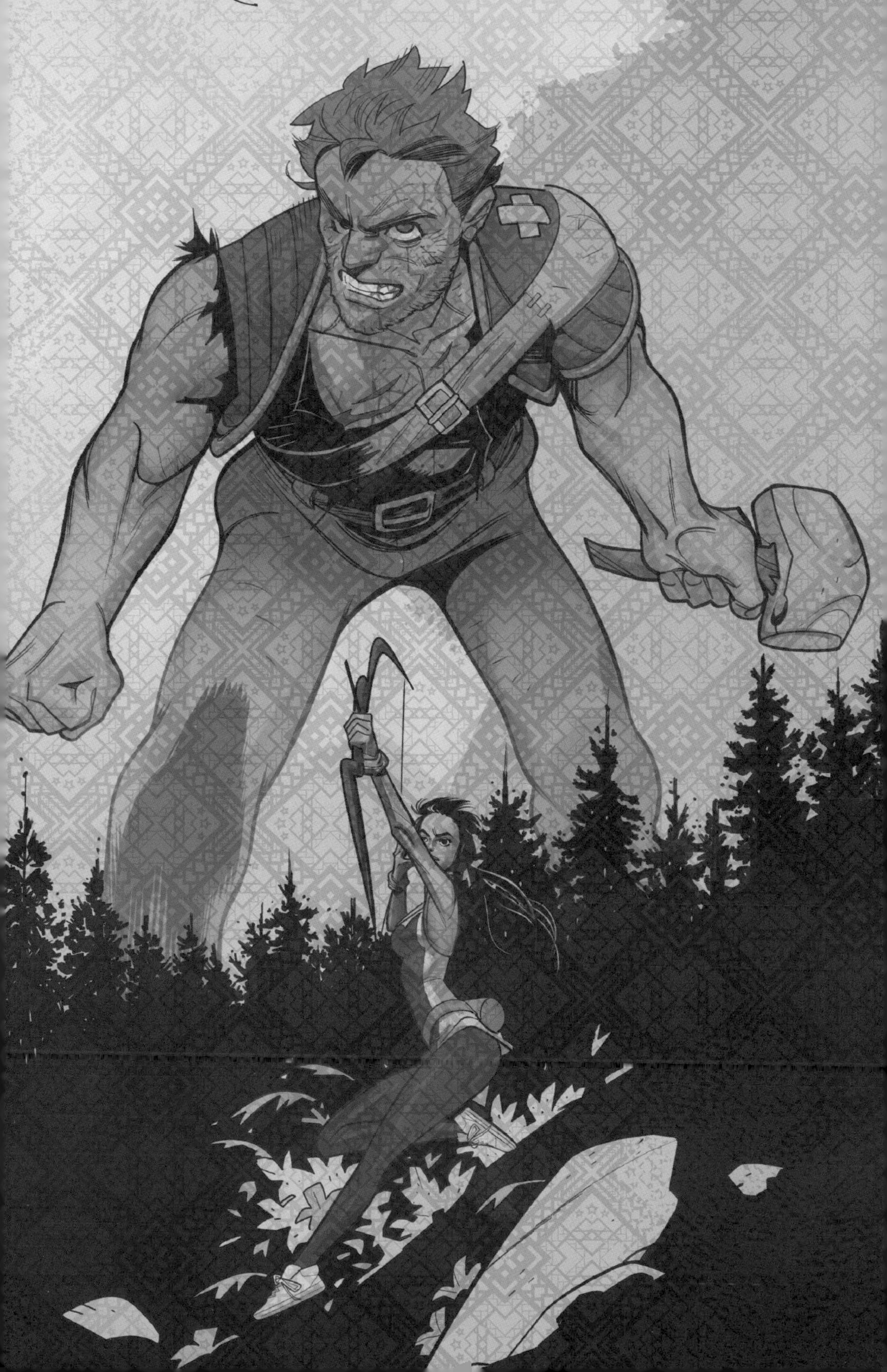

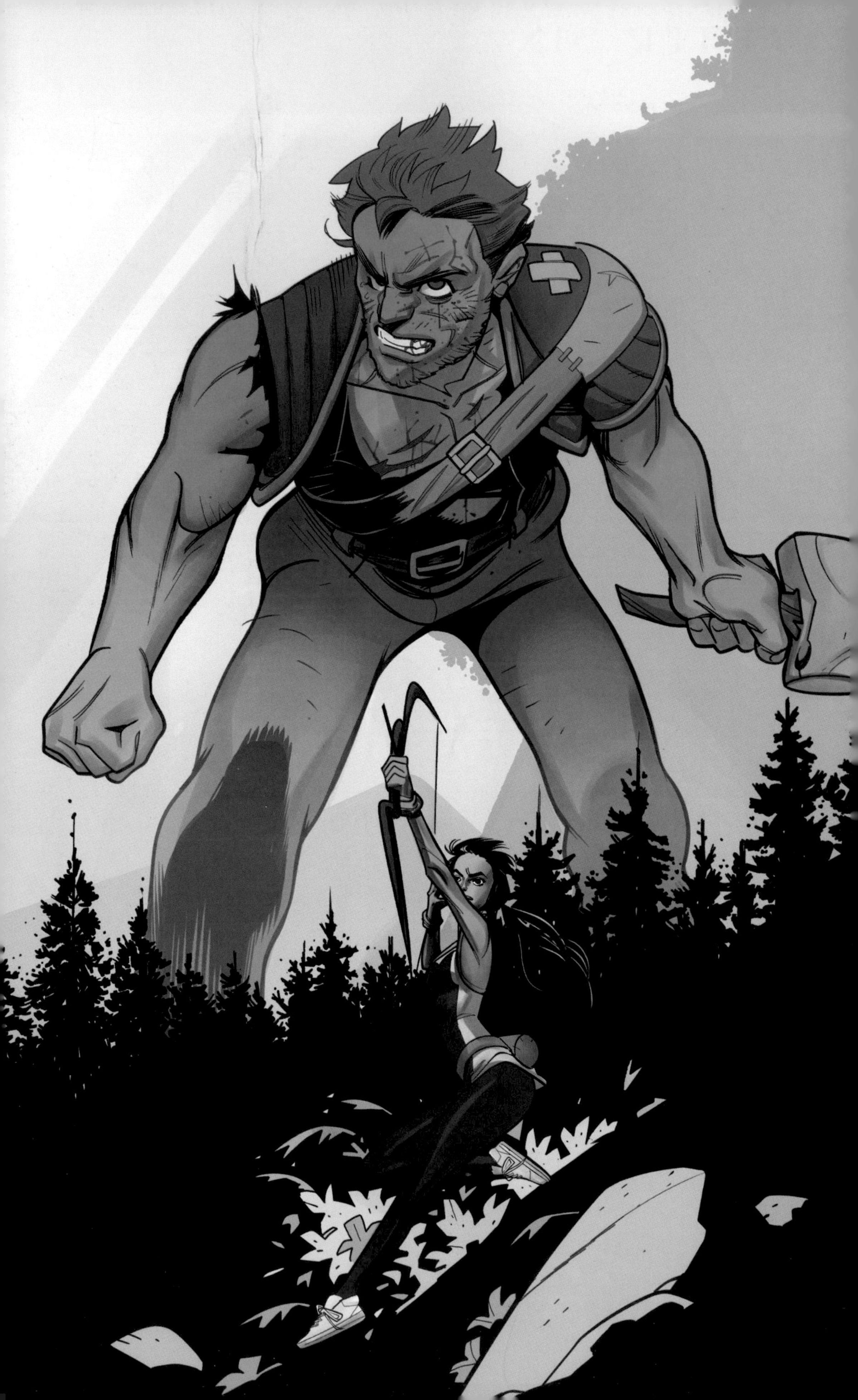

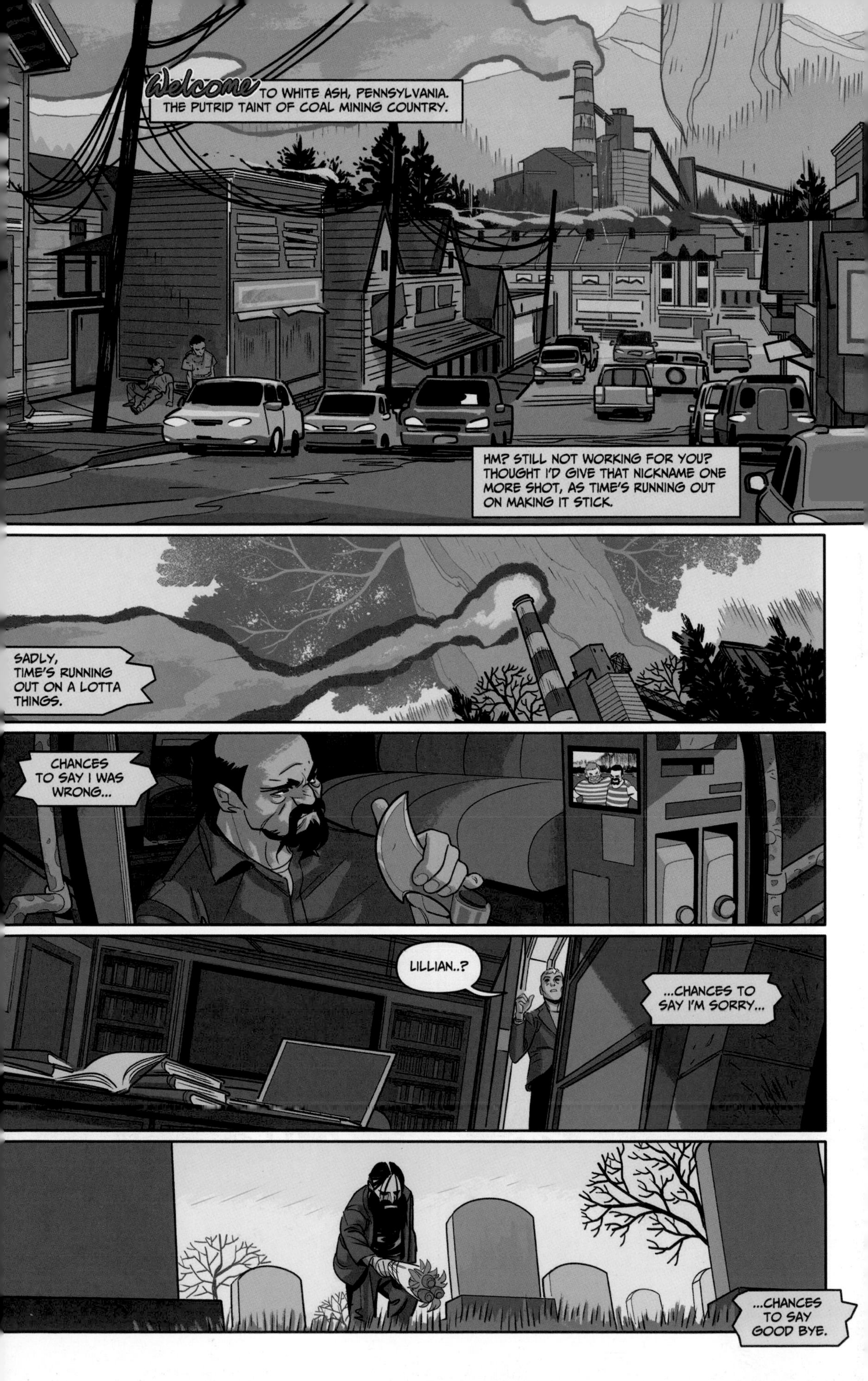
Welcome TO WHITE ASH, PENNSYLVANIA. THE PUTRID TAINT OF COAL MINING COUNTRY.
HM? STILL NOT WORKING FOR YOU? THOUGHT I'D GIVE THAT NICKNAME ONE MORE SHOT, AS TIME'S RUNNING OUT ON MAKING IT STICK.
SADLY, TIME'S RUNNING OUT ON A LOTTA THINGS.
CHANCES TO SAY I WAS WRONG...
LILLIAN..?
...CHANCES TO SAY I'M SORRY...
...CHANCES TO SAY GOOD BYE.

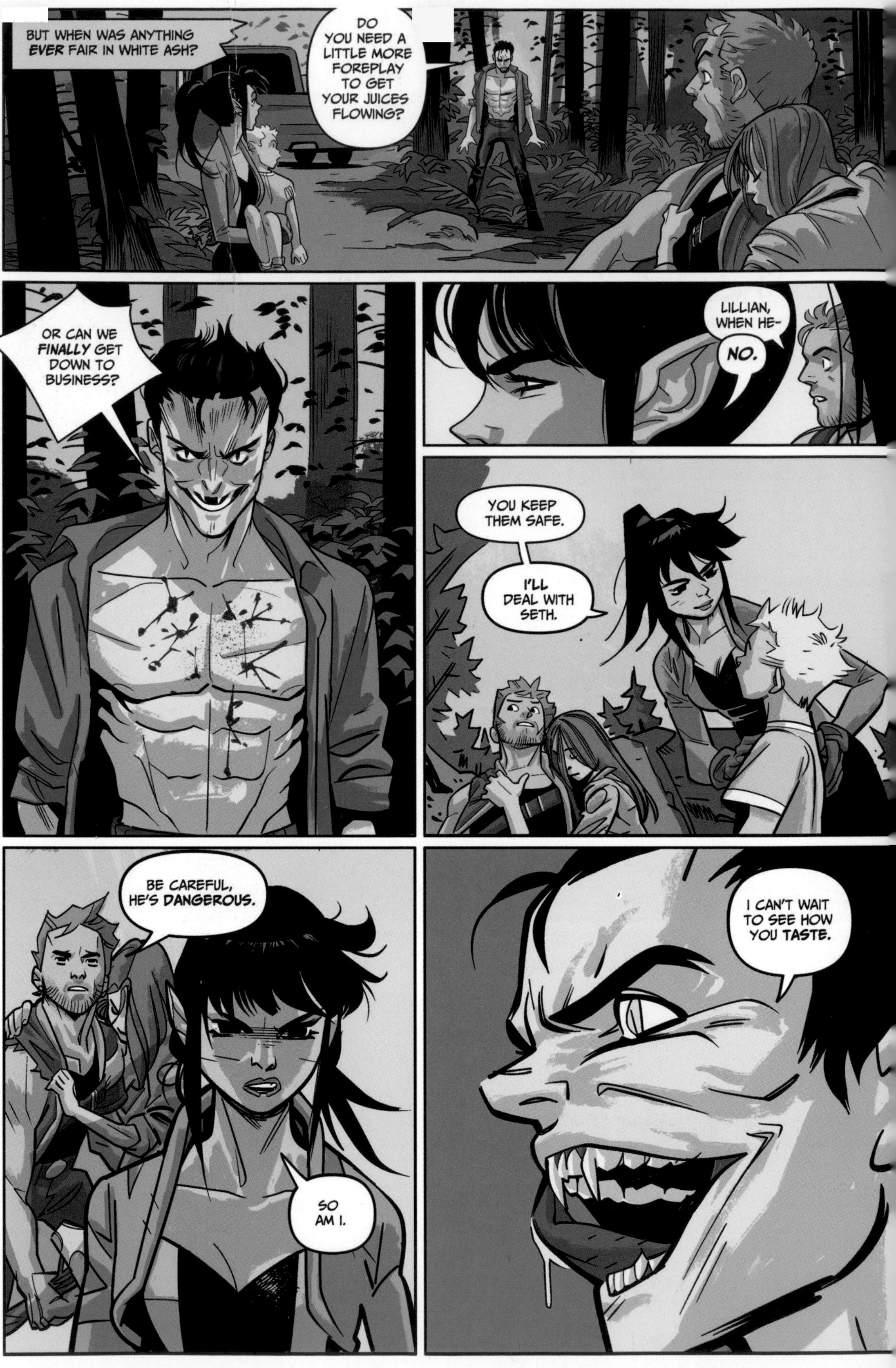

BUT WHEN WAS ANYTHING EVER FAIR IN WHITE ASH?
DO YOU NEED A LITTLE MORE FOREPLAY TO GET YOUR JUICES FLOWING?
OR CAN WE FINALLY GET DOWN TO BUSINESS?
LILLIAN, WHEN HE-
NO.
YOU KEEP THEM SAFE.
I'LL DEAL WITH SETH.
BE CAREFUL, HE'S DANGEROUS.
SO AM I.
I CAN'T WAIT TO SEE HOW YOU TASTE.

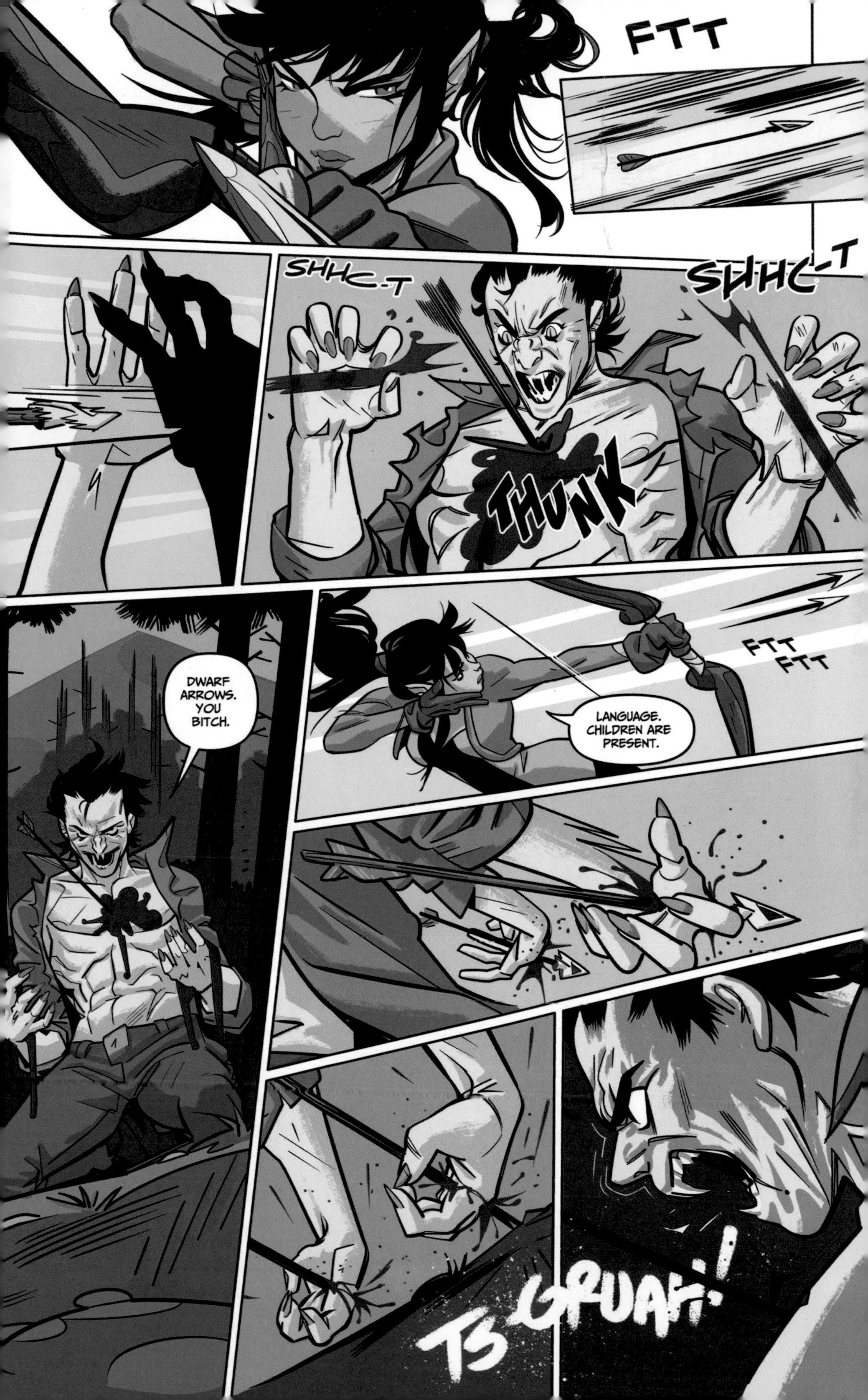

FTT
SHHC-T
SHHC-T
THUNK
DWARF ARROWS. YOU BITCH.
FTT FTT
LANGUAGE. CHILDREN ARE PRESENT.
TS GRUAH!

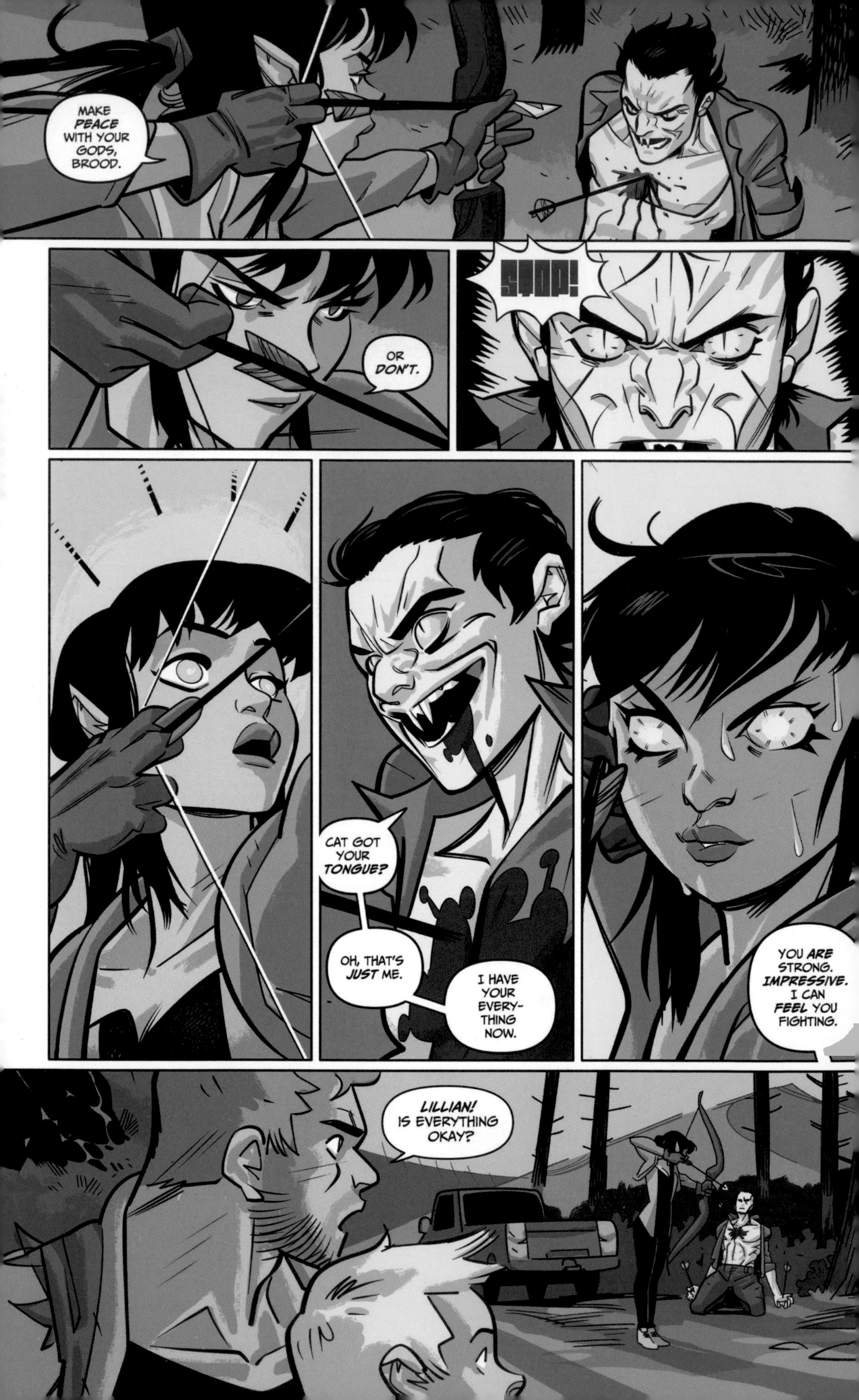
MAKE PEACE WITH YOUR GODS, BROOD.
OR DON'T.
STOP!
CAT GOT YOUR TONGUE?
OH, THAT'S JUST ME.
I HAVE YOUR EVERY-THING NOW.
YOU ARE STRONG. IMPRESSIVE. I CAN FEEL YOU FIGHTING.
LILLIAN! IS EVERYTHING OKAY?

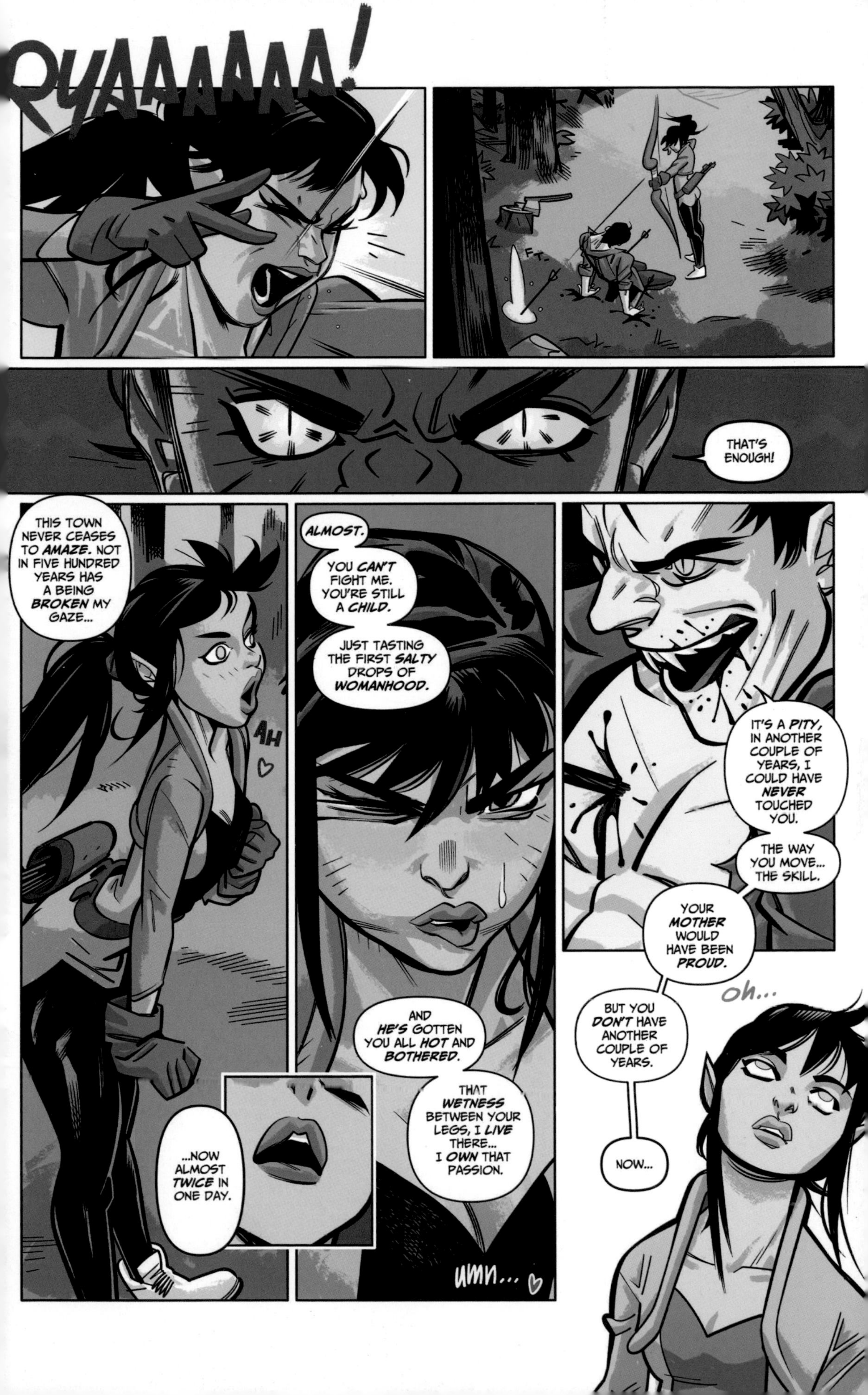
RYAAAAAAA!
F-T.
THAT'S ENOUGH!
THIS TOWN NEVER CEASES TO AMAZE. NOT IN FIVE HUNDRED YEARS HAS A BEING BROKEN MY GAZE...
AH ♡
...NOW ALMOST TWICE IN ONE DAY.
ALMOST.
YOU CAN'T FIGHT ME. YOU'RE STILL A CHILD.
JUST TASTING THE FIRST SALTY DROPS OF WOMANHOOD.
AND HE'S GOTTEN YOU ALL HOT AND BOTHERED.
THAT WETNESS BETWEEN YOUR LEGS, I LIVE THERE... I OWN THAT PASSION.
umn... ♡
IT'S A PITY, IN ANOTHER COUPLE OF YEARS, I COULD HAVE NEVER TOUCHED YOU.
THE WAY YOU MOVE... THE SKILL.
YOUR MOTHER WOULD HAVE BEEN PROUD.
BUT YOU DON'T HAVE ANOTHER COUPLE OF YEARS.
NOW...
oh...

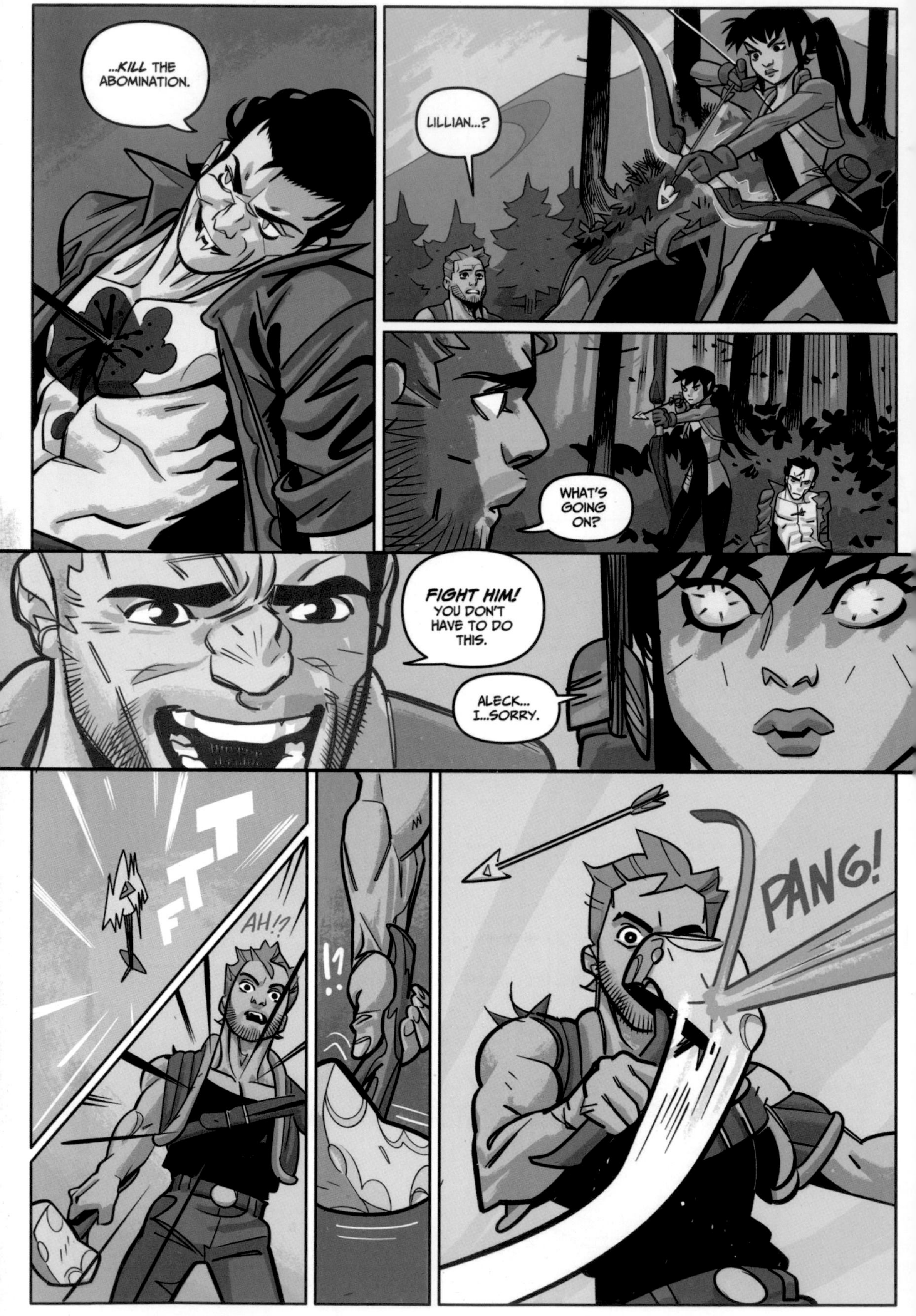
...KILL THE ABOMINATION.
LILLIAN...?
WHAT'S GOING ON?
FIGHT HIM! YOU DON'T HAVE TO DO THIS.
ALECK... I...SORRY.
FTT
AH!?
!?
PANG!

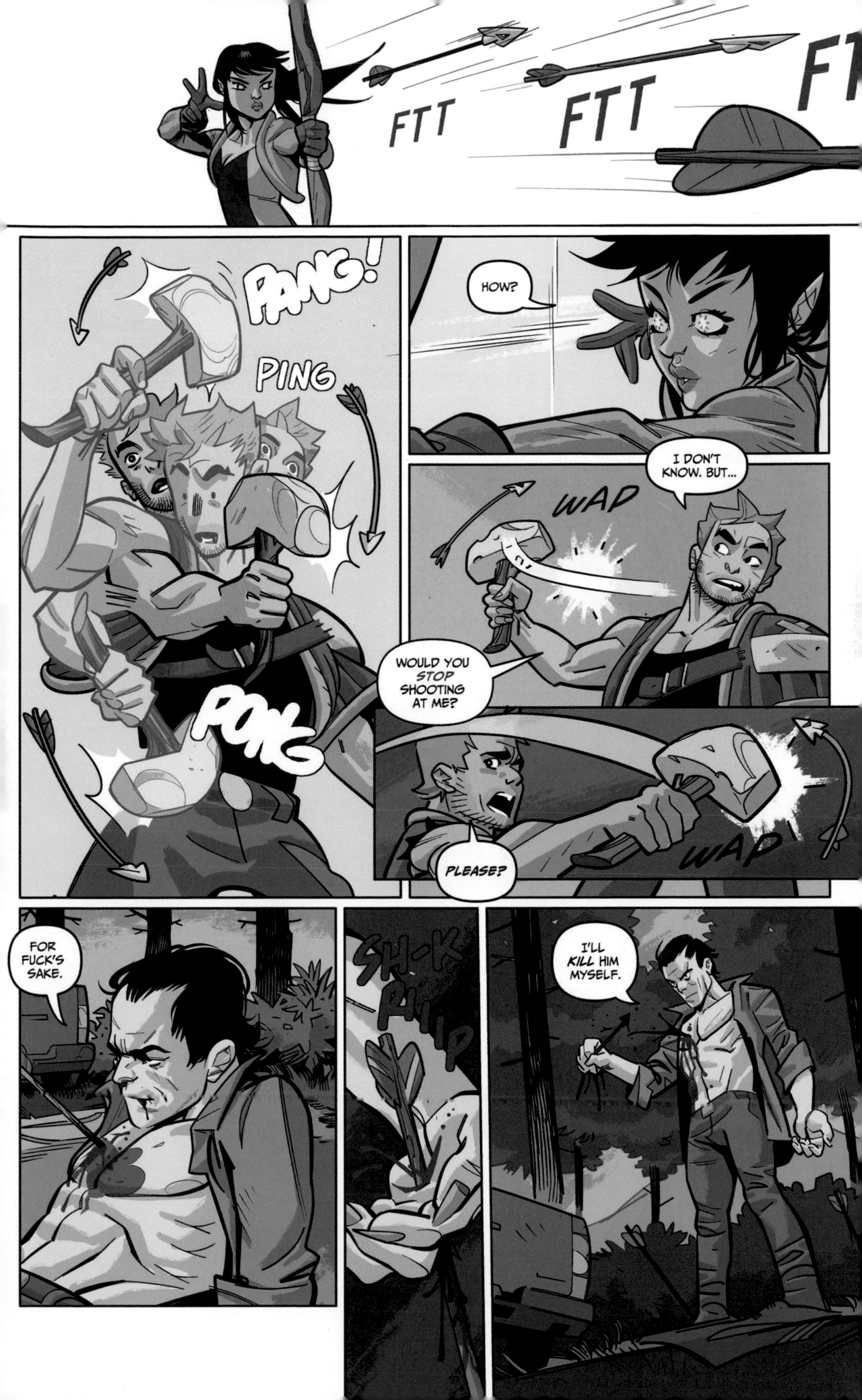
FTT
FTT
FT
PANG!
PING
PONG
HOW?
I DON'T KNOW. BUT...
WAP
WOULD YOU STOP SHOOTING AT ME?
WAP
PLEASE?
FOR FUCK'S SAKE.
SH-K
RHIP
I'LL KILL HIM MYSELF.

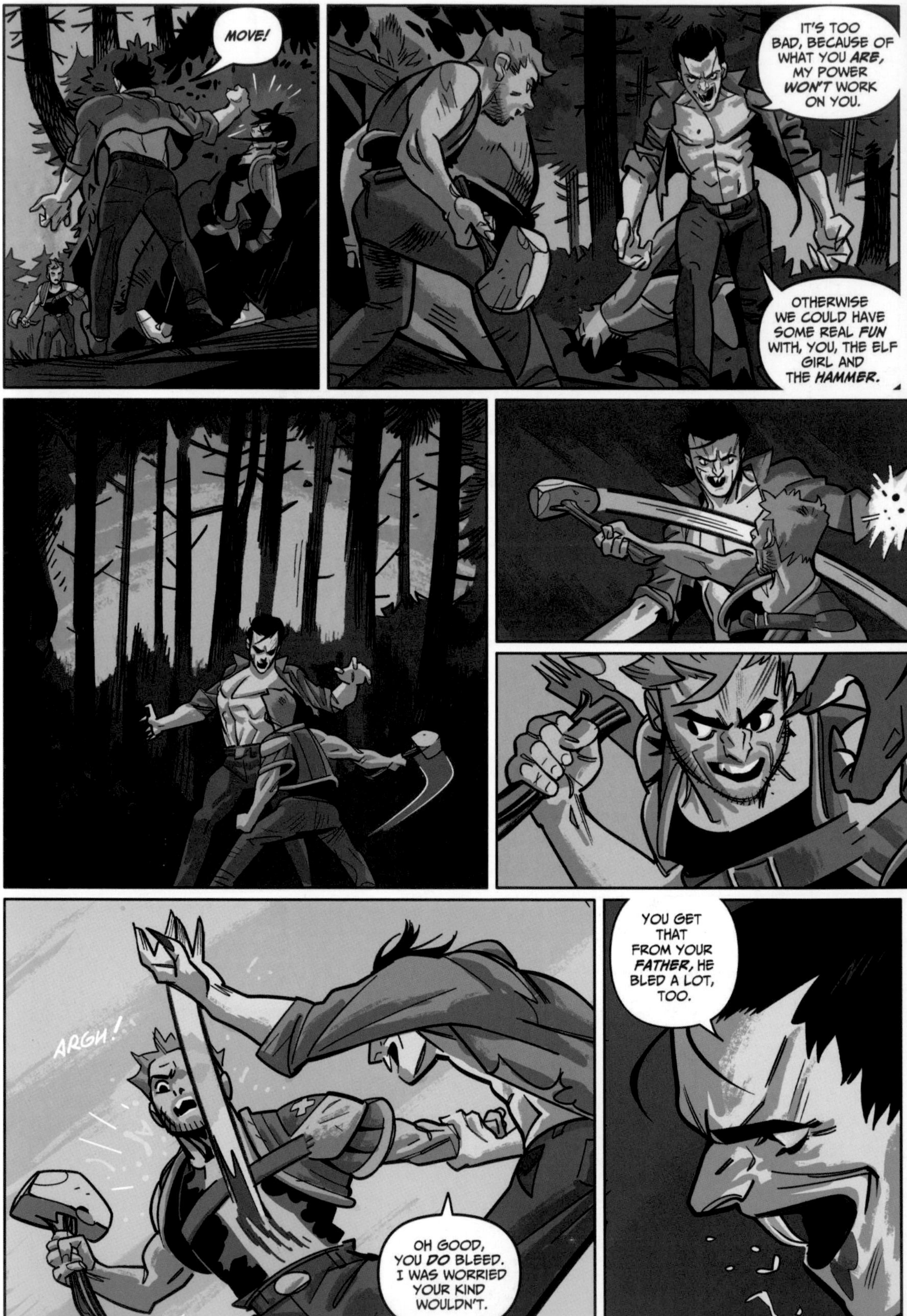
MOVE!
IT'S TOO BAD, BECAUSE OF WHAT YOU ARE, MY POWER WON'T WORK ON YOU.
OTHERWISE WE COULD HAVE SOME REAL FUN WITH, YOU, THE ELF GIRL AND THE HAMMER.
ARGH!
OH GOOD, YOU DO BLEED. I WAS WORRIED YOUR KIND WOULDN'T.
YOU GET THAT FROM YOUR FATHER, HE BLED A LOT, TOO.

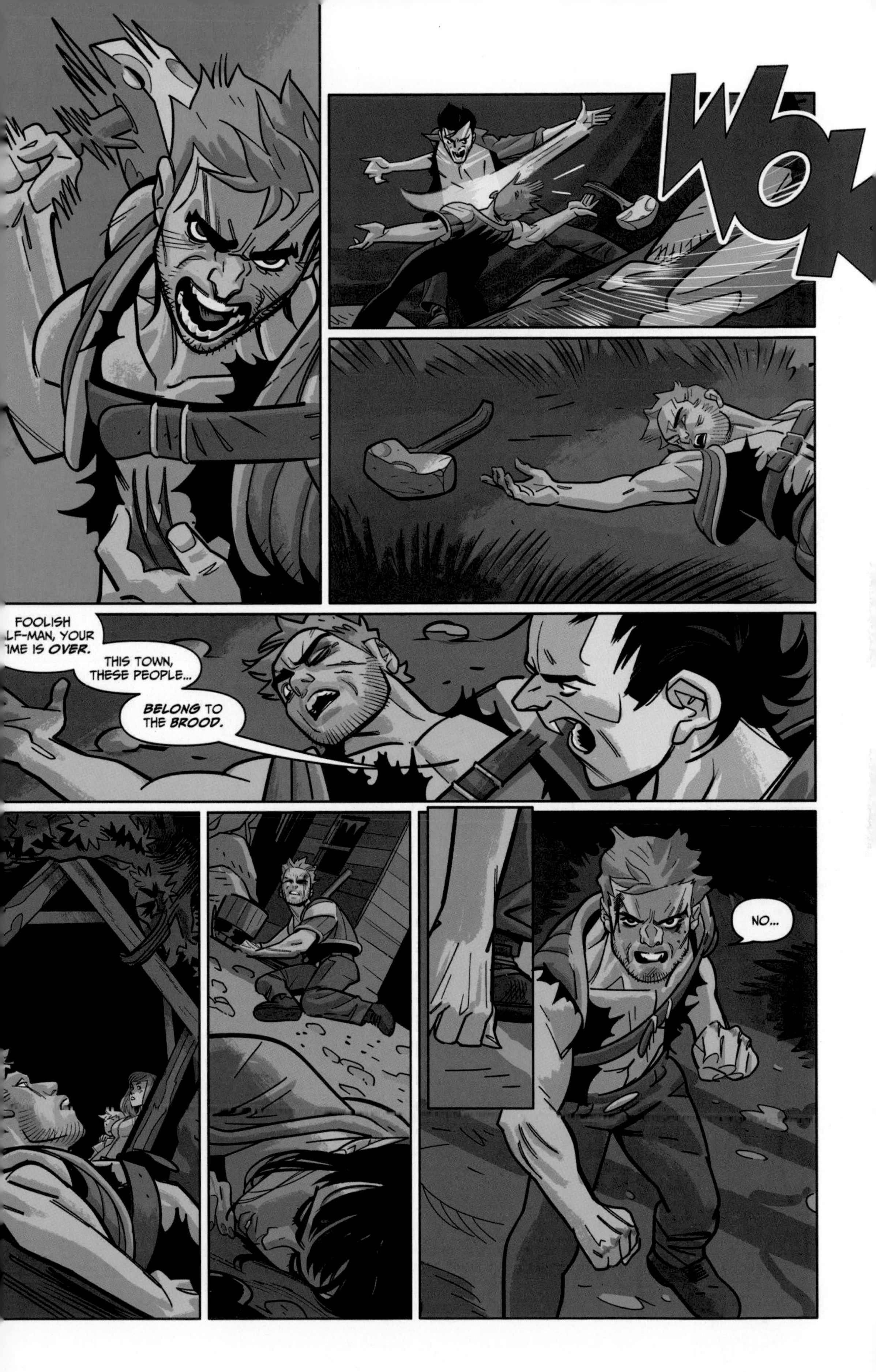
WOK
FOOLISH
ALF-MAN, YOUR
IME IS OVER.
THIS TOWN,
THESE PEOPLE...
BELONG TO
THE BROOD.
NO...

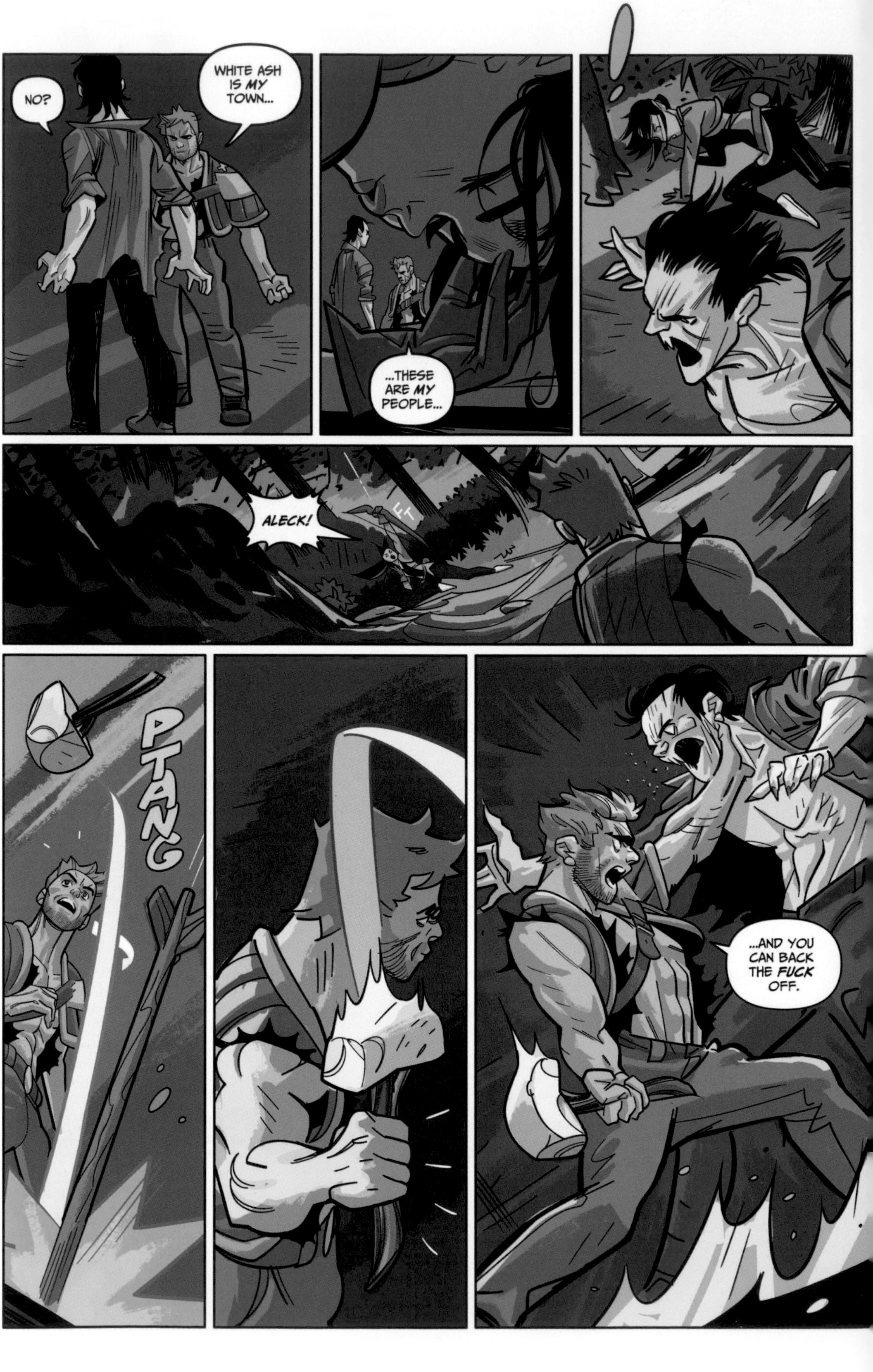

NO?
WHITE ASH IS MY TOWN...
...THESE ARE MY PEOPLE...
!
ALECK!
PTANG
...AND YOU CAN BACK THE FUCK OFF.

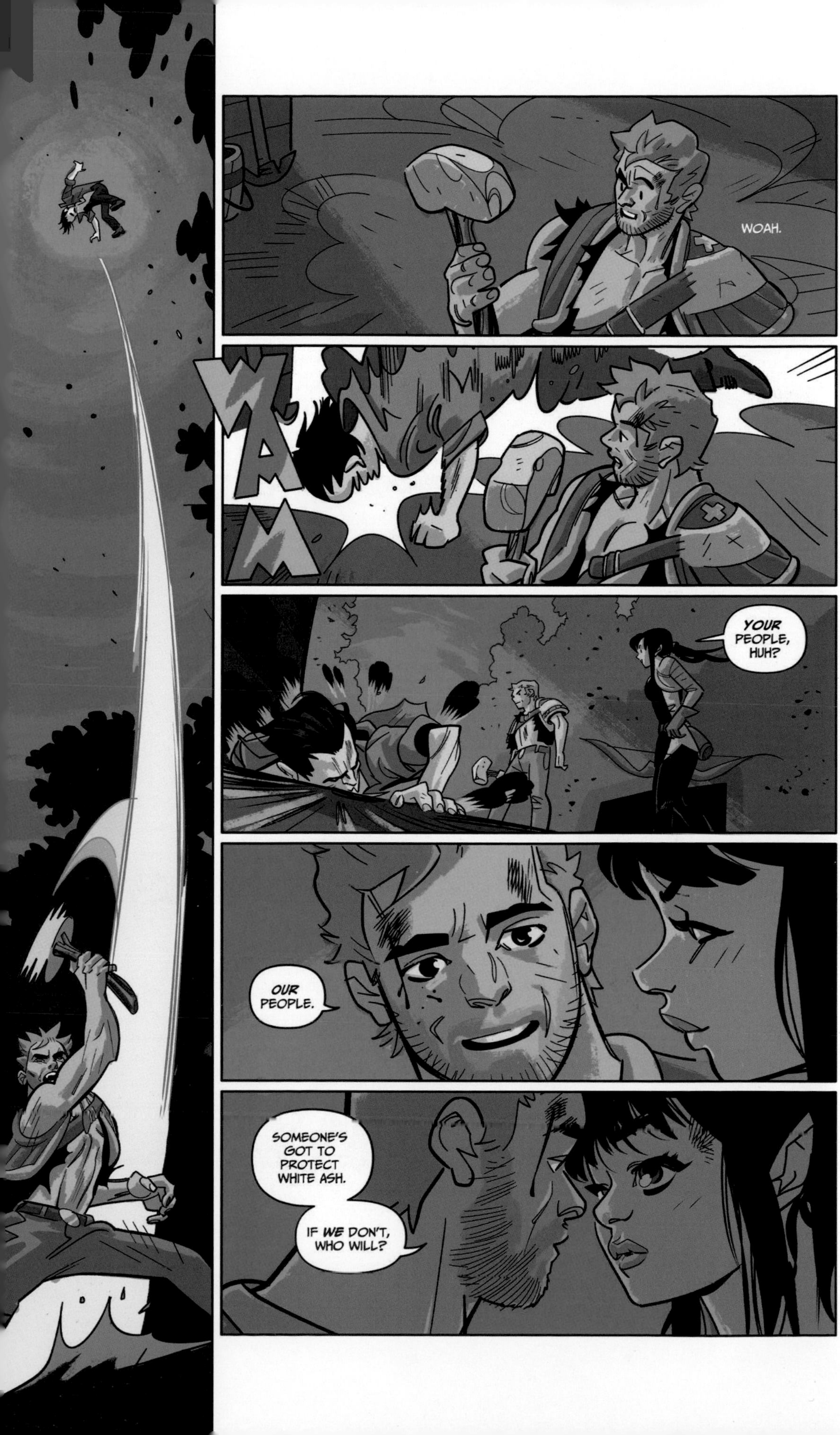
WOAH.
WAM
YOUR PEOPLE, HUH?
OUR PEOPLE.
SOMEONE'S GOT TO PROTECT WHITE ASH.
IF WE DON'T, WHO WILL?

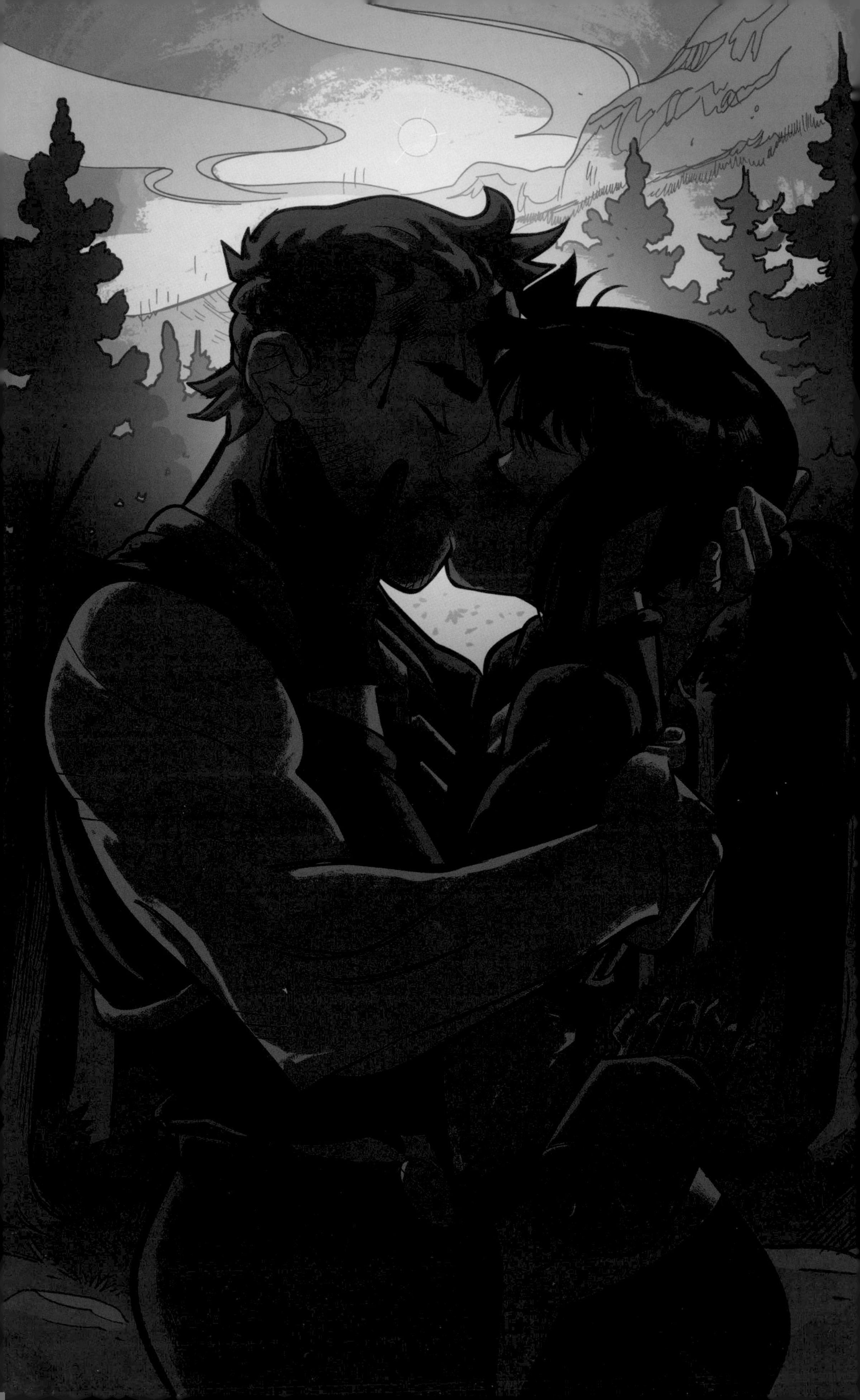

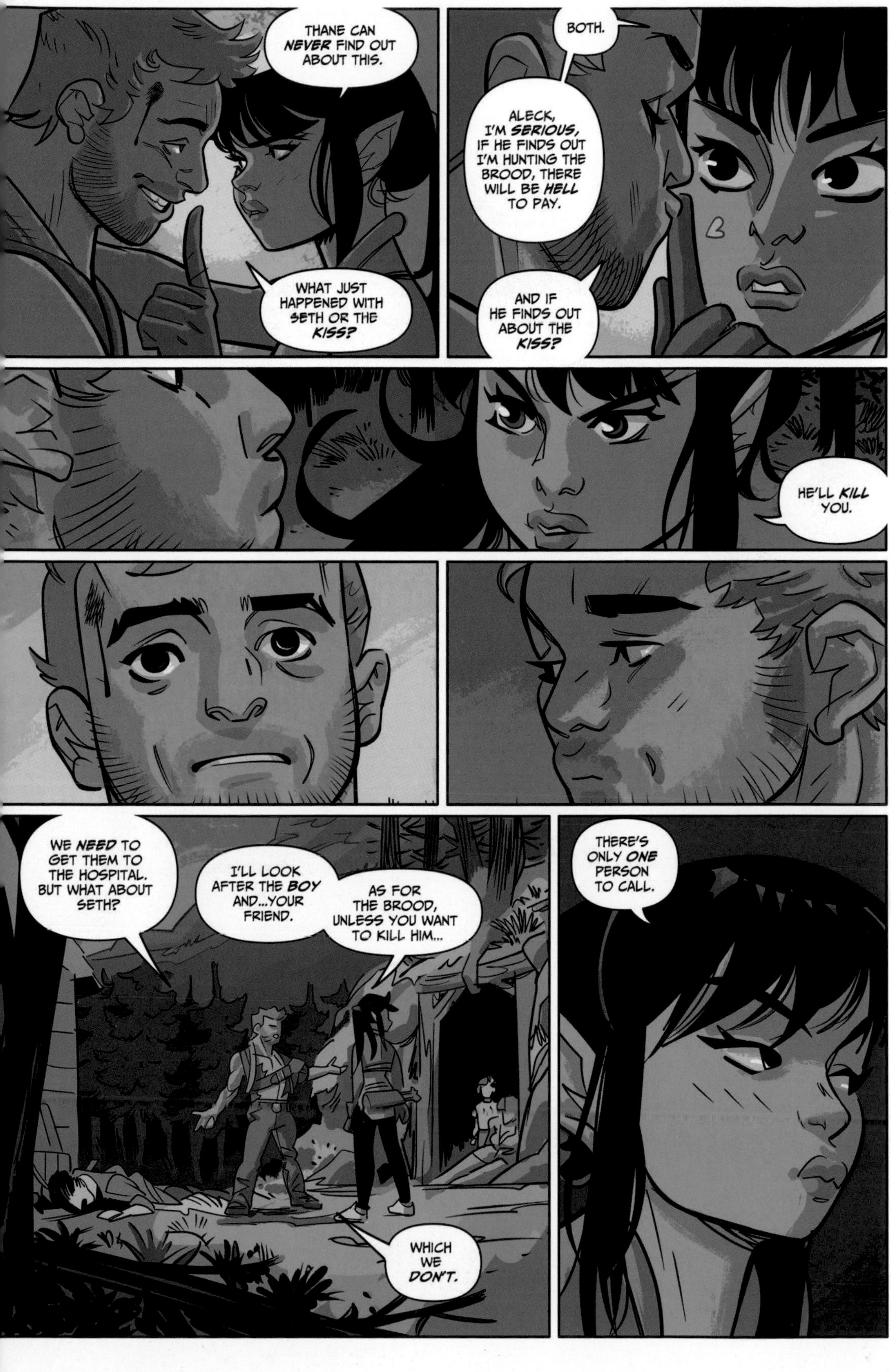
THANE CAN NEVER FIND OUT ABOUT THIS.
WHAT JUST HAPPENED WITH SETH OR THE KISS?
BOTH.
ALECK, I'M SERIOUS, IF HE FINDS OUT I'M HUNTING THE BROOD, THERE WILL BE HELL TO PAY.
AND IF HE FINDS OUT ABOUT THE KISS?
HE'LL KILL YOU.
WE NEED TO GET THEM TO THE HOSPITAL. BUT WHAT ABOUT SETH?
I'LL LOOK AFTER THE BOY AND...YOUR FRIEND.
AS FOR THE BROOD, UNLESS YOU WANT TO KILL HIM...
WHICH WE DON'T.
THERE'S ONLY ONE PERSON TO CALL.

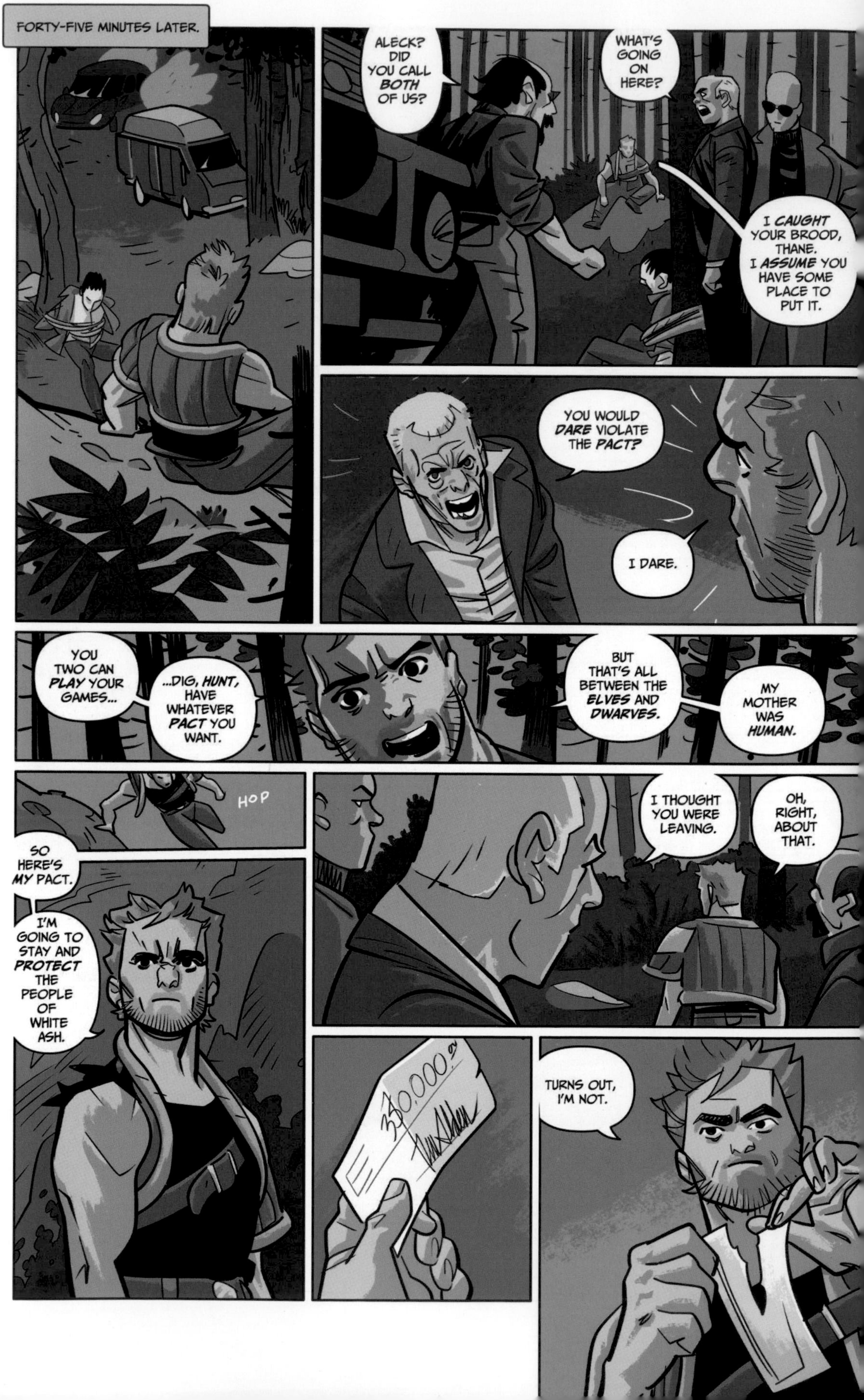
FORTY-FIVE MINUTES LATER.
ALECK? DID YOU CALL BOTH OF US?
WHAT'S GOING ON HERE?
I CAUGHT YOUR BROOD, THANE. I ASSUME YOU HAVE SOME PLACE TO PUT IT.
YOU WOULD DARE VIOLATE THE PACT?
I DARE.
YOU TWO CAN PLAY YOUR GAMES...
...DIG, HUNT, HAVE WHATEVER PACT YOU WANT.
BUT THAT'S ALL BETWEEN THE ELVES AND DWARVES.
MY MOTHER WAS HUMAN.
HOP
SO HERE'S MY PACT.
I'M GOING TO STAY AND PROTECT THE PEOPLE OF WHITE ASH.
I THOUGHT YOU WERE LEAVING.
OH, RIGHT, ABOUT THAT.
350,000.00
TURNS OUT, I'M NOT.

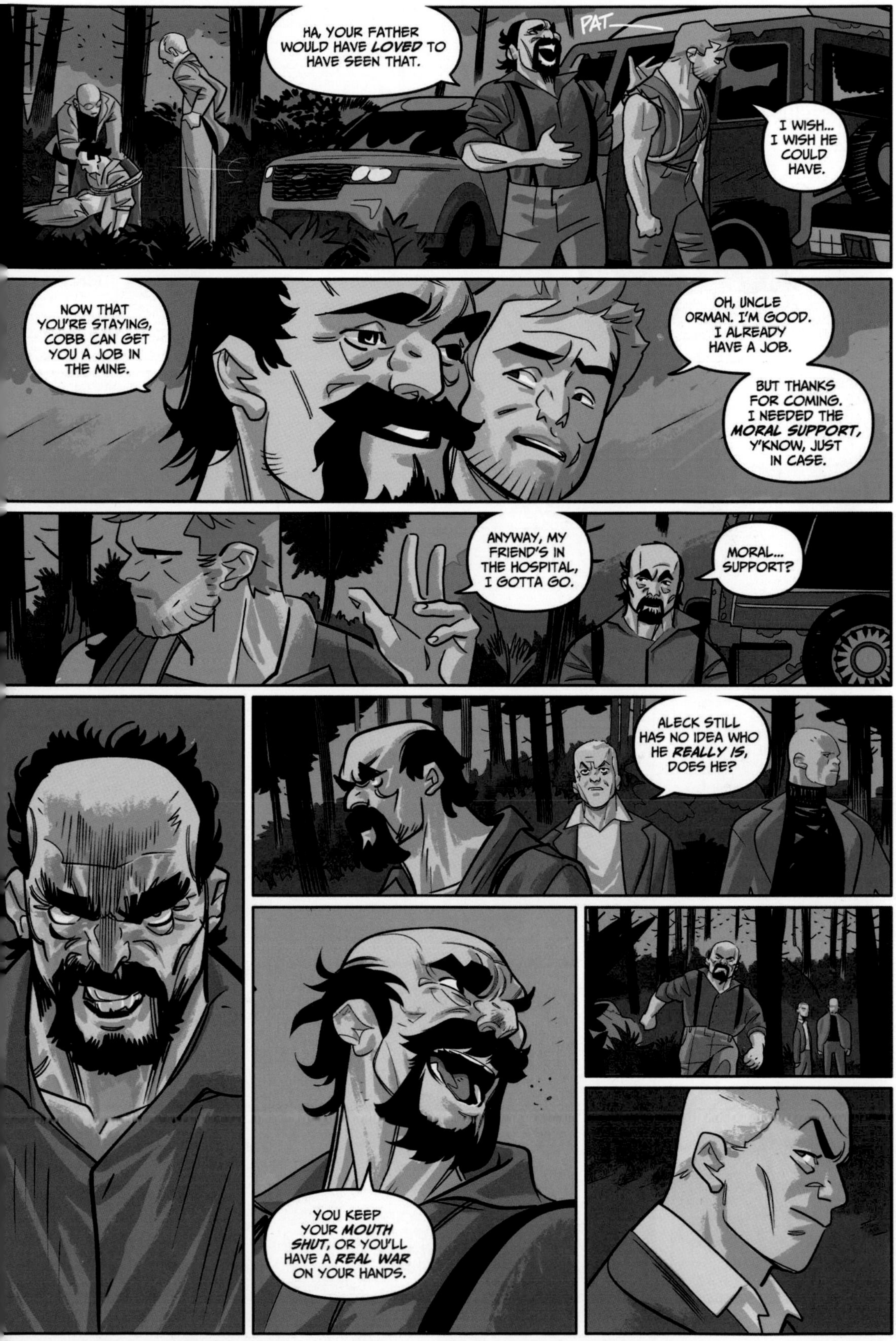
HA, YOUR FATHER WOULD HAVE LOVED TO HAVE SEEN THAT.
PAT
I WISH... I WISH HE COULD HAVE.
NOW THAT YOU'RE STAYING, COBB CAN GET YOU A JOB IN THE MINE.
OH, UNCLE ORMAN. I'M GOOD. I ALREADY HAVE A JOB.
BUT THANKS FOR COMING. I NEEDED THE MORAL SUPPORT, Y'KNOW, JUST IN CASE.
ANYWAY, MY FRIEND'S IN THE HOSPITAL, I GOTTA GO.
MORAL... SUPPORT?
ALECK STILL HAS NO IDEA WHO HE REALLY IS, DOES HE?
YOU KEEP YOUR MOUTH SHUT, OR YOU'LL HAVE A REAL WAR ON YOUR HANDS.

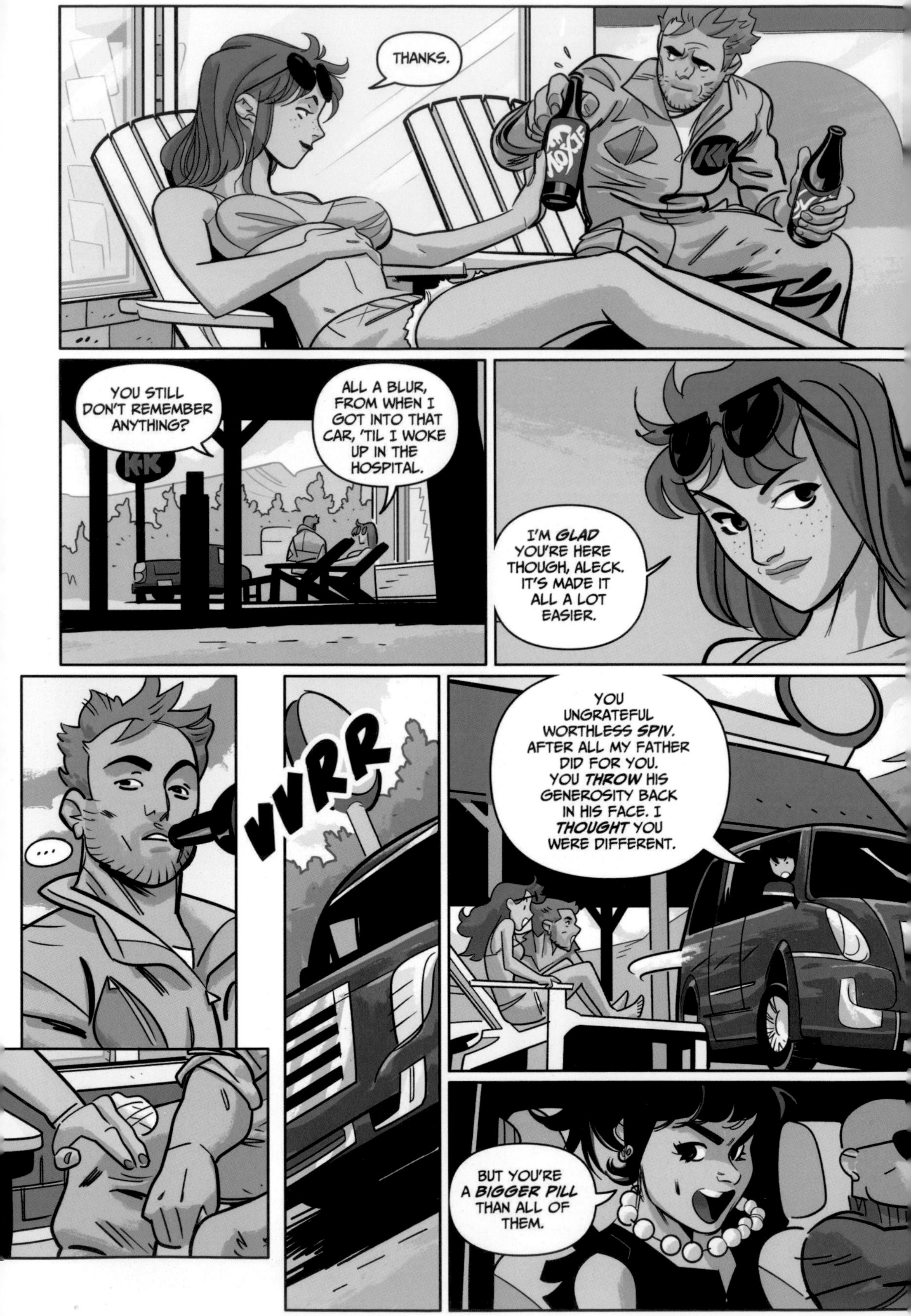
THANKS.
YOU STILL DON'T REMEMBER ANYTHING?
ALL A BLUR, FROM WHEN I GOT INTO THAT CAR, 'TIL I WOKE UP IN THE HOSPITAL.
I'M GLAD YOU'RE HERE THOUGH, ALECK. IT'S MADE IT ALL A LOT EASIER.
...
VVRR
YOU UNGRATEFUL WORTHLESS SPIV. AFTER ALL MY FATHER DID FOR YOU. YOU THROW HIS GENEROSITY BACK IN HIS FACE. I THOUGHT YOU WERE DIFFERENT.
BUT YOU'RE A BIGGER PILL THAN ALL OF THEM.

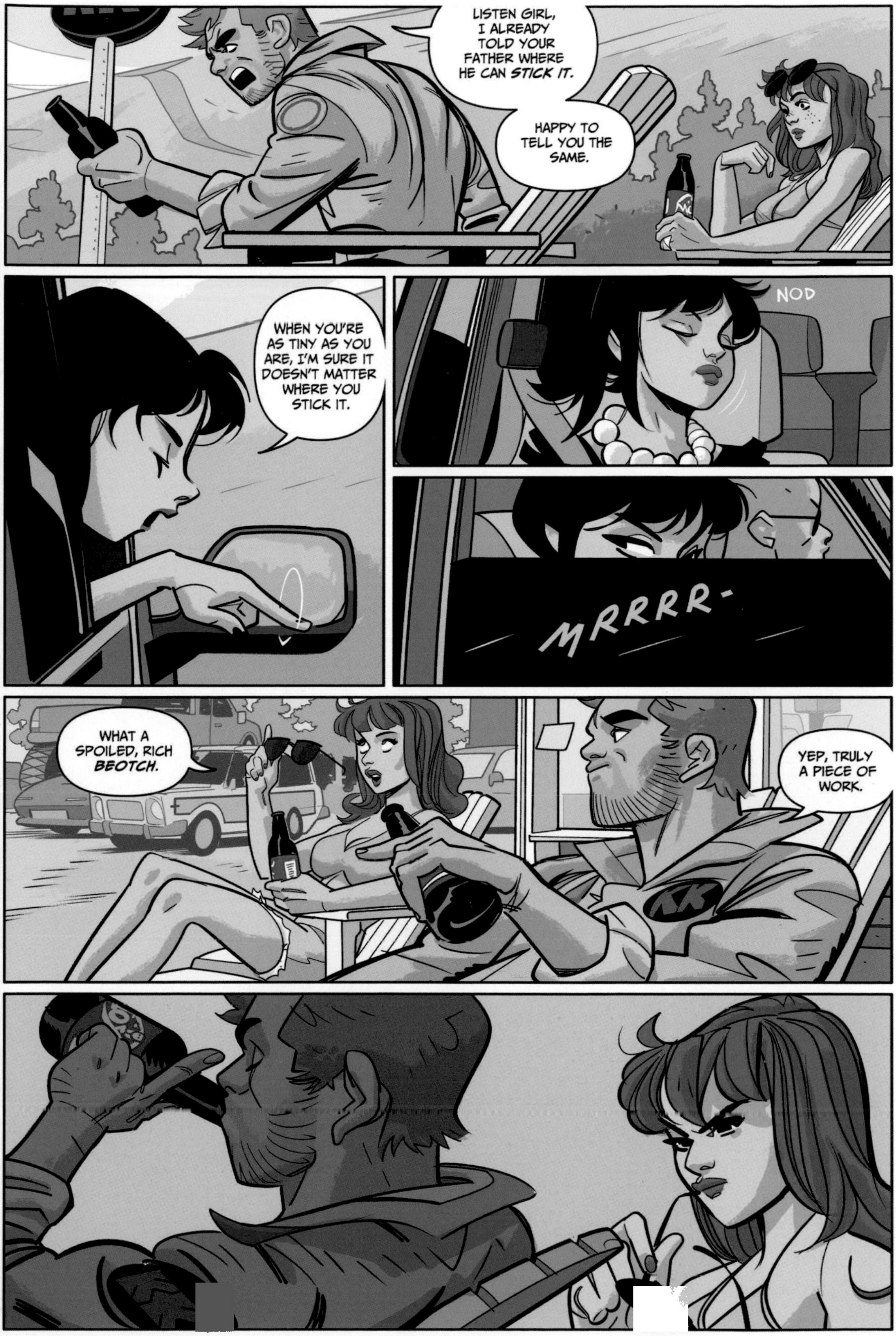
LISTEN GIRL, I ALREADY TOLD YOUR FATHER WHERE HE CAN STICK IT.
HAPPY TO TELL YOU THE SAME.
WHEN YOU'RE AS TINY AS YOU ARE, I'M SURE IT DOESN'T MATTER WHERE YOU STICK IT.
NOD
MRRRR-
WHAT A SPOILED, RICH BEOTCH.
YEP, TRULY A PIECE OF WORK.

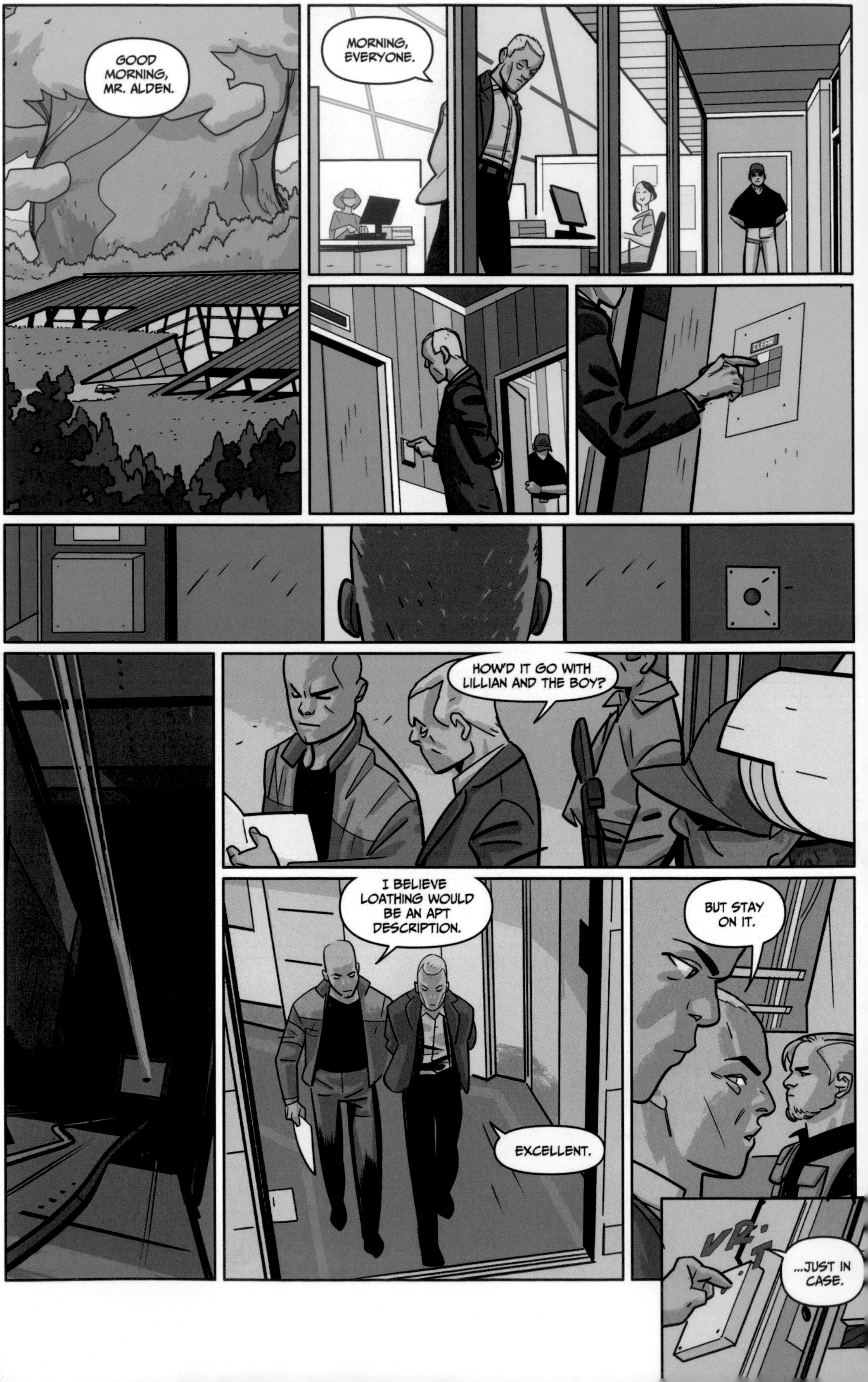
GOOD MORNING, MR. ALDEN.
MORNING, EVERYONE.
CLEAR
HOW'D IT GO WITH LILLIAN AND THE BOY?
I BELIEVE LOATHING WOULD BE AN APT DESCRIPTION.
EXCELLENT.
BUT STAY ON IT.
VRT
...JUST IN CASE.

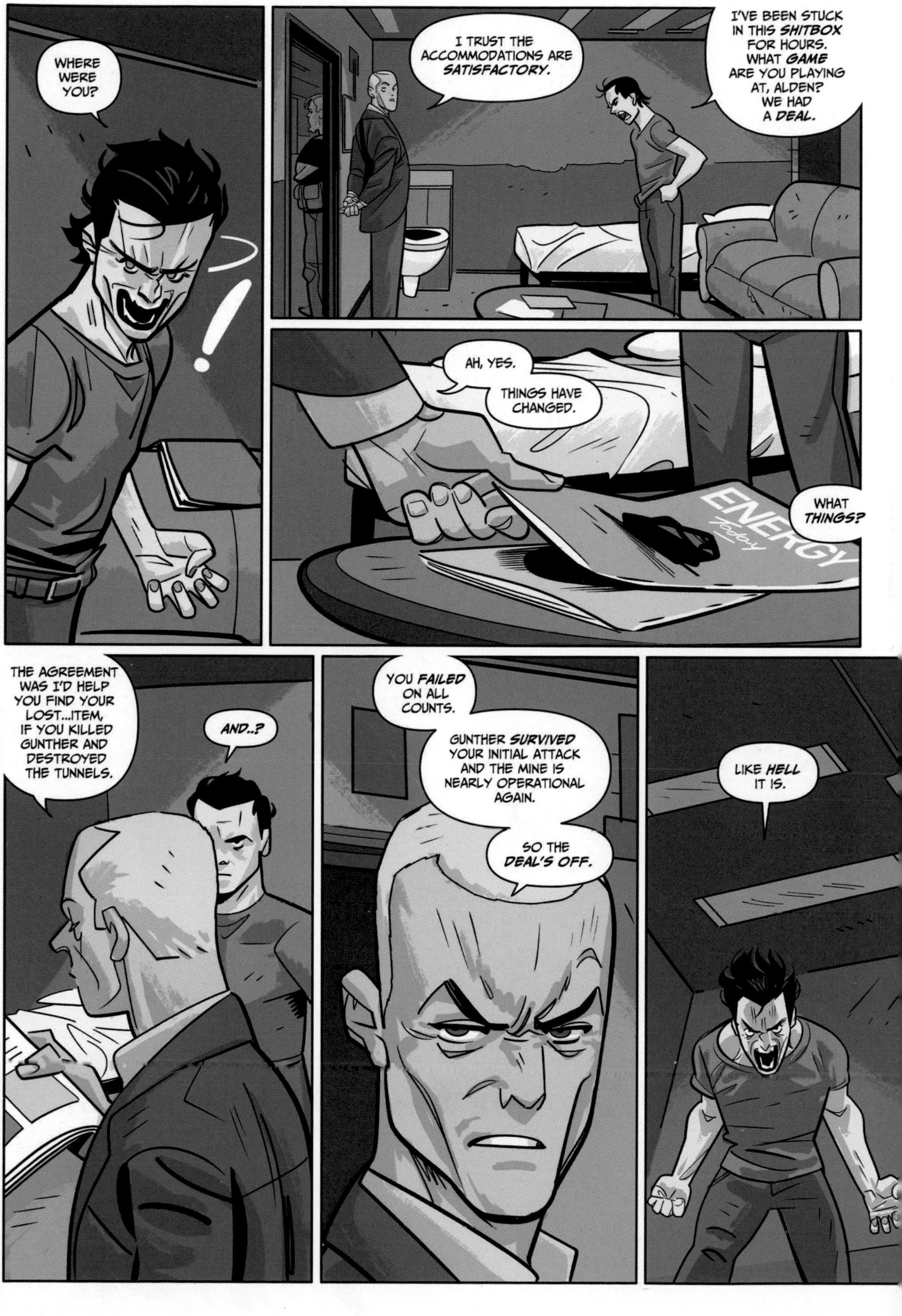
WHERE WERE YOU?
I TRUST THE ACCOMMODATIONS ARE SATISFACTORY.
I'VE BEEN STUCK IN THIS SHITBOX FOR HOURS. WHAT GAME ARE YOU PLAYING AT, ALDEN? WE HAD A DEAL.
AH, YES.
THINGS HAVE CHANGED.
ENERGY Today
WHAT THINGS?
THE AGREEMENT WAS I'D HELP YOU FIND YOUR LOST...ITEM, IF YOU KILLED GUNTHER AND DESTROYED THE TUNNELS.
AND..?
YOU FAILED ON ALL COUNTS.
GUNTHER SURVIVED YOUR INITIAL ATTACK AND THE MINE IS NEARLY OPERATIONAL AGAIN.
SO THE DEAL'S OFF.
LIKE HELL IT IS.

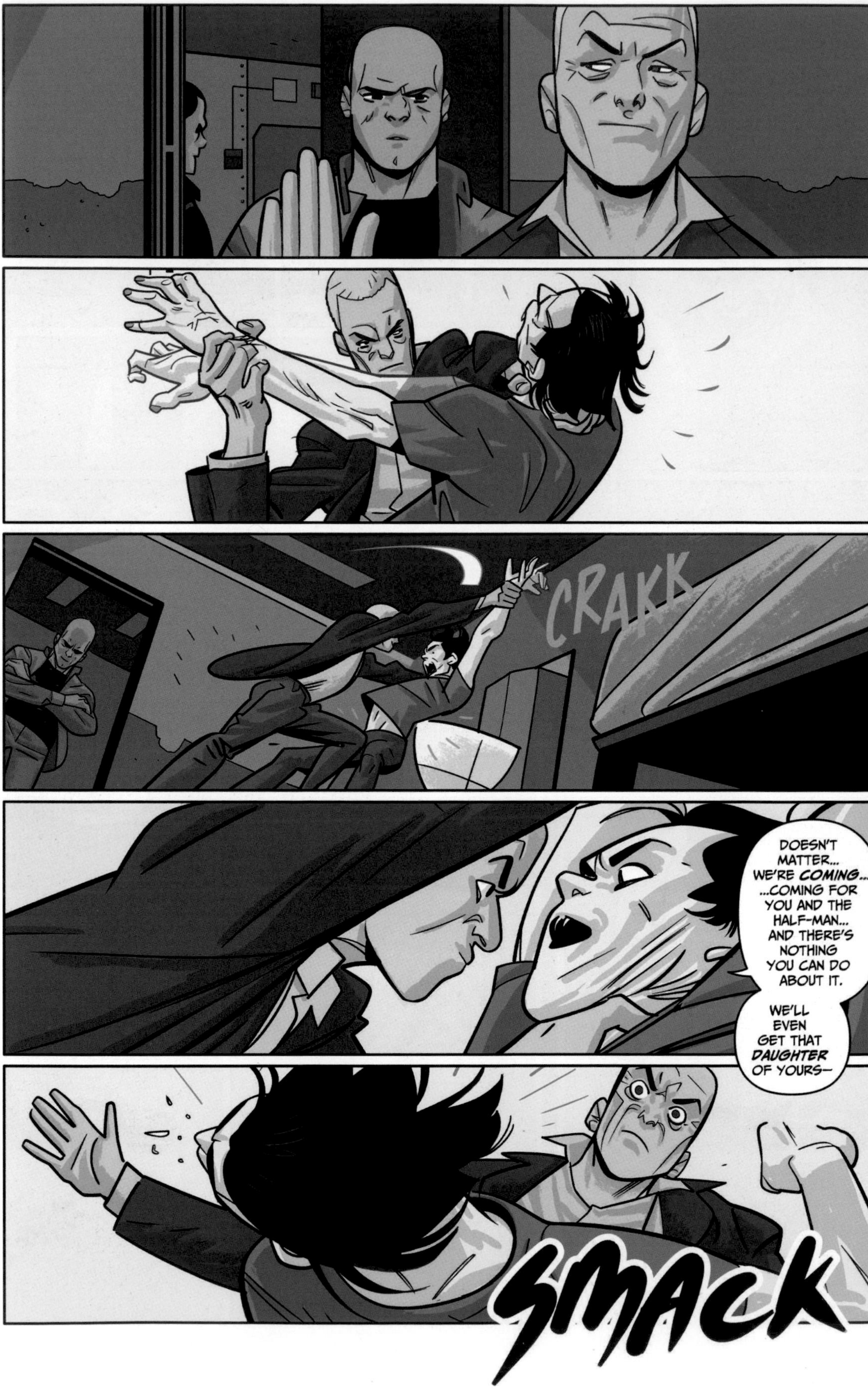
CRAKK
DOESN'T MATTER... WE'RE COMING... ...COMING FOR YOU AND THE HALF-MAN... AND THERE'S NOTHING YOU CAN DO ABOUT IT.
WE'LL EVEN GET THAT DAUGHTER OF YOURS—
SMACK

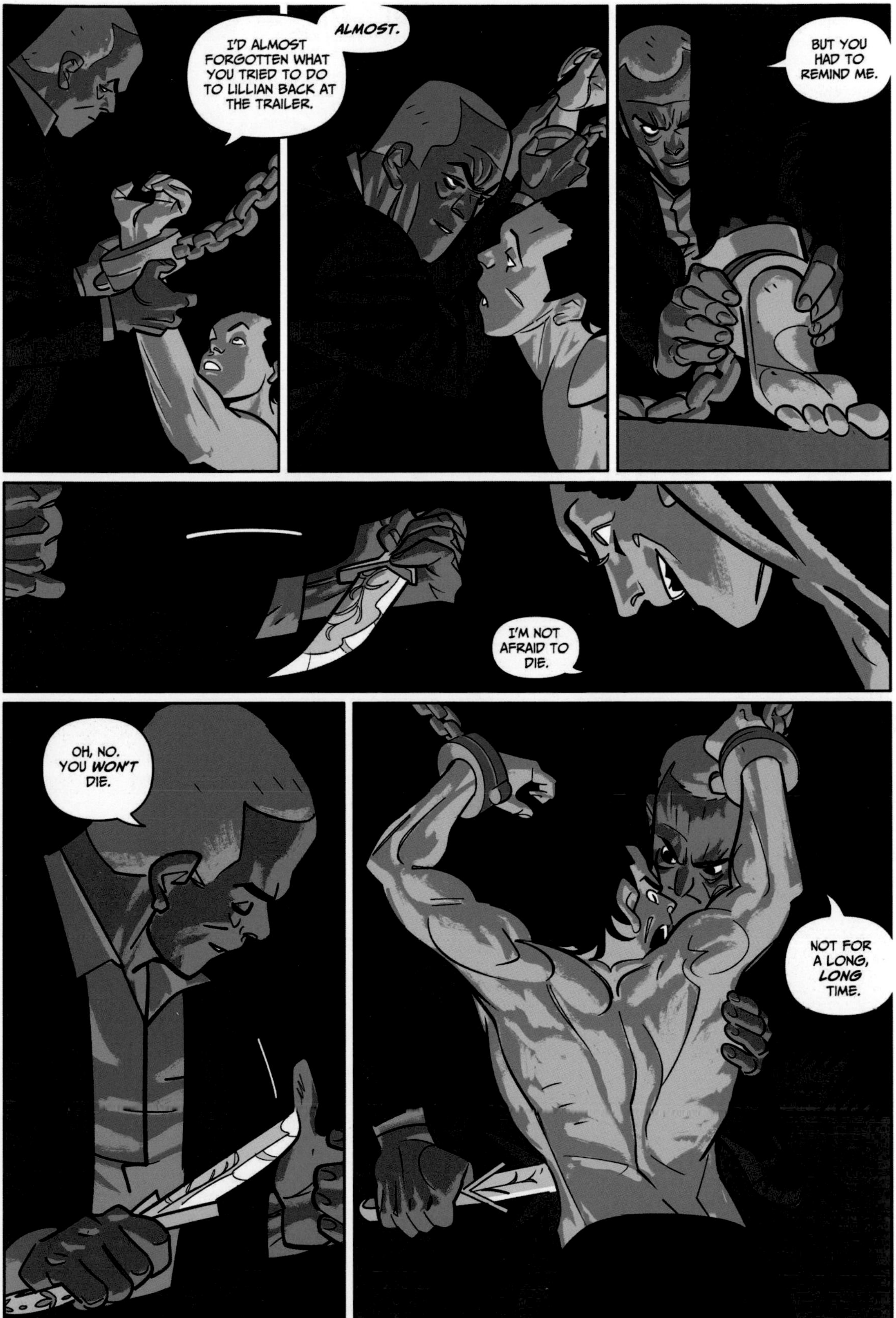
I'D ALMOST FORGOTTEN WHAT YOU TRIED TO DO TO LILLIAN BACK AT THE TRAILER.
ALMOST.
BUT YOU HAD TO REMIND ME.
I'M NOT AFRAID TO DIE.
OH, NO. YOU WON'T DIE.
NOT FOR A LONG, LONG TIME.

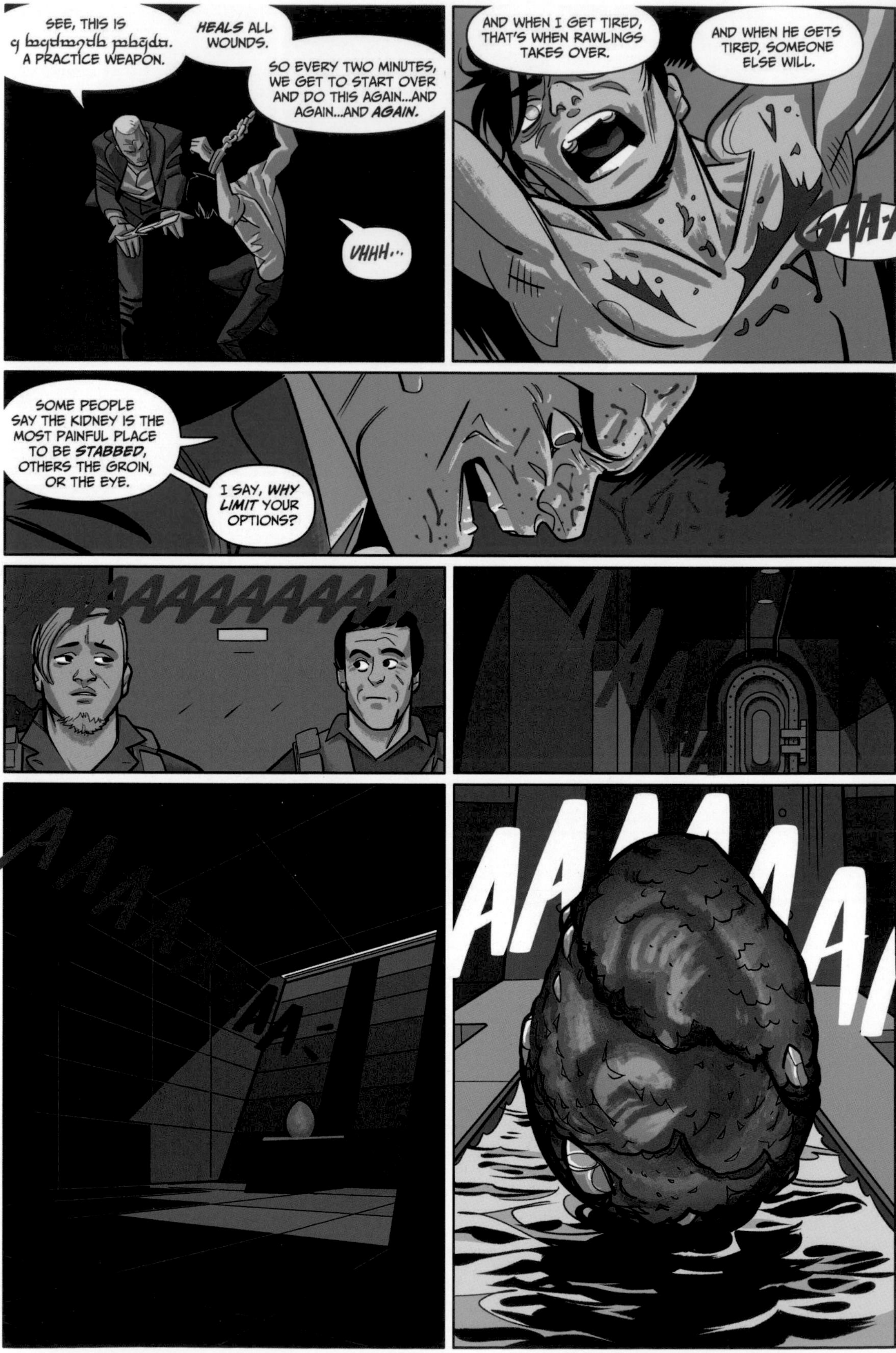
SEE, THIS IS
A PRACTICE WEAPON.
HEALS ALL WOUNDS.
SO EVERY TWO MINUTES, WE GET TO START OVER AND DO THIS AGAIN...AND AGAIN...AND AGAIN.
UHHH...
AND WHEN I GET TIRED, THAT'S WHEN RAWLINGS TAKES OVER.
AND WHEN HE GETS TIRED, SOMEONE ELSE WILL.
GAA-A
SOME PEOPLE SAY THE KIDNEY IS THE MOST PAINFUL PLACE TO BE STABBED, OTHERS THE GROIN, OR THE EYE.
I SAY, WHY LIMIT YOUR OPTIONS?

THE
PROCESS

CHARACTER DESIGN

The following are the initial character sketches I sent to Charlie upon reading up on the characters. These sketches were the first in a learning process of getting to know them. Part of the joy of comics is getting to really live inside your characters and become them by acting them out on the page and over a long process become familiar.

Artists will first get a synopsis of the character, a snapshot, like a Facebook profile. So, like a facebook profile, you might get where they work or the broad strokes of their interests. However you don't know that their favorite restaurant is that Mexican joint on 18, or that they had a tire swing accident in the woods when they were a kid and that had a strong influence on the person they would become.

In the process of drawing the characters, what first was maybe a shadow, or a snapshot of their personality, becomes more fully fleshed out and three dimensional. In that regard, I see changing with your characters as part of the process. Initially, I was drawn to lean on reference for the actors who might be inspiration for the characters, but as time went on that was less and less necessary. It's fairly visible with Lillian, who had multiple actresses that were being drawn upon to create the sort of dynamic elements that make her interesting.

CONOR HUGHES

ALECK

Short (obviously), immaculate groomed stubble (think Hemsworth in Thor). Hair should be modern. Trendy. Though he's short, he doesn't have the traditional Dwarf physique. More of a swimmers body. Same goes for his face. He can have distinctive features, but not the traditional dwarven nose, brows, etc. He's very good looking (and knows it). Stylish as he can afford.

Also, though he can come off as full of himself, we need be able to root for Aleck. He's our co-hero (along with Lillian) and this is his journey. So he needs that roguish charm. His other plus is, he's honest, like his father Gunther. What you see is what you get.

LILLIAN

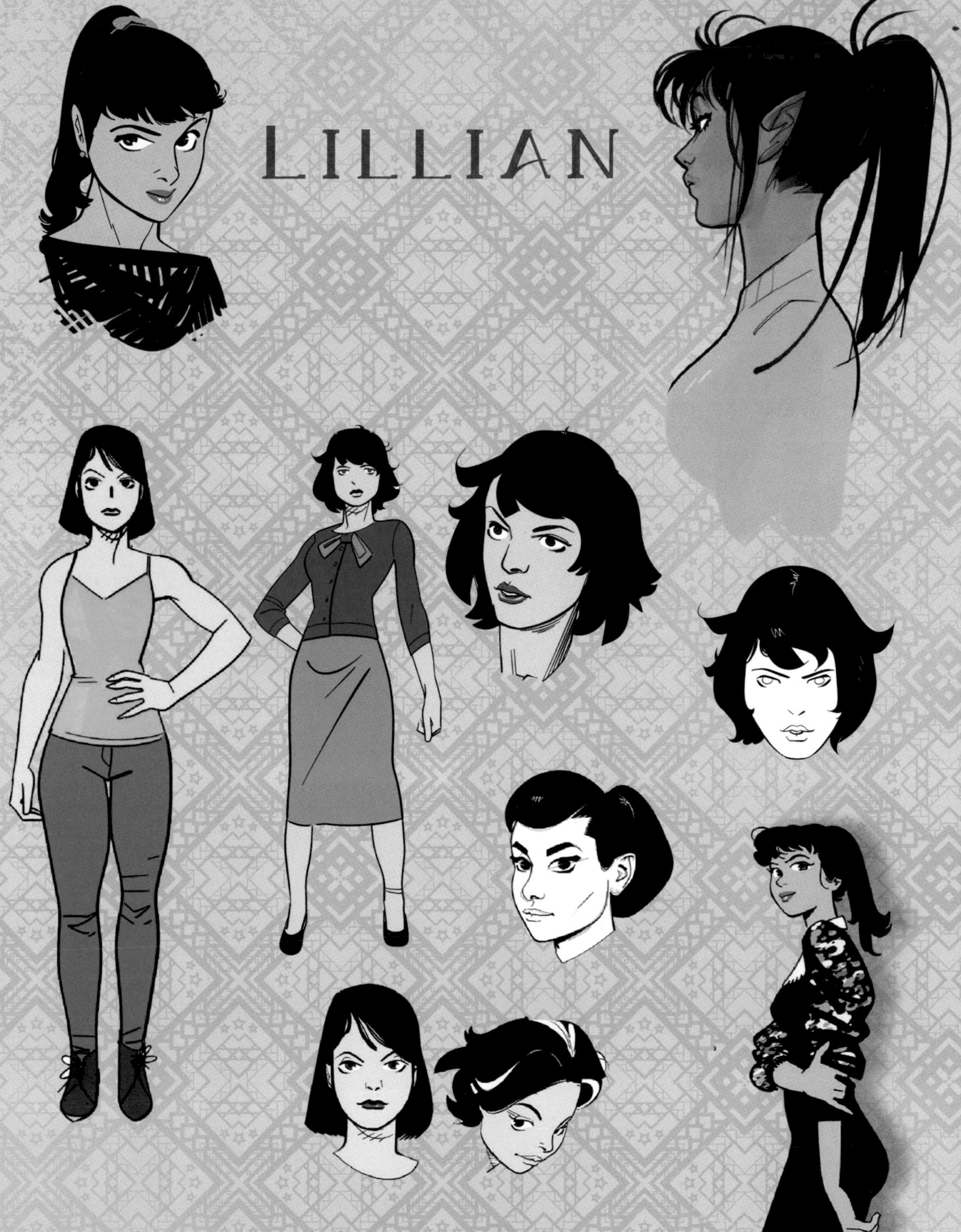

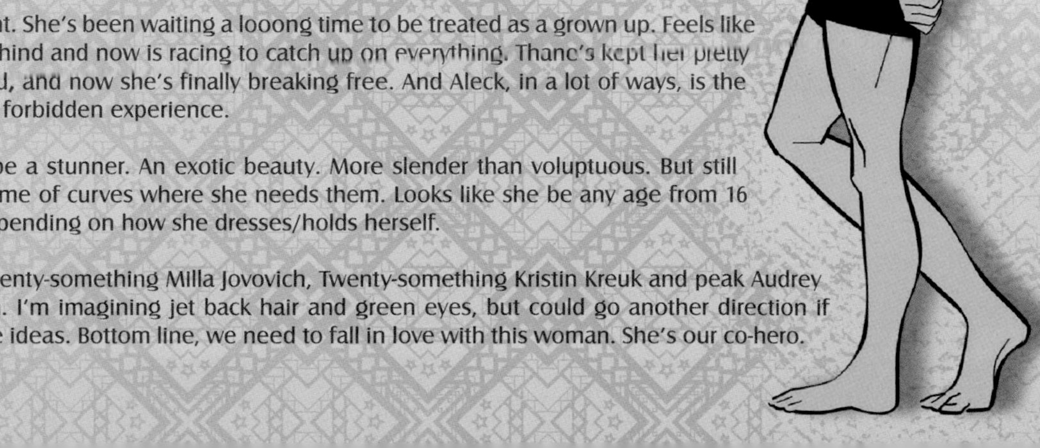

Impatient. She's been waiting a looong time to be treated as a grown up. Feels like she's behind and now is racing to catch up on everything. Thane's kept her pretty sheltered, and now she's finally breaking free. And Aleck, in a lot of ways, is the ultimate forbidden experience.

Should be a stunner. An exotic beauty. More slender than voluptuous. But still has a some of curves where she needs them. Looks like she be any age from 16 to 35 depending on how she dresses/holds herself.

Think twenty-something Milla Jovovich, Twenty-something Kristin Kreuk and peak Audrey Hepburn. I'm imagining jet back hair and green eyes, but could go another direction if you have ideas. Bottom line, we need to fall in love with this woman. She's our co-hero.

THANE

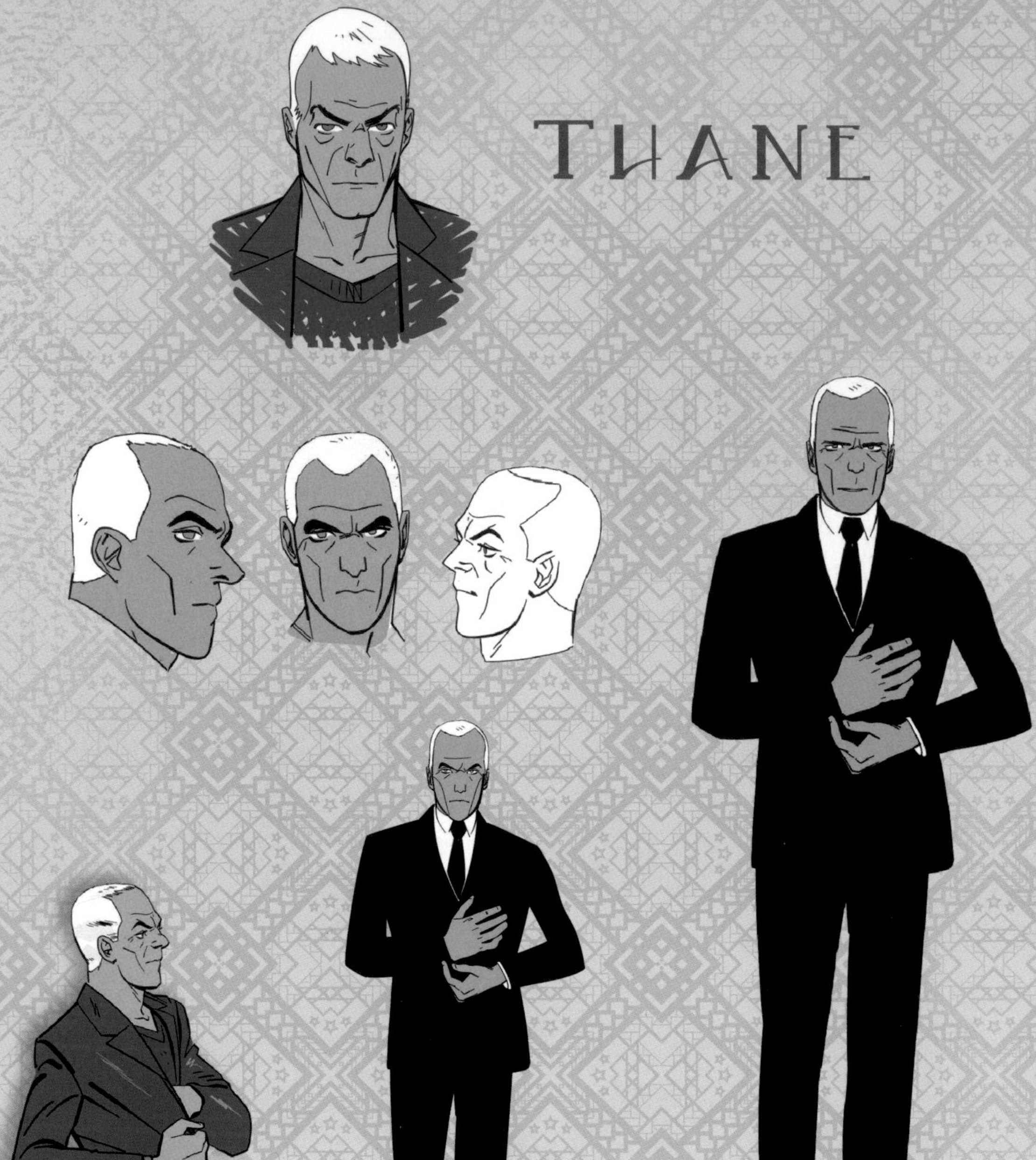

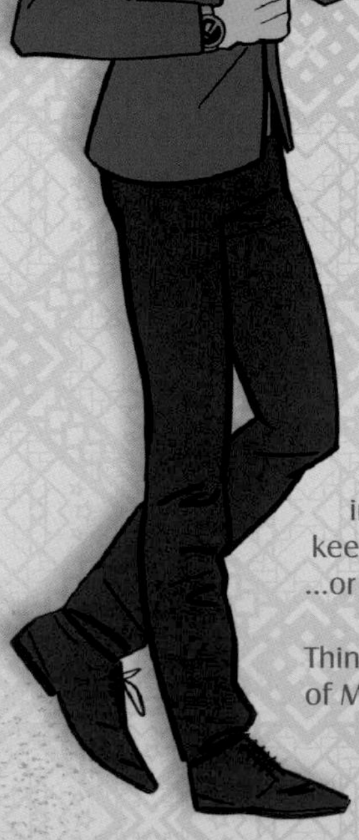

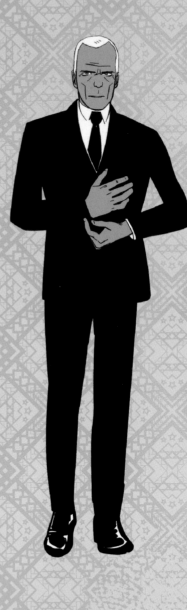

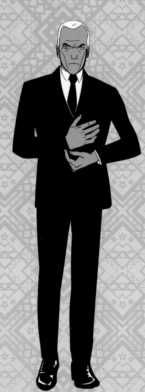

Arrogant, erudite, almost always in control of his emotions. His one button that can be pushed is Lillian. He will do anything to keep her safe. Machiavellian in his machinations. Holds all the cards. In the town of White Ash, Thane is the keeper of all the secrets...
...or almost all of them.

Think a cross between Hugo Weaving and Jason Isaacs topped off with a dash of Malcolm McDowell. Tall, imposing, with fiery blue eyes and short white hair.

SETH

Part beautiful man. All evil. Think Tom Hiddleston as Loki. Should be a bit snakelike in his movements and gestures. Has a way of mesmerizing people with his eyes. Should be lean, lanky and always ready to strike.

THE ART PROCESS

Thumbs or thumbnails are where a lot of the comic is really made. That's when one takes the script and applies it to the page. For White Ash, I've been working digitally, which means I use a digital tablet to draw and for the most part the workhorse of White Ash has been Clip Studio, with a little Photoshop. Here the panel numbers are made final if they are outlined in the script, and their layout. From there, the composition of each panel is roughed in, usually with stick figures and a general sense of what the environment looks like. Pictured here is an example of relatively tight thumbnails for me. When the thumbs are done, the majority of the decisions are made regarding pacing, composition, possibly black spotting. From there, the next step is...

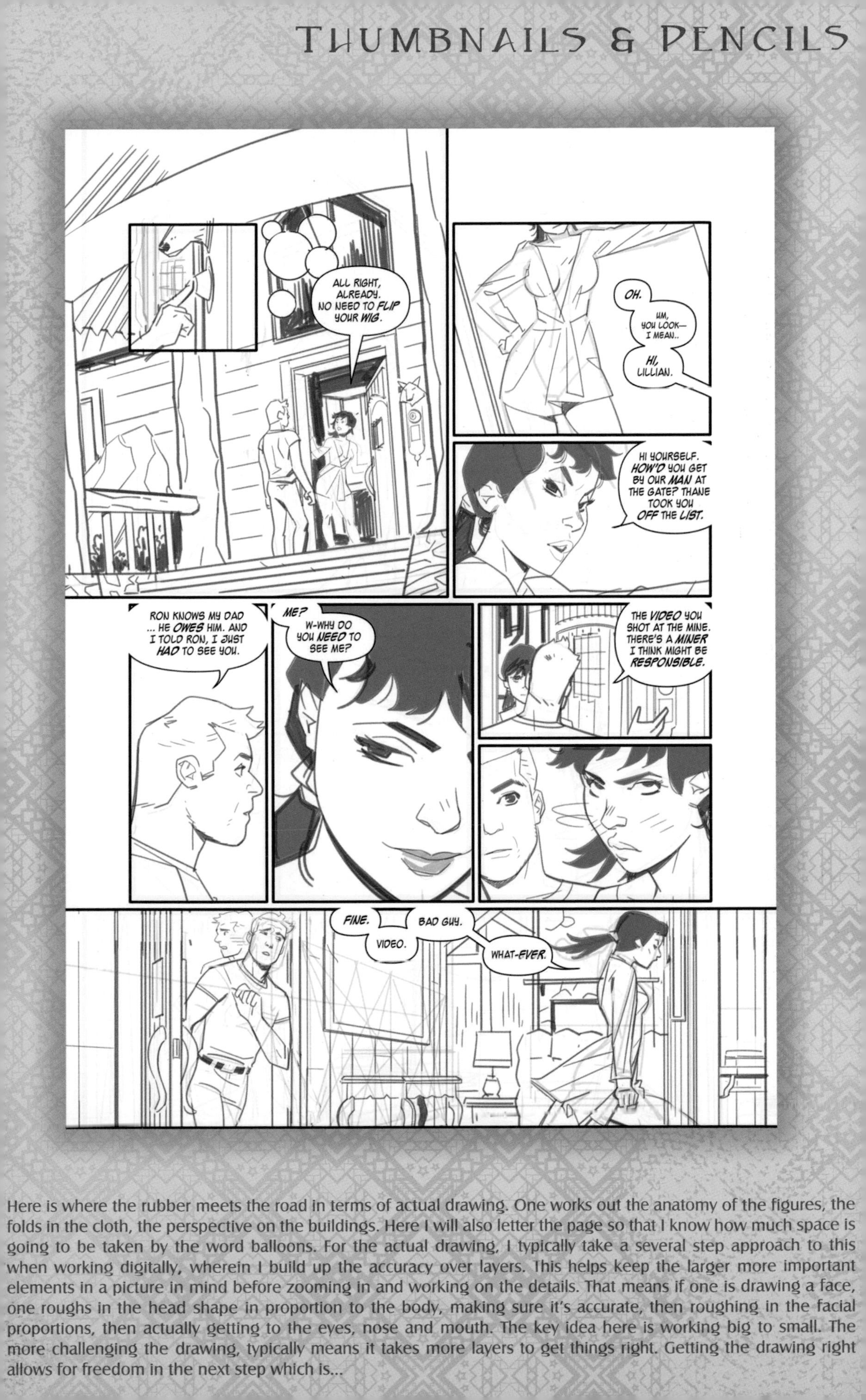
ALL RIGHT, ALREADY. NO NEED TO FLIP YOUR WIG.
OH.
UM, YOU LOOK— I MEAN..
HI, LILLIAN.
HI YOURSELF. HOW'D YOU GET BY OUR MAN AT THE GATE? THANE TOOK YOU OFF THE LIST.
RON KNOWS MY DAD ... HE OWES HIM. AND I TOLD RON, I JUST HAD TO SEE YOU.
ME? W-WHY DO YOU NEED TO SEE ME?
THE VIDEO YOU SHOT AT THE MINE. THERE'S A MINER I THINK MIGHT BE RESPONSIBLE.
FINE.
VIDEO.
BAD GUY.
WHAT-EVER.

Here is where the rubber meets the road in terms of actual drawing. One works out the anatomy of the figures, the folds in the cloth, the perspective on the buildings. Here I will also letter the page so that I know how much space is going to be taken by the word balloons. For the actual drawing, I typically take a several step approach to this when working digitally, wherein I build up the accuracy over layers. This helps keep the larger more important elements in a picture in mind before zooming in and working on the details. That means if one is drawing a face, one roughs in the head shape in proportion to the body, making sure it's accurate, then roughing in the facial proportions, then actually getting to the eyes, nose and mouth. The key idea here is working big to small. The more challenging the drawing, typically means it takes more layers to get things right. Getting the drawing right allows for freedom in the next step which is...

THE ART PROCESS

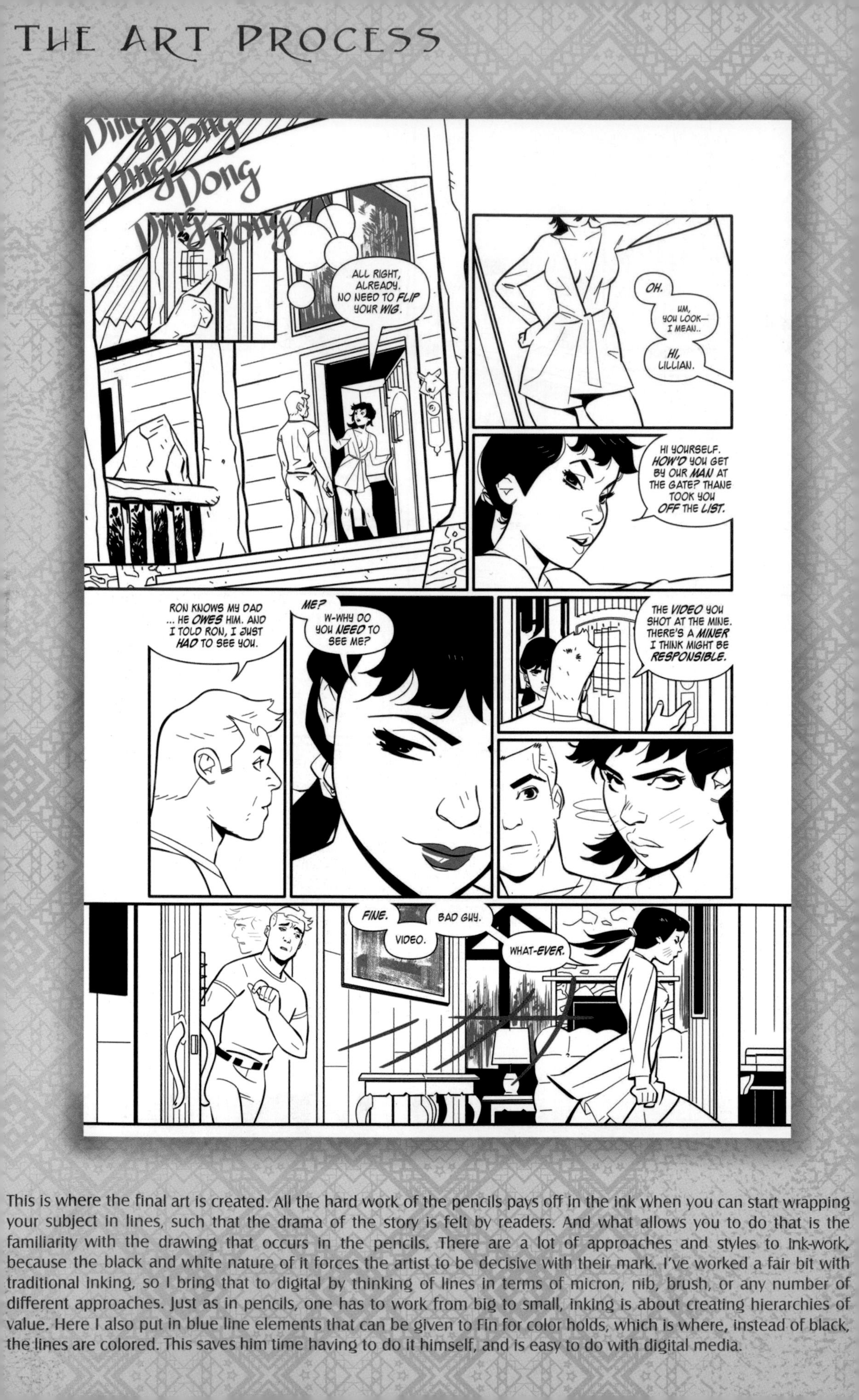

Ding Dong
Ding Dong
ALL RIGHT, ALREADY. NO NEED TO *FLIP* YOUR *WIG*.
OH.
UM, YOU LOOK— I MEAN..
HI, LILLIAN.
HI YOURSELF. *HOW'D* YOU GET BY OUR *MAN* AT THE GATE? THANE TOOK YOU *OFF* THE *LIST*.
RON KNOWS MY DAD ... HE *OWES* HIM. AND I TOLD RON, I JUST *HAD* TO SEE YOU.
ME?
W-WHY DO YOU *NEED* TO SEE ME?
THE *VIDEO* YOU SHOT AT THE MINE. THERE'S A *MINER* I THINK MIGHT BE *RESPONSIBLE*.
FINE.
VIDEO.
BAD GUY.
WHAT-*EVER*.

This is where the final art is created. All the hard work of the pencils pays off in the ink when you can start wrapping your subject in lines, such that the drama of the story is felt by readers. And what allows you to do that is the familiarity with the drawing that occurs in the pencils. There are a lot of approaches and styles to ink-work, because the black and white nature of it forces the artist to be decisive with their mark. I've worked a fair bit with traditional inking, so I bring that to digital by thinking of lines in terms of micron, nib, brush, or any number of different approaches. Just as in pencils, one has to work from big to small, inking is about creating hierarchies of value. Here I also put in blue line elements that can be given to Fin for color holds, which is where, instead of black, the lines are colored. This saves him time having to do it himself, and is easy to do with digital media.

And here is the final page, after Fin has worked his magic.

CONOR HUGHES

THE COLORING PROCESS

The starting point. The 11X17 600 dpi file I get sent from Conor.

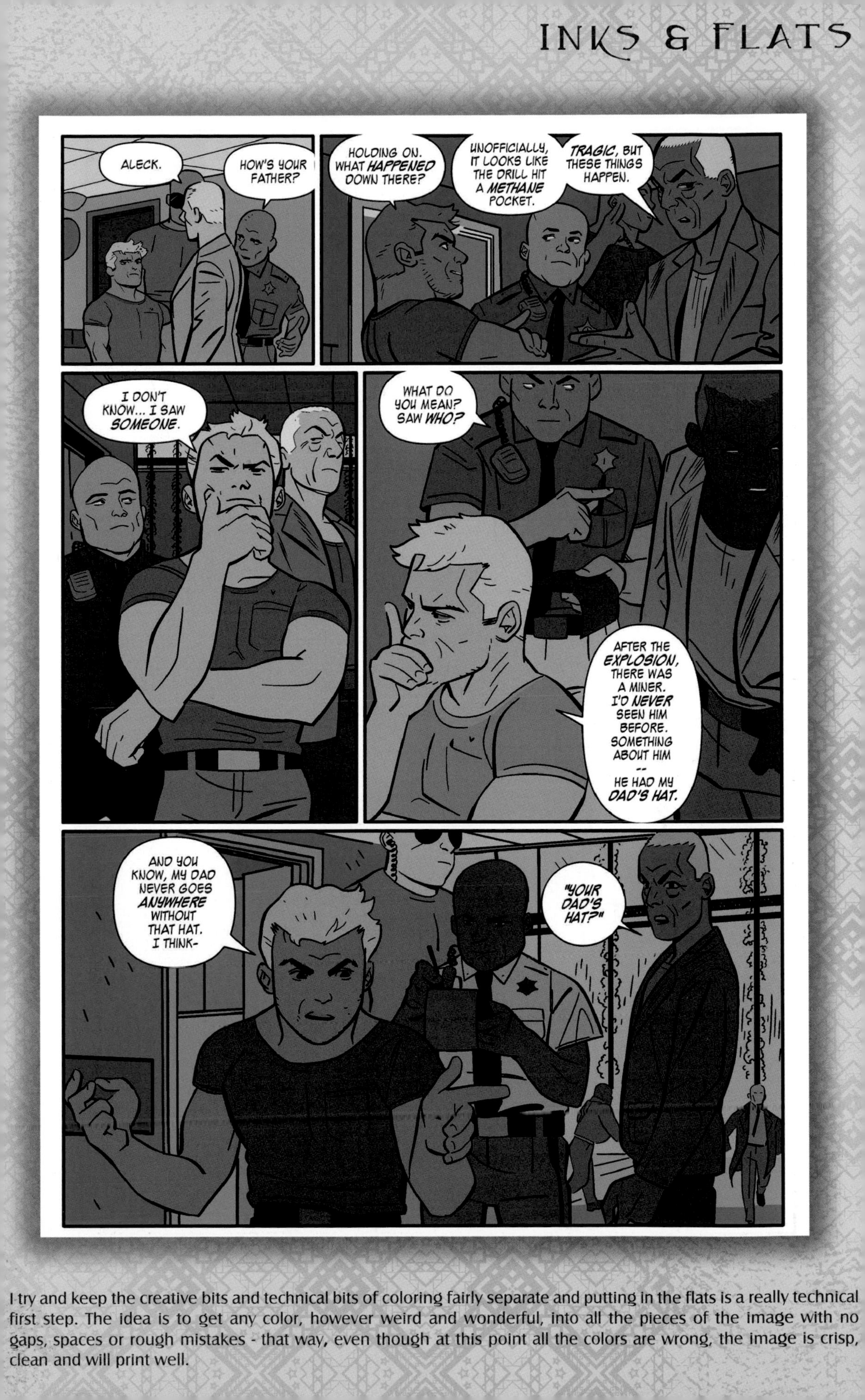
ALECK.
HOW'S YOUR FATHER?
HOLDING ON. WHAT HAPPENED DOWN THERE?
UNOFFICIALLY, IT LOOKS LIKE THE DRILL HIT A METHANE POCKET.
TRAGIC, BUT THESE THINGS HAPPEN.
I DON'T KNOW... I SAW SOMEONE.
WHAT DO YOU MEAN? SAW WHO?
AFTER THE EXPLOSION, THERE WAS A MINER. I'D NEVER SEEN HIM BEFORE. SOMETHING ABOUT HIM --
HE HAD MY DAD'S HAT.
AND YOU KNOW, MY DAD NEVER GOES ANYWHERE WITHOUT THAT HAT. I THINK-
"YOUR DAD'S HAT?"

I try and keep the creative bits and technical bits of coloring fairly separate and putting in the flats is a really technical first step. The idea is to get any color, however weird and wonderful, into all the pieces of the image with no gaps, spaces or rough mistakes - that way, even though at this point all the colors are wrong, the image is crisp, clean and will print well.

THE COLORING PROCESS

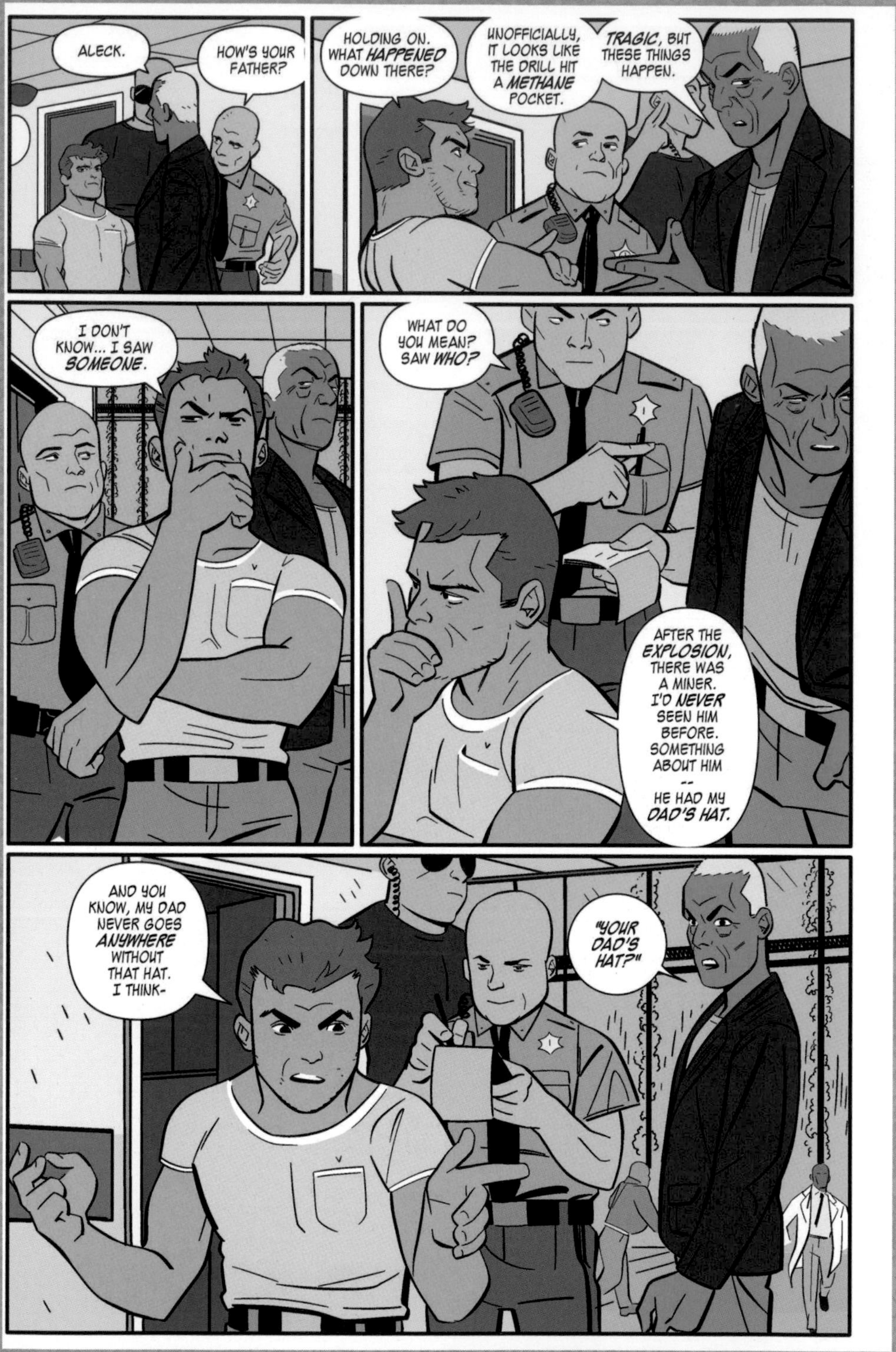
ALECK.
HOW'S YOUR FATHER?
HOLDING ON. WHAT HAPPENED DOWN THERE?
UNOFFICIALLY, IT LOOKS LIKE THE DRILL HIT A METHANE POCKET.
TRAGIC, BUT THESE THINGS HAPPEN.
I DON'T KNOW... I SAW SOMEONE.
WHAT DO YOU MEAN? SAW WHO?
AFTER THE EXPLOSION, THERE WAS A MINER. I'D NEVER SEEN HIM BEFORE. SOMETHING ABOUT HIM -- HE HAD MY DAD'S HAT.
AND YOU KNOW, MY DAD NEVER GOES ANYWHERE WITHOUT THAT HAT. I THINK-
"YOUR DAD'S HAT?"

Putting in the basic colors is when you really start to color the page. I replace the flats with local colors which are correct in the general sense, making sure characters' skin tones or costume colors are correct and that basic things in the world are an appropriate color and have a rough harmony to them. If I have a strong sense of a certain palette, color scheme or lighting idea I'll often kick it off here, but if not, making sure skies are blue and grass is green is a good start. At this point it's definitely not at its best, but if you absolutely had to go to print, the page would make sense and the comic would be readable.

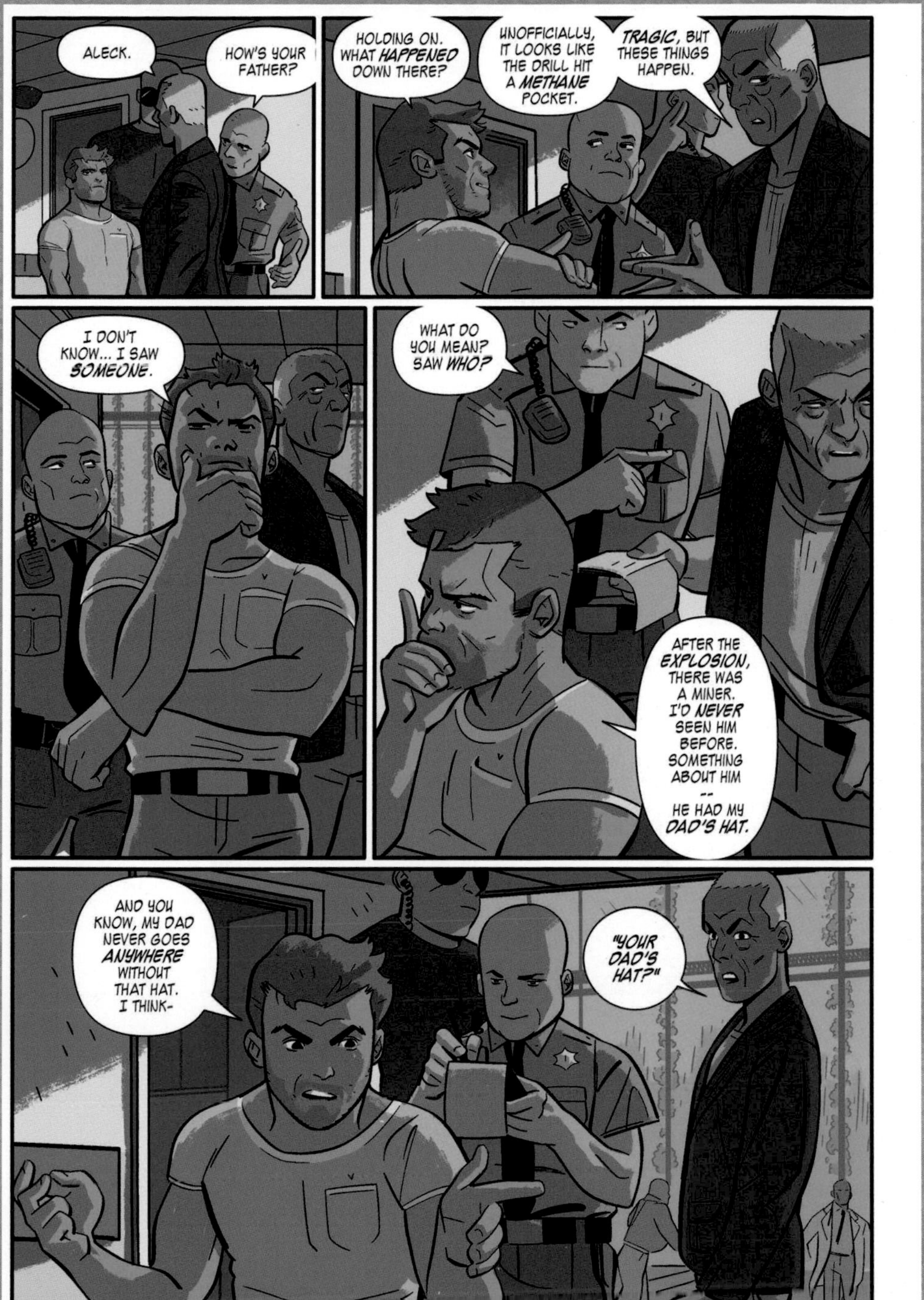
ALECK.
HOW'S YOUR FATHER?
HOLDING ON. WHAT HAPPENED DOWN THERE?
UNOFFICIALLY, IT LOOKS LIKE THE DRILL HIT A METHANE POCKET.
TRAGIC, BUT THESE THINGS HAPPEN.
I DON'T KNOW... I SAW SOMEONE.
WHAT DO YOU MEAN? SAW WHO?
AFTER THE EXPLOSION, THERE WAS A MINER. I'D NEVER SEEN HIM BEFORE. SOMETHING ABOUT HIM -- HE HAD MY DAD'S HAT.
AND YOU KNOW, MY DAD NEVER GOES ANYWHERE WITHOUT THAT HAT. I THINK-
"YOUR DAD'S HAT?"

his is the fun bit, the least technical and most creative. The final colors for me are all about atmosphere, lighting, one etc. I start to think "is it cold? Warm? Stifling?" or "How should we feel? Uneasy? Joyful? What does that look ke?" and "How can I best help, support the script and the drawing? How can I tell the story?". Since I already know e page will print cleanly, and I have basic colors locked down, I can treat them and shift them however I want - dd shadows, push an environmental atmosphere or make the colors represent the characters' emotions. For me, at kind of experimenting is where the magic happens and how pages can really come to life.

FIN CRAMB

THE CREATORS

CHARLIE STICKNEY

Charlie Stickney is Co-Publisher of Scout Comics, and writer of comics like *White Ash*, *Glarien*, *The Game* and *The Adept*. A twenty-year veteran of the non-comic Entertainment Industry, Charlie produced the award-winning documentary *The Entertainers* and helped create the animated series *Horrible Histories* and *Cosmic Quantum Ray*.

Charlie's career in comics started with an internship in the editorial offices of Marvel. After a prolonged dalliance creating stories with pictures that move, Stickney has happily returned to his favorite medium. Charlie lives in Los Angeles with his amazing wife and two (mostly) lovely children.

CONOR HUGHES

Conor Hughes likes to draw comics and his breakout works have been the popular Kickstarter comics *White Ash* and *The Game*.

You can troll him on Twitch at *twitch.tv/conorhughes*, where he can often be found making comics, as well as in Hopewell NJ, with his amazing wife and giggle monster baby girl.

FIN CRAMB

Fin loves all things comics and can usually be found happily working into the wee, small hours in his studio in Edinburgh, Scotland. Fin's previous credits include working on *Savant* (Dark Horse), *Planet of the Apes* (Madefire), *Peter Pan the Graphic Novel* (Birlinn) and the *Johnny Cash Project*.

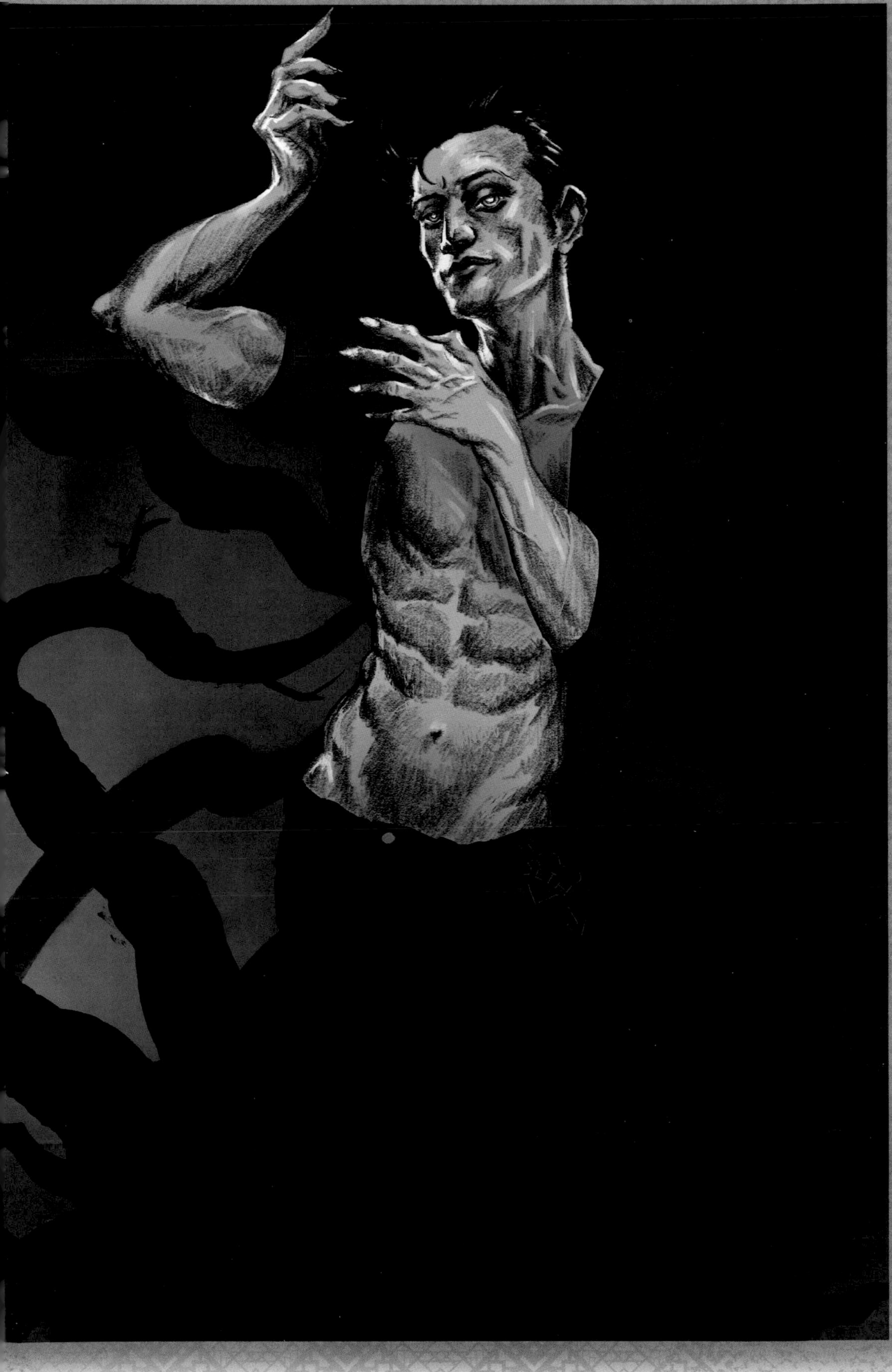

FIN CRAMB

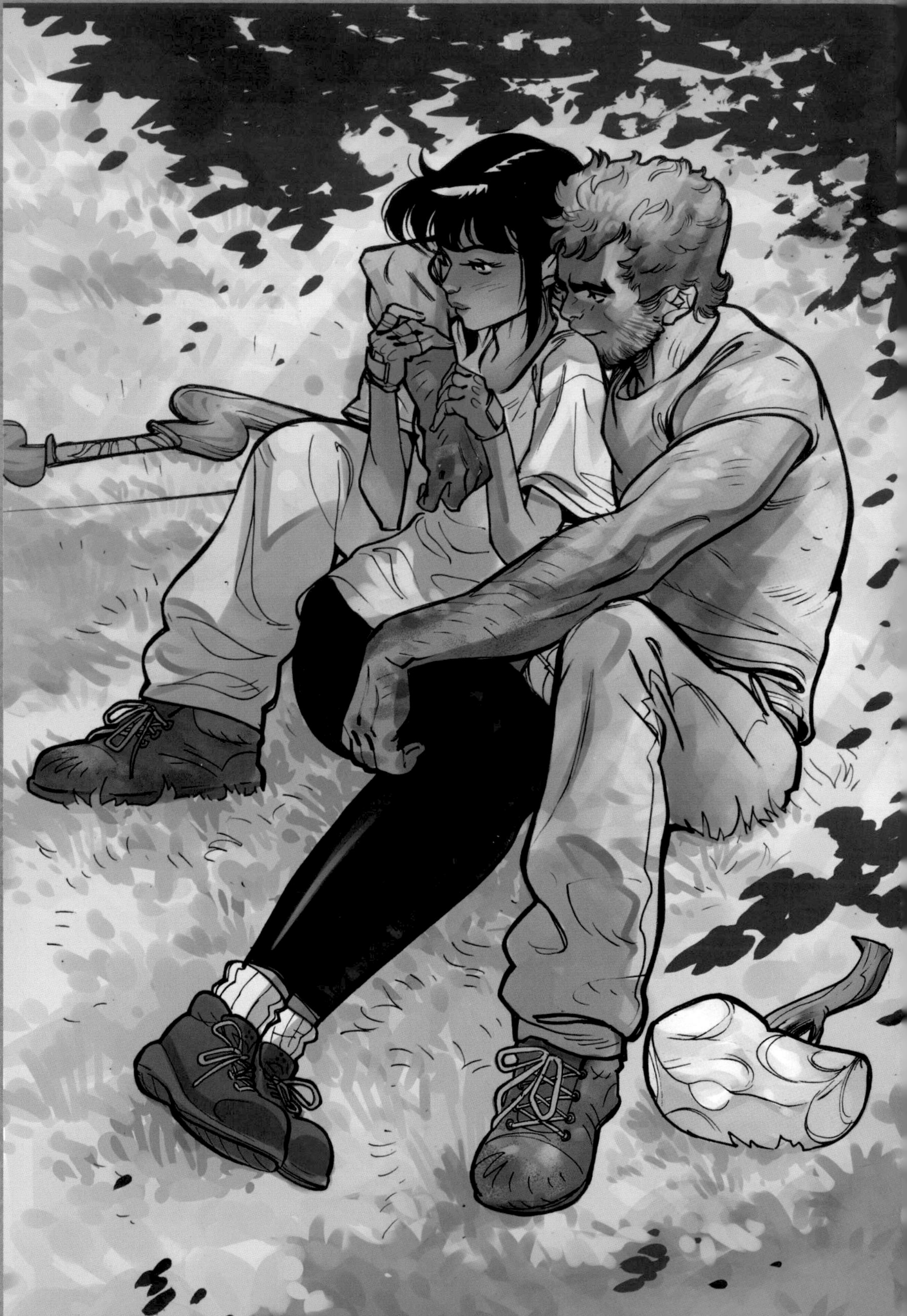

CONOR HUGHES

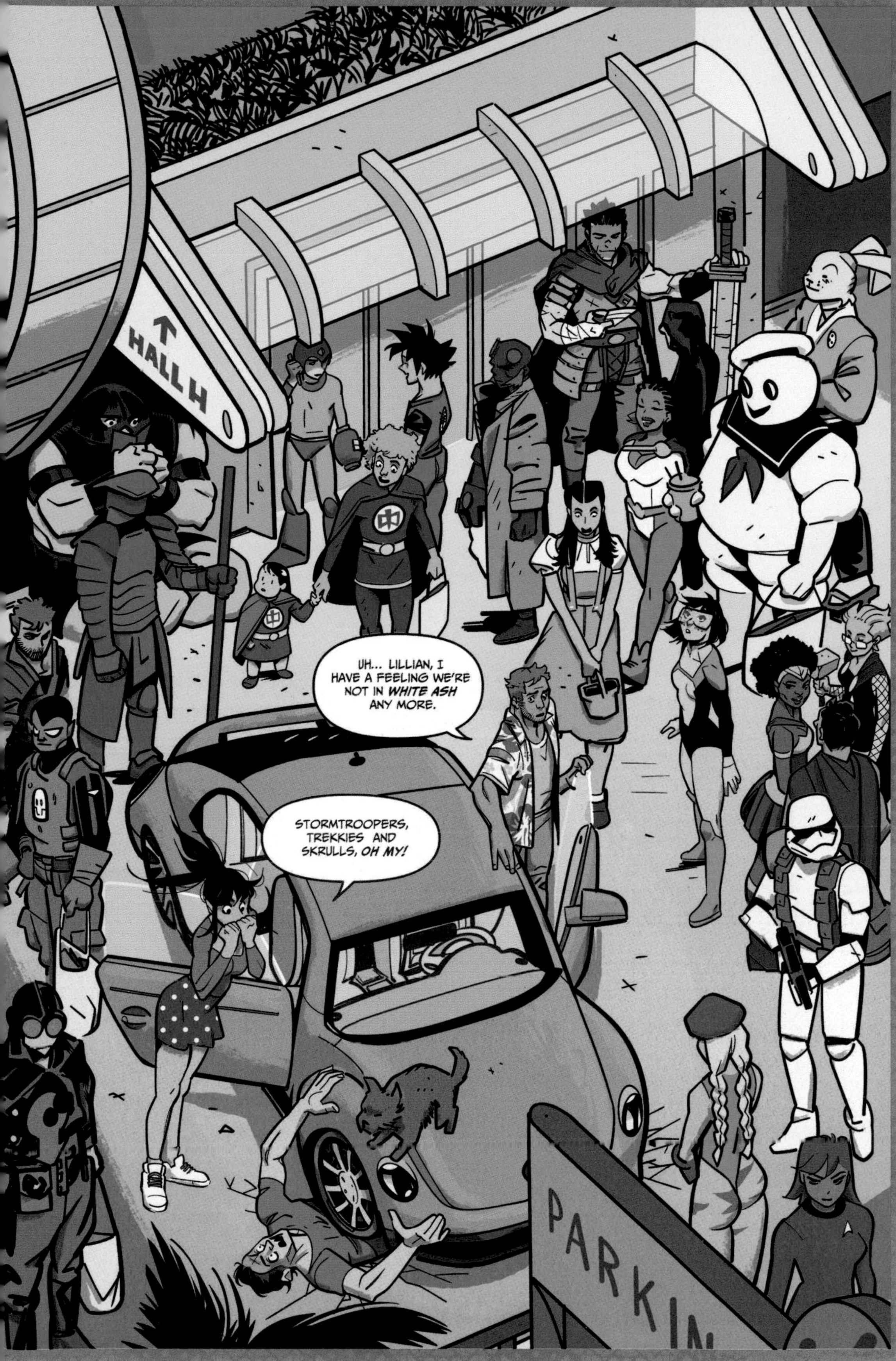
HALL H
UH... LILLIAN, I HAVE A FEELING WE'RE NOT IN *WHITE ASH* ANY MORE.
STORMTROOPERS, TREKKIES AND SKRULLS, *OH MY!*
PARKIN

CONOR HUGHES